THE PLAYS OF
SHAKESPEARE

THE PLAYS OF
SHAKESPEARE

A Thematic Guide

VICTOR L. CAHN

GREENWOOD PRESS
Westport, Connecticut • London

Library of Congress Cataloging-in-Publication Data

Cahn, Victor L.
  The plays of Shakespeare : a thematic guide / Victor L. Cahn.
    p. cm.
  Includes bibliographical references and index.
  ISBN 0–313–30981–7 (alk. paper)
    1. Shakespeare, William, 1564–1616—Themes, motives. 2. Shakespeare, William,
  1564–1616—Handbooks, manuals, etc. 3. Shakespeare, William, 1564–1616—Outlines,
  syllabi, etc. I. Title.
  PR2987.C28 2001
  822.3'3—dc21   00–022337

British Library Cataloguing in Publication Data is available.

Library of Congress Catalog Card Number: 00–022337
ISBN: 0–313–30981–7

First published in 2001

Greenwood Press, 88 Post Road West, Westport, CT 06881
An imprint of Greenwood Publishing Group, Inc.
www.greenwood.com

Printed in the United States of America

(∞)™

The paper used in this book complies with the
Permanent Paper Standard issued by the National
Information Standards Organization (Z39.48–1984).

10 9 8 7 6 5 4 3 2 1

To my mother,
Evelyn Baum Cahn

Thou art thy mother's glass, and she in thee
Calls back the lovely April of her prime . . .
—Shakespeare, Sonnet 3

Contents

Contents

Contents

Introduction

Every work of art deserves to be enjoyed and evaluated on its own merits. When we consider an artist of stature, however, the temptation to see each effort as part of an entire oeuvre is irresistible. Such is the case especially with William Shakespeare, author of the greatest, most influential body of literature that one person has ever written.

This volume is devoted to Shakespeare's dramatic output, which he created over a period of approximately two decades, beginning about 1590. The thirty-seven plays encompass tragedies, histories, comedies, and romances. Few dramatists have achieved remotely comparable success in any one of these genres, and none has triumphed in so wide a range of forms, nor has any matched Shakespeare's linguistic imagination and beauty of expression. He stands alone, the pinnacle of Western literature.

Perhaps most remarkable is the popularity of his plays, which remain in continual production around the world, often as a part of annual festivals devoted solely to Shakespeare. In addition, new filmed versions of his works are offered with amazing regularity. He is also a pervasive presence in literature classes at every level, and rare is the college or university that does not have at least one course devoted exclusively to his works. Clearly something in his plays reaches audiences universally, something beyond the glorious language, the skill at stagecraft, and the stories that reflect the extraordinary world of the Renaissance, both in England and across Europe.

That "something" is Shakespeare's understanding of our experiences throughout life. Over the centuries, individual societies have changed profoundly, but the fundamental conflicts and crises that human beings must resolve have not. Thus although almost all of Shakespeare's plots are borrowed from other sources, written in verse or elevated prose, and set in cultures far distant from those of our own time, the social, moral, and political issues that his characters face still touch us profoundly.

This book is devoted to exploring those issues. The title refers to various "themes," but the word is used liberally. Some themes encompass categories of characters, like "Clerics" and "Fools," while others emerge from questions specific to Shakespeare's day, like "Divine Right" and "Fate." Most themes, however, are traditional ones for artists, such as "Generations," "Mortality," and "War." Each theme is developed with focus on how the subtlety of the characters' psychology is revealed through their specific actions and the richness of their language. Emphasis is also placed on the theatricality of these plays, which are treated not as purely literary texts, but as scripts created for performance.

Thirty-five themes are arranged alphabetically in this volume. Although these chapters may be read in sequence, each stands independently. To be sure, some themes blend with others. Any discussion of "Politics," for instance, must include reference to "Order" and "Power," while Shakespeare's portrait of "Marriage" leads directly to how he presents "Gender" and "Love and Romance." Furthermore, certain major scenes are discussed from several different points of view. The opening of *King Lear*, for example, has ramifications about "Appearance versus Reality," "Fathers and Daughters," and several other motifs, while the trial scene in *The Merchant of Venice* is analyzed from the perspective of "Justice," "Money," and "Revenge." The approach will, I hope, help readers understand how virtually everything that is part of the human experience became part of Shakespeare's dramatic universe.

The thematic view also enriches the study of an individual play, first by placing it in the context of Shakespeare's entire output, then by demonstrating how its themes are developed in different works. For instance, a reader concerned with one particular play could look up the title in the index and note all the chapters in which that play is discussed. By moving from chapter to chapter, the reader could thereby construct an overview of the major themes of that work.

All plays in the traditional Shakespearean canon are discussed here, but particular attention is devoted to those that are most often presented onstage and studied in the classroom: the tragedies *Romeo and Juliet, Julius Caesar, Hamlet, Othello, King Lear*, and *Macbeth*; the comedies *The Taming of the Shrew, A Midsummer Night's Dream*, and *The Merchant of Venice*; the histories of the second Henriad (*Richard II, Henry IV, 1* and *2*, and *Henry V*); and the romance *The Tempest*.

My text is *The Riverside Shakespeare* (Houghton Mifflin), and all quotations, noted by act, scene, and line, are from that volume. Brackets around quoted words indicate that the enclosed material is open to quesitons of texual authority.

Finally, let us remember that Shakespeare was a man of the commercial theater. The audiences he sought to entertain encompassed all levels of society: from the well-to-do and educated to the poor and illiterate.

Perhaps they are one reason that he created an equally extensive range of characters, placed them in a multitude of settings, and evoked so rich a variety of moods. But whatever the inspiration for his genius, it leaves us both grateful and humble. After all, to borrow from James Joyce's *Ulysses* (citing Alexandre Dumas, *père*), "After God Shakespeare has created most."

Acting

That Shakespeare's plays are suffused with images of acting and the stage should be no surprise. After all, Shakespeare was himself an actor, and we can assume that for the twenty years or so that he was a practicing playwright (averaging nearly two scripts a year), his life revolved around the other members of his company and the environment of the theater.

What may take us aback, however, is the variety of meanings and denotations that the theme of "acting" invokes. In some plays, the references imply metaphoric parallels between a character onstage and a human being functioning in the "real world." In other works, the implications of "acting" resonate more deeply, involving the very attitude with which a character proceeds through life. These figures, Shakespeare suggests, may be aware of the artificiality and fleeting nature of the "roles" they play. Such characters often conclude that they are performing a part in the drama of events that surround them, improvising lines and actions that maintain their performance. Furthermore, when we consider the aggregate of these characters and Shakespeare's implications about them, we are forced to question the nature of our own existence. To what extent are we, too, playing roles? Ultimately we may ask, both about Shakespeare's characters and ourselves, to what extent do such roles supersede our own personality? Or is that personality nothing more than the sum of the many parts that we assume, such as spouse, employee, friend, or sibling?

Let us begin with those characters who mention theatrical imagery only briefly, but to sharp effect. In *King Lear*, for instance, the title character, who has been expelled from his home and stranded on the heath, and who now stands battered and nearly mad with grief, removes his crown of weeds and flowers and reflects:

When we are born, we cry that we are come
To this great stage of fools.

(IV, vi, 182–183)

This image suggests that human beings are blind to the nature of our condition, that we fail to appreciate what matters in life and to dismiss what is incidental. With these words, Lear also condemns his own actions and attitudes.

In *Macbeth*, on the other hand, the title character, emotionally deadened after the series of murders that he has committed or ordered, as well as the death of his wife, speaks in similar imagery:

Life's but a walking shadow, a poor player,
That struts and frets his hour upon the stage,
And then is heard no more. It is a tale
Told by an idiot, full of sound and fury,
Signifying nothing.

(V, v, 24–28)

Here is a statement of utter resignation. Having sunk to the nadir of the moral scale and believing himself unredeemable, Macbeth has no concern for, nor does he believe in, anything or anyone.

Both characters speak in terms of the stage with yet another implication: the brevity of each human life. In the face of such a vision, however, the two react differently. Lear seeks a reordering of priorities, for by this juncture, he has learned that before he is King, he is but a man, with the same needs and feelings of other men. Now he accepts responsibility for his errors, and as his life dwindles away, he seeks only reconciliation with his daughter Cordelia. For him, the image of the stage suggests recognition and understanding. Macbeth, however, is reduced to the belief that existence is meaningless. He sees himself as the victim of temptation by the witches and his wife, a man who under their urging committed senseless violence. First he murdered King Duncan. Then, trying to break free of the witches' predictions and the future they seemed to set out for him, he murdered Banquo, his erstwhile comrade, and his rival Macduff's wife and children. Now he presents himself as a pathetic actor, blankly mouthing a pointless script, bereft of all values and therefore all priorities.

The brevity of life that Macbeth invokes is expressed most memorably in Shakespeare's final play, *The Tempest*. Here Prospero, the Duke who is soon to leave his island of exile and regain political power, uses his magic to create a supernatural theatrical spectacle. Suddenly, however, he remembers that his enemies still flourish, and he dismisses the performers:

Acting

These our actors
(As I foretold you) were all spirits, and
Are melted into air, into thin air,
And like the baseless fabric of this vision,
The cloud-capp'd tow'rs, the gorgeous palaces,
The solemn temples, the great globe itself,
Yea, all which it inherit, shall dissolve,
And like this insubstantial pageant faded
Leave not a rack behind. We are such stuff
As dreams are made on; and our little life
Is rounded with a sleep.

(IV, i, 148–158)

Since *The Tempest* was almost certainly the final play that Shakespeare wrote alone, most audiences conclude that this speech should be understood as the playwright's farewell to his art. Prospero dwells on the transience of all human effort, and the reference to "the globe," the name of the theater where so many of Shakespeare's works were performed, seems to imply that the playwright believes that his own works are themselves transitory. Like so much of human existence, they will live for only so long as the people of his time can remember. Is Shakespeare commenting upon the impermanence of theatrical art, which perishes at the end of each performance, or, indeed, of all human endeavour? Or is he perhaps suggesting that such impermanence makes the entire human experience that much more precious?

Prospero's tone is wistful. Another equally famous, yet far grimmer statement about the theatrical quality of human life is uttered in *As You Like It* by the forest philosopher, Jaques. He begins:

All the world's a stage,
And all the men and women merely players;
They have their exits and their entrances,
And one man in his time plays many parts,
His acts being seven ages.

(II, vii, 139–143)

The opening tone is gentle, but what follows is a bitter catalogue that presents human life from an increasingly gloomy perspective. Humanity proceeds from infancy, "Mewling and puking" (II, vii, 144), to unhappy schoolboy, to pining lover, to brutal soldier, to severe judge, to aging lothario, to helpless victim of age: "Sans teeth, sans eyes, sans taste, sans every thing" (II, vii, 166). Jaques presents life as a compilation of miseries, one unhappy posture after the other. At every moment, he implies, we should be conscious that we are forever aging and dying.

The title character of Shakespeare's late tragedy *Coriolanus* also experiences a revelation about the quality of his life. After the Roman general Martius conquers the city of Corioles and earns the title "Coriolanus," he is urged by his supporters to campaign, as it were, for consul of Rome by standing before its citizens and revealing his wounds. Martius replies:

> It is a part
> That I shall blush in acting, and might well
> Be taken from the people.
>
> (II, ii, 144–146)

He understands that performance is a necessary aspect of politics, but believes himself unable to carry it out properly. After he fails, though, he is urged by his ambitious mother, Volumnia, to try again, and once more he invokes the image of acting, this time with different implications:

> Why did you wish me milder? Would you have me
> False to my nature? Rather say, I play
> The man I am.
>
> (III, ii, 14–16)

Coriolanus suggests that he has always behaved violently, but only because his mother encouraged him to act according to this aspect of his personality. The audience understands, however, that Coriolanus's personality has been shaped totally by his mother, that this violent predilection is the product of her indoctrination. We never see the young Martius, but we are led to believe that even had he been born with different inclinations, his mother's instruction would have destroyed them. In other words, she set out a role in life for him to play, and he has carried it off brilliantly, if unhappily. Only now is he beginning to realize as much:

> You have put me now to such a part which never
> I shall discharge to th' life.
>
> (III, ii, 105–106)

He understands that the role of politician is one for which he is entirely unsuited. By the end of the play, however, he articulates that his entire life has been the performance of a part that he has always despised:

> Like a dull actor now
> I have forgot my part, and I am out,
> Even to a full disgrace.
>
> (V, iii, 40–42)

Whatever other instincts and talents young Martius might have had were crushed under the authority of Volumnia's discipline. The role as a soldier usurped his personality completely.

The title character of *Richard II* is likewise an actor, although, unlike Martius, he is less conscious of the theatrical nature of his performance, yet ironically far more successful when he indulges it. For instance, when he surrenders the crown to Bullingbrook, the future Henry IV, Richard "performs" his abdication with more brilliance than he ever "performed" his duties as King:

> With mine own tears I wash away my balm,
> With mine own hands I give away my crown,
> With mine own tongue deny my sacred state,
> With mine own breath release all duteous oaths ...
> (IV, i, 207–210)

Clearly, a master showman is at work. The Duke of York, however, Richard's uncle and a fervent supporter of the crown, pierces to the core of Richard's kingship. Earlier he commented:

> Yet looks he like a king! Behold, his eye,
> As bright as is the eagle's, lightens forth
> Controlling majesty. Alack, alack, for woe,
> That any harm should stain so fair a show!
> (III, iii, 68–71)

Once Richard has abdicated, York completes the image:

> As in a theatre the eyes of men,
> After a well-graced actor leaves the stage,
> Are idly bent on him that enters next,
> Thinking his prattle to be tedious,
> Even so, or with much more contempt, men's eyes
> Did scowl on gentle Richard.
> (V, ii, 23–27)

In his final soliloquy, the King at last sees the truth:

> Thus play I in one person many people,
> And none contented. Sometimes am I king;
> Then treasons make me wish myself a beggar,
> And so I am. Then crushing penury
> Persuades me I was better when a king ...
> (V, v, 31–35)

That Richard has always been at heart an actor and poet who is hopelessly ill-suited to the throne makes him, like Coriolanus, a sympathetic figure.

All the characters discussed thus far have been analyzed as actors on what we might call "the stage of life." In *A Midsummer Night's Dream*, Shakespeare dramatizes an even closer connection between life and theater by creating an actual play-within-a-play. When Bottom and his fellow mechanicals of the acting company prepare their version of "Pyramus and Thisbe," they struggle with the concept of how their audience will distinguish the action onstage from reality. For instance, Bottom suggests that someone must take on the role of "Wall"; otherwise the spectators will have to imagine the chink through which the lovers whisper (III, i, 67–71). Similarly, he worries that any enactment of a lion will frighten the audience (III, i, 29–34) and that the death of Pyramus, as played by Bottom himself, will prove so realistic as to disturb the ladies. We laugh at his inability to grasp that those who watch a dramatic presentation understand that what they see onstage is fiction. Yet Bottom does in fact intuit a more important truth: that all audiences have the capacity to suspend disbelief, that part of the magic of theater is our eagerness to believe what we know to be patently false. Thus when the hilariously bizarre version of "Pyramus and Thisbe" is performed before the royal couple, Hippolyta, Queen of the Amazons who is betrothed to Theseus, says of the tormented Pyramus, "Beshrew my heart, but I pity the man" (V, i, 290). Her words move us, because we who have been watching the antics of the four lovers, Hermia, Helena, Lysander, and Demetrius, have been inspired to laughter and emotion by their plight. Through the burlesque of Bottom and his cohorts, therefore, Shakespeare reminds us of the power of drama to arouse passions possibly stronger than those inspired by life itself. Hence the attraction and fascination of the stage and, indeed, of all art.

The apotheosis of many of Shakespeare's implications about the relationship of acting and theater to life may be found in the mind of one character: Hamlet. From virtually his opening lines, we realize that he is preoccupied with acting and the need to distinguish a person's genuine personality from any role that he or she assumes. For instance, speaking to Queen Gertrude, his mother, about the grief which she claims he is affecting, Hamlet says of his behavior:

> These indeed seem,
> For they are actions that a man might play,
> But I have that within which passes show,
> These but the trappings and the suits of woe.
> (I, ii, 83–86)

He is obsessed with honesty, tormented by the hypocrisy that Gertrude, King Claudius, and others in the court exude. Thus to Hamlet, acting is a vehicle for dishonesty.

Yet after he greets the company of Players, Hamlet's soliloquy shows that he also believes that theater is a vehicle for revelation:

> Hum—I have heard
> That guilty creatures sitting at a play
> Have by the very cunning of the scene
> Been strook so to the soul, that presently
> They have proclaim'd their malefactions . . .
>   (II, ii, 588–592)

Hamlet suggests that a work of art can bring from an audience responses that might otherwise remain submerged. We are more honest in our reactions to art than to life.

At this juncture, Hamlet also resolves to use an imaginary stage to fulfill the mission that has frustrated him: he plans to carry out his role of revenger in a theater of his own creation. Thus far, he has been unable to follow the directive of his father, the Ghost, and unable to take action against Claudius. Now Hamlet resolves to escape his own self, in a sense, and become an actor playing the part of revenger on the stage of the court of Elsinore. Playing such a part will give Hamlet the freedom he spoke of earlier in this speech, when he envied the Player's capacity to mourn in character more effectively than Hamlet as himself (II, ii, 551–567). Thus for Hamlet, the stage, the mode of acting, provides the freedom to carry out his deepest desires, to reveal himself more completely than he dares to do in the "real world."

In Act III, scene ii, Hamlet confronts the Players with specific directions about how they should perform the script that he has composed for them. We may take this counsel on several levels. The first is literal: Hamlet genuinely seeks to have his text performed properly. The second may be insinuation by Shakespeare himself, advising his own actors how they should perform: by speaking clearly, refraining from excessive gesture, and controlling passion (III, ii, 1–14). On a third level, however, we may interpret Hamlet's advice as self-instruction:

> Be not too tame neither, but let your own
> discretion be your tutor. Suit the action to the word,
> the word to the action, with this special observance,
> that you o'erstep not the modesty of nature: for any
> thing so o'erdone is from the purpose of playing,
> whose end, both at the first and now, was and is, to
> hold as 'twere the mirror up to nature; to show virtue

7

her feature, scorn her own image, and the very age and
body of the time his form and pressure.

(III, ii, 16–24)

Yet as much as he advocates moderation, Hamlet in his own personal
performance will be unable to maintain control. During the production
of "The Murder of Gonzago," when Hamlet hopes to trap Claudius by
presenting before the King the reenactment of a murder carried out in
much the same manner as Claudius's murder of Hamlet's father, the
Prince is so outlandish with his interruptions and asides that he oblit-
erates his earlier dictum: ". . . the play's the thing / Wherein I'll catch the
conscience of the King" (II, ii, 604–605). Instead, Hamlet overplays his
part, disrupts the performance, and destroys his own standing in the
court.

Finally, one last level of meaning in the passage quoted above may
remind us of Shakespeare's own faith in the power of all art: the capacity
to reveal humanity to itself. After all, what may a playwright and a
company of actors be said to do but take our daily experiences, crystal-
lize them into compositions built of action and language, and thereby
reveal the glories, defeats, absurdities, and sorrows of the human experience? That is the cause to which Shakespeare devoted his life, and the
result is a single volume of plays that represents one of the wondrous
achievements in the history of the human spirit.

Appearance versus Reality

Throughout Shakespeare's plays, one of the most effective plot strategies springs from characters who are deceived by another's demeanor or language. When these otherwise intelligent men and women observe a sequence of action or hear an address, they tend to accept the implications of what confronts them without probing further or even questioning the motives of those involved. Such lack of perception is frequently dramatized in imagery of sight, almost always with implications of "insight," and the consequences of this "blindness" may be either comic or tragic. For Shakespeare, how characters respond when they distinguish between appearance and reality reveals a great deal about the characters themselves.

In Shakespeare's comedies, the conflict usually has psychological overtones related specifically to romance. In *The Taming of the Shrew*, for instance, when Petruchio arrives for his wedding with the shrewish Katherine, his servant, Biondello, describes the groom's garb as outlandishly unsuitable for so dignified a ceremony (III, ii, 43–63). Tranio, another servant, understands, however, that Petruchio "hath some meaning in his mad attire" (III, ii, 124). That meaning, we soon learn, is to teach Katherine to refrain from judging people by clothing or other superficial evidence:

> Our purses shall be proud, our garments poor,
> For 'tis the mind that makes the body rich;
> And as the sun breaks through the darkest clouds,
> So honor peereth in the meanest habit.
> (IV, iii, 171–174)

Later, after Kate has undergone Petruchio's brutal, if well-intentioned, punishment, she learns this lesson as well as many others, and consequently the uncertain meaning of appearance becomes the stuff of humor. For instance, during their journey back to Padua, the couple banters playfully, first about whether the source of light above them is the sun or the moon, then about whether a fellow traveler is a young virgin or an old man (IV, v, 1–50). As the pair exchange badinage, we realize, along with the two of them, that they are playing a game, and their capacity to indulge in such byplay reflects a profound bond based on their capacity to view life from a similar perspective, to judge appearances skeptically, and to distinguish posturing from uprightness.

Indeed, the entire plot of *The Taming of the Shrew* is built on the unmasking of false appearance. Katherine, who initially seems a shrew, is revealed to be a woman of warmth, wit, and passion. Her sister, Bianca, who at the start appears obliging and charming, turns out to be the true shrew. Baptista, father to the two girls, claims to have affection for both, but in fact regards them as no more than prizes to be offered to the highest bidder (II, i, 341–345). Lucentio, Gremio, and Hortensio, who pretend to be steadfast suitors, all disguise themselves shamefully. Virtually no one in the cast proceeds honestly except Petruchio, whose early protestations about Katherine's beauty and good nature turn out to be uncannily accurate:

> Now, Kate, I am a husband for your turn,
> For by this light whereby I see thy beauty,
> Thy beauty that doth make me like thee well,
> Thou must be married to no man but me . . .
> (II, i, 272–275)

Petruchio alone sees beneath her veneer, and he alone understands that her nature has been thwarted by the patriarchal society in which she has been raised. Ultimately, he is the one who "sees" the truth about her.

All these elements are suggested in the opening "Induction," when the drunken tinker, Christopher Sly, is subject to a prank by the other patrons of the alehouse. When he is asleep, they dress him in fine clothes and insist that he is a lord. In the words of the Huntsman: "He is no less than what we say he is" (Induction, i, 71). Upon awakening, Sly quickly accepts his new role:

> Am I a lord, and have I such a lady?
> Or do I dream? Or have I dream'd till now?
> I do not sleep: I see, I hear, I speak;
> I smell sweet savors, and I feel soft things.
> Upon my life, I am a lord indeed,
> And not a tinker, nor Christopher Sly.
> (Induction, ii, 68–73)

His behavior suggests how the nature of a human personality is subject to external influence, how what we see and hear about ourselves substantially shapes us. In the context of the entire play, this revelation insinuates that for her whole life Katherine has been too powerful a personality for the taste of the male populace of Padua. Yet by boldly revealing her frustration at this predicament, she has invited others to conclude that she is merely a shrew. As a result, she has isolated herself even further and simultaneously increased her misery. Once Petruchio enters, however, and alters the "appearance" of both the woman herself and the world as she sees it, her "reality" shines through.

This motif recurs throughout Shakespeare's oeuvre. In the romance *The Winter's Tale*, written near the end of his career, Polixenes, King of Bohemia, meets Perdita, the daughter of Leontes, King of Sicilia. The girl has long been thought dead, but in fact has grown up and lived the quiet life of a peasant. As Polixenes listens to her, however, he intuits something singular in her manner:

> This is the prettiest low-born lass that ever
> Ran on the green-sord. Nothing she does, or seems,
> But smacks of something greater than herself,
> Too noble for this place.
>
> (IV, iv, 156–159)

His sensitivity gives him the capacity to perceive Perdita's true nature that lies beneath her simple exterior.

The theme of "appearance versus reality" is presented more fully in *A Midsummer Night's Dream*, in which from the outset we are confronted with the matter of perspective, particularly about love. Egeus, a citizen of Athens, has decreed that his daughter, Hermia, must marry Demetrius, but she prefers Lysander, and expresses her passion in terms that permeate the play: "I would my father look'd but with my eyes" (I, i, 56). Theseus, Duke of Athens, regards the matter differently, although he maintains the imagery: "Rather your eyes must with his judgment look" (I, i, 57). Later, Helena, the final member of the quartet of young lovers, reflects on the peculiar nature of affection:

> Things base and vile, holding no quantity,
> Love can transpose to form and dignity.
> Love looks not with the eyes but with the mind;
> And therefore is wing'd Cupid painted blind.
>
> (I, i, 232–235)

Helena is partially correct. Eyes can be deceiving, but at other times a person can "see" through appearance and into the reality of a situation.

For instance, when Titania, Queen of the Fairies, awakens under the influence of the magic flower whose juice has been dropped in her eyes by the spirit Puck, she falls in love with the first creature she sees, which happens to be Nick Bottom, the weaver wearing an ass's head:

> I pray thee, gentle mortal, sing again.
> Mine eye is much enamored of thy note;
> So is mine eye enthralled to the shape.
>
> (III, i, 137–139)

Her sight and hearing are distorted, however. The implication of the scene is that love is not so much an intellectual passion as an infatuation of the senses that lies beyond rational explanation. Titania's next line hits the truth: "Thou art as wise as thou art beautiful" (III, i, 148). She may not literally "see" everything, but she certainly "sees" the truth about Bottom. Later, when her husband, Oberon, awakens Titania and explains the truth about her passion, she recoils: "O, how mine eyes do loathe his visage now!" (IV, i, 79). She reverts to the woman who judges only by the surface of things. But does she truly understand Bottom? Shakespeare suggests that in his ass's head, Bottom appears monstrous, but is in fact gentle and loving. Hence appearance and reality clash.

As they do with the young lovers. Thanks to Puck's interference, the affections of Lysander and Demetrius change at a dizzying pace, but when the two pairs are at last sorted out, Hermia reacts tellingly:

> Methinks I see these things with parted eye,
> When every thing seems double.
>
> (IV, i, 189–190)

She intuits how love can deceive and that affections may waver without reason, sentiments expressed most dramatically by Theseus:

> Lovers and madmen have such seething brains,
> Such shaping fantasies, that apprehend
> More than cool reason ever comprehends.
> The lunatic, the lover, and the poet
> Are of imagination all compact . . .
> The lover, all as frantic,
> Sees Helen's beauty in a brow of Egypt . . .
> Or in the night, imagining some fear,
> How easy is a bush suppos'd a bear!
>
> (V, i, 4–22)

Thus in *A Midsummer Night's Dream*, the appearance and the reality of love are at times interchangeable. This theme has melancholy overtones, however, for at the end of the play we realize that Demetrius, although smitten with Helena, lives as yet under the influence of Puck's magic drops. Has Demetrius's fundamental character changed, or could he one day awaken and again become infatuated with Hermia? How steadfast are these lovers, particularly the males? Those questions lurk beneath the weddings and the ostensibly happy resolution.

Perhaps the most powerful example of "appearance versus reality" in Shakespeare's comedies may be found in a theatrical gambit that pervades the plays: women disguising themselves as men. Since no female actors were permitted on the Elizabethan stage, all women's parts were played by men or boys, and thus this device was natural. What is of particular interest, however, is that not only are these masquerades invariably successful, but they are, in their own ironic way, revealing. Works in which the tactic is utilized include *The Two Gentlemen of Verona*, *The Merchant of Venice*, and *As You Like It*, but in no play is it more theatrically or thematically compelling than in *Twelfth Night*.

From the start, Viola, the young woman stranded in Illyria, alerts us to this key motif of the play, as she requests of the Captain of the ship that rescued her:

> I prithee (and I'll pay thee handsomely)
> Conceal me what I am, and be my aid
> For such disguise as haply shall become
> The form of my intent.
>
> (I, ii, 52–55)

Subsequently, the two relationships she shares, one with Orsino, Duke of Illyria, and the other with Olivia, a rich countess, resound with questions of "appearance versus reality." Orsino falls in love with the feminine beauty of Viola disguised as "Caesario" (I, iv, 31–35), believing the bold young servant to be a man, while Olivia is smitten with Caesario's feminine sensibilities, while simultaneously admiring his gentlemanly bearing and manner (I, v, 290–297). In both cases, the infatuated older person intuits a reality that lies underneath the trappings of appearance, and as the play proceeds, the complications that spring from these conflicting desires grow more passionate. Thus throughout the text the denotations and connotations of "masculine" and "feminine" become blurred, and we in the audience are led to question the essence of these qualities whose attributes we normally take for granted. Such is the case in all the comedies where similar disguise is employed.

The subplot of the *Twelfth Night* also invokes the theme of "appearance versus reality." The duping of Olivia's steward, Malvolio, by her uncle, Sir Toby Belch, and his cohorts succeeds in making Malvolio "appear" so bizarre that the "reality" of his sanity becomes suspect. As Olivia says, upon seeing him enter "cross-garter'd" with yellow stockings, "Why, this is very midsummer madness" (III, iv, 56), a suggestive echo of an earlier play. Even when Malvolio is imprisoned, Feste the clown, playing the role of Sir Topas, toys with Malvolio about perspective and vision, while Malvolio struggles to proclaim himself sane: "I am not mad, Sir Topas, I say to you this house is dark" (IV, ii, 40–41).

Finally, the rampant confusion that arises when Viola and her brother, Sebastian, both wander through Illyria provides great fun for us, as Orsino, Olivia, Sir Toby, Sir Andrew, and Sebastian's friend Antonio continually mistake one sibling for the other. In this context as well, though, we are reminded of the thematic importance of the crises. First, Viola senses the truth of things:

> Prove true, imagination. O, prove true,
> That I, dear brother, be now ta'en for you.
> (III, iv, 375–376)

Later, after Sebastian has been mistaken by several people for Viola, he remarks to himself:

> . . . Yet doth this accident and flood of fortune
> So far exceed all instance, all discourse,
> That I am ready to distrust mine eyes,
> And wrangle with my reason that persuades me
> To any other trust but that I am mad.
> (IV, iii, 11–15)

Such reflection reminds us of many characters throughout Shakespeare's comedies, both male and female, whose progress is at least partly based on their capacity to distinguish truth from illusion.

The concept of "appearance versus reality" also has political implications. Many of the leading figures in Shakespeare's history plays and political tragedies are aware of how, to invoke a phrase from twentieth-century parlance, "image is everything." No one, however, is more conscious of the importance of perception than Henry IV's son Hal, who eventually becomes Henry V. In the second scene of *Henry IV, Part 1*, when Hal is still regarded as a wastrel by everyone, including his father, the young Prince reveals a political acumen that becomes his dominant quality throughout the three plays in which he takes a leading part. Here, onstage alone, he reflects on his behavior and unsavory companions:

> So when this loose behavior I throw off
> And pay the debt I never promised,
> By how much better than my word I am,

By so much shall I falsify men's hopes,
And like bright metal on a sullen ground,
My reformation, glitt'ring o'er my fault,
Shall show more goodly and attract more eyes
Than that which hath no foil to set it off.
I'll so offend, to make offense a skill,
Redeeming time when men least think I will.

(I, ii, 208–217)

Soon the Prince becomes utterly absorbed with the importance of appearance and his presentation of self before the world. In *Henry IV, Part 2*, for instance, Hal, brooding over the serious illness of his father, inquires of his comrade, Poins: "What wouldst thou think of me if I should weep?" (II, ii, 52–53).

For the rest of Hal's life, as Shakespeare dramatizes it, the young man never makes a move without anticipating how his actions will "appear" before the multitudes: whether the "reality" of his political and military tactics will communicate the picture of himself that he seeks to promote. Throughout *Henry V*, especially, the newly crowned King always phrases decisions in terminology that suggests he is ruling in accordance with a rigorous moral code. For instance, he orders the executions of the traitors Grey, Scroop, and Cambridge in God's name (II, ii, 177–182), and later threatens the citizens of Harfleur with destruction, but only after insisting that they will bear blame for their own ruin (III, iii, 1–42).

The need to stress appearance in the political realm is also vital to *Julius Caesar*. The conspirators against Caesar want desperately to have the patrician Brutus ally himself with them, not because of any great affection they hold for him, but because, in the words of the conspirator Casca:

And that which would appear offense in us,
His countenance, like richest alchymy,
Will change to virtue and to worthiness.

(I, iii, 158–160)

Even Caesar, seemingly untouchable, feels the need to maintain appearances. When Calphurnia, his wife, relates the dream which she believes foreshadows Caesar's death, Caesar initially assents to her wishes that he remain home that day. When, however, Decius, another member of the conspiracy, reinterprets that dream, and intimates that for Caesar to withdraw would make him seem frightened in the eyes of the Roman plebeians, Caesar hurriedly agrees to go to the Senate (II, ii 105–107).

The conflict between appearance and reality, however, can have overtones beyond the romantic and the political. When characters of enormous stature and power are deceived, then act in accordance with flawed visions of the world, the consequences can be disastrous. Such is the pattern of events in several of Shakespeare's monumental tragedies.

In *Macbeth*, King Duncan's trust in outward gestures of friendship makes him especially vulnerable. First he speaks of the Thane of Cawdor, recently executed as a traitor: "He was a gentleman on whom I built/ An absolute trust" (I, iv, 13–14). Yet Duncan remains blind, even as he approaches his cousin Macbeth's home, where the King is soon to be killed:

> This castle hath a pleasant seat, the air
> Nimbly and sweetly recommends itself
> Unto our gentle senses.
>   (I, vi, 1–3)

The character most deceived by appearances, however, is the title figure himself. From the earliest, ambiguous predictions by the witches, Macbeth constantly tries to distinguish between illusion and certainty, as when he contemplates the notorious dagger:

> I have thee not, and yet I see thee still.
> Art thou not, fatal vision, sensible
> To feeling as to sight? or art thou but
> A dagger of the mind, a false creation,
> Proceeding from the heat-oppressed brain?
>   (II, i, 36–39)

Furthermore, although Macbeth's downfall springs from his inability to withstand the allure of power, the enticing visions the witches present drive him, even as they embody the contrast between what he anticipates and what occurs. Throughout the play, the witches dangle half-truths before Macbeth, but he never has the will, strength, or desire to withstand the temptation or the appearance of good fortune.

The contrast between appearance and reality is even more fundamental to the tragedy of Othello. At the outset of the play, Iago, Othello's ensign, emphasizes this crucial gap, especially in terms of servants who maintain one attitude for the public while inwardly holding a different view:

> Were I the Moor, I would not be Iago.
> In following him, I follow but myself . . .
>   I am not what I am.
>   (I, i, 57–58, 65)

In addition, on countless occasions he refers to himself as "honest," and this self-created image seeps into all the characters' phraseology. Indeed, hardly anyone mentions Iago's name without placing the adjective "honest" before it. Iago emphasizes this irony when he focuses on specific tactics calibrated to prey on Othello's weaknesses. Speaking of Cassio, Othello's lieutenant, Iago says:

> He hath a person and a smooth dispose
> To be suspected—fram'd to make women false.
> The Moor is of a free and open nature,
> That thinks men honest that but seem to be so,
> And will as tenderly be led by th' nose
> As asses are.
>
> (I, iii, 397–402)

In sum, Othello cannot distinguish between what he thinks he sees and what he in fact witnesses.

The entire tragedy is made more poignant because the love between Othello and Desdemona, the foundation of the story, is itself based on illusion. Othello affirms this condition when he comments to Brabantio, Desdemona's father, how she fell in love with Othello after his long narrative about his travels:

> My story being done,
> She gave me for my pains a world of [sighs];
> She swore, in faith 'twas strange, 'twas passing strange;
> 'Twas pitiful, 'twas wondrous pitiful.
> She wish'd she had not heard it, yet she wish'd
> That heaven had made her such a man.
>
> (I, iii, 158–163)

Clearly Desdemona is infatuated with the hero at the core of this story, someone she romanticizes; thus she does not know Othello as a man, but only as a fantasy figure. Othello then reveals that he reciprocates both the manner and the substance of her affection:

> She lov'd me for the dangers I had pass'd,
> And I lov'd her that she did pity them.
>
> (I, iii, 167–168)

He does not know her well either, but because of his innocence in worldly matters, intertwined with his own considerable ego that has been buttressed by his military stature, he is taken with her because she has shown him such passion. Again, what strikes us is how this relationship is based almost solely on appearance.

The downfall of Othello and Desdemona's marriage also occurs because of clashes between what is apparent and what is true. Iago manages to shift the blame for starting a fight in the streets onto Cassio; Othello then accepts Iago's version without question and dismisses Cassio. Even more sinister is the lengthy and remarkable "seduction," as Iago takes a few fleeting incidents and twists them into so vivid a picture that Othello's mind creates an entirely new reality for him (III, iii). Once more, Othello's naivete and pride, perhaps in combination with the insecurity that emerges from his place as the only black man in a white world, leads him to believe Iago's "evidence," which is no more than a series of fictions, or a collection of facts presented and thereafter interpreted in a distorted manner.

Othello desires to remain judicious, but he fails to appreciate the painful irony embodied in his own warnings:

> No, Iago,
> I'll see before I doubt; when I doubt prove,
> And on the proof, there is no more but this—
> Away at once with love or jealousy!
> (III, iii, 189–192)

Later he shouts with stunning ferocity:

> Be sure of it. Give me the ocular proof,
> Or by the worth of mine eternal soul,
> Thou hadst been better have been born a dog
> Than answer my wak'd wrath!
> (III, iii, 360–363)

In sum, he wants to "see" before he believes. Not long after, Othello is finally convinced that he does have proof, when, as he hides in degradation, he observes Cassio exchanging ribald laughter with Iago. Othello quickly assumes the discussion to be about Desdemona; thus the appearance of the conversation deceives him, as does the reentrance of the prostitute Bianca, who scolds the comically intimidated Cassio. Iago also knows how to echo Othello's threats and shrewdly invokes the Moor's own metaphor: "Did you perceive how he laugh'd at his vice?" (IV, i, 171). This line is followed by: "And did you see the handkerchief?" (IV, i, 173).

The final speech of the play reinforces the theme of appearance versus reality, when the Venetian noble Lodovico comments that the entire story "poisons sight" (V, ii, 364). Thus one crucial aspect of the play is how a vulnerable human being may be made to "see" what someone else intends, how individual weaknesses may be used to lead a great person down a path of destruction.

In no play of Shakespeare's, however, is the gap between what we believe and what is true more thrillingly dramatized than in *King Lear*. Indeed, from the start, the text is saturated with images of sight and understanding.

In the very first lines between Lear's loyal servant, Kent, and the Earl of Gloucester, the King's judgment is called into question, as the two men comment on the comparative worth of the King's sons-in-law, Albany and Cornwall. When Lear begins his division of the kingdom, however, the imagery of sight takes over. First his oldest daughter, Goneril, in response to her father's demand for an expression of love, offers a curious tribute:

> Sir, I love you more than [words] can wield the matter,
> Dearer than eyesight, space, and liberty . . .
> (I, i, 55–56)

We understand that "space" and "liberty" are fundamental human rights that would naturally be "dear" to Goneril. Why, however, does she mention "eyesight" first? Perhaps she subtly mocks Lear, implying that were he more "perceptive," he would avoid the blunder he is about to make.

After Lear's second daughter, Regan, offers her own oily tribute to her father, Cordelia, his youngest, has her opportunity, but she is unable to participate in this charade. Instantly, Lear rises in humiliation and outrage at her apparent insolence. The moment is unbearable for the audience, for we recognize Cordelia's worth, as well as Lear's tragic misstep in failing to distinguish between the reality of her genuine love (which she will not taint with public demonstration) and the fraudulent statements of affection by Goneril and Regan. In fury, the King expels Cordelia with painful irony: "Hence, and avoid my sight!" (I, i, 124). When Kent protests, Lear threatens him in almost identical terms, but the undaunted servant retorts with the same image:

> See better, Lear, and let me still remain
> The true blank of thine eye.
> (I, i, 158–159)

Like the audience, Kent understands the reality of the people involved, but cannot make Lear "see."

The subplot with Gloucester and his sons also uses imagery of sight, for Gloucester, too, is unable to distinguish the comparative worth of his children. When he comes across his bastard son, Edmund, ostentatiously hiding a paper, Gloucester demands to peruse it: "Come, if it be nothing,

19

I shall not need spectacles" (I, ii, 34–35). The letter, supposedly composed by the legitimate son, Edgar, is a sham, but Gloucester does not realize so. Both he and Lear are too "blind" to recognize that they are being duped, and much of the tragedy of the play is the suffering that they undergo before they "see" the difference between the reality of true love and the appearance of false love.

Numerous passages could be cited to suggest this gradual discovery, but a few must suffice. One occurs when Lear has been thrust out of Goneril's home:

> Does any here know me? This is not Lear.
> Does Lear walk thus? speak thus? Where are his eyes?
> (I, iv, 226–227)

Lear has dispensed with the royal "we" that has until this point dominated his speech. For the first time, he regards himself not simply as King, but as a man, subject to human miseries and frailties. In doing so, he acknowledges the truth of the identity that lies beneath the royal facade. Later in the same scene, he berates himself:

> Old fond eyes,
> Beweep this cause again, I'll pluck yet out,
> And cast you, with the waters that you loose,
> To temper clay.
> (I, iv, 301–304)

We sense that he holds his eyes responsible for the calamitous error in judgment that has left him and his kingdom in such turmoil.

Perhaps the most unbearable instance of the revelation of reality occurs with the blinding of Gloucester by Regan's husband, Cornwall, a horror perpetrated with Edmund's permission. As one eye, then the other, is literally torn out, Gloucester cries out in physical and emotional anguish:

> O my follies! then Edgar was abus'd.
> Kind gods, forgive me that, and prosper him!
> (III, vii, 91–92)

Before Cornwall is himself fatally wounded, he refers to Gloucester as "that eyeless villain" (III, vii, 96). We recognize the dramatic irony that while Gloucester now is literally "eyeless," he figuratively understands all. As Lear later comments with mad poignancy, "A man may see how this world goes with no eyes" (IV, vi, 150–151).

Even in Lear's final lines, the imagery of sight resounds tellingly:

Do you see this? Look on her! Look her lips,
Look there, look there!

(V, iii, 311–312)

Does the feather on her lips move? Or is Lear deceived by appearance? Perhaps he actually wants to be deceived. In any case, Lear's struggle to discern the truth reminds us of the fundamental flaw that contributed so mightily to his downfall.

The capacity for insight, the ability to distinguish between appearance and reality, is a gift shared by some of the cleverest of Shakespeare's characters. Thus here we might also have considered Richard III, Falstaff, and Hamlet. Those who are discussed in this section, though, are the ones whose lives are touched with particular intensity by the need to search beneath language and action, to understand how insight into human character reveals truths that may save us from suffering that is either self-imposed or imposed on us by others.

Clerics

The world of Shakespeare's plays is Christian. To be sure, several of the plays are set in classical or other non-Christian locales. Yet even in these works, the characters seem to function with an understanding of Christian principles. At the same time, the tone of the plays, the combination of plot and dramatic tension, is essentially secular. Organized religion is usually peripheral to the stories, while religious issues *per se* are presented only in the context of other social and political themes. Thus comparatively few members of the clergy appear in the plays, and most who do are considerably less than holy. Indeed, whatever the depth of their religious feeling, their convictions are usually subordinate to their desire to participate in more earthly activities. Why should Shakespeare have presented clerics in such an unflattering light? Perhaps the answer is related to England's break from the Catholic Church in Rome in 1533 over the matter of Henry VIII's divorce. Whatever the reason, religious figures in Shakespeare's plays generally devote themselves to matters worldly rather than spiritual.

One of Shakespeare's more daunting clerical figures is the Bishop of Carlisle from *Richard II*. A fierce proponent of the principle of the divine right of kings, Carlisle initially tries to bolster the spirits of the beseiged monarch, whose will is tottering under attack from troops led by Henry Bullingbrook:

> Fear not, my lord, that Power that made you king
> Hath power to keep you king in spite of all.
> (III, ii, 27–28)

Carlisle later speaks on behalf of Norfolk, once the King's most trusted operative, but months earlier exiled by Richard, and at this moment the object of accusations by Aumerle. When Bullingbrook promises to investigate the charges, Carlisle reveals that Norfolk has died in exile:

Many a time hath banish'd Norfolk fought
For Jesu Christ in glorious Christian field,
Streaming the ensign of the Christian cross
Against black pagans, Turks, and Saracens,
And toil'd with works of war, retir'd himself
To Italy, and there at Venice gave
His body to that pleasant country's earth,
And his pure soul unto his captain Christ,
Under whose colors he had fought so long.
(IV, i, 92–100)

Carlisle's implication is clear: that by fighting for England and Richard II, Norfolk also fought for Christianity. When, however, Bullingbrook announces his intention to take the throne in Richard's place, Carlisle's rage overflows:

O, forfend it, God,
That in a Christian climate souls refin'd
Should show so heinous, black, obscene a deed!
I speak to subjects, and a subject speaks,
Stirr'd up by God, thus boldly for his king.
(IV, i, 129–133)

Even after Richard surrenders his throne without struggle, and internal warfare seems to have been averted, Carlisle speaks in a tone filled with dread:

The woe's to come; the children yet unborn
Shall feel this day as sharp to them as thorn.
(IV, i, 322–333)

Thus Carlisle asserts himself into the world of politics, but without desire for personal reward. This unselfishness is acknowledged by Bullingbrook when he becomes Henry IV, for at the end of *Richard II*, when the new King dispenses punishment and reward to those who have been involved on both sides of the usurpation, he speaks generously to Carlisle:

Carlisle, this is your doom:
Choose out some secret place, some reverent room,
More than thou hast, and with it joy thy life.
So as thou liv'st in peace, die free from strife,
For though mine enemy thou hast ever been,
High sparks of honor in thee have I seen.
(V, vi, 24–29)

Perhaps the new King's solicitude toward Carlisle emerges from a desire to avoid offending both the court and God, or perhaps Henry genuinely accepts Carlisle's dedication to the country. Whatever the case, the estimate of Carlisle's worth is fair.

No other clergy in the second Henriad carry themselves with Carlisle's dignity. In *Henry IV, Part 2*, Archbishop Scroop berates his colleagues who initially supported Henry's taking the throne, but who have grown angry over his unwillingness to grant them the political rewards they expected:

> So, so, thou common dog, didst thou disgorge
> Thy glutton bosom of the royal Richard,
> And now thou wouldst eat thy dead vomit up,
> And howl'st to find it. What trust is in these times?
> They that, when Richard liv'd, would have him die,
> Are now become enamor'd on his grave.
> (I, iii, 97–102)

Although he, too, despises the King and the environment that his actions have caused, Scroop shrewdly notes the pettiness and envy that mark those one-time allies who have become Henry's enemies. Despite such insight, however, Scroop's ugly vocabulary does not befit a clergyman and thus derogates his office. How apt, then, that when the rebels against Henry are ready for battle, Scroop, usually suspicious of everyone's behavior, agrees to the offer from the King's son, Prince John of Lancaster, that both sides disperse. Thereafter Scroop is immediately arrested for treason (IV, ii, 109). Even more fitting is John's remark that he will redress the rebels' grievance with "Christian care" (IV, ii, 115), a phrase that mocks Scroop's religious title.

Henry V presents us with two even more politically-minded clerics, the Archbishop of Canterbury and the Bishop of Ely. When they follow the Chorus at the start of the play proper, their voices are quiet, but their words suggest how removed they are from matters of the spirit and how involved they have become in the power struggles of the court. Canterbury shows particular concern over a bill that would cost the church much of its income. Ely comments quietly: "This would drink deep" (I, i, 20), but we sense his desire to maintain wealth. Similarly, Canterbury's brief response communicates equal desperation masked by a calm demeanor: " 'Twould drink the cup and all" (I, i, 21). The two then move to a discussion of the new king, Henry V, who has surprised the country by maturing since his wilder days, which were dramatized in *Henry IV*. They also admire his military exploits, as well as his capacity to unravel difficult moral and legal issues (I, i, 43–46). All these qualities lead to yet another reason for Canterbury to be pleased with Henry's attitude:

For I have made an offer to his Majesty,
Upon our spiritual convocation
And in regard of causes now at hand,
Which I have open'd to his Grace at large,
As touching France, to give a greater sum
Than ever at one time the clergy yet
Did to his predecessors part withal.
(I, i, 75–81)

The words "spiritual convocation" cannot disguise the political maneuvering that Canterbury has carried out in an effort to inspire the new King to fight a war against France that the Church will support. Canterbury also hints that the war will distract Henry from consideration of the bill which could cost the Church so much money.

In the next scene, the King formally solicits justification from Canterbury for beginning a military conflict with France. In response, the Archbishop provides a remarkably convoluted explanation of Salique Law (which barred succession through a female line). This analysis leads to examples of numerous precedents which, Canterbury insists, provide the requested legal basis. Yet so perplexing is this address that at its conclusion the King is forced to ask once more: "May I with right and conscience make this claim?" (I, ii, 96). After Canterbury recalls Henry's glorious family history, Ely pursues a decidedly nontheological approach to the issue:

Awake remembrance of these valiant dead,
And with your puissant arm renew their feats,
You are their heir, you sit upon their throne;
The blood and courage that renowned them
Runs in your veins; and my thrice-puissant liege
Is in the very May-morn of his youth,
Ripe for exploits and mighty enterprises.
(I, ii, 115–121)

He never mentions the bloodshed and inevitable loss of life that could result from warfare. Clearly, political and military considerations here superseded the moral and ethical standards by which men of the cloth traditionally stand. But then Shakespeare's clerics are hardly traditional.

One of the most overtly power-hungry characters in the entire *Henry VI* sequence is the Bishop of Winchester, later Cardinal. As one of the great-uncles to the young and ineffectual King, Winchester is close enough to the center of political power to touch it, but he is always blocked by Gloucester, the King's uncle, as well as his officially sanctioned Protector. Early in *Henry VI, Part 1*, Gloucester captures the core of Winchester's character by recalling his unsavory past:

> Stand back, thou manifest conspirator,
> Thou that contrivedst to murther our dead lord,
> Thou that giv'st whores indulgences to sin.
> I'll canvass thee in thy broad cardinal's hat,
> If thou proceed in this thy insolence.
> (I, iii, 33–37)

For the rest of his life, Winchester continually plots with other nobles, shifting from one alliance to another, but his fundamental goal remains his own political advantage. One moment when he exposes his agenda occurs in *Henry VI, Part 1*, after the marriage of Henry to the daughter of Earl of Arminack seems inevitable. Winchester hopes that the union will both bring him the political leverage he seeks and destroy his most hated rival:

> Humphrey of Gloucester, thou shalt well perceive
> That neither in birth, or for authority,
> The Bishop will be overborne by thee.
> I'll either make thee stoop and bend thy knee,
> Or sack this country with a mutiny.
> (V, i, 58–62)

Time and again in this tetralogy, individuals whom we recognize as dangerous make their malevolence evident by rationalizing chaos as an alternative to defeat by legal means. Here Winchester proves as ruthless as any secular politician in the court. When in *Henry VI, Part 2* he is stricken by a mysterious ailment and dies unrepentant, Warwick sums up the Cardinal's story: "So bad a death argues a monstrous life" (III, iii, 30). No further comment about him follows.

Perhaps the most insidious religious figure in all of Shakespeare's plays is Pandulph in *King John*. He enters as a representative of the Pope, intending to force the beleaguered King John to accept Stephen Langton, the Pope's selection, for Archbishop of Caunterbury. We should note that this play is set in the early thirteenth century, more than 200 years before England broke from the Church in Rome. For Shakespeare's audience, then, Pandulph's entrance aroused immediate antagonism. Furthermore, Pandulph's order that the King conform to his wishes inspires John's best moment:

> What earthy name to interrogatories
> Can taste the free breath of a sacred king?
> Thou canst not, Cardinal, devise a name
> So slight, unworthy, and ridiculous,
> To charge me to an answer, as the Pope.
> (III, i, 147–151)

John is surely bold here, but by insulting the Pope and turning his back on Rome, he ruins any chance for a political alliance with France and thereafter any opportunity for reuniting the two countries with himself in charge.

Pandulph, ever the politician, schemes to exacerbate John's dilemma:

> . . . Thou shalt stand curs'd and excommunicate,
> And blessed shall he be that doth revolt
> From his allegiance to an heretic,
> And meritorious shall that hand be call'd . . .
> (III, i, 173–176)

Pandulph thus puts a price on John's head, leaving King Philip of France trapped. He wants to be loyal to the Church and therefore must obey Pandulph, but he has agreed with John to a political marriage that will save his country from war. Philip's solution reflects his weakness, as he turns to Pandulph to provide a compromise. Instead, the Cardinal gives Philip an ultimatum:

> O, let thy vow
> First made to heaven, first be to heaven perform'd.
> That is, to be the champion of our Church!
> (III, i, 265–267)

So intense is the pressure applied by Pandulph, in conjunction with Lewis, Prince of France, that Philip succumbs, and the alliance is shattered.

Thus Pandulph becomes the embodiment of a Church that, in Shakespeare's view, seeks to control the temporal world as well as the spiritual one. But Pandulph has not finished. John's schism with Philip has caused turmoil in England, where his loudest opponent is Constance, mother of John's nephew, Arthur, whom she is pushing to occupy the throne. Therefore she laments the misery that she claims John has created:

> No, I defy all counsel, all redress,
> But that which ends all counsel, true redress:
> Death, death. O amiable lovely death!
> Thou odiferous stench! sound rottenness!
> (III, iv, 23–26)

Pandulph then insinuates himself into the situation by accusing her of madness (III, iv, 43). She retorts, legitimately: "Thou art [not] holy to belie me so . . . (III, iv, 44). Pandulph, however, is undeterred, and next moves to counsel young Lewis. First he suggests that John plans to have

Arthur killed (III, iv, 131–140), but far from finding such an act morally repulsive, Pandulph sees potential benefits for Lewis himself:

> You, in the right of Lady Blanch your wife,
> May then make all the claim that Arthur did.
> (III, iv, 142–143)

Lewis expresses skepticism that the strategy will work, but Pandulph responds with the cynical tone of a seasoned political tactician: "How green you are and fresh in this old world!" (III, iv, 145). He then demonstrates his understanding of the common people by warning Lewis that if Arthur is killed, the mob will revolt against John.

Such discernment makes Pandulph a compelling figure. In a play full of vacillating characters, he is single-minded in the pursuit of his own power through the instrument of the Church. After convincing Philip to invade England, a move the French people will support when they learn that the English under Faulconbridge the Bastard have ransacked churches (III, iv, 171–181), Pandulph leaves with smug delight.

No doubt the cleric in Shakespeare's plays who achieves the greatest political heights is Cardinal Wolsey in *Henry VIII*. After the opening celebration between Henry and the King of France at the Field of the Cloth of Gold, the Duke of Buckingham expresses to the Duke of Norfolk the general feeling toward Wolsey that is held by the other nobles:

> The devil speed him! no man's pie is freed
> From his ambitious finger. What had he
> To do in these fierce vanities? I wonder
> That such a keech can with his very bulk
> Take up the ray's o' th' beneficial sun,
> And keep it from the earth.
> (I, i, 51–57)

As always in Shakespeare, the word "sun" has overtones of the King himself, and thus Buckingham implies that Henry remains unaware of Wolsey's activities. We should note that the portrait of the King that emerges in this play is not that of the bloated hedonist familiar from history, but of a fundamentally benign ruler with the best interests of his country at heart. After all, Henry VIII was the father of the recently deceased Elizabeth I, and Shakespeare had to portray him delicately. Thus at the start of the play, the King is unaware of Wolsey's machinations, but gradually acquires the political mastery that brings Wolsey down and simultaneously elevates himself.

For a time, however, the Cardinal controls matters ruthlessly. For instance, moments after Buckingham offers that early judgment, he is arrested. Although the order is said to come from Henry, Buckingham knows that Wolsey gave the command (I, i, 122–126). Soon afterwards, a matter of taxation is brought before the King, who remains strangely detached from the matter: "Taxation?/ Wherein? and what taxation" (I, ii, 37–38). When he turns to Wolsey for advice, the Cardinal deflects responsibility:

> . . . I have no further gone in this than by
> A single voice, and that not pass'd me but
> By learned approbation of the judges.
> (I, ii, 69–71)

When, however, Henry pardons those punished unfairly for protesting the tax (I, ii, 98–102), Wolsey orders his confederate to ensure that the King's decree seems to be the product of Wolsey's own intervention (I, ii, 103–107). His capacity for political gamesmanship, though despicable, is undeniable.

Eventually Wolsey meets his downfall, though more because of coincidence than his own flaws. As Norfolk eagerly reports:

> The King hath found
> Matter against him that for ever mars
> The honey of his language.
> (III, ii, 20–22)

The Duke of Suffolk clarifies the situation:

> The Cardinal's letters to the Pope miscarried,
> And came to th' eye o' th' King, wherein was read
> How that Cardinal did entreat his Holiness
> To stay the judgment o' th' divorce . . .
> (III, ii, 30–33)

When the King reveals his knowledge of Wolsey's dealings, the trapped Cardinal lashes out against those who rejoice in his defeat:

> How eagerly ye follow my disgraces
> As if it fed ye, and how sleek and wanton
> Ye appear in every thing may bring my ruin!
> Follow your envious courses, men of malice!
> (III, ii, 240–243)

Those vengeful nobles, particularly Surrey, in turn assault Wolsey with a catalogue of his plots and betrayals, until the Lord Chamberlain objects:

Press not a falling man too far! 'tis virtue.
His faults lie open to the laws, let them,
Not you, correct him. My heart weeps to see him
So little of his great self.
(III, ii, 333–336)

This outcry, in combination with Wolsey's own egotistical reflections, almost give the Cardinal a measure of tragic stature, as does his sudden self-awareness and vulnerability:

My high-blown pride
At length broke under me, and now has left me,
Weary and old with service, to the mercy
Of a rude stream that must for ever hide me.
Vain pomp and glory of this world, I hate ye!
(III, ii, 361–365)

How much of this conversion is legitimate or the expression of a defeated power-broker is uncertain. Nonetheless, for all his unscrupulousness, Wolsey brings irresistible energy and wit to the proceedings.

Occasionally Shakespeare dramatizes how clergy can be used for advantage by shrewd political leaders. In *Richard III*, for instance, the would-be King appears before the public positioned between two ministers, while his henchman Buckingham claims that here is evidence of the King's lack of concern for power:

Two props of virtue for a Christian prince,
To stay him from the fall of vanity;
And see, a book of prayer in his hand—
True ornaments to know a holy man.
Famous Plantagenet, most gracious prince,
Lend favorable ear to our requests,
And pardon us the interruption
Of thy devotion and right Christian aid.
(III, vii, 96–103)

The theatricality of this moment is brilliant, as Richard seizes on what seems to be a universal phenomenon: the bond between religion and politics. Whatever the society, the presence of a secular ruler under the sanction of a religious authority comforts the populace, a strategy Shakespeare here mocks through the figure of the most unholy of kings.

Shakespeare sometimes presents even beneficent clergy in an unpleasant light. In *Romeo and Juliet*, Friar Lawrence wants to help the young lovers, but he cannot grasp the depth of their love and unwittingly contributes to their downfall. For instance, learning of Romeo's affections, the Friar warns: "Wisely and slow, they stumble that run fast" (II, iii, 93). Romeo later comments on the absurdity of this advice, given Romeo's passionate nature: "Thou canst not speak of that thou does not feel" (III, iii, 64). Later, it is the Friar who conceives the plan involving the apothecary and Juliet's pretending to commit suicide by poison. The scheme is so convoluted as to invite mishap, and in that sense it reflects the Friar's own ways. Finally, when Romeo's death is revealed, the Friar urges Juliet to escape:

> Come, come away.
> Thy husband in thy bosom lies dead;
> And Paris too. Come, I'll dispose of thee
> Among a sisterhood of holy nuns.
> (V, iii, 154–157)

Even the suggestion of such a recourse for Juliet suggests the Friar's blindness to her feeling. Finally, when he hears intruders, the Friar lacks the fortitude to remain and face responsibility: "I dare no longer stay" (V, iii, 159). True, he returns later to explain what has occurred, but by then he has lost our respect.

If Shakespeare demonstrates antagonism to clerical figures themselves, religious beliefs and values do buttress his plays. In *Hamlet*, for example, the officer Marcellus tries to understand why the Ghost of Hamlet's father should have scurried away so quickly in the early morning:

> Some say that ever 'gainst that season comes
> Wherein our Savior's birth is celebrated,
> This bird of dawning singeth all night long,
> And then they say no spirit dare stir abroad . . .
> (I, i, 158–161)

Later, in his first soliloquy, pondering the possibility of suicide, Hamlet broods:

> . . . Or that the Everlasting had not fix'd
> His canon 'gainst [self]-slaughter!
> (I, ii, 131–132)

Thus we are always conscious that as Hamlet seeks answers to his crises, he includes Christian values as he tries to balance the ethical equation. Yet in the same play, after Laertes, son of the court advisor Polonius, warns Ophelia to be careful about giving herself to Hamlet, she retorts:

> But, good my brother,
> Do not, as some ungracious pastors do,

Show me the steep and thorny way to heaven,
Whiles, [like] a puff'd and reckless libertine,
Himself the primrose path of dalliance treads,
And reaks not his own rede.

(I, iii, 46–51)

Here again Shakespeare upholds the principles of Christianity, but not necessarily the actions of those who would teach such principles.

Indeed, Christian values underlie all his work. He unleashes scorn, however, on those clergy who would take the moral authority that society bestows upon their profession and use it for personal aggrandizement and profit. Throughout his plays, Shakespeare reveals his antagonism for political hypocrisy of all varieties, but he seems to reserve special venom for those who would hide it behind a mask of piety.

Commoners

Shakespeare's audience included all levels of society, ranging from the educated aristocracy to the poor and illiterate "groundlings" who occupied the seats immediately in front of the stage. To appeal to such a heterogeneous group, the playwright created an equally wide roster of characters: royals and nobles, gentry and yeomen, thieves and bawds. Over the past centuries, most critical and audience attention understandably has focused on those characters from the upper class, who speak in sophisticated voices and seem to face issues of greater import. But Shakespeare's attitude toward the great mass of people in the lower strata of society is also intriguing, for it is a curious amalgam of perspectives. He shows great sympathy for certain individuals of little social status, whom he presents as simple, honest folk standing in sharp relief to more cosmopolitan, powerful individuals who dictate the course of the day-to-day world. Yet when Shakespeare depicts hordes of untutored citizens or peasants trying to act in concert, he usually presents them as not only vulnerable to manipulation, but also potentially violent.

Among those admirable, unpretentious figures Shakespeare offers is the Gardener in *Richard II*, who appears after the King has been removed from the throne by Henry Bullingbrook, soon to become Henry IV. At first, one of the Gardener's subordinates questions the meaning of his own work:

> Why should we in the compass of a pale
> Keep law and form and due proportion,
> Showing as in a model our firm estate,
> When our sea-walled garden, the whole land,
> Is full of weeds . . .
>
> (III, iv, 40–44)

If the entire country is falling apart, queries this man, why should he, or anyone, maintain his duty? The Gardener has two replies. The first reflects Richard's own negligence:

> Hold thy peace.
> He that hath suffered this disordered spring
> Hath now himself met with the fall of leaf.
> (III, iv, 47–49)

The Gardener recognizes that the King himself must bear blame for the chaotic state into which England has fallen. Thus the Gardener articulates a faith in universal justice, the conviction that those who commit crimes inevitably pay the punishment. Second, the Gardener adds that in their own way, he and his men maintain the integrity of the country:

> Superfluous branches
> We lop away, that bearing boughs may live;
> Had he done so, himself had borne the crown,
> Which waste of idle hours hath quite thrown down.
> (III, iv, 63–66)

Richard failed to sustain discipline among his followers and allowed the political system to slip into decay. The parallel thus becomes unmistakable between the garden and England itself. Both are living entities that must be nurtured. Neglect of responsibility, whether by a ruler or by a gardener, causes degeneration. In this brief scene, then, the Gardener becomes the embodiment of the English people, struggling to preserve their way of life and survive the political turmoil that besets their nation.

An even more moving example of a single citizen caught up in the greater whirl around him is Feeble, the ladies' tailor who faces military service in *Henry IV, Part 2*. From watching Falstaff in *Henry IV, Part 1* and *Part 2*, we know that he allows richer citizens to bribe their way out of military service. Thus the forces he is ordered to supply turn out to be ragtag troops with no idea what the greater issues of the war might be, but who nonetheless are "pressed" into service. Here Falstaff asks of this befuddled recruit, whose name reflects his status and, we assume, his stature:

> Wilt thou make as many holes
> in an enemy's battle as thou has done in a woman's
> petticoat?
> (III, ii, 153–155)

Feeble answers simply: "I will do my good will, sir, you can have no more" (III, ii, 156). The straightfowardness of this reply stands in contrast to the convoluted reasonings that wealthier figures invoke to justify their fighting for one cause or another. Later, Feeble adds:

> By my troth I care not; a man can die but
> once, we owe God a death. I'll ne'er bear a base mind.
> And't be my dest'ny, so; and't be not, so. No man's too
> good to serve 's prince, and let it go which way it will,
> he that dies this year is quit for the next.
>   (III, ii, 234–238)

His dignity inspires comparison with Hamlet's reflections on the fall of a sparrow before his climactic sword fight (V, ii, 219–224). Feeble may lack Hamlet's capacity for introspection, but in the face of conflict and likely death, both men summon the same perspective. One great difference between the two, though, is that Hamlet has meditated on such issues for his whole life, while Feeble encounters them here for the first time. Nonetheless, Feeble's directness, what we might even term a certain "nobility," pierces through the bombast and hypocrisy that characterize so many operatives in the history plays. In addition, Feeble's expression about owing "God a death" echoes Hal's remark to Falstaff in *Henry IV, Part 1* (V, i, 126), suggesting that wisdom may come from surprising sources.

One more character from that world deserves comment. In *Henry V*, before the climactic battle of Agincourt, the King, perhaps seeking a return to his carefree days dramatized in *Henry IV, Part 1* and *2* when he frequented the taverns with Falstaff, disguises himself and wanders through the camp of his troops. There he encounters three soldiers named Bates, Court, and Williams, whose views on war and death challenge the King's own values.

As the conversation begins, the King seeks reassurance that his policies have wide support:

> Methinks I could not die any
> where so contented as in the King's company, his cause
> being just and his quarrel honorable.
>   (IV, i, 126–128)

The word "honorable" is always suspect, as we shall consider in the chapter on "Honor." Michael Williams, however, stands unimpressed:

> I am afeard there are few die
> well that die in a battle; for how can they charitably
> dispose of any thing, when blood is in their argument?
> Now, if these men do not die well, it will be a black

matter for the King that led them to it; who to disobey
were against all proportion of subjection.
                    (IV, i, 141–146)

Throughout the play, Henry has tried to insist, both to himself and to everyone else, that by declaring war on the French he has not acted unilaterally, but has followed legal and religious sanction. Williams, however, does not permit the King to claim such a pose. In response, Henry offers an intricate series of arguments to justify how the King is not responsible for each man's life, but still Williams refuses to relent (IV, i, 197–202). Frustrated, Henry finally challenges Williams to a duel, an action that diminishes the King, at least momentarily. Thus with just a few lines, Williams makes us wonder even more deeply about the nature of military conflict and the role of the soldier who stands torn between self-preservation and loyalty to his government.

Hence the Gardener, Feeble, and Williams, all of whom have a brief time onstage, emerge as voices of reason and conscience. They also stand apart from the masses of people of similar rank, who are portrayed by Shakespeare in far less flattering terms.

Consider the mob that follows the rebel Jack Cade in *Henry VI, Part 2*. When he moves to the fore, the English crown is almost literally up for grabs. Henry VI holds it, but because he is a Lancaster and the grandson of the usurper Henry IV, who deposed Richard II, Henry VI's right to sit on the throne is under attack from the Yorks, who believe that in light of certain complicated laws of inheritance, they can legitimately claim the throne (see the chapter on "Divine Right"). As a result, the country is in the early stages of the Lancaster-York conflict, known subsequently as the War of the Roses.

Cade himself is a charismatic leader, a distant relative of some of the Yorks. Nonetheless, his sporadic recitation of his family history (IV, ii, 39–44) puts the entire Lancaster-York conflict in an unpleasant light. We know that those nobles squabbling over the order of ancestry seek to maintain law. When, however, Cade shouts: "All the realm shall be in common" (IV, ii, 68), he invites the breakdown of the social structure. So does his cohort Dick the Butcher, who urges the oft-quoted: "The first thing we do, let's kill all the lawyers" (IV, ii, 76). Cade and his followers unleash such savagery that they almost make us long for the machinations of Suffolk, York, and Queen Margaret.

Cade's followers first condemn a nameless clerk, ostensibly because he can read and write (IV, ii, 105–110). Then Sir Humphrey Stafford and his brother are brought in, and after the mob calls for their execution (IV, ii, 173), Cade reminds the audience where his values lie: "But then are we in order when we are most out of order" (IV, ii, 189–190). To Shakespeare's listeners, for whom anarchy and the breakdown of governmental structure was a paramount fear, Cade's words could not be more distressing. Here is the threat that a mob poses, and it is a threat that Shakespeare makes painfully graphic.

What follows is a series of brief scenes which reflect the chaos that ensues when a mob runs amok. A random soldier is killed simply for shouting Cade's name (IV, vi, 7–8). Before Lord Say suffers the same punishment, Cade confesses his fear of intelligence in any quarter:

> The proudest peer in
> the realm shall not wear a head on his shoulders,
> unless he pays me tribute.
> (IV, vii, 119–121)

He revels in blind acceptance by the mob. Yet Cade is hardly a fool. When Buckingham and Clifford, the King's ambassadors, announce Henry VI's willingness to pardon the rebels (IV, viii, 7–10) who cheer such news, Cade berates his followers:

> But you are all recreants and dastards,
> and delight to live in slavery to the nobility.
> (IV, viii, 27–28)

Even one who has received such enthusiastic loyalty from the mob loses patience with their mindlessness. When the horde temporarily transfers allegiance back to Cade, only to switch again at Clifford's urging, Cade mocks the fickleness which Shakespeare often ascribes to them: "Was ever feather so lightly blown to and fro as this multitude?" (IV, viii, 55–56).

The manner of Cade's death is appropriate, coming at the hands of Iden, another simple individual whose life is the antithesis of the unbridled ambition that characterizes so many in the play:

> I seek not to wax great by others' [waning],
> Or gather wealth, I care not with what envy.
> (IV, x, 20–21)

Yet even though Iden commits the murder, we can say that Cade dies at the hands of the commoners on whom he relied and who ultimately betray him.

Even when the mob in Shakespeare's plays does not actually turn violent, it must be flattered, for the threat of explosion is eternally present, and the politician who cannot work to soothe the masses faces trouble indeed. Richard II acknowledges that truth, when he comments about Bullingbrook, the man who threatens his throne:

How he did seem to dive into their hearts
With humble and familiar courtesy . . .
                    (I, iv, 25–26)

In his resentment of the strength of the people and his envy of an opponent with the skill to control them, Richard speaks for many rulers throughout literature and history.

Shakespeare releases his full fury at the mob in his Roman plays, such as his late tragedy *Coriolanus*, as cynical a study of politics as he ever created. At the time when the play is set, approximately 490 B.C., Rome is a republic, but real power lies in the hands of a few. Nevertheless, any candidate for leadership must indulge the Roman version of rituals that are always intrinsic to political life. As the play opens, the masses mill about aimlessly, blaming their great general Martius for their lack of food. For instance, the First Citizen shouts: "Let us kill him, and we'll have corn at our own price" (I, i, 10–11). As is usual in Shakespeare, the mob offers a simplistic solution to a complicated problem. The shrewd Menenius, however, as smooth a patrician and politician as Rome offers, diffuses their anger with the famous tale of the belly, a fable in which the aristocrats are symbolized by that organ, which devours what it needs, then distributes to the other parts. The mob is not remotely bothered by Menenius's distortion of logic, for common sense would suggest that the ruling class should be pictured as the head of the body, not its chief consumer. Nonetheless, when Menenius concludes by referring to the First Citizen as "the great toe of the assembly" (I, i, 155), the merriment is intoxicating.

Martius, though, lacks Menenius's grace, and instead berates the crowd:

> He that will give good words to thee will flatter
> Beneath abhorring. What would you have, you curs,
> That like nor peace nor war? The one affrights you,
> The other makes you proud. He that trusts to you,
> Where he should find you lions, finds you hares;
> Where foxes, geese.
>
>   (I, i, 167–172)

His scorn proves prophetic. Martius, however, is not alone in his distrust of the great mass of citizens. Even their own representatives, Brutus and Sicinius, care little for the people whose interests they supposedly serve (II, i, 205–221). They anticipate the moment when Martius, now named "Coriolanus" in honor of his victory at Corioles, campaigns for the office of consul by revealing his wounds. As predicted, Coriolanus despises the overtly political gesture of flattering the voters:

> Think upon me? Hang 'em,
> I would they would forget me, like the virtues
> Which our divines lose by 'em.
>> (II, iii, 56–58)

When the electorate approaches, he adds: "Bid them wash their faces,/ And keep their teeth clean" (II, iii, 60–61). In his Roman plays, Shakespeare regularly uses the image of the mob's stinking breath to characterize their general demeanor.

The more Coriolanus is forced to campaign, the more he comes to hate the mob. We must regard his attitude with some suspicion, for we know that his mother, Volumnia, urges him to seek office. He despises everything she wants, yet so totally does she dominate him that he has no outlet but to follow the course she has set out. Thus we ask whether Coriolanus's distaste for the people emerges from his own upbringing, or from the innate loathesomeness of those he seeks to rule. Perhaps the answer involves some combination of the two. Still, the masses are an ugly group, as they demonstrate when their spokesmen Brutus and Sicinius talk them into following this strategy:

> Lay
> A fault on us, your tribunes, that we labor'd
> (No impediment between) but that you must
> Cast your election on him.
>> (II, iii, 226–229)

Naturally the mob agrees, earning further abuse from Coriolanus, who accuses his fellow patricians of pandering:

> Thus we debase
> The nature of our seats and make the rabble
> Call our cares fears; which will in time
> Break ope the locks a' th' Senate, and bring in
> The crows to peck the eagles.
>> (III, i, 135–139)

Moments earlier he referred to them as "Hydra" (III, i, 93), invoking the mythological nine-headed beast slain by Hercules. We might think the judgment cruel, but later in the same scene the plebeians, goaded by Brutus and Sicinius, are ready to throw Martius off the Tarpeian rock, from where all who acted against the state were hurled to their death.

Coriolanus eventually offers grudging apologies, but his attitude reverts quickly, and he resolves to take action on his own:

You common cry of curs, whose breath I hate
As reek a' th' rotten fens, whose love I prize
As the dead carcasses of unburied men
That do corrupt my air—I banish you!
(III, iii, 120–123)

He does not escape, in fact, for in being true to his own behavior, he must fight somewhere, and thus he joins the army of his longtime enemy, Aufidius and the Volsces. Menenius first blames Sicinius and Brutus for Coriolanus's defection:

You have made fair hands,
You and your crafts! You have crafted fair!
(IV, vi, 117–118)

But he also assaults the plebeians, who prove timidly hypocritical by insisting that they never wanted Coriolanus expelled (IV, vi, 139–145). However childish or maladjusted we judge Coriolanus to be, the mob is always worse.

The manner of Coriolanus's death is fitting. After his mother and wife fail to persuade him to rejoin Rome, Coriolanus finds himself muddled, unable to commit fully to anyone but himself. Still, the Volscean mob, like their Roman counterparts, initially cheer their new ally who had recently killed their children in war (V, vi, 51–63). But when the Volsces attack and Coriolanus tries to establish a peace that brings glory to both cities, Aufidius brands him a traitor, and the Volsces, ever fickle, recall his past conquests of them and join in the accusation. Within moments Coriolanus is killed: not by one man, but by the crowd.

Perhaps Shakespeare's most famous portrait of the mob is in *Julius Caesar*, where in some respects it may even be judged the central character, the one whom all the principals fear and to whom all the principals gear their actions. True, Rome of 44 B.C. is not a democracy. Yet its politicians understand that any individual who hopes to gain power must have the support of the people.

Their unruliness is apparent in the first scene, as they ramble aimlessly while two tribunes, Murellus and Flavius, seek to rally popular support against Caesar. After the commoners exit, Flavius notes acidly:

See whe'er their basest metal be not mov'd;
They vanish tongue-tied in their guiltiness.
(I, i, 61–62)

He recognizes how malleable they are. An equally cynical note is injected by the conspirator Casca, who describes the mob's attitude after Caesar publically declined a crown:

> ... the rabblement howted, and
> clapp'd their chopp'd hands, and threw up their
> sweaty night-caps, and utter'd such a deal of stinking
> breath because Caesar refused the crown, that it had,
> almost, chok'd Caesar ...
>
> (I, iii, 244–248)

The familiar image of the mob's breath, in the context of such sneering, confirms the attitude that the politicians in this play have toward the masses whose support they must win.

Even Caesar worries about their mood. When his wife, Calphurnia, relates her dream that shows the masses bathing in blood running from Caesar's statue, he agrees that for her sake he will remain home from the Senate (II, ii, 71). However, at the mere suggestion by the conspirator Decius that the people will laugh if Caesar yields to his wife's fears, the great general immediately changes his mind (II, ii, 105–107). The mob inspires that much fear.

The most astonishing glimpse of the masses occurs after the assassination of Caesar, when first Brutus, then Antony, takes control in the Forum. Initially, the crowd responds to Brutus's thin words about honor, but they do so in curious phrases. "Let him be Caesar" (III, ii, 51) shouts one, and "Caesar's better parts/ Shall be crown'd in Brutus" (III, ii, 51–52) adds another. Despite Brutus's hopes for them, the people do not seek freedom. They desire a ruler, an authority to set down laws and regulate lives. Thus the chaos of the play's opening scene mirrors the community state of mind.

Antony's oration, however, leaves the crowd constantly off balance. In his opening lines, he stands over Caesar's corpse and seems to accede to the mob's immediate desires: "I come to bury Caesar, not to praise him" (III, ii, 74). But immediately, and with apparent humility, Antony recreates scenes from Caesar's life, simultaneously glorifying him and diminishing the stature of the men who killed him (III, ii, 87–103). Slowly the plebeians turn his way: "Methinks there is much reason in his sayings" (III, ii, 107), says one. The gambit of showing Caesar's will drives the mob into a well-timed frenzy, for as they grow desperate to learn its contents, Antony claims that he does not mean to disclose any stipulations, then further entices them: "You are not wood, you are not stones, but men ..." (III, iii, 142). Eventually he sends the crowd charging in one direction, then waves the parchment and with comic adroitness pulls them back: "You have forgot the will I told you of" (III, ii, 238).

Antony's most effective stroke, though, is bringing the mob around Caesar's body, then holding up the ripped and bloody cloak, which was worn, Antony claims: "That day he overcame the Nervii" (III, ii, 173). He then graphically points to where each assassin's knife supposedly entered Caesar's body. He cannot, of course, know where and by whom individual blows were struck, but he conjures up a scenario of one blade after another ripping Caesar's body, and with every stab the mob feels the blade within themselves. Caesar's wounds become their own, and they quickly label the conspirators as "traitors" (III, ii, 255).

Although Antony is brilliant, two lines reveal his icy detachment:

> Now let it work. Mischief, thou art afoot,
> Take what course thou wilt!
>
> (III, ii, 259–260)

The mob, racing off to commit destruction and murder (III, ii, 254–261), is terrifying.

The funeral oration is usually regarded as the climax of the play, but the brief scene that follows is the dramatic high point. It lasts only thirty-seven lines, but it is a fearful portrait of humankind reveling in savagery. In a moment that recalls the actions of Jack Cade's followers against the clerk, the Roman people realize that Cinna the Poet is not the conspirator they seek, but kill him anyway (III, iii, 33–34).

This scene is the mob's final appearance, and therefore what remains with us is the montage of men running the streets like the "dogs of war" Antony invoked earlier (III, i, 273). The image carries over even to plays where the mob does not actually appear, but in which this sense of them looms. In *Hamlet*, for example, a messenger reports that Laertes, in fury over the death of his father, Polonius, and his sister, Ophelia, has aroused the rabble who "call him lord" (IV, v, 103). Claudius remains convinced that as King he can hold authority (IV, v, 124–126), and he does manage to diffuse Laertes' threat, but the actions of the populace in support of Laertes affirms once more Shakespeare's fear of mob rule.

Throughout his plays, Shakespeare suggests that the brutish energy of the masses must be controlled by an authoritative government. Indeed, as the plebeians in *Julius Caesar* and *Coriolanus* suggest, the mob wants and needs control by an outside agent. True, Shakespeare demonstrates sympathy and respect for some of his humblest characters, but never does he let us forget that when individuals join in action, they may lose rationality, morality, and even their fundamental decency.

Cynicism

One of the most intriguing fronts any theatrical character can offer is cynicism. Those figures who comment derisively upon the actions and values of others can be a daunting presence, puncturing dignity and revealing hypocrisy. In real life as well, this attitude sometimes provides a certain pleasure for onlookers. Yet although Shakespeare presents several cynical figures, and although at first blush they may prove enjoyable, their cynicism is ultimately revealed to be destructive: not only to others, but also to themselves.

For instance, in *Romeo and Juliet*, the attitude of Mercutio contrasts with the romantic instincts of his younger friend, Romeo, who rhapsodizes about his vulnerability to love:

> Is love a tender thing? It is too rough,
> Too rude, too boist'rous, and it pricks like thorn.
>> (I, iv, 25–26)

Mercutio offers a simple solution:

> If love be rough with you, be rough with love;
> Prick love for pricking, and you beat love down.
>> (I, iv, 26–27)

He resists romance, adding that his callousness ensures that he will never be hurt. Yet his confidence has another side. Presently, in the celebrated speech that describes the adventures of Queen Mab, who inspires sleepers to dream of their greatest desires, Mercutio demonstrates his captivating wordplay:

> And in this state she gallops night by night
> Through lovers' brains, and then they dream of love;

> [O'er] courtiers' knees, that dream on cur'sies straight;
> O'er lawyers fingers, who straight dream on fees . . .
>> (I, iv, 70–73)

By the end of the recitation, however, the playful images degenerate into ugliness, as soldiers cut throats and maids suffer virtual rape. Thus Mercutio's latent frustration and hostility overcome his charm. Finally, Romeo cuts him off:

> Peace, peace, Mercutio, peace!
> Thou talk'st of nothing.
>> (I, iv, 95–96)

Mercutio concurs:

> True, I talk of dreams,
> Which are the children of a idle brain,
> Begot of nothing but vain fantasy.
>> (I, iv, 96–98)

He recognizes his hollowness; yet he cannot cure this condition. For instance, when Romeo races off to pursue Juliet, his new infatuation, Mercutio reduces this affection to a crude joke:

> O, Romeo, that she were, O that she were
> An open-[arse], thou a poprin pear!
>> (II, i, 37–38)

Romeo recognizes his friend's weakness: "He jests at scars that never felt a wound" (II, ii, 1). Unable to give love, Mercutio scorns what he cannot experience. His wit may have casual appeal, as when he jokes lewdly with Juliet's lusty Nurse (II, iv), but beneath the attractive surface lies a pitiable core.

Still, Mercutio's aggressive humor reflects passion inside him. This energy, which must come out in some form, emerges when he enters in the heat of midday, bantering with his friend Benvolio and seemingly looking for a fight:

> Thy head is as full of quarrels as an egg is
> full of meat, and yet thy head hath been beaten as
> addle as an egg for quarrelling.
>> (III, i, 22–24)

We sense in Mercutio's language a latent violence, a restlessness that may well emanate from lack of love. Then, as if seizing upon a target for this thwarted emotion, Mercutio refuses to let Tybalt, his rival from the Capulet family, pass calmly. In response, Romeo attempts to placate the anger of Tybalt, Juliet's cousin:

> I do protest I never injured thee,
> But love thee better than thou canst devise,
> Till thou shalt know the reason of my love . . .
> (III, i, 68–70)

Outraged by the seeming capitulation of a Montague to one of the hated Capulets, Mercutio explodes: "O calm, dishonorable, vile submission!" (III, i, 73), and a moment later he attacks Tybalt. Although Romeo tries to act as peacemaker, Mercutio is fatally wounded, and in his last moments turns to universal denunciation: "A plague a' both houses!" (III, i, 91), blaming his death on the two rival families. We, however, recognize the truth. Even though Mercutio dies punning about being "a grave man" (III, i, 98), he instigated this confrontation and thereby destroyed himself. His wit could not supplant the need to give and receive the love that he mocked.

Another character who casts a cynical eye on love is Enobarbus in *Antony and Cleopatra*. He is a soldier, the closest aid to Mark Antony, who, along with Lepidus and Octavius Caesar, is one of the triumvirate that rules Rome. Antony, however, has become obsessed with Cleopatra, the Queen of Egypt, and therefore has neglected his Roman duties. Enobarbus thus finds himself in the awkward position of struggling to maintain loyalty to a great man gone astray.

Yet Enobarbus's attitude is complicated because, on the one hand, he enjoys the salacious humor of Cleopatra's court, and even participates with his own coarse remarks: "Mine, and most of our fortunes to-night, shall be—drunk in bed" (I, ii, 45–46). He also jests with Antony about Cleopatra's sexual inclinations (I, ii), and their byplay clarifies that the two men see preposterousness in both Antony's dalliance and all sexual activity. On the other hand, when Maecenas, one of Caesar's men, suggests that Antony will tire of Cleopatra, Enobarbus offers eloquent tribute to her:

> Never, he will not.
> Age cannot wither her, nor custom stale
> Her infinite variety. Other women cloy
> The appetites they feed, but she makes hungry
> Where most she satisfies . . .
> (II, ii, 233–237)

Although Enobarbus lives without romantic attachment, he appreciates the depth of feeling such passion can inspire in Antony, who has the capacity to surrender himself completely to love.

In place of marriage to a woman, Enobarbus has created a marriage to service. His devotion to Antony's charge fulfills the void within him, although Antony's faltering under Cleopatra's influence tests Enobarbus's devotion. As he says:

> . . . yet he that can endure
> To follow with allegiance fall'n lord
> Does conquer him that did his master conquer,
> And earns a place i' th' story.
> (III, xiii, 43–46)

Before long, though, Antony's military failures leave Enobarbus's faith shattered:

> When valor [preys on] reason,
> It eats the sword it fights with. I will seek
> Some way to leave him.
> (III, xiii, 198–200)

Even a cynic needs to believe in something, and when Enobarbus is denied such an object, he becomes lost. Antony's subsequent forgiveness, then, leaves Enobarbus seeing himself as a betrayer, and his subsequent death should be seen as the product of a broken heart as much as the result of any physical wound. We might even take his passing as recognition that his own mocking perspective contributed to his downfall.

Enobarbus seeks to compensate for his view of life and love by attaching himself to the military, specifically to Antony. Mercutio tries to fill the void inside him with humor and friendship. Neither succeeds, for cynicism, as dramatized by Shakespeare, tends to destroy the cynic. Without any outlet, however, cynicism may also turn outward, where its consequences can damage others as well.

Such is the case with Iago in *Othello*. First, as Othello's ensign, he mocks the promotion of Cassio to Othello's lieutenant (I, i, 20–30). Then he scorns the notion of service (I, i, 42–65). Finally, and perhaps most significantly, he torments Brabantio, Desdemona's father, by conjuring up a series of brutal images about her relationship with Othello:

> Your heart is burst, you have lost half your soul;
> Even now, now, very now, an old black ram
> Is tupping your white ewe.
> (I, i, 87–89)

Cynicism

> I am one, sir, that comes to tell you your
> daughter and the Moor are [now] making the beast
> with two backs.
>
> (I, i, 115–117)

The preoccupation with matters sexual and racial seems at the heart of Iago's anger. Whenever we grapple with the tantalizing question of his motivation to destroy the marriage of Othello and Desdemona, we return to the sexual imagery that dominates his language. For instance, to his dupe, Roderigo, Desdemona's would-be suitor, Iago scorns sexual appetite:

> The food
> that to him now is as luscious as locusts, shall be to
> him shortly as [acerb] as [the] coloquintida. She
> must change for youth; when she is sated with his
> body, she will find the [error] of her choice.
>
> (I, iii, 347–351)

Unlike Mercutio, Iago has no friends with whom he can share his wit and thereby release frustration. Unlike Enobarbus, Iago has no political or social cause to which he can devote himself. Trapped in a loveless marriage to Emilia, Iago has only himself; thus his cynicism festers. Again and again we feel Iago in torment over the emotional and physical joy shared by Othello, a black man, and Desdemona, a younger white woman, and this torment takes the form of bitter humor that Iago uses to drive Othello to a frenzy of jealousy. After Iago has brought Othello to the brink of madness by suggesting that Desdemona and Cassio have had an affair, Iago reflects on how commonplace such behavior is:

> There's millions now alive
> That nightly lie in those unproper beds
> Which they dare swear peculiar . . .
>
> (IV, i, 67–69)

The image furthers Iago's plan by infuriating Othello, but it also soothes Iago's frustration about himself, for he has been scorned by women. In his eyes, they are nothing but immoral predators. Hence their lack of interest in him is actually a point in his favor, and his cynical attitude is justified. We also note how often Iago urges others to assert their "manhood." He does so to Roderigo (I, iii, 335), and to Othello (III, iii, 374 and IV, i, 65). Iago also speaks constantly in images of manhood. All these references suggest that he is uncertain of his own masculinity, an implication that makes his cynicism an all-the-more desperate attempt to salvage his ego.

What becomes especially gripping is how Iago consciously uses his fury to drive himself to vengeance:

> I hate the Moor,
> And it is thought abroad that 'twixt my sheets
> [H'as] done my office. I know not if't be true,
> But I, for mere suspicion in that kind,
> Will do as if for surety.
>
> (I, iii, 386–390)

The idea that Othello has slept with Emilia is ludicrous, as Iago admits. Yet so twisted is he by his own cynicism that he does not care. Indeed, part of the fascination of Iago is that he never clarifies his goals. In the opening of the play, he refers to "my peculiar end" (I, i, 60), and he never becomes more specific. The ruination of Othello and Desdemona, even if successful, would not help him, but he continually spurs himself to action: "This is the night/ That either makes me, or foredoes me quite" (V, i, 128–129). Never, though, does he articulate what the completion of his plan will accomplish. In fact, he has no reason. Rather his cynicism has manifested itself in destruction carried out for its own sake.

At the end of the play, when Iago's treachery has been revealed, his final words are terrifyingly appropriate:

> Demand me nothing: what you know, you know:
> From this time forth I never will speak word.
>
> (V, ii, 303–304)

What could he say, even if he wanted to explain himself? The roots of his fury are unknown, even to him. All he has is his cynical pose, the product of a profound dissatisfaction with his social and marital status, and his concomitant desire to prove himself worthy of being judged "a man."

Perhaps the most cynical character in Shakespeare's plays is at the core of what may be his most cynical text, *Troilus and Cressida*. This is Shakespeare's version of Homer's *Iliad*, the most celebrated military adventure in history, which the playwright turns upside down and inside out. Achilles, Agamemnon, Ulysses, Ajax, Menelaus: the noble figures familiar from Homer's epic are reduced to greedy, treacherous squabblers, full of bluster and selfishness. Even those few who retain some stature, such as the Trojan hero Hector and his wife, Andromache, are deluded about the glories of war.

At the center of this turmoil is Thersites, described by Shakespeare as "a deformed and scurrilous Greek." His language is always marked by physical imagery, with the implication that as individual bodies in this play are scarred and diseased, so the body politic on both the Greek and Trojan sides is equally corrupted. Perhaps he is a mock version of the chorus familiar from Greek tragedy, although at times his denunciations are comically direct:

> Agamemnon is a fool, Achilles is a fool,
> Thersites is a fool, and, as aforesaid, Patroclus
> is a fool.
> (II, iii, 58–60)

Agamemnon is leader of the Greek forces, Achilles is the greatest of the Greek warriors, and Patroclus is Achilles' lover, with whom the great soldier dallies in his tent while the battle awaits. At other moments, however, Thersites reminds us of the reality underneath the savagery of the battle: that all was started over the theft of Helen, wife of King Agamemnon's brother, Menelaus, by the Trojan prince Paris. In Thersites' eyes, nothing grand about these figures remains. Nor in our own eyes, once Thersites has finished:

> Here is such patchery, such juggling, and
> such knavery! All the argument is a whore and a
> cuckold, a good quarrel to draw emulous factions and
> bleed to death upon. [Now the dry suppeago on the
> subject, and war and lechery confound all!]
> (II, iii, 71–75)

Thersites repeats that last sentiment at several times, confirming his view that the most memorable battle in history was motivated by elemental, even bestial, desires.

Thersites' part in the play is comparatively small. Yet with each entrance, he forces us to consider the other characters from the most ruthless of perspectives. Here he derides the behavior of Achilles and Patroclus:

> With so much blood and too little brain,
> these two may run mad, but, if with too much brain
> and too little blood they do, I'll be a curer of
> madmen.
> (V, i, 48–51)

Later he offers a corrosive diatribe on the leaders of both the Greek and Trojan sides (IV, iv, 1–17), and subsequently, at the sight of Menelaus and Paris fighting, Thersites sneers: "The cuckold and the cuckold-maker are at it. Now, bull! now dog!" (V, vii, 9–10). How can we regard any of this action seriously? The commentary of the cynic reduces the pageant of the Trojan War to a barbaric farce.

We would be wrong, however, to assume that Thersites speaks for Shakespeare. The situation is more complicated than such obscene commentary would suggest, and the political and military strategies followed on both sides, along with Hector's attempt to conduct himself with dignity, and the suffering of his wife, Andromache, leave us more in despair than laughter. After all, Thersites may see the folly of others, but he himself is merely a figure on the periphery of events, as unpleasant and empty as the action before him. Like the other cynics considered in this section, he amuses us with his caustic wit, which reduces all to rubble. Inevitably, however, the cynics in Shakespeare's plays become trapped in destruction, their own existence as impoverished as that of those they mock.

Divine Right

One of the fundamental cultural beliefs of Shakespeare's time was the medieval conviction that a king's position on the throne was divinely sanctioned. As such, the monarch was the linchpin between the microcosm (our daily existence) and the macrocosm (the surrounding universe). Moreover, the strength and stability of the kingship was reflected on those two planes. A strong royal presence manifested itself in a stable world, while a throne in chaos was mirrored by a kingdom equally in disorder.

Throughout Shakespeare's plays, however, especially the two series of four plays that dramatize English history from 1399 to 1485, we see the growing politicization of this sacred position. Leading figures of the Renaissance, such as the political theorist Machiavelli, contributed to an environment in which the unquestioned authority of divine right was increasingly vulnerable to the force of popular approval, as well as to the machinations of political contention. Thus although the principle of "divine right" still held sway over Shakespeare's time and thought, the nature of the office became complicated by individual struggles for authority.

This conflict dominated Shakespeare's era; nonetheless, the playwright dramatized aspects of the issue against a variety of historical settings. For instance, in the first scene of *King Lear*, which takes place during the timeless generations of ancient England, Lear responds to his daughter Cordelia's refusal to flatter him by reminding her and all listeners of the source of his royal stature:

> For by the sacred radiance of the sun,
> The [mysteries] of Hecat and the night;
> By all the operation of the orbs,
> From whom we do exist and cease to be . . .
> (I, i, 109–112)

Lear believes that his divine ordination must force everyone to submit to his command. Yet one of the great tensions of the play is the growing resistance to such authority, articulated first by the Earl of Gloucester's illegitimate son, Edmund, who begins a memorable soliloquy as follows: "Thou, Nature, art my goddess, to thy law/ My services are bound" (I, ii, 1–2). Edmund offers tribute to a different divinity, one that embodies a primitive, even bestial drive toward power. Indeed, the play as a whole may be regarded as a war between two convictions: first, traditional religious belief and, second, the secular assumption that the right to authority belongs to whoever has the strength to seize and keep it.

Shakespeare also brings out the theme of divine right in plays set beyond the boundaries of England. In *Hamlet*, for example, King Claudius comforts his wife, Gertrude, over the threatening presence of Laertes, enraged over the murder of his father, Polonius:

> Let him go, Gertrude, do not fear our person;
> There's such divinity doth hedge a king
> That treason can but peep to what it would,
> Acts little of his will.
>
> (IV, v, 123–126)

Indeed, the authority of divine right is so strong that here the populace embraces it, even when the legitimacy of the King is uncertain. Such is the case in the final scene of *Hamlet*, when the dying Laertes blames Claudius for poisoning Gertrude and conspiring to envenom the swords with which Laertes and Hamlet have fatally wounded each other. After Hamlet stabs Claudius, the onlookers nevertheless shout "Treason, treason!" (V, ii, 323), standing by the King even when his crimes are of such magnitude.

To understand the full power of divine right, however, we must look at Shakespeare's history plays, in which the nature of kingship is one of the central themes. *King John*, for instance, set at the end of the twelfth century, focuses on the immediate descendants of Henry II, including the title character, who eventually signed the Magna Charta. As the play starts, the King's position is already shaky, for according to the strict laws of succession, the throne should belong to Arthur, Duke of Britain. The guiding principle decreed that after the death of a childless monarch, in this case Richard I (also known as "Richard the Lionhearted"), the crown should pass to the oldest surviving brother. In this situation, however, because that brother, Geoffrey, had already died, the next in line should have been Arthur, Geoffrey's son, not John, Richard's second-oldest brother. The crux of the drama rests in the reality that John has violated the law by seizing the crown. Indeed, so militant is his claim that he announces himself willing to go to war to retain it (I, i, 19–20).

Even John's mother, Elinor, recognizes that legally the throne belongs to Arthur (I, i, 40–41), but John's resolve may be seen in two lines when he confirms his willingness to fight: "Our abbeys and our priories shall pay/ This [expedition's] charge" (I, i, 48–49). Here John reveals both his ruthlessness and determination. He has the insolence to steal from churches, and thus he clarifies that he will not hesitate to break laws to secure his position. He therefore promises an authoritative kingship that might well violate accepted rights, but which should also maintain the strength of the country. Arthur, on the other hand, reveals himself to be weak on several counts, and this dilemma leads to the central question. Who is preferable as ruler: the aggressive, even dictatorial John, or the legitimate but passive Arthur? Neither proves satisfactory.

The situation grows more complicated when King Philip of France accuses John of violating the principle of divine right:

> But thou from loving England art so far
> That thou hast under-wrought his lawful king,
> Cut off the sequence of posterity,
> Outfaced infant state, and done a rape
> Upon the maiden virtue of the crown.
>
> (II, i, 94–98)

Then Philip reaffirms the place of God in the matter of royal succession. He points to the city of Angiers ("this" [II, i, 106]), and speaks of it as an inheritance to Arthur from God. The implication is that John, by claiming possession, goes against divine will. John's retort would have stirred Shakespeare's audience: that Philip is using support from the Church to interfere in England's political life (II, i, 118). Thus one difficulty the play poses is Shakespeare's attitude toward John. He has taken the crown by usurpation, but he is an Englishman heroically standing against the Church of Rome.

Eventually, John's innate corruption causes him to lose political authority, which is picked up and thereafter borne nobly by his half-brother, Philip the Bastard, the illegitimate son of Richard the Lionhearted. Still, with his powers waning and the country in disarray, John falls so far as to establish a treaty with the Pope, which the Bastard decries:

> O inglorious league!
> Shall we, upon the footing of our land,
> Send fair-play orders and make compromise,
> Insinuation, parley, and base truce
> To arms invasive?
>
> (V, i, 65–69)

Thereafter the Bastard leads his nation's armies, so that England is united. Still, because of John's desperation to retain his throne, and a selfishness that spread throughout the royal world and by extension into the kingdom at large, the country was for a time fragmented. The play as a whole thus reaffirms that divine right was the foundation upon which the political, religious, and social order of England rested.

The violation of that order reaches extraordinary dimensions in Shake-speare's aforementioned tetralogies. The story begins in 1398, during the reign of Richard II, when the principle of divine right still remained unquestioned. In *Richard II*, the Duchess of Gloucester berates her brother-in-law, John of Gaunt, because of his unwillingness to act against the King, whom both suspect of ordering the murder of the Duke of Gloucester, Gaunt's brother and the Duchess's husband. Gaunt's answer sets a tone for the entire sequence of plays:

> God's is the quarrel, for God's substitute,
> His deputy anointed in His sight,
> Hath caus'd his death, the which if wrongfully,
> Let heaven revenge, for I may never lift
> An angry arm against His minister.
> (I, ii, 37–41)

Gaunt has lived his entire life under the precept of divine right, and he cannot give way on so essential an aspect of his being. No such scruples, however, inhibit Gaunt's son, Henry Bullingbrook, who returns from exile in direct disobedience of King Richard's order. York, Bullingbrook's uncle, clarifies the orthodox position held by his and Gaunt's generation:

> Thou art a banish'd man, and here art come,
> Before the expiration of thy time,
> In braving arms against thy sovereign.
> (II, iii, 110–112)

Bullingbrook, however, retorts that other principles must be considered:

> I am a subject,
> And I challenge law. Attorneys are denied me,
> And therefore personally I lay my claim
> To my inheritance of free descent.
> (II, iii, 133–136)

Everyone onstage and off knows that after the death of Gaunt, Richard confiscated land and monies that were legally Bullingbrook's inheritance. Thus, according to Bullingbrook's perspective, Richard, under the claim

of divine right, has clashed with a fundamental precept of English society—primogeniture, or inheritance by the oldest son. Bullingbrook then
insists that once the King has broken the latter principle, Bullingbrook
himself need no longer stand by the former.

The consequences of this action resound through the second Henriad,
but not without further debate. First, the Bishop of Carlisle, seeking to
bolster Richard's dwindling courage, reaffirms the authority of divine
right:

> The means that heavens yield must be embrac'd,
> And not neglected; else heaven would,
> And we will not.
> (III, ii, 28–30)

At these words, Richard is momentarily comforted:

> Not all the water in the rough rude sea
> Can wash the balm off from an anointed king;
> The breath of worldly men cannot depose
> The deputy elected by the Lord . . .
> (III, ii, 54–57)

Bullingbrook, however, remains relentless, and with the support of most
of the English nobility, forces Richard II to step down from the throne
so that Bullingbrook, who also holds the title "Duke of Herford," can
take over. This usurpation earns ferocious rebuke from Carlisle:

> My Lord of Herford here, whom you call king,
> Is a foul traitor to proud Herford's king
> And if you crown him, let me prophecy,
> The blood of English shall manure the ground,
> And future ages groan for this foul act.
> (IV, i 134–138)

Shakespeare's audience, who lived approximately 190 years after the
deposition of Richard, would have recognized that what Carlisle anticipates is what we have come to know as the War of the Roses, the sixty-
year battle for the English throne waged by two noble families, the Lancasters and the Yorks.

Richard, too, envisions such turmoil. He warns Northumberland, Bullingbrook's chief ally, to beware the new King's attitude:

> He shall think that thou, which knowest the way
> To plant unrightful kings, wilt know again

Being ne'er so little urg'd, another way
To pluck him headlong from the usurped throne.
(V, i, 62–65)

Richard accurately forecasts that once divine right has been challenged successfully, subsequent monarchs are more vulnerable than ever to insurrection by dissatisfied nobles.

We must also recognize that in Shakespeare's eyes, the English throne under Richard's stewardship became susceptible to other political influences that we would recognize as endemic to our own time. For instance, Richard II ruefully notes how comfortably Bullingbrook deals with the populace at large:

What reverence he did throw away on slaves,
Wooing poor craftsmen with the craft of smiles . . .
(I, iii, 27–29)

Richard resents how the need to appeal to the public has become part of the responsibilities of a king. Yet by the beginning of *Henry IV, Part 1*, the newly crowned Henry finds that even his considerable political skills are not sufficient to alleviate the turmoil his actions have caused, and this deficiency, combined with the willingness of certain nobles to overthrow the throne once more, creates a crisis for the King. The result is a rebellion that creates disorder in the country and personal agony for Henry, as he confesses to his son, Hal:

I know not whether God will have it so
For some displeasing service I have done,
That in his secret doom, out of my blood
He'll breed revengement and a scourge for me . . .
(III, ii, 4–7)

Not only is the country burdened by the consequences of Henry's actions, but the King suffers personally: first, from the incessant barrage of political opposition; second, by a crippling, leprosy-like disease; and, finally, by the failure of his oldest son, Hal, to conduct himself as the Prince of Wales should. Instead, Hal has been frequenting the taverns and carousing with the riffraff of England, including Sir John Falstaff. Still, Henry refuses to apologize for his actions against Richard:

The skipping King, he ambled up and down,
With shallow jesters, and rash bavin wits,
Soon kindled and soon burnt, carded his state,
Mingled his royalty with cap'ring fools . . .
(III, ii, 60–63)

Divine Right

Whatever guilt Henry acknowledges, the theme of divine right remains at the forefront. Before the climactic battle at Shrewsbury, Sir Walter Blunt, the king's loyal supporter, accuses the rebels of treachery:

> And God defend but still I should stand so,
> So long as out of limit and true rule
> You stand against anointed majesty.
>
> (IV, iii, 38–40)

How ironic that a king who rebelled in spite of the religious sanctioning of the throne should now stand by that authority, even though he himself is a usurper who bears the weight of his crime.

In *Henry IV, Part 2*, with yet another rebellion threatening his reign, the King, now painfully aged, reflects on the path his life has followed:

> Then you perceive the body of our kingdom
> How foul it is, what rank diseases grow,
> And with what danger, near the heart of it.
>
> (III, i, 38–40)

He cannot escape the conviction that his own poor health is manifested in the struggles within his kingdom. Later, when still another insurrection against Henry IV is underway, the Earl of Westmoreland, in the name of King Henry, criticizes the rebels in familiar terms:

> What peer hath been suborn'd to grate on you?
> That you should seal this lawless bloody book
> Of forg'd rebellion with a seal divine?
>
> (IV, i, 90–92)

Even on his deathbed, the King must acknowledge his transgression:

> God knows, my son,
> By what by-paths and indirect crook'd ways
> I met this crown, and I myself know well
> How troublesome it sate upon my head.
> To thee it shall descend with better quiet,
> Better opinion, better confirmation,
> For all the soil of the achievement goes
> With me into the earth.
>
> (IV, v, 183–190)

Henry IV's prediction, however, or perhaps it is a desperate wish, does not come true. In *Henry V*, for instance, the young King includes tributes to God in virtually every major speech, as if trying to assure himself and others that although he is the son of a usurper, and thus in the eyes of a substantial portion of the kingdom still an illegal interloper on the throne, the blessings of God are on him, and he is in fact divinely ordained. One instance among many occurs when the King inquires whether he may rightly exercise his claim to the French throne by going to war. First, Henry couches the issue in polite terms:

> For God doth know how many now in health
> Shall drop their blood in approbation
> Of what your reverence shall incite us to.
> (I, ii, 18–20)

He simultaneously acknowledges his respect for God and deflects responsibility for the upcoming military action. When the legitimacy of the cause is finally established by the Bishop of Eli and the Archbishop of Canterbury, Henry maintains this tone:

> Now are we well resolv'd, and by God's help
> And yours, the noble sinews of our power,
> France being ours, we'll bend it to our awe.
> (I, ii, 222–224)

Henry subtly implies that not only is the upcoming invasion divinely sanctioned, but that any nobles who question the King's legitimacy would themselves be going against God.

Yet even as Henry V proceeds with such political adroitness, the weight of his father's actions weigh upon him. Before the monumental battle of Agincourt, he recounts bitterly the burden he and his countrymen have been forced to carry:

> Not to-day, O Lord,
> O, not to-day, think not upon the fault
> My father made in compassing the crown!
> I Richard's body have interred new,
> And on it have bestowed more contrite tears,
> Than from it issued forced drops of blood.
> (IV, i, 292–297)

The guilt over the usurpation will never escape the King nor his descendants.

Henry does triumph in this battle, but his reign is comparatively short, and when he is succeeded on the throne by his infant son, Henry VI, England endures a terrible period of unrest. Shakespeare dramatized this era earlier in his career, in the first tetralogy of history plays: *Henry VI, Part 1*; *Henry VI, Part 2*; *Henry VI, Part 3*; and *Richard III*. Throughout that series, events of the usurpation are retold several times, with descendants of Henry IV's family, the Lancasters, perpetually justifying his actions against Richard. Meanwhile, members of the opposing family, the Yorks, seek to establish their own right to the crown through the intricate, yet religiously ordained, laws of succession.

One example of such clarification takes place in *Henry VI, Part 1*, when the historical background is presented in overwhelming detail (II, v, 61–92). The essence of the squabble is delineated by Edmund Mortimer, a figure whom Shakespeare has misidentified, but who nonetheless clarifies the situation. Mortimer himself is descended from Clarence, the third son of Edward III, while the current King, Henry VI, is a great-grandson of John of Gaunt, the fourth son of Edward III. Richard, Duke of York, is the son of Edward's fifth son. This Richard married Anne Mortimer, also a descendant of Clarence. Thus the Yorks claim that through this marriage, the throne belongs to their family. On this subtle point, taken up on either side by a good many massive egos and ambitious family members, the battle raged for decades.

With that historical reality before us, we must face the all-important question of Shakespeare's verdict about Henry IV's actions. Was his removal of Richard II in violation of divine right, and did the usurpation bring England decades of political uncertainty and intra-family bloodshed? Or were Richard's actions against the people, including his confiscation of Bullingbrook's inheritance, and the probable murder of Gloucester (indeed, his entire governance of England) of such criminal magnitude that he deserved to be deposed?

The answer to both questions is, paradoxically, "yes."

Henry's action was wrong, but necessary. The usurpation of the throne was an action against God, but it was an action demanded by the moment. King Henry V, regarded by many as the most heroic ruler in English history, would never have reached the throne had the childless Richard's plan for succession been carried out. Yet after the death of Henry V, England continued to pay severe consequences. These, however, had to be endured so that the two families, the Lancasters and the Yorks, could unite in the placement of King Henry VII on the throne, and the country might thereafter benefit from a newly enfranchised kingship. Henry IV's crimes thus began a new age of English rule, one more responsive to increasing pressures and responsibilities, both in England and throughout the world.

Fate

Perhaps the most important thematic difference between the tragedies of Shakespeare and those of the great classical Greek dramatists Aeschylus, Sophocles, and Euripides is the freedom that individual characters possess. In Greek tragedy, the gods can ordain the outcome of events, and no matter how human beings struggle, divine will is irresistible. Such is the case, for example, with the title figure of Sophocles' *Oedipus Rex*. Because of transgressions committed before he was born, Oedipus is condemned by the gods to murder his father and marry his mother, and despite his parents' attempts to spare themselves this fate, Oedipus does indeed kill his father, Laius, and marry his mother, Jocasta. The tension of the play is Oedipus's gradual discovery that these crimes have plunged his city into suffering, and that he himself is the purveyor of the evil that he seeks to purge.

In Shakespeare's tragedies, on the other hand, we are always conscious that characters are free to determine the course of their own lives. True, certain figures look to the heavens to explain or excuse their own blunders or the missteps of others, and at times supernatural elements seem to control events. Ultimately, however, Shakespeare insists that human beings are responsible for their own actions.

In *Titus Andronicus*, Shakespeare's first tragedy, the tribune Marcus, brother of the title character, has witnessed a series of horrors, including the rape and mutilation of Titus's daughter, Lavinia. In the depths of his misery, Marcus cries out:

> O why should nature build so foul a den,
> Unless the gods delight in tragedies?
> (IV, i, 59–60)

The audience, however, realizes that blame for the brutality that has preceded does not lie with the gods. To the contrary, we have seen Titus order the sacrifice of Alarbus, son of Tamora, Queen of the Goths. We have seen Titus also kill his own son, Lucius, who dared block his father's way for just an instant. We have witnessed Lavinia's insults to Tamora; Emperor Saturninus's callousness against his brother, Bassianus; and Bassianus's stealing away with Lavinia. Therefore we do not blame the stars, but human participants in the story. Marcus is the earliest of several characters in Shakespeare's tragedies who look to the stars for explanation of events of earth, but in every case that character proves misguided.

In *Romeo and Juliet*, the issue is raised in the Prologue of the play, as the Chorus announces:

> From forth the fatal loins of these two foes
> A pair of star-cross'd lovers take their life;
> Whose misadventur'd piteous overthrows
> Doth with their death bury their parents' strife.
> (Prologue, 5–8)

Remarkably, the Prologue reveals the plot of the story, suggesting, by use of the words "fatal" and "star-cross'd," that all subsequent action is determined. Such a reading, however, fails to take into account how the laying out of the story compels us to ponder not details of plot, but the significance of the overall situation. Why do events occur as they do? The answer, again, lies with human behavior. Romeo is impetuous, sometimes foolishly so. Mercutio, Romeo's close friend, is hot-tempered, as is Juliet's cousin Tybalt. Both the Montague and Capulet parents are immersed in the feud and preoccupied with their own plans. Juliet's Nurse is prattling and egoistic, while Friar Lawrence, Romeo's confidant, concocts a plan for the young lovers' escape that proves too convoluted and therefore subject to human error. All these characters, with generally good intentions, are victimized by their own weaknesses and impel the play toward its tragic end.

After Romeo has tried to stop the sword fight between Mercutio and Tybalt, and thereby caused Mercutio's death, he tries to evade responsibility: "O, I am fortune's fool!" (III, i, 136). We recognize, though, that the blame for Mercutio's death rests with the actions of the three individuals involved, any one of whom could have avoided the quarrel. On the other hand, to have done so would have been in conflict with their personalities: not with the stars, but with their own traits and inclinations.

Near the end of the play, when Romeo lies dead in the tomb and the Friar must acknowledge that his plan has failed, he tries to explain the reason to Juliet: "A power greater than we can contradict/ Hath thwarted our intents" (V, iii, 153–154). Even Friar Lawrence does not have the courage to admit his own bungling.

In *Hamlet*, the title character also tries to excuse what he perceives as his failings by looking to the heavens. Before the fatal encounter with Laertes, Hamlet acknowledges how he has not fulfilled the Ghost's request to carry out revenge against King Claudius, and hence has fallen short in the most important challenge of his life. Trying to justify his inefficacy, or at least to explain it, Hamlet muses to his friend Horatio:

> Our indiscretion sometime serves us well
> When our deep plots do pall, and that should learn us
> There's a divinity that shapes our ends,
> Rough-hew them how we will—
> (V, ii, 8–11)

Hamlet seeks to excuse his own inaction by blaming forces beyond his power. Later he becomes even more resigned:

> There is special
> providence in the fall of a sparrow. If it be [now],
> 'tis not to come; if it be not to come, it will be
> now; if it be not now, yet it [will] come—the
> readiness is all. Since no man, of aught he leaves,
> knows what is't to leave betimes, let be.
> (V, ii, 219–224)

Hamlet has reached his nadir; he does not even care whether he survives the fight. Here is the expression of a man who judges himself a profound disappointment to his father and his nation, but rather than accept blame for that disappointment, he chooses instead to believe in the helplessness of humanity.

Othello, too, reaches such a point of resignation, after his ensign Iago's treachery has been revealed, and Iago's wife, Emilia, lies dead, murdered by her husband after revealing the truth. At this moment, Othello, with his own wife, Desdemona, lifeless before him, cries out: "Who can control his fate?" (V, ii, 265). Moments later he kills himself, but not before seeking solace through evading guilt. We, however, recognize that Othello was manipulated masterfully by Iago, and that Othello's own temper, pride, and insecurity led him to follow his course of action.

One of the sharpest presentations of this issue occurs in *King Lear*. After Lear has banished his daughter Cordelia, Gloucester reads a letter supposedly written by the son he has always trusted, Edgar. The letter purports to communicate Edgar's anger with his father's "oppression of aged tyranny" (I, ii, 49–50), and a stupefied Gloucester inquires of his bastard son, Edmund, where and when the letter was found. When Edmund, the author of the forgery, identifies the piece as Edgar's, Gloucester is at a loss to explain the volcanic events that have left the kingdom in a state of such unrest:

> These late eclipses in the sun and moon
> portend no good to us. Though the wisdom of nature
> can reason it thus and thus, yet nature finds itself
> scourg'd by the sequent effects.
>
> (I, ii, 103–106)

The answer to this proposition comes from Edmund, who minces no words:

> This is the excellent foppery of the world,
> that when we are sick in fortune—often the
> surfeits of our own behavior—we make guilty
> of our disasters the sun, the moon, and stars,
> as if we were villains of necessity, fools by
> heavenly compulsion, knaves, thieves, and treachers
> by spherical predominance; drunkards, liars and
> adulterers by an enforc'd obedience of planetary
> influence, and all that we are evil in, by a
> divine thrusting on.
>
> (I, ii, 118–126)

That this statement comes from the ruthless Edmund is not comforting. Nonetheless, we recognize its accuracy. Lear himself has made the terrible misjudgment of turning on Cordelia and bestowing her share of his kingdom on her two unprincipled sisters, Goneril and Regan. Gloucester, too, has been so blind as to trust Edmund, when all along he has known the worth of Edgar.

Later, when his eyes have been torn out by the vengeful Regan and her husband, Cornwall, Gloucester moans to the heavens:

> As flies to wanton boys are we to th' gods,
> They kill us for their sport.
>
> (IV, i, 36–37)

Such a nihilistic description puts the source of human error in the hands of impersonal, even malignant, outside agencies. Yet such is never the case in Shakespeare's plays, for here, too, the missteps of Lear and Gloucester are always apparent.

The play in which elements of the supernatural and fate take part most profoundly is *Macbeth*. The brief opening scene with the three witches confirms their concentration on the title character, and from this point on we wonder to what extent Macbeth is a free agent, and to what extent, if any, the witches control his actions. One early line answers this question, when the Sergeant, returning from battle bloody with wounds, recounts the action:

> For brave Macbeth (well he deserves that name),
> Disdaining Fortune with his brandish'd steel . . .
>
> (I, ii, 16–17)

The implication is clear: Macbeth controls himself. He is not the helpless plaything of outside forces.

When the witches do tempt him with predictions that he will become Thane of Cawdor, then King of Scotland, Macbeth's reaction is telling:

> My thought, whose murther yet is but fantastical,
> Shakes so my single state of man that function
> Is smother'd in surmise, and nothing is
> But what is not.
>
> (I, iii, 139–142)

The witches have not implanted in Macbeth the idea of murdering King Duncan. Rather, the thought was present before, and the witches' predictions only bring to the surface feelings that had been churning inside him. Indeed, Macbeth soon resolves to "proceed no further in this business" (I, vii, 31), but after a few minutes of persuasion from Lady Macbeth, he changes his mind, when she touches one of his points of vulnerability:

> Art thou afeard
> To be the same in thine own act and valor
> As thou art in desire?
>
> (I, vii, 39–41)

Sensitive to any suggestion that undermines his masculinity, Macbeth resolves to carry out the plot. No fate or supernatural energy does him in. He proceeds on the basis of his own need to prove his manhood to his wife, to fulfill his own ambition, and to release his own capacity for violence.

The extent of Macbeth's freedom is emphasized by his actions against the family of Macduff. After the witches parade the three apparitions before Macbeth, he not only accepts these images as true, but goes beyond them:

> The castle of Macduff I will surprise,
> Seize upon Fife, give to th' edge o' th' sword

His wife, his babes, and all unfortunate
That trace him in his line.

(IV, i, 150–154)

Nothing the witches do forces Macbeth to proceed this way. The children he is supposed to fear are Banquo's, not Macduff's. Yet so consumed is Macbeth by his appetite for murder that he follows his own instincts and orders a series of murders that are utterly pointless.

Is there any sense, then, in which Shakespeare implies that fate rules human action? Perhaps, if we extend the definition of "fate" to go beyond individual action. For instance, in *King Lear*, after Kent, Lear's loyal servant now disguised as Caius, has been condemned by Cornwall and Regan to sit in the stocks for a night, he reflects: "Fortune, good night; smile once more, turn thy wheel" (II, ii, 173). Kent trusts in the ultimate rightness of things, an eternal justice that holds sway over the world. Later, the dying Edmund, defeated in trial by a mysterious knight who turns out to be his brother, Edgar, admits: "The wheel is come full circle, I am here" (V, iii, 175). Throughout his life he has scorned faith in anything but his own capacities; now Edmund assents to a strength greater than his own, and his surrender suggests recognition that the universe is ultimately a benign entity.

We feel the weight of this belief at the end of virtually every play Shakespeare wrote. In the comedies and romances, the conclusion customarily involves a marriage or series of marriages that reestablish social balance. In the histories and tragedies, political order is reasserted. Whatever the dramatic form, an inevitable resolution of conflicts, what might be termed "fate," asserts itself.

Another way "fate" may be said to influence events is suggested in *King Lear* by Edgar, just a few lines prior to Edmund's admission quoted above. Having fatally wounded his brother, Edgar tries to comfort him:

The gods are just, and of our pleasant vices
Make instruments to plague us . . .

(V, iii, 171–172)

Edgar suggests that our own faults lead us to make errors, that the "fate" of which we are victim is the one which we cause. Indeed, he implies that a combination of character and circumstance creates a sense of inevitability that might be mistaken for destiny.

We see evidence of this perspective repeatedly in Shakespeare's plays. In *King Lear*, the catastrophic decisions Lear makes in the opening scene are a direct result of his personality. His need for flattery is the reason he asks his daughters to declaim publicly the depth of their love for him. His pride is wounded when Cordelia, with seeming perverseness, refuses to compromise her integrity. Finally, his temper and rashness lead him to expel Cordelia and relinquish her share of the kingdom to Goneril and Regan.

In *Macbeth*, the witches gleefully carry out their malicious schemes, but they do not choose just any man on whom to work. Rather, they choose Macbeth, and lead him down a road toward which he is already inclined to travel. We know from his success in battle that Macbeth is violent and impulsive. When the witches tempt him with promise of the throne, and when Lady Macbeth taunts him about his lack of courage, his instinct is spurred, and thereafter his own capacity for destruction consumes him. After all, when Lady Macbeth comes across the sleeping Duncan, she cannot kill him (II, ii, 10–13), but Macbeth proceeds directly with the murder. Immediately afterwards, his conscience takes over, but his warrior drives, those of a man who has killed often, help him carry out his desires.

In *Hamlet*, the young Prince is an artistic, sensitive man, an unlikely candidate for violence. Yet when the Ghost of his father orders him to take action against Claudius, Hamlet is thrust into a situation where his own character makes successful resolution impossible. In desperation, Hamlet shouts, "My fate cries out . . ." (I, iv, 82). But that "fate" is the result of one particular man with one particular personality, finding himself in one singular set of circumstances. The stars do not control him.

Othello, too, is trapped between character and circumstance. He is probably the only black man of his rank in Venice: proud, yet unschooled in the ways of that cosmopolitan city. In this way, he may be considered naive, and thus when Iago begins to inject his poison, all of Othello's doubts, fears, and insecurities emerge. Were Iago not to intrude, we imagine Othello and Desdemona could survive happily. Again, character and circumstance unite to create the sense of "fate."

Finally, in *Romeo and Juliet*, the Prologue reminds us that the family conflict is "ancient," that the "strife" has been handed down by the parents, and that "civil blood makes civil hands unclean." The inescapable conclusion is that despite all their passion, Romeo and Juliet are trapped in a situation that crushes their aspirations. Thus we might regard "fate" here as the weight of the past working with the oppressive environment of the present, in combination with the personalities of all the characters involved. The "star-cross'd" element is that, given such a society and the intensity of the love between Romeo and Juliet, the tragic outcome is inevitable. In sum, we are more conscious than ever that the human personality is helpless against itself, a theme that recurs throughout the Shakespearean canon.

Fathers and Daughters

Of the great variety of relationships that Shakespeare dramatizes, one of the richest is between fathers and daughters. In legal terms, male parents in Shakespeare's plays have almost complete authority over their children, in particular the daughters. Yet many of these young women seek to exercise their own wills. The resulting tension is intensified by the universal conflict that exists between generations, as well as by the timeless male chauvinism that compels fathers to shield their daughters from worldly matters, including emotional and sexual attachment. These clashes resolve in a variety of ways, but the basis of the struggle is always how both generations are challenged to accept each other's values. In this way, the daughters may be seen as standing up against the strictures of medieval society, as well as representing the values of the Renaissance and its emphasis on individual social, political, intellectual, and economic freedom.

In *A Midsummer Night's Dream*, for example, the plot is set off by the citizen Egeus's demand that his daughter, Hermia, marry not the man she loves, Lysander, but the man Egeus prefers, Demetrius. In the great comic tradition that extends back to the theater of Greece and Rome, Egeus is a bully who fails to appreciate his daughter's intelligence and capacity to love, as well as the attractiveness of the suitor she desires. He reveals these aspects of himself early:

> Thou, thou, Lysander, thou has given her rhymes,
> And interchang'd love-tokens with my child;
> Thou has by moonlight at her window sung
> With faining voice verses of faining love,
> And stol'n the impression of her fantasy
> With bracelets of thy hair, rings, gawds, conceits,
> Knacks, trifles, nosegays, sweetmeats—messengers
> Of strong prevailment in unhardened youth.

With cunning hast thou filch'd my daughter's heart,
Turn'd her obedience (which is due to me)
To stubborn hardness.
                                        (I, i, 28–38)

The last two lines in particular raise the question as to whether Egeus objects to Lysander because of the young man's artful rituals of courtship, or because of Hermia's boldness in choosing Lysander without seeking her father's approval. Whatever the cause, Egeus climaxes his tirade with a threat that sends the plot whirling: "Either to die the death, or to abjure/ For ever the society of men" (I, i, 65–66). Despite this grim warning, we cannot regard Egeus with deep concern, for theatrical convention in comedy assures us that his demands will be thwarted. Still, Hermia and Lysander must endure severe trial in the woods before all resolves happily. Even afterwards, Egeus still grumbles:

Enough, enough, my lord; you have enough.
I beg the law, the law, upon his head.
They would have stol'n away, they would, Demetrius,
Thereby to have defeated you and me:
You of your wife, and me of my consent,
Of my consent that she should be your wife.
                                        (IV, i, 154–159)

But when Demetrius announces that he has switched allegiance to Helena, who loves him, and Duke Theseus approves both unions, Egeus is left to stew in his own frustration.

In *The Taming of the Shrew*, the mistreatment of a young woman by her father has different repercussions. Katherine has acquired the reputation of a shrew, and from her initial appearance, her harsh behavior justifies that renown. Yet as her father, Baptista, reveals his preference for his younger daughter, Bianca, Katherine's fury becomes more understandable. As she says:

She is your treasure, she must have a husband;
I must dance barefoot on her wedding-day,
And for your love to her lead apes to hell.
Talk not to me, I will go sit and weep,
Till I can find occasion of revenge.
                                        (II, i, 32–36)

Baptista's attitude has created in Katherine an anger that she turns against the world. She is further tormented by her isolation, for unlike Hermia, she has yet to find a suitor worthy of her. The vapid men of Padua are charmed by the surface attractions of Bianca, but too shallow to appreciate Katherine's worth. Only when the alluring newcomer Petruchio enters her life, bringing a mind and wit equal to hers, is Katherine able to escape the shackles of her father's authority.

At the end of the play, when during the banquet Katherine comes forth contentedly at Petruchio's beckoning, Baptista is impressed:

> Now fair befall thee, good Petruchio!
> The wager thou hast won, and I will add
> Unto their losses twenty thousand crowns,
> Another dowry to another daughter,
> For she is chang'd, as she had never been.
>   (V, ii, 111–115)

Throughout the play, Baptista has been preoccupied with money, going so far as to offer Bianca's hand in marriage to that suitor with the most firmly guaranteed solvency. When he here again expresses delight in financial terms, we wonder if he appreciates how Katherine's warmth has blossomed under Petruchio's influence, or whether Baptista still assumes that money is the only requirement for happiness.

A different kind of shackle is apparent in *The Merchant of Venice*, in which two fathers attempt to impose rules on their daughters. Portia, a dynamic woman with beauty, wit, and wealth, is nonetheless trapped into passivity by her late father's dictum that she belongs to the man who chooses her picture from among three caskets. From her very first line, we recognize Portia's discontent: "By my troth, Nerissa, my little body is a-weary of this great world" (I, ii, 1–2). Like Katherine, Portia is unhappy, but because she has her woman-in-waiting Nerissa in whom she may confide, Portia's discontent has been transformed into restlessness rather than fury.

In the same play, we see another daughter who feels trapped by her father: Jessica, daughter of Shylock. Her hatred, though, is aimed directly at him:

> Alack, what heinous sin is it in me
> To be ashamed to be my father's child!
> But though I am a daughter to his blood,
> I am not to his manners. O Lorenzo,
> If thou keep promise, I shall end this strife,
> Become a Christian and thy loving wife.
>   (II, iii, 16–21)

Jessica seeks to be part of the society around her. Indeed, she has completely accepted its values, including anti-Semitism, and she sees her salvation, both literal and metaphoric, in escape from her father's home.

Both young women eventually achieve independence. Bassanio, the one man Portia desires, chooses her picture from the lead casket, although we feel that her true means of freeing herself is through her portrayal of the male lawyer Balthazar. As she says before leaving for court:

> I have within my mind
> A thousand raw tricks of these bragging Jacks,
> Which I will practice.
>
> (III, iv, 76–78)

We sense that for much of her life Portia has been waiting to release the full force of her intellect and spirit. Now that she has opportunity to prove herself the equal of the men around her, she holds nothing back. Even after she has trapped Shylock in court and contributed to the series of cruel punishments inflicted upon him, she still toys with Bassanio, demanding the ring that he promised her (as Portia) he would never surrender. All Portia's actions reflect her need to stand on her own by liberating herself from society's male influence, particularly that of the father who condemned her to years of inactivity.

Jessica, too, breaks from her father's control, but she does so by joining society through marriage to Lorenzo, a Christian. Just how sympathetic we are to her actions depends on how sympathetic we are to Shylock, but no doubt Shakespeare's audience would have applauded her as one with the courage to flout a brutal, even grotesque father who tries to impose on his daughter not only his religion, but also the antisocial practices that make him so unlikeable:

> Lock up my doors, and when you hear the drum
> And the vile squealing of the wry-neck'd fife,
> Clamber not you up to the casements then,
> Nor thrust your head into the public street
> To gaze upon Christian fools with varnish'd faces . . .
>
> (II, v, 29–33)

Yet even when the trial has ended, and Jessica and Lorenzo should be entirely happy, she remarks: "I am never merry when I hear sweet music" (V, i, 69). We wonder if Jessica retains some of Shylock's attitude toward such popular entertainment. Perhaps she is her father's daughter after all, whether she cares to acknowledge so or not.

Thus far we have considered father-daughter relationships only in the comedies. The presentations of this bond differ in the tragedies and romances, where the emphasis is more on the moral lessons to be drawn from the daughter's striving for individuality.

For example, in *Romeo and Juliet*, after Tybalt, Juliet's cousin, has slain

Mercutio, and Romeo has foolishly avenged his friend's death by killing Tybalt, her father still insists that she marry the County Paris. When Juliet begs to be free from that relationship, he responds brutally:

> Hang thee, young baggage! disobedient wretch!
> I tell thee what: get thee to church a' Thursday,
> Or never after look me in the face.
>   (III, v, 160–162)

Capulet is more concerned with imposing his wishes on his daughter than with ensuring her happiness. At the close of the play, he expresses grief over Juliet's body, but never articulates how his actions and attitudes contributed to her tragic end.

In *Hamlet*, Polonius tries to exert paternal authority over Ophelia, stifling her sexual desires and warning her, with characteristic circumlocution, of the danger the Prince poses:

> In few, Ophelia,
> Do not believe his vows, for they are brokers,
> Not of that dye which their investments show,
> But mere [implorators] of unholy suits,
> Breathing like sanctified and pious bonds,
> The better to [beguile]. This is for all:
> I would not, in plain terms, from this time forth
> Have you so slander any moment leisure
> As to give words or talk with the Lord Hamlet.
>   (I, iii, 127–134)

Later, when Hamlet has appeared before Ophelia in what seems to be a state of disorder, Polonius initially blames Ophelia for Hamlet's behavior: "What, have you given him any hard words of late?" (II, i, 104). When Ophelia insists that she has followed her father's orders by refusing to see Hamlet, Polonius reverses himself and attributes Hamlet's antics to Ophelia's neglect. Whatever way she turns, Ophelia is trapped between the man she loves, who has apparently scorned her, and the father who forbids her to mend the relationship. Thus when Hamlet kills Polonius, Ophelia is lost, with no one to whom she can turn. Thereafter she enters in a state of madness, singing obscene ditties that reflect her desperate need for love. Her subsequent suicide is the inevitable outcome of her father's repression and Hamlet's rejection.

In *Othello*, the actions of Desdemona leave her father, Brabantio, in panic. Indeed, her marriage to Othello shatters his world, as he clarifies when Iago breaks the news in the middle of the night:

> What tell'st thou me of robbing? This is Venice;
> My house is not a grange.
>
> (I, i, 105–106)

How, Brabantio wonders, can such sexual license be carried out by his daughter in his home and his city? Soon he confronts Othello:

> O thou foul thief, where has thou stow'd my daughter?
> Damn'd as thou art, thou has enchanted her,
> For I'll refer me to all things of sense,
> If she in chains of magic were not bound . . .
>
> (I, ii, 62–65)

All of Brabantio's values are embodied in his daughter, who has betrayed him, and therefore his life has lost its foundation. Unable to face that reality, he insists that Othello could have seduced Desdemona only through magic (I, ii, 63–66).

Desdemona, however, offers a different explanation:

> I am hitherto your daughter. But here's my husband;
> And so much duty as my mother show'd
> To you, preferring you before her father,
> So much I challenge that I may profess
> Due to the Moor, my lord.
>
> (I, iii, 185–189)

Her declaration, so formal in tone, raises the question of how much of her speech emerges purely out of love for Othello, and how much reflects her need to make a stand against her father. In any case, her will is irresistible, and Brabantio has no choice but to let her leave, although he issues this warning:

> Look to her, Moor, if thou hast eyes to see;
> She has deceived her father, and may thee.
>
> (I, iii, 292–293)

Later, when Othello nears the depths of his misery, Iago recalls this sentiment (III, iii, 206). By then, however, the action of the play has moved to the Venetian colony of Cyprus, and we have not seen Brabantio for some time. At the end of the play, we learn that he has died. As his brother, Gratiano, reports to Othello: "Thy match was mortal to him, and pure grief/ Shore his old thread in twain" (V, ii, 205–206). In this play, therefore, father and daughter never achieve reconciliation.

Such is not the case in Shakespeare's romances, all of which are infused with the spirit of acceptance. In *Pericles*, for instance, the reunion between the title character and his daughter, Marina, who has seemingly been lost, touches us, for although the two do not recognize each other, something profound stirs within them. As Pericles says: "Pray you turn your eyes upon me./ You're like something that—" (V, i, 101–102). The gradual discovery of their identities, a process that Shakespeare extends almost unbearably, reaffirms Pericles' faith and inspires a dream that leads him to find Thaisa, his wife. Thus his daughter becomes his vehicle for salvaging his hopes.

In *Cymbeline*, the title character, the King of Britain, banishes his daughter, Imogen, who has married Posthumus against Cymbeline's wishes. Much later, after Cymbeline has been captured in military conflict, he broods upon his initial misjudgment that has led him to such a crisis:

> It had been vicious
> To have mistrusted her; yet, O my daughter,
> That it was folly in me, thou mayst say,
> And prove it in thy feeling. Heaven mend all!
> (V, v, 65–68)

Eventually Imogen, so long disguised as Fidele, reveals herself to her father, and their reunion embodies the uniting of both their family that has been torn apart and the country suffering under war.

In *The Winter's Tale*, Leontes, King of Sicilia, is obsessed with the suspicion that his wife, Hermione, has had an affair with his best friend, Polixenes. No denial can alleviate Leontes' madness, although when Hermione gives birth to a baby girl, the child's attendant, Paulina, hopes that the infant will assuage Leontes' rage:

> We do not know
> How he may soften at the sight o' th' child:
> The silence often of pure innocence
> Persuades when speaking fails.
> (II, ii, 37–40)

Leontes' reaction, however, is precisely the opposite, and he orders that the child be exiled: "To some remote and desert place quite out/ Of our dominions" (II, iii, 176–177). In true theatrical tradition, and in a plot device inspired by several myths, including that of Oedipus, the child survives. Years later, when circumstances bring the grown daughter, Perdita, before Leontes, he seems to intuit her identity, for her presence reminds him of Hermione, whom he believes dead: "I thought of her,/ Even in these looks I made" (V, i, 227–228). The actual scene of recognition between the two takes place offstage, but we are assured by some gentlemen that it was profoundly moving: "a sight which was to be seen, cannot be spoken of" (V, ii, 42–43). Thus here, too, a daughter restores a father's faith and allows him to express his regret over his earlier misjudgments.

In the last of Shakespeare's romances, *The Tempest*, Prospero's daughter, Miranda, is above all an audience to whom he may tell the story of his life as Duke of Milan, where his throne was usurped by his brother, Antonio, and from where Prospero and Miranda were set adrift, only to end up on the island where they have lived for twelve years. Miranda is also one of the few members of Prospero's present kingdom, and he rules her firmly. When, for instance, Miranda falls in love at the sight of Ferdinand, the son of her father's enemy, she begs of Prospero:

> O dear father,
> Make not too rash a trial of him, for
> He's gentle, and not fearful.
> (I, ii, 467–469)

Prospero, however, quashes her speaking so boldly: "What, I say,/ My foot my tutor?" (I, ii, 469–470). He insists on exerting the prerogatives of father and ruler. Still, the love between Ferdinand and Miranda cannot be suppressed, and Prospero is at last stirred by his daughter's capacity for affection. Although he sentences Ferdinand to hard labor to win Miranda's hand, Prospero reflects: "Poor worm, thou art infected!" (III, i, 32). Later, at the sight of the two of them, he adds:

> Fair encounter
> Of two most rare affections! Heaven rain grace
> On that which breeds between 'em!
> (III, i, 74–76)

The innocent love of Miranda gradually moves Prospero to surrender his own antagonism toward those against whom he seeks vengeance, but he is not totally transformed. First he reminds both Miranda and Ferdinand of his paternal authority by establishing rules for courtship:

> But
> If thou dost break her virgin-knot before
> All sanctimonious ceremonies may
> With full and holy rite be minist'red,
> No sweet aspersion shall the heavens let fall
> To make this contract grow . . .
> (IV, i, 14–19)

Here is another father seemingly horrified by the thought of his daughter's sexuality. Later, when for the first time Miranda sees Ferdinand's father, Alonso, the King of Naples, and Antonio, along with his confederate, Sebastian, Alonso's brother, Miranda exclaims:

> How many goodly creatures are there here!
> How beauteous mankind is! O brave new world
> That has such people in't!
>
> (V, i, 182–184)

Prospero retorts: " 'Tis new to thee" (V, i, 184). Even the innocent optimism of Miranda cannot erase Prospero's bitterness.

In no play of Shakespeare's is the father-daughter bond so moving as in *King Lear*. Indeed, the crux of the plot is the rift that emerges between Lear and his youngest and favorite daughter, Cordelia. In the opening scene, while Lear prepares to renounce responsibility and divide his kingdom among his three daughters, Cordelia waits in agony as her two older sisters, Goneril and Regan, falsely claim their love, as their father has commanded. Finally, Lear invites her to speak so as "to draw/ A third more opulent than your sisters'?" (I, i, 85–86). He makes clear to all that he has already decided who will receive which territory, so in fact he is not conducting a competition, as he earlier insisted. Nevertheless, Cordelia cannot or will not violate her relationship with her father by turning it into a vehicle for his public self-aggrandizement. Thus she offers the fatal reply: "Nothing, my lord" (I, i, 87). Despite Lear's insistence, Cordelia is stubborn, and in his refusal to forgive her stubbornness, Lear unintentionally demonstrates just how much this parent and child share. Moments later, he expels her, with the pathetic confession: "I lov'd her most, and thought to set my rest/ On her kind nursery" (I, i, 123–124). We recognize that Lear is not evil, but that he is foolishly allowing pride to get the best of him.

In the world of this play, however, even a temporary lapse of judgment proves cataclysmic, and Lear's blunder results in unbearable suffering for him, since his two remaining daughters expel him from their houses and leave him stranded and helpless. Cordelia does not reappear until the middle of Act IV, when she and her father reunite in a scene of unbearable beauty. Lear, barely in possession of his faculties, struggles to ask forgiveness:

> I know you do not love me, for your sisters
> Have (as I do remember) done me wrong:
> You have some cause, they have not.
>
> (IV, vii, 72–74)

Cordelia's heartrending answer, however, soothes him: "No cause, no cause" (IV, vii, 74). Later, when the two become prisoners of the army of Edmund, Duke of Gloucester, Lear begs only that he and his daughter remain together:

> Come, let's away to prison:
> We two alone will sing like birds i' th' cage;
> When thou dost ask me blessing, I'll kneel down
> And ask of thee forgiveness.
> (V, iii, 8–11)

We recognize that Lear has learned about the worth of people, and his desperate request suggests that the only part of life he now cherishes is the love of his daughter. Although Shakespeare leads us to suspect that he and Cordelia will be saved, Lear does not find such solace, for Edmund sends orders that the two should be executed. Eventually he rescinds the command, but not until Cordelia is dead. In perhaps the most terrible moment in all of Shakespeare's plays, Lear enters *"with Cordelia in his arms"* (V, iii, 257). He holds only one thought:

> This feather stirs, she lives! If it be so,
> It is a chance which does redeem all sorrows
> That ever I have felt.
> (V, iii, 266–268)

At last he realizes that before he is a king, he is a man, with all of a man's needs and feelings.

Cordelia's life and death teach Lear values he should have held all his life, but, sadly, that knowledge comes too late. Indeed, few of Shakespeare's fathers even learn such profound lessons. Still, we understand how daughters, limited in their capacity to act on their own, can force confrontations between the old and the new. In the resolution of those conflicts, daughters thereby influence the beliefs of both their fathers and the ever-changing society around them.

Fidelity

As men and women in Shakespeare's plays struggle to find happiness through romantic love, one of the obstacles that blocks their path is fidelity. More specifically, female characters are often forced to endure the conduct of men whose sense of commitment wavers alarmingly. As Friar Lawrence, Romeo's confidante in *Romeo and Juliet*, says after Romeo proclaims his newly discovered affections for Juliet:

> Holy Saint Francis, what a change is here!
> Is Rosaline, that thou didst love so dear,
> So soon forsaken? Young men's love then lies
> Not truly in their hearts, but in their eyes.
> (II, iii, 65–68)

The young man to whom these words are spoken, Romeo, never turns away from Juliet, but other romantic heroes prove less devoted. As a result, many of the women in Shakespeare's plays, particularly the comedies, must settle for the best of an assortment of mediocre suitors, while their male counterparts appear lucky to marry as fortunately as they do. Shakespeare's unmistakable implication is that women hold more steadfastly to their love than men do, one reason why we often feel that Shakespeare's women are superior, both intellectually and morally, to the men they marry.

In Shakespeare's first comedy, *The Comedy of Errors*, Adriana expresses concern over the whereabouts of her missing husband, Antipholus, but her sister, Luciana, dismisses such worry:

> A man is master of his liberty:
> Time is their master, and when they see time,
> They'll go or come; if so, be patient, sister.
> (II, i, 7–9)

Luciana, who is single, has no stake in male behavior. Adriana, however, feels keenly the helplessness of a married woman's position (II, i, 34–41), and we understand that she is trapped between contradictory emotions. She admits being possessive, but she is equally eager that her intense devotion will be reciprocated. She is bitter at her husband's callous treatment, but hopes that his pleasure in her will be revived. All she can do in this predicament, however, is articulate her desperation:

> His company must do his minions grace,
> Whilst I at home starve for a merry look . . .
> (II, i, 88–89)

Later, Luciana tries to explain to Antipholus of Syracuse why a husband should treat his wife more kindly:

> Alas, poor women, make us [but] believe
> (Being compact of credit) that you love us;
> Though others have the arm, show us the sleeve;
> We in your motion turn, and you may move us.
> (III, ii, 21–24)

That Luciana speaks to the wrong twin does not detract from the import of her words. Passivity is part of the plight that the women of Shakespeare's day had to endure, and his female characters reflect such frustration.

Despite her pain, Adriana pays her husband's debt to the goldsmith, Angelo, rather than see Antipholus imprisoned for insanity. She does so even after he heaps abuse on her for the slights he imagines she has committed against him:

> Dissembling harlot, thou art false in all,
> And art confederate with a damned pack
> To make a loathsome abject scorn of me . . .
> (IV, iv, 101–103)

The scene suggests that women who seek happiness must accept their husbands' foibles. The Abbess confirms this lesson:

> The consequence is then, thy jealous fits
> Hath scar'd thy husband from the use of wits.
> (V, i, 85–86)

To be sure, this viewpoint does not encompass Shakespeare's entire perspective on relationships between husbands and wives (see the chapter on "Marriage"), but he does suggest that female understanding is essential if a relationship is to thrive. At the same time, however, his sympathy in this matter is virtually always with the woman.

Such is certainly the case in *The Two Gentlemen of Verona*. Neither of the title characters, Proteus, with his stereotypical infatuations, nor Valentine, with his equally familiar scorn of love, is an attractive figure. Thus our loyalties lie with the women with whom these two become involved. The first, Julia, is inexplicably attracted to Proteus, a relationship encouraged by her lady-in-waiting, Lucetta:

> I have no other reason but a woman's reason:
> I think him so, because I think him so.
>   (I, ii, 23–24)

Later, when Proteus has been ordered by his father to leave Verona to join Valentine in Milan, Proteus gives no sign that he intends to be disloyal to Julia, but his last line about her proves ironically accurate: "For truth hath better deeds than words to grace it" (II, ii, 17). He prefers to be judged by his actions, not by his statements of love.

We recall this claim when Proteus instantly falls in love with the object of Valentine's devotion, Silvia (II, iv, 191–195). So intense is Proteus's infatuation that he plots against his best friend:

> O, but I love his lady too too much,
> And that's the reason I love him so little.
>   (II, iv, 205–206)

Before long, he has dismissed Julia:

> I will forget that Julia is alive,
> Rememb'ring that my love to her is dead . . .
>   (II, vi, 27–28)

We may partially excuse Proteus's behavior by rationalizing that he is a headstrong young man; nonetheless, his moral gyrations remain irritating. As if sensing Proteus's actions, Julia resolves to hurry after him, although she claims to have faith in him:

> His words are bonds, his oaths are oracles,
> His love sincere, his thoughts immaculate,
> His tears pure messengers sent from his heart,
> His heart as far from fraud as heaven from earth.
>   (II, vii, 75–78)

The irony of her trust is painful.

When she reaches Milan disguised as Sebastian, she overhears Proteus proclaim his affections for Silvia while simultaneously belittling his feelings for Julia:

> I grant, sweet love, that I did love a lady;
> But she is dead.
>
> (IV, ii, 105–106)

In disguise, Julia must withhold her torment:

> Not so; but it hath been the longest night
> That e'er I watch'd, and the most heaviest.
>
> (IV, ii, 139–140)

After Julia, still disguised as Sebastian, tries unsuccessfully to convince Proteus to return to her, she bemoans her dilemma:

> Alas, poor fool, why do I pity him
> That with his very heart despiseth me?
> Because he loves her, he despiseth me;
> Because I love him, I must pity him.
>
> (IV, iv, 93–96)

The complexity of her feelings reflects those of other Shakespearean heroines who cannot explain why they love a man who mistreats or disappoints them. Yet something inside these women compels them to offer that love.

.The supposedly happy resolution of this confusion fails to satisfy us. When the four lovers find themselves in the forest, Proteus's lust for Silvia so overwhelms him that he threatens to rape her. His awkward apology that follows Valentine's interference (V, iv, 73–77) may be understood as Proteus's recognition of the obsessive ardor that drove him to the brink of madness, and Valentine's equally unwieldy acceptance and offer of Silvia's hand to Proteus may be taken as a supreme gesture of male friendship. Nevertheless, the plight of the two women left to deal with these unpleasant men is not comforting. For instance, after everything that has transpired, and Julia's identity is at last revealed, Proteus claims her as his own, but only in backhanded fashion:

> What is in Silvia's face, but I may spy
> More fresh in Julia's with a constant eye?
>
> (V, iv, 114–115)

Valentine then claims Silvia for himself, but he seems to do so primarily to thwart the intentions of his rival Thurio. Neither suitor inspires admiration nor alleviates suspicions that both women could have had better luck in love.

Even in *A Midsummer Night's Dream*, male fidelity is in question. Hermia claims to her father, Egeus, that she is in love with Lysander, but when the pair are in the woods together, she speaks of "all the vows that ever men have broke/ (In number more than women ever spoke)" (I, i, 175–176). Moreover, her suspicions prove accurate, first when Lysander inexplicably tells Helena of his plans with Hermia (I, i, 209–213), and second when Lysander becomes attracted to Helena. True, at that moment Lysander is under the influence of the magic juice that Puck squeezes out of the flower, but Lysander's passions for Helena seem stronger than any he has offered to Hermia:

> Not Hermia, but Helena I love.
> Who will not change a raven for a dove? . . .
> Reason becomes the marshall to my will,
> And leads me to your eyes, where I o'erlook
> Love's stories written in Love's richest book.
> (II, ii, 113–122)

Meanwhile, his sudden hatred for Hermia inspires more intense and more believable emotions than any that his love brought forth:

> For as a surfeit of the sweetest thing
> The deepest loathing to the stomach brings . . .
> (II, ii, 137–138)

At the end of the play, we note that Lysander's rival, Demetrius, has finally allowed himself to be won by Helena, but he still operates under the influence of Puck's magic. Thus Shakespeare leaves open the possibility that should the spell wear off, Demetrius will revert to his old, surly self.

Male characters in Shakespeare's plays also betray women in more subtle ways. In *Much Ado About Nothing*, although Claudio's marriage to Hero has been arranged, he professes that he has profound feeling for her. Yet several of his statements underlie that declaration. First he comments to Benedick: "Can the world buy such a jewel?" (I, i, 181), implying that he seeks to possess her as if she were primarily a source of financial profit. Then he adds: "In mine eye, she is the sweetest lady that ever I look'd on" (I, i, 187–188). In a play where characters are frequently unable to judge appearance from truth, Claudio's love seems based on surface values. Later he asks whether Leonato, Hero's father, has any sons (I, i, 293), as if in fear that Hero's fortune will have to be shared with siblings.

A more serious point of weakness about Claudio is his willingness to accept the bastard Don John's insinuations that his brother, Don Pedro, Prince of Aragon, is wooing Hero for himself. Here Claudio reveals his own shallowness:

> Friendship is constant in all other things
> Save in the office and affairs of love . . .
> (II, i, 175–176)

Presently, Claudio seems to forget his doubts, but not long after, when Don John claims to have observed Hero's unfaithfulness, Claudio's suspicions take command of him:

> If I see any thing to-night why I should
> not marry her, to-morrow in the congregation,
> where I should wed, there will I shame her.
> (III, ii, 123–125)

Claudio is not stupid, but he is gullible and seems eager to punish the woman whom he supposedly loves. After an offstage incident in which he witnesses the disguised Borachio, Don John's confederate, speaking at Hero's window, Claudio carries out his threat in brutal fashion, interrupting his wedding vows:

> There, Leonato, take her back again.
> Give not this rotten orange to your friend . . .
> She knows the heat of a luxurious bed;
> Her blush is guiltiness, not modesty.
> (IV, i, 31–42)

Why does he go out of his way to humiliate Hero publicly, along with her father and the entire assemblage?

Even the Friar's announcement of Hero's supposed death does not alter Claudio's manner. He refuses to apologize for his behavior (V, i, 72) and, in what should be a moment of pain, banters tastelessly with Don Pedro and Benedick. This attitude is so repulsive as to earn rebuke from the normally lighthearted Benedick:

> You are a villain. I jest
> not; I will make it good how you dare, with what you
> dare, and when you dare. Do me right; or I will protest
> your cowardice. You have kill'd a sweet lady,
> and her death shall fall heavy on you. Let me hear
> from you.
> (V, i, 145–150)

Claudio, however, ignores this threat. He is also perfectly content to accept Leonato's offer to marry his "other" daughter (V, i, 288–292), even though he has never met her. Does the lure of money still hold him? He enters the wedding ceremony grimly: "Which is the lady I must seize upon?" (V, iv, 53). Finally, at the moment of revelation, when Hero removes her mask, Claudio offers only a brief exclamation: "Another Hero!" (V, iv, 62). Perhaps we are to take him as one stunned into joyful silence, but he never apologizes for his past insults, nor does he express renewed faith in her. Thus Claudio is not precisely unfaithful to Hero, but his lack of substance and his failure to trust her does not bode well for their marriage.

One of Shakespeare's most ironic dramatizations of male infidelity is in *Twelfth Night*, as Orsino, the Duke of Illyria, who is supposedly in love with Olivia, tries to convince Viola, disguised as Caesario, about the nature of male passion:

> There is no woman's sides
> Can bide the beating of so strong a passion
> As love doth give my heart; no woman's heart
> So big, to hold so much; they lack retention.
> (II, iv, 93–96)

Even as he speaks, his affection for Caesario is running wild, contradicting all his protestations about male devotion.

Perhaps Shakespeare's strongest judgment about fidelity, however, is articulated by an unlikely source: Emilia, Iago's wife in *Othello*. When her lady Desdemona weeps over Othello's accusations that she has been unfaithful, Emilia's weary tone reflects the experience of a woman who has seen too much of life to maintain any illusions:

> But I do think it is their husband's faults
> If wives do fail . . .
> Why we have galls; and though we have some grace,
> Yet have we some revenge. Let husbands know
> Their wives have sense like them; they see, and smell,
> And have their palates both for sweet and sour,
> As husbands have. What is it that they do
> When they change us for others? Is it sport?
> I think it is. And doth affection breed it?
> I think it doth. Is't frailty that thus errs?
> It is so too. And have we not affections,
> Desires for sport, and frailty, as men have?
> Then let them use us well; else let them know,
> The ills we do, their ills instruct us so.
> (IV, iii, 86–104)

She decries what is known today as "the double standard," insisting that women have the same physical desires as men, but that rules of society prevent women from satisfying these desires. How ironic, then, that Emilia should be married to Iago, who time and again reiterates how women and men both are prey to sexual urges that he describes in animalistic terms.

Yet Emilia's statement also implies, and here it should be seen in the context of Shakespeare's other plays, that women have a capacity for emotional commitment that raises them above such primitive response. Indeed, none of Shakespeare's romantic heroines proves as fickle as most of his heroes. Did Shakespeare then approve of such behavior on the part of men? A far more likely explanation is that Shakespeare's capacity to identify with all aspects of the human experience includes sympathy for how women, whatever their legal rights, have a moral claim to the same understanding and affection that they grant to the men they love. The outcomes of his plays, however, suggest that few women are so fortunate as to be the beneficiaries of such devotion.

Fools

No group of Shakespeare's characters is more treasured by audiences than those known as "fools." On the surface, they are merely a source of amusement, providing comic relief under generally serious circumstances. Furthermore, their parts are rarely large and may actually be peripheral to the main action. In spite of this separation, however, or perhaps because of it, their perspectives mirror our own uncertainty, wonder, or frustration.

During Shakespeare's time, the term "fool" was applied to jesters of the medieval court who entertained royal personages. Because fools had no official status, they were entitled to utter all sorts of humorous, even rude remarks which, if emanating from any other source, would have been risky indeed. In this discussion, however, the word "fool" is used more generously to encompass those characters whom Shakespeare describes sometimes as "fools" and at other times as "clowns." All offer respite from the primary tensions; yet their reflections also provide insight about the leading players. These "fools" may be divided into two general categories: (1) buffoons who unintentionally create broad comedy with physical antics and eccentric vocabulary; and (2) wits who aim their agile wordplay at specific targets.

One of Shakespeare's earliest, yet most charming clowns is Dull in *Love's Labor's Lost*. Above all, he is prone to corruptions of language that guarantee laughter:

> I myself reprehend his own person, for I am
> his Grace's farborough; but I would see his own
> person in flesh and blood.
> (I, i, 183–185)

Such malapropisms, though, provide more than humor. In a play where so many of the upper-class lovers are prone to linguistic grandiloquence behind which they disguise their feelings, Dull's honest gracelessness is a relief. In addition, pedants like the schoolmaster, Holofernes, may be more sophisticated than Dull, but they are also objects of ridicule, since under the guise of erudition they purvey nonsense.

Dull may be seen as a forerunner of one of Shakespeare's most beloved comic figures, Dogberry in *Much Ado About Nothing*. Officially an officer of the law, Dogberry can utter scarcely a sentence that does not offer some delightful corruption of language:

> You are thought here to be the most
> senseless and fit man for the constable of the watch;
> therefore bear you the lanthorn.
>
> (III, iii, 22–24)

Yet Dogberry, too, is a significant thematic presence. First, his appearance onstage creates an aura of innocence. No matter how malicious Don John's schemes, or how cruelly Claudio, Hero's fiance, and Leonato, her father, behave because of her supposed transgressions, Dogberry alleviates the spirit of malice. Second, several of the major characters in this play hide behind their own language. The romantic antagonists, Beatrice and Benedick, for instance, insult each other repeatedly, refusing to acknowledge their mutual attraction that is obvious to everyone else. That Dogberry manages to communicate meaning despite his verbal missteps points up the foibles of the other, more elevated characters.

One of Dogberry's memorable moments occurs during the inquisition of Don John's underlings, Borachio and Conrade, the latter of whom refers to Dogberry as "an ass." The officer responds to this insult with fury:

> But, masters, remember that
> I am an ass; though it be not written down, yet forget
> not that I am an ass.
>
> (IV, ii, 76–78)

His outrage is endearing, yet oddly touching, a combination of qualities shared by many of Shakespeare's fools. Dogberry also provides relief when Benedick has finally lost patience with the heartless actions of Claudio and accuses him of having killed Hero, "a sweet and innocent lady" (V, i, 190–191). At this point Dogberry enters, prepared to condemn Borachio and Conrade for their part in the conspiracy against Hero. Infused with his mission, he states to Don Pedro:

> Marry, sir, they have committed false report;
> moreover they have spoken untruths: secondarily,

they are slanders; sixt and lastly, they
have belied a lady; thirdly, they have
verified unjust things; and to conclude, they
are lying knaves.

(V, i, 215–219)

During this muddled sequence of accusations, we recognize that the same charges could be leveled at Claudio. Even more satisfying is Don Pedro's response, which parodies Dogberry's unique verbal thrusts:

First, I ask thee what they have
done; thirdly, I ask thee what's their offense; sixt
and lastly, why they are committed; and to conclude,
what you lay to their charge.

(V, i, 220–223)

That the aristocratic Don Pedro can at this tense moment join Dogberry's inadvertent merriment assures us that all will resolve happily.

Dull and Dogberry were probably created by the same member of Shakespeare's acting company, the large, yet agile Will Kemp. A clown who excelled in physical comedy, he almost certainly originated the role of Bottom in *A Midsummer Night's Dream* and may well have been the first Falstaff in *Henry IV*. Kemp, however, was prone to ad-libbing and upstaging, and eventually left the company. He died in 1603, before some of Shakespeare's greatest comic parts were written, and his place was taken by Robert Armin, a gentler, more musical stage presence, whose persona probably influenced the nature of Shakespeare's later fools.

One of the most insightful of Shakespeare's clowns may be found in *Hamlet*. The two gravediggers, as they are more often designated, reflect in leisurely fashion on the nature of their calling and on life itself, for they see a symmetry to human existence. After all, everyone of every status ultimately comes under their care, and not surprisingly, their remarks bear on the play as a whole.

The first clown is the more talkative, and sets out a problem:

Here lies the water; good.
Here stands the man; good. If the man go to this water
and drown himself, it is, will he, nill he, he goes,
mark you that. But if the water come to him and drown
him, he drowns not himself; argal, he that is not
guilty of his own death shortens not his own life.

(V, i, 15–20)

He asks whether one who is the target of forces greater than himself can be guilty of failing to act properly. That query certainly applies to Hamlet, who was thrust into the position of revenger by his father, the Ghost. He did not seek that responsibility, nor does he want to fulfill it. To what extent, then, can we blame Hamlet for his failure? And to what extent do we sympathize with and even pity him for finding himself unable to resolve the crisis?

When the second gravedigger departs, Hamlet, accompanied by his friend Horatio, approaches the remaining man and reflects on the actions of this laborer:

> That skull had a tongue in it, and could
> sing once. How the knave jowls it to the ground,
> as if 'twere Cain's jaw-bone, that did the first
> murder! This might be the pate of a politician,
> which this ass now o'erreaches, one that would
> circumvent God, might it not?
>
> (V, i, 75–80)

Without speaking, the gravedigger suggests to Hamlet images of Claudius, who murdered his brother and thereby circumvented God by grabbing the crown of Denmark. The skull also reminds Hamlet of Polonius, who died at Hamlet's hand, then of Rosencrantz and Guildenstern, who were executed following Hamlet's rewriting of Claudius's letter to the King of England. Later the gravedigger's holding up the jester Yorick's skull leads Hamlet to reflect on age and mortality, how even Alexander, a prince who once conquered the entire world, now stops "a beer-barrel" (V, i, 212). Thus for Hamlet, the gravedigger's task leads to the conclusion that all of life is meaningless, and that therefore Hamlet's inaction is as meaningless as anything else.

A figure from another tragedy who does not bear the title "clown," yet who belongs in that tradition, is the drunken porter from *Macbeth*. He truly serves as comic relief, for Macbeth and Lady Macbeth have just carried out the murder of King Duncan, and Macbeth's conscience has already begun to torment him. He imagines voices calling "Sleep no more" (II, ii, 38), and he hears the knocking at the castle door, a noise that he now hopes will wake the dead Duncan. At this moment, though, the Porter appears to muse on the plight of the "porter of Hell Gate" (II, iii, 2), as fitting a description as any of Macbeth's castle.

As the knocking from outside continues, the Porter contemplates its source:

> Faith, here's an equivocator, that could
> swear in both the scales against either scale,

who committed treason enough for God's sake, yet
could not equivocate to heaven.

(II, iii, 8–11)

This portrait ironically reflects Macbeth, who equivocated, or lied, his way to murder and committed treason by killing the King, but who now cannot pray even hypocritically for forgiveness. The Porter then moves to the subject of drink, describing it as another kind of equivocator:

... it makes him, and it mars him; it sets him
on, and it takes him off; it persuades him, and
disheartens him ...

(II, iii, 31–33)

Thus the parallel is established between intoxication from drink and intoxication from ambition. Macbeth has been inspired by ambition to kill, but as the Porter suggests, the same quality cannot carry Macbeth to triumph. In just a few passages, then, the Porter articulates the pith of Macbeth's dilemma.

Not all of Shakespeare's clowns succeed in lightening the pressure created by tense moments. In *Othello*, for instance, a Clown enters (III, iv) when Othello is at the height of his agony over Desdemona's supposed infidelity, and seconds after Iago and Othello have sworn mutual loyalty (III, iii, 480). The Clown makes a few puns on the matter of "lying," suggesting sexual connotations as well as the deception that dominates Iago's lines. Still, the moment is weak. Perhaps the intrusion of a Clown is irrelevant in a tragedy where so much ironic humor is offered by Iago.

The bitterest fool in Shakespeare's plays is Apemantus of *Timon of Athens*. He uses his wit to expose everyone's foibles, including those of Timon and the Poet, who pretends to admire the King so as to gain funds from him: "He that loves to be flatter'd is worthy o' th' flatterer" (I, i, 226–227). Yet Apemantus is not without feeling for Timon:

O you gods! what a number
of men eats Timon, and he sees 'em not! It grieves
me to see so many dip their meat in one man's blood,
and all the madness is, he cheers them up too.
I wonder men dare trust themselves with men.

(I, ii, 39–44)

Like a parent berating a naughty child, Apemantus feels both anger and compassion for his King. Yet Apemantus also sees the essence of Timon's folly: "The middle of humanity thou never knewest, but the extremity of both ends" (IV, iii, 300–301). Apemantus therefore confirms that strong wit must be buttressed by understanding.

The most touching of Shakespeare's fools is the "Fool" in *King Lear*. He appears after Cordelia has been expelled by Lear and departed for France with her future husband. The Fool also exits permanently before Cordelia returns. Therefore they are never onstage together, and tradition holds they that were played by the same actor. Not surprisingly, then, the two characters fulfill much the same function: each acts as Lear's conscience. Cordelia does so in court, and the Fool serves when Lear is stranded on the heath. In addition, Lear's final speech of the play begins "And my poor fool is hang'd!" (V, iii, 306). Does he refer to one of these figures or both?

Indeed, they are complementary from virtually the first mention of the Fool, who is described by a knight:

> Since my young lady's going into France,
> sir, the Fool hath much pin'd away.
>
> (I, iv, 74)

When the Fool enters, he immediately reinforces the magnitude of the blunder Lear has committed by mutilating his realm:

> When thou clovest thy [crown] i' th' middle and
> gav'st away both parts, thou bor'st thine ass on
> thy back o'er the dirt. Thou hadst little wit in
> thy bald crown when thou gav'st thy golden one
> away.
>
> (I, iv, 160–163)

The image of the egg suggests that Lear has fractured his bond not only with his children, but also with his kingdom, which is in his charge as well. The word "golden," in reference to the crown, refers to the literal wealth that Lear has surrendered, but also to Cordelia, whom Lear has lost. The Fool even parodies Lear's brusque, ironic dismissal of Cordelia to exile: "Nothing. I have sworn. I am firm" (I, i, 245). At that moment, the King bitterly echoed her own earlier regret that she had "nothing" to say in response to his request for a statement of her love for him (I, i, 85–91). Now the Fool forces Lear to confront his own predicament: "I am a Fool, thou art nothing" (I, iv, 193–194).

In some ways, the Fool's most important contribution to the play is not verbal, but physical. By his very presence, he humanizes Lear, as when the two men wander helplessly in the ferocious storm. When they come across a tiny hovel, Lear does not seek to shield himself, but ushers the Fool in first:

Take physic, pomp,
Expose thyself to feel what wretches feel,
That thou mayst shake the superflux to them,
And show the heavens more just.

(III, iv, 33–36)

The Fool's influence has helped Lear acquire the compassion to become the great King he never was. The moment is made more terrible, however, by the presence of Gloucester's son Edgar, disguised as Tom o' Bedlam. Suddenly we are confronted by the sight of Lear, who borders on madness; Edgar, who feigns madness; and the Fool, whose wit stands on the edge of madness, all sheltering and supporting one another. Two brief scenes later, they attempt to conduct a mock trial of his daughters, and at the end, the Fool quietly takes his leave: "And I'll go to bed at noon" (III, vi, 85). The implication is that he can no longer stand to see such suffering as Lear endures.

Like the Fool in *King Lear*, Feste in *Twelfth Night* was probably originated onstage by Robert Armin. Both characters have a melancholy demeanor, and both sing to express their deepest selves. Feste is perhaps Shakespeare's richest clown, and in some ways the most memorable figure in *Twelfth Night*. His songs are especially touching, for instance:

Where is love? 'Tis not hereafter;
Present mirth hath present laughter;
What's to come is still unsure.
In delay there lies no plenty,
Then come kiss me sweet and twenty;
Youth's a stuff will not endure.

(II, iii, 47–52)

The words reflect the uncertain, transient nature of love, a central theme here, since all the major characters, especially Olivia, Viola, and Orsino, grapple with their emotions and desires. Perhaps more significant is that although Feste mixes within the riotous circle of Sir Toby, Sir Andrew, and Maria, and does participate in their torment of the puritanical Malvolio, he never shares their drunken revels. Rather, he remains apart, offering comments addressed to no one in particular, but whose chief purpose is apparently to amuse himself. For example, he meddles in the byplay between Sir Toby and Malvolio with interjections that each of the antagonists approves, then scorns (II, iii). Feste, meanwhile, seems oblivious to both men and entertains himself.

Perhaps more than anyone else, Viola sees the truth in Feste's words. When they banter, Feste offers a characteristically grim view of life and love:

> Foolery, sir, does walk about the orb like the
> sun, it shines every where. I would be sorry, sir,
> but the fool should be as oft with your master as with
> my mistress. I think I saw your wisdom there.
>
> (III, i, 38–41)

Even though Feste does not recognize that Viola is disguised as Caesario, he seems to see through her pose, so that she is tempted to reveal herself. Nonetheless, after Feste has left the stage, she says of him:

> This fellow is wise enough to play the fool,
> And to do that well craves a mind of wit.
> He must observe their mood on whom he jests,
> The quality of persons and the time . . .
>
> (III, i, 60–63)

Hers is as accurate a portrait of Feste as anyone offers.

Perhaps the episode when Feste gives full reign to his comic inventiveness occurs when he harasses the supposedly mad Malvolio, who has been imprisoned in darkness. The scene has cruel aspects, but Feste softens that feeling by performing not so much to torture the pitiable Malvolio as to indulge his own joy in masquerade. Indeed, we wonder why Feste bothers to dress up as Sir Topas the Curate, when, as Maria points out, Malvolio cannot see him and therefore cannot be deceived by the disguise (IV, ii, 64–65). Nonetheless, for Feste the game is everything, and he switches voices and dances about for his own entertainment. Suddenly, though, he switches to another song:

> I am gone, sir,
> And anon, sir,
> I'll be with you again;
> In a trice
> Like to the old Vice,
> Your need to sustain . . .
>
> (IV, ii, 120–125)

Even this episode cannot cure his sadness over conditions he has witnessed.

After all the confusions of identity have been resolved, and the lovers have sorted themselves out, Feste remains to sing the play to its conclusion. One of his verses has lines in common with a song by King Lear's Fool (III, ii, 74–77):

> When that I was and a little tiny boy,
> With hey ho, the wind and the rain,

A foolish thing was but a toy,
For the rain it raineth every day.

(V, i, 389–392)

His emphasis is the brevity of human existence. Feste sees our lives as short and therefore laughable, and the vanity and egoism that are the dominant traits of virtually every other character in this play are thus all the more ridiculous. At the same time, because our lives are so short and laughable, Feste sees such vanity and egoism as sad. His attitude throughout the play is thus the product of this dual vision.

Moreover, such a complicated approach to life seems to reflect many of the "fools" Shakespeare creates. The comedy they convey gives us great pleasure. At the same time, their befuddlement or isolation is tinged with a melancholy that makes our smiles turn wistful.

Forgiveness

One of the most ingratiating aspects of Shakespeare's works is the playwright's seemingly limitless affection for his characters. No matter what their vices or crimes, no matter how misguided or even brutal they may be, Shakespeare invests virtually every one with humanity, often manifested through expressions of forgiveness. Such reconciliation occurs at the end of many plays in different genres, contributing both to the catharsis that is essential to the tragic experience and to the joy that is part of the comic form.

In *Romeo and Juliet*, for instance, the final moments of the play find the surviving members of the Capulet and Montague families mourning the deaths of the title characters. First, Friar Lawrence recounts the events that have transpired, at last taking blame on himself:

> . . . and if aught in this
> Miscarried by my fault, let my old life
> Be sacrific'd some hour before his time,
> Unto the rigor of severest law.
>
> (V, iii, 266–269)

The Prince, however, refuses to condemn the Friar: "We still have known thee for a holy man" (V, iii, 270). This line suggests a theme that pervades Shakespeare's canon: that decent people may, in moments of crisis, be capable of indecent acts, and that therefore we must judge people by their entire lives, not by instances of weakness. Moments later, the two families join in mutual penance, although we note that a measure of competition may remain after Capulet offers his hand in friendship, and Montague offers to go one step further by building a statue: "But I can give thee more" (V, iii, 298). Despite this small bump, however, the path of reconciliation seems clear.

Such is also the tone at the end of *Julius Caesar*, when the forces of the

99

conspirators Brutus and Cassius have been defeated. As the conquering Antony looks down at the corpse of Brutus, who has fallen on his sword, Antony, once willing to "let slip the dogs of war" (III, i, 273) so that Caesar's assassination might be avenged, nonetheless forgives Brutus:

> This was the noblest Roman of them all:
> All the conspirators, save only he,
> Did that they did in envy of great Caesar;
> He, only in a general honest thought
> And common good to all, made one of them.
> (V, v, 68–72)

Antony recognizes Brutus's decency, and this acknowledgement buttresses the play's tragic stature.

Even in *Hamlet*, a play that ends with a series of murders, the spirit of forgiveness lives. The dying Laertes, once obsessed by the desire to revenge the deaths of his father, Polonius, and his sister, Ophelia, but now fatally wounded by his own poisoned sword, asks of Hamlet: "Exchange forgiveness with me..." (V, ii, 329), and a few lines later, Hamlet does so. We recognize, however, that Hamlet is not completely overtaken by generosity, for he offers no pardon to his uncle, Claudius, nor even to his mother, Gertrude.

Perhaps the most complicated expression of mutual forgiveness takes place at the end of the comedy *As You Like It*, when almost every principal character in the play joins in that spirit. The effect is almost like a great chorus. Dominated by the reunion of the Duke Senior and his daughter, Rosalind, and under the care of the god Hymen, expressions of love and forgiveness cascade before us. Hymen blesses several marriages: Rosalind and Orlando; Celia and the now-reformed Oliver; Phebe and Silvius, to whom she is urged strongly to return; and even the cynical Touchstone and the simple Audrey. The tone of the moment is underlined by Orlando's brother Jaques de Boys, who enters to report that Duke Frederick, who had earlier threatened to kill his brother, the Duke Senior, encountered "an old religious man" (V, iv, 160), and was miraculously converted to a peaceful mode. Thus the changed Duke has relinquished his claims, and all lands have been restored to the Duke Senior. The speed of some of these transformations may seem unlikely, but the play has been built upon the regenerative, even magical, powers of the forest of Arden, and we may therefore accept how marriage and reconciliation, comic forms of forgiveness, might occur under such circumstances.

Forgiveness does not conclude every play, however. At the end of *Othello*, for instance, the title character has been forced by Iago's wife, Emilia, to acknowledge the terrible truth that it was Othello's ensign Iago who tricked the general into believing that Desdemona was unfaithful. When Emilia makes this realization public, Iago stabs her to death. In response, Othello tries to kill Iago, but only wounds him, and thereafter seeks forgiveness for Othello's own cataclysmic misjudgments:

> An honorable murderer, if you will;
> For nought I did in hate, but all in honor.
>
> (V, ii, 294–295)

No one, however, speaks on Othello's behalf. Instead, Iago responds from his own perspective:

> Demand me nothing; what you know, you know:
> From this time forth I never will speak word.
>
> (V, ii, 303–304)

To this insolence, the Venetian nobleman Lodovico answers: "What? not to pray?" (V, ii, 305), but Iago revels in his evil and has no desire for absolution. True, given how murky his motivations have been, we may assume that even did he desire forgiveness, he would be unable to explain what led him to carry out his diabolical schemes. Nonetheless, his refusal to invite sympathy is striking.

Also compelling are those moments where we wonder just how believeable certain expressions and acceptances of forgiveness are. Near the end of *Richard II*, for example, the Duke of York brings in his son, Aumerle, whom York suspects of treachery against the newly enthroned Henry IV. The young man's mother, the Duchess of York, pleads for him before the King: "I do not sue to stand;/ Pardon is all the suit I have in hand" (V, iii, 129–130). At once, Henry answers with apparent generosity: "I pardon him as God shall pardon me" (V, iii, 131). Is Henry, however, truly forgiving Aumerle? Or does he hope that his action will inspire absolution for Henry's own transgressions in removing Richard from the throne? Or is the new King seeking merely to mend political fences? Perhaps all three reasons lead him to speak as he does.

In *Much Ado About Nothing*, we are also left uncertain as to characters' feelings. After the falseness of the accusations about Hero's infidelity to her fiance, Claudio, has been exposed, the Friar boasts to Leonato, Hero's father: "Did I not tell you she was innocent?" (V, iv, 1). Leonato, however, brings his own attitude to the matter:

> So are the Prince and Claudio, who accus'd her
> Upon the error that you heard debated.
> But Margaret was in some fault for this,

Although against her will, as it appears
In the true course of all the question.
(V, iv, 2–5)

He seems more intent upon exonerating himself and others than upon seeking his daughter's forgiveness for having assumed that she was guilty. We are therefore denied the pardon for which we wait. Moreover, at the wedding that follows, Hero is unmasked before Claudio, who has assumed that he would be marrying a different woman. At the sight of Hero, though, his only response is: "Another Hero?" (V, iv, 62). To which she replies:

Nothing certainer:
One Hero died defil'd, but I do live,
And surely as I live, I am a maid.
(V, iv, 62–64)

We hear nothing more from either of them. Claudio never apologizes for believing the worst about the woman he claims to love, nor does Hero seem to feel the need to exonerate him for his assumption against her. Perhaps we should conclude that the two have been stunned into silence and that later they will exchange appropriate expressions of affection, but surely the moment is awkward.

Perhaps the most dramatically unwieldy pardon occurs in *The Two Gentlemen of Verona*. First Proteus, infatuated with his friend Valentine's love, Silvia, threatens to rape her: "I'll force thee to yield to my desire" (V, iv, 59). At this point, Valentine steps forward to accuse his friend of treachery:

Proteus,
I am sorry I must never trust thee more,
But count the world a stranger for thy sake.
(V, iv, 68–70)

Now follows two twists that strain credulity. First, Proteus is suddenly overcome by remorse:

My shame and guilt confounds me.
Forgive me, Valentine; if hearty sorrow
Be a sufficient ransom for offense,
I render't here: I do as truly suffer
As e'er I did commit.
(V, iv, 73–77)

102

The shift is credible only if we see Proteus as a man who earlier was possessed by a desire so fierce that he lost all reason, including affection for his best friend. Under such circumstances, abrupt repentance is as believable as abrupt infatuation.

Equally difficult to explain is Valentine's acceptance of this plea: "All that was mine in Silvia I give thee" (V, iv, 83). Perhaps Valentine is in his own way conforming to the Renaissance ideal of male friendship. A more likely explanation is that he, once a skeptic about love, is reverting to his former self and yielding to his friend's impetuosity.

At this moment, however, Julia, still disguised as Sebastian, faints, and within moments all identities are revealed. The last 100 lines of the scene, therefore, are marked by reconciliation. Proteus comes to his senses and realizes that Julia is his true love, and a silent Silvia is embraced by Valentine. Even the Duke enters, first to forgive Valentine for purusing Silvia: "I do applaud thy spirit, Valentine . . ." (V, iv, 140). Then he pardons the band of thieves in the forest. Such generosity springing forth instantly may seem artificial, but then this play is built upon sudden and unexpected alterations of attitude.

Some of the most moving instances of forgiveness may be found in the romances, Shakespeare's final four plays. Indeed, all these works conclude with extensive episodes of family reunion, and always after lengthy times of separation. Here we feel Shakespeare trying to create his own dramatic universe, where the good are rewarded and the evil punished, where all complications resolve smoothly, and everyone lives happily ever after.

Discussion of two romances should suffice to clarify this point. In the final moments of *The Winter's Tale*, Leontes, King of Sicilia, is brought before a statue of his wife, Hermione, whom he has thought long dead. For a few moments, he contemplates the figure sadly, bitterly ruing the insane jealousy that sent her, he thinks, to her death:

> O royal piece,
> There's magic in thy majesty, which has
> My evils conjur'd to remembrance, and
> From thy admiring daughter took the spirits,
> Standing like stone with thee.
>
> (V, iii, 38–42)

Under the prodding of his faithful servant, Paulina, he prays for Hermione's deliverance, when suddenly, in a moment of stage magic, she steps from her pedestal to embrace him. Hermione is then reunited with her daughter, Perdita, whom she thought lost forever. Hermione's subsequent sentiments embody the spirit of the entire work:

> You gods, look down
> And from your sacred vials pour your graces
> Upon my daughter's head!
>
> (V, iii, 121–123)

A few lines later, in the play's closing speech, Leontes accepts the pardon of his surviving household and embraces them, and all leave the stage with unalloyed joy. We feel how the passing years have wiped away the pain caused by Leontes' earlier behavior and how a transcedent purification has been achieved through mutual understanding.

Forgiveness is also an essential part of the finale of *The Tempest*, when Prospero is prepared to punish Alonso, King of Naples, his brother Sebastian, and Prospero's brother, Antonio, all of whom he blames for his expulsion from the throne of Milan and his years of exile on the island. As Prospero explains to his enslaved sprite, Ariel:

> Let them be hunted soundly. At this hour
> Lies at my mercy all mine enemies.
> Shortly shall all my labors end, and thou
> Shalt have the air at freedom.
>
> (IV, i, 262–265)

Ariel, however, invokes gentler terms, recalling Prospero's successful magic:

> Your charm so strongly works 'em
> That if you now beheld them, your affections
> Would become tender.
>
> (V, i, 17–19)

Prospero is uncertain: "Dost thou think so, spirit?" (V, i, 19), to which Ariel answers: "Mine would, sir, were I human" (V, i, 20). A few lines later, Ariel offers one more sentiment that has profound implications throughout Shakespeare's work: "The rare action is/ In virtue than in vengeance" (V, i, 27–28). This expression will be considered more fully in the chapter on revenge, but it clearly implies the ennobling quality of forgiveness that Prospero obeys. Not that such an act always transforms evil. At the end of this play, for instance, Antonio never apologizes for his plottings. Like Iago, he strides offstage silently, and we suspect that when opportunity for mischief arises again, he will revert to his calculating self.

Surely the most powerful scenes of reconciliation and forgiveness occur in *King Lear*. Late in the play, the King enters, exhausted mentally and physically from his ordeal on the heath, as well as from the emotional suffering he has endured. When he is reunited with his daughter, Cordelia, whom he has not seen since he expelled her from the kingdom in the first scene, he speaks in simple, gentle language, reflecting the spiritual transformation that has overtaken him:

> I know you do not love me, for your sisters
> Have (as I do remember) done me wrong:
> You have some cause, they have not.
> (IV, vii, 72–74)

Cordelia's response could not be more eloquent: "No cause, no cause" (V, vii, 74). She has always recognized what Lear has finally learned: that true love does not turn away in the face of error. Here Cordelia echoes one of Shakespeare's sonnets: ". . . love is not love/ Which alters when it alteration finds," a sentiment followed a few lines later by: "Love alters not with his brief hours and weeks,/ But bears it out even to the edge of doom" (Sonnet 116). Now, in his humility, Lear understands the nature of that emotion as he never has before: "Pray you now forget, and forgive; I am old and foolish" (V, vii, 84).

Much of the rest of the play builds upon this reconciliation. As Lear says when the two have been taken prisoner by Edmund's forces:

> Come, let's away to prison:
> We two alone will sing like birds i' th' cage;
> When thou dost ask me blessing, I'll kneel down
> And ask of thee forgiveness.
> (V, iii, 8–11)

Not long after, Edmund himself is defeated in combat. We have seen him conspire heartlessly against his own father and join with Regan, Cornwall, and Goneril to destroy Lear and his kingdom. Now, with death imminent, even Edmund seeks the repose of forgiveness and therefore asks his masked conqueror:

> But what art thou
> That hast this fortune on me? If thou'rt noble,
> I do forgive thee.
> (V, iii, 165–167)

The mysterious knight then reveals the truth:

> My name is Edgar, and thy father's son.
> The gods are just, and of our pleasant vices
> Make instruments to plague us.
> (V, ii, 170–172)

For Edgar, as probably for Shakespeare himself, the spirit of forgiveness reflects faith in the ultimate rightness of the universe. By revealing our capacity to grow, see, and finally understand, the act of reconciliation elevates human beings, an essential part of comic, romantic, and tragic drama.

Gender

Is any theme in literature more provocative than the differences between men and women? Countless artists draw inspiration from the nature of masculine and feminine identity, and the variety of sensibilities that characterize each gender. Such issues resound with particular force in Shakespeare's plays, even though they were written when women were forbidden to appear on the English stage, and all female roles were portrayed by young men or boys. Although we may assume that Shakespeare's audience accepted the illusion, his writing under such a constriction must have shaped his vision. Furthermore, many of his plots involve female characters dressing up as males, a deception that leads to all sorts of intriguing situations in which the intrinsic biological differences between men and women, as well as those created by society, come to the fore. To encapsulate Shakespeare's views on this subject in a sentence or two is impossible. We can say with assurance, though, that in his plays, the categories of what we call "masculine" and "feminine" are hardly absolute. Rather, they tend to overlap within characters, at times indistinguishably, and sometimes clashing violently.

No play better epitomizes the war between masculine and feminine instincts than *Macbeth*. Indeed, the first characters we meet, the three witches, are described later as women with beards (I, iii, 46), and thus from the outset the genders mix uncomfortably. Macbeth is soon introduced as a soldier of pure brutality: "Valor's minion" (I, ii, 19), a stereotypical masculine image, but we soon learn that he has no children. The witches predict that one day he will have the crown of Scotland, but also that it shall be passed on to his rival Banquo's children. We may surmise, therefore, that Macbeth has failed in the most fundamental responsibility of a man: to be a father. The question therefore arises as to whether his battlefield exploits are some form of compensation to prove the manhood that is suspect because of his failure to sire offspring.

Our first impression of Lady Macbeth intensifies the issue of gender.

After she reads her husband's letter detailing the witches' prophesies, her reaction is chilling:

> Yet I do fear thy nature,
> It is too full o' th' milk of human kindness
> To catch the nearest way.
> (I, v, 16–18)

Her imagery hints that Macbeth is too feminine, that he lacks the masculine aggression necessary to take command. Moments later, she prays perversely for her own masculine attributes to be released:

> Come, you spirits
> That tend on mortal thoughts, unsex me here,
> And fill me from the crown to the toe topful
> Of direst cruelty! Make thick my blood,
> Stop up th' access and passage to remorse,
> That no compunctious visitings of nature
> Shake my fell purpose, nor keep peace between
> Th' effect and [it]! Come to my woman's breasts,
> And take any milk for gall, you murth'ring ministers . . .
> (I, v, 40–48)

She envisions herself trapped between two forces: her womanliness, in the form of certain biological phenomena, and society's rules that limit her options. She cannot achieve power by herself and therefore is forced to try to do so through her husband.

When, however, Macbeth seeks to set aside their plan to kill King Duncan, Lady Macbeth knows what buttons to push to provoke her husband into action:

> Art thou afeard
> To be the same in thine own act and valor
> As thou art in desire?
> (I, vii, 39–41)

She questions only his courage, but Macbeth takes her challenge to have different implications:

> I dare do all that may become a man;
> Who dares [do] more is none.
> (I, vii, 46–47)

Lady Macbeth is relentless, though, and drives home the point of vulnerability:

What beast was't then
That made you break this enterprise to me?
When you durst do it, then you were a man;
And to be more than what you were, you would
Be so much more the man . . .

    I have given suck, and know
How tender 'tis to love the babe that milks me;
I would, while it was smiling in my face,
Have pluck'd my nipple from his boneless gums,
And dash'd the brains out, had I so sworn as you
Have done to this.

                    (I, vii, 46–58)

Not only does she insinuate that her husband lacks manhood. She also mocks her own femininity by saying that she herself is more of a man than he is, for even when fulfilling the biological responsibilities at the core of her womanhood, she had more masculine resolve than Macbeth has now.

Her strategy works, for she does inspire, or perhaps the proper word is "bully," her husband into murdering Duncan. We note, however, that when the opportunity to kill presents itself to her, she refrains from committing the act: "Had he not resembled/ My father as he slept, I had done't" (II, ii, 12–13). Although she claims that she has the necessary brutality within her, something in Lady Macbeth's character forbids her from taking a life. Moreover, throughout the rest of the play, she weakens under the knowledge of her part in the assassination. By the end, she is sleepwalking, reduced to tonelessly reciting images that represent previous events. For all her bravado, her conscience overwhelms her, and this collapse suggests that what might be judged to be her femininity supersedes her more masculine ambition.

Meanwhile, under the weight of his actions, Macbeth becomes emboldened, if madly so. In an attempt to possess the crown seemingly forever, he orders the killing of Banquo and his son, Fleance, for whom the witches have ordained the throne. Following the failure of that scheme, Macbeth orders the slaughter of the family of his suspicious rival, Macduff, even though none of these people has been connected to Macbeth's own predicament. Macbeth thus becomes imbued with "masculine" violence, and even goes beyond any predictions that the witches had decreed. Nonetheless, our supposition that he is compensating for insecurity about his manhood is echoed by Macduff when he learns of the slaughter of his own children: "He has no children. All my pretty ones?" (IV, iii, 216). Thus we are perpetually aware of the conflict within both the play and the title character over the forces of masculinity and femininity, as well as the havoc these opposing instincts may wreak within an individual.

Other plays of Shakespeare dramatize aspects of this theme. In *Coriolanus*, the title character's mother, Volumnia, is trapped by her identity as a woman and seeks to use her son to triumph vicariously in both the military and political arenas. As she explains to her son's wife, Virgilia:

> I tell thee, daughter, I sprang not more
> in joy at first hearing he was a man-child than now
> in first seeing he had prov'd himself a man.
> (I, iii, 15–17)

Like Lady Macbeth, Volumnia is a woman whose male aggressiveness is prisoner to both her biology and the role that her society imposes on her.

In *Henry VI, Part 1*, written very early in Shakespeare's career, the playwright does portray a woman who succeeds in the traditionally masculine world of war. Nonetheless, even the French themselves, whose triumphs Joan of Pucelle guides, regard her as demonic because of her actions and her flaunting her sexuality. Indeed, the French King almost resents her victories (I, vi, 17–18). One implication of the play, therefore, is that Joan's position is part of the unnaturalness that pervades the world and contributes to the general upset intertwined with the Hundred Years War between England and France, as well as the imminent War of the Roses between the English royal families of Lancaster and York. Indeed, the rest of *Henry VI*, as well as part of *Richard III*, which completes the story, is dominated by Henry VI's wife, Margaret, who is described in *Henry VI, Part 3* by her rival and victim York:

> She-wolf of France, but worse than wolves of France,
> Whose tongue more poisons than the adder's tooth!
> How ill-beseeming is it in thy sex
> To triumph like an Amazonian trull
> Upon their woes whom fortune captivates!
> (I, iv, 111–115)

As much as any character, Margaret embodies the chaos of this tetralogy by breaking all bounds of traditional gender roles.

Shakespeare's most interesting dramatizations of distinctions between what we call "masculine" and "feminine" are to be found in his romantic stories. In *Antony and Cleopatra*, for instance, the Queen describes to her attendant Charmian an incident when Cleopatra dressed a drunken Antony in her "tires and mantles" while she wore his sword (II, v, 19–23). What attraction, we wonder, did she find in blurring the lines between their identities, feminizing the manly Roman general, while taking on for herself the image of the triumphant military leader? Apparently Shakespeare sees aspects of both genders within even the most heterosexual of relationships.

In *As You Like It*, Rosalind, the banished Duke's daughter, cannot explain why she finds herself strangely unsettled. She therefore inquires of her cousin, Celia, whether such a condition could be cured by love. Celia's reply resounds through the Shakespearean canon:

> Marry, I prithee do, to make sport withal.
> But love no man in good earnest, nor no further
> in sport neither, than with safety of a pure
> blush thou mayest in honor come off again.
> (I, ii, 26–29)

She implies that under the influence of infatuation, characters may try to control their desires, but the power of love is such that when individuals fall under its influence, they are helpless to withstand its allure. Moreover, the eagerness of these two girls to mock the fortunes of others suggests that both are ripe for a lesson about love.

When Duke Frederick banishes Rosalind from court because, as a relative of his exiled brother, she poses a threat to his throne, she disguises herself as a man, Ganymed, and, along with Celia, seeks refuge in the Forest of Arden. There she comes across an extravagant love poem written to her, and demands to know its author. She recognizes that the verses are maudlin; yet she is struck by their unfettered emotion:

> Is he of God's making? What manner of
> man? Is his head worth a hat? Or his chin
> worth a beard?
> (III, ii, 205–207)

She is desperate to know who has so touched her. Here is a key moment, for without even seeing the man in question, Rosalind realizes that she desires him. Her affections are not based on his appearance or accomplishments. Rather through his poetry, she sees the inner man, and we are thus aware of her capacity to intuit his qualities. In general, Shakespeare's women are similarly insightful. They can probe and thereafter understand human feelings with a perception that leaves males far behind.

Yet Rosalind can also be girlishly giddy, as when she discovers that the author she loves is Orlando, with whom she was smitten earlier:

What did he when thou saw'st him?
What said he? How look'd he? Wherein went he?
What makes he here? Did he ask for me? Where
remains he? How parted he with thee? And when
shalt thou see him again? Answer me in one word.
(III, ii, 220–224)

Despite her self-possession and wit, Rosalind is still vulnerable to her desire, and hence her mind and heart begin to battle each other. This war of emotion is characteristic of many of Shakespeare's women.

It intensifies in Rosalind later in this scene, when Orlando appears. According to the conventions of the Elizabethan stage, he fails to recognize her in disguise, even when she talks about his poems. After Orlando proclaims he is the "love-shak'd" author (III, ii, 367), Rosalind insists he prove that love:

Me believe it? You may as soon make her
that you love believe it, which I warrant she is
apter to do than she confesses she does.
(III, ii, 387–389)

Unable to confess her desires, Rosalind tries to inspire Orlando to take action on his own. Here is yet another aspect of the female predicament. Given the social conditions under which women live, they cannot be aggressors in romance; rather, they must wait for men to take the lead, and often these men are too blind, awkward, or incompetent to do so.

Even more subtle differences between men and women surface when Rosalind, still in disguise as Ganymed, lectures the haughty Phebe, who scorns the lovesick Silvius:

But, mistress, know yourself, down on your knees,
And thank heaven, fasting, for a good man's love . . .
Cry the man mercy, love him, take his offer . . .
(III, v, 57–61)

Rosalind realizes that although the conventions of love may appear ridiculous, love itself is not, and so stirring is Rosalind's depth of feeling that Phebe instantly falls in love with her (III, v, 81–82). The moment has several implications: first, that women talk of love on a plane far above that of men, as well as with greater intensity and directness; second, that only women truly understand what other women feel; and, third, that women seek in love a depth of emotional response that only women can provide.

We see further evidence of these convictions in the next scene when, under Rosalind's coaching, Orlando attempts to rehearse the presentation of his affections:

> Come, woo me, woo me; for now I am in a
> holiday humor, and like enough to consent.
> What would you say to me now, and I were your
> very very Rosalind?
>
> (IV, i, 68–71)

Orlando reluctantly begins, but with almost every line he utters, Rosalind amends his delivery or word usage, refining his expression so that it touches her just the right way. Her battle to teach him, while simultaneously controlling her own longing to break free of her disguise and express her passion openly, moves us profoundly. She is trapped by her femininity, as well as by social conventions of the day and the crisis at hand. Nonetheless, we are conscious of how her masculine and feminine attributes, while blending together, also tug against one another.

We see further examples of such distinctions in *Twelfth Night*, which was likely the comedy that Shakespeare wrote immediately after *As You Like It*. Here our sympathies lie primarily with Viola, who is stranded in Illyria after the shipwreck that separates her from her brother, Sebastian. After she retreats to the court of Duke Orsino, she immediately falls in love with him, even as she takes on the role of the male Cesario. Meanwhile, Orsino finds himself aroused by the disguised young woman, and he grapples with his urges:

> Diana's lip
> Is not more smooth and rubious; thy small pipe
> Is as the maiden's organ, shrill and sound,
> And all is semblative a woman's part.
>
> (I, iv, 31–34)

He senses Viola's womanliness, but at the moment he does not know her identity. We are therefore forced to ponder the nature of physical attraction: does Orsino truly seek a member of the opposite gender, or is he simply attracted to femininity, whether in the form of a man or a woman? Moreover, that the role of Viola must have been originally played by a boy complicates the dilemma further.

The plot becomes more intricate, and the problem of gender more perplexing, when Viola is forced, in Orsino's name, to woo his love, Olivia. Playing this part, Viola offers expressions of devotion which are so touching that she wins over Olivia almost at once:

> Make me a willow cabin at your gate,
> And call upon my soul within the house;

Write loyal cantons of contemned love,
And sing them loud even in the dead of night . . .
                    (I, v, 268–271)

Olivia is quietly taken: "You might do much" (I, v, 276). Thereafter we ask whether she is attracted to the elegance of Viola's poetry, the feminine sensibility therein, or the delicacy of the young suitor's features. After all, before Cesario departs, Oliva adds:

Thy tongue, thy face, thy limbs, actions, and spirit
Do give the fivefold blazon.
                    (I, v, 292–293)

Clearly, physical attraction bubbles within her; yet Viola and she can never become a match. Thus even at this point, we predict that Sebastian will appear and become the object of Olivia's desire.

Viola, too, appreciates Olivia's quandary. After Malvolio returns the ring that Cesario has supposedly left behind, Viola anguishes over how she has caused another woman such pain:

How easy is it for the proper-false
In women's waxen hearts to set their forms!
Alas, [our] frailty is the cause, not we,
For such as we are made [of], such we be.
                    (II, ii, 29–32)

She is both puzzled and intrigued by the confusion of which she is part:

As I am man,
My state is desperate for my master's love;
As I am woman (now alas the day!),
What thriftless sighs shall poor Olivia breathe!
O time, thou must untangle this, not I,
It is too hard a knot for me t' untie.
                    (II, ii, 36–41)

Her reflections show the mixture of masculine and feminine qualities within her. Even more important, she may also manifest Shakespeare's conviction of how genders merge within all of us.

This confusion is compounded when Viola, still as Cesario, returns to Olivia's house, and the two bandy back and forth playfully. First Olivia demands: "I prithee tell me what thou think'st of me" (III, i, 138). To which Viola replies: "That you do think you are not what you are" (III, i, 139). Olivia senses that Viola's remark has additional implications: "If I think so, I think the same of you" (III, i, 140). Viola tries to shy away:

"Then you think right; I am not what I am" (III, i, 141). But Olivia insists: "I would you were as I would have you be" (III, i, 142). A few lines later, she adds:

> I love thee so, that maugre all thy pride,
> Nor wit nor reason can my passion hide.
> Do not extort thy reasons from this cause,
> For that I woo, thou therefore has no cause . . .
> (III, i, 151–154)

Olivia articulates how the lure of romance is so great as to reach beyond her ken or control. As much as any character in Shakespeare's plays, she suggests the unfathomable nature of attraction between people and between masculine and feminine qualities. We see as much when Antonio, whose devotion to Viola's brother, Sebastian, may have sexual overtones, interrupts the duel between Viola and Sir Andrew Aguecheek, who seeks to marry Olivia. Antonio mistakes Viola for Sebastian, and for his pains is taken away to prison. Yet Antonio is steadfast in his loyalty, as we realize when he is brought before Orsino and speaks of Viola's behavior:

> For his sake
> Did I expose myself (pure for his love)
> Into the danger of this adverse town,
> Drew to defend him when he was beset . . .
> (V, i, 82–85)

We are again reminded of Olivia's earlier implication, and of Shakespeare's, that a natural unity exists between masculine and feminine, but that neither of these qualities is to be found exclusively in males or females. Rather, they may join in both the human form and the human spirit.

Indeed, wherever exigencies of plot lead Shakespeare's female characters to appear in male garb, this theme arises: in *The Two Gentlemen of Verona*, *The Merchant of Venice*, and *Cymbeline*, to name three more. In such cases, we find ourselves speculating about Shakespeare's vision of the causes of sexual attraction, the meaning of sexual identity, and, ultimately, the essence of gender. Perhaps we must therefore acknowledge what Shakespeare himself seems to accept: here is one more insoluble puzzle about the nature of the human animal.

Generations

No theme dominates the history of tragic drama so profoundly as the relationship between one generation and those that follow. Certainly the plots of most Greek tragedies dramatize how children pay for the sins of their ancestors. In the *Agamemnon* of Aechylus, for instance, present events are virtually dictated by the evil actions of earlier generations of the House of Atreus. In Sophocles' *Oedipus the King*, because of transgressions by the parents of the title character, he is condemned to kill his father and marry his mother. Thereafter, Oedipus's own actions shape the lives of his children.

In most of the plays of Shakespeare, however, the power of one generation over another is not so specifically determined; the gods do not decree inevitable consequences. Rather, throughout the tragedies, comedies, histories, and romances, children struggle with their parents' values and the implications of certain behaviors and traditions. Yet the younger generation must also establish its own codes of morality.

The opening lines of *Romeo and Juliet*, for example, clarify how the two young lovers have grown up in the midst of a long-standing familial conflict:

> . . . Doth with their death bury their parents' strife,
> The fearful passage of their death-mark'd love,
> And the continuance of their parents' rage,
> Which, but their children's end, nought could remove . . .
> (Prologue, 8–11)

From the outset, the plot is laid out: only through the deaths of their children will the parents' animosity be erased. Yet the children themselves are not mere pawns in the struggle. They grapple with the bloody rivalry that possesses their families and their city, and their attempts to surmount it are among the most compelling moments of the play. Juliet, the cooler, more rational of the two lovers, articulates the dilemma that she and Romeo share, when in the famous balcony scene, she pleads with him:

> O Romeo, Romeo, wherefore art thou Romeo?
> Deny thy father and refuse thy name . . .
> (II, ii, 33–34)

She establishes the central crisis of the play. When she urges Romeo to separate himself from his family, she hopes that he will reject the hatred and code of revenge which have held sway for as long as anyone can remember. One intriguing aspect of this play is that Romeo never understands this issue. Instead, at the key moment of the drama, after Juliet's cousin, Tybalt, through Romeo's interference, kills Mercutio in the sword fight, Romeo surrenders to the values of his father's generation and steps up to kill in the name of his friend's death. Immediately afterwards, Lord and Lady Capulet insist that despite Tybalt's death, Juliet must obey their wishes and marry Paris, whatever her feelings for him (III, iv). The result of all this generational oppression is doom for the love between two young people who are unable to break free of their parents' values. By the end of the play, however, when the families gather in mourning, we sense that the shared sacrifice may have at last purged the city of the bloody feud.

In *Othello*, Desdemona makes clear from virtually her first words that in marrying Othello, a Moor, she is separating herself from her father and the prejudices of his generation:

> But here's my husband;
> And so much duty as my mother show'd
> To you, preferring you before her father,
> So much I challenge that I may profess
> Due to the Moor, my lord.
> (I, iii, 185–188)

As the play proceeds, Desdemona's love for Othello grows more intense, even as irrational jealousy possesses him. At this point, though, we recognize that rebellion against her father's dictum is at least part of Desdemona's motivation for marriage to a man so alien to her immediate world.

Whenever Shakespeare dramatizes romance, as he does in all the comedies, one essential element is the need for the lovers to detach themselves from their parents' authority. In *The Taming of the Shrew*, the values of the community, as articulated by Baptista, are that the richest suitor shall obtain his desirable daughter, Bianca, in marriage, and then only after his eldest daughter, Katherine, is married (II, i, 342–344). In the meantime, Petruchio has entered the town of Padua, ostensibly with one aim in mind: to marry a wealthy woman (I, ii, 75–76). By the end of the play, however, he and Katherine have broken away from such principles and established love on their own mutually satisfying terms.

In *A Midsummer Night's Dream*, Hermia and Lysander wish to marry against the wishes of her father, Egeus, who pleads his case to Theseus, the Duke of Athens:

> I beg the ancient privilege of Athens:
> As she is mine, I may dispose of her;
> Which shall be either to this gentleman,
> Or to her death, according to our law
> Immediately provided in that case.
>
> (I, i, 41–45)

Theseus seems to concur with Egeus's claim. Eventually, however, the Duke overrules this judgment and allows the lovers to choose for themselves. The entire situation is undercut, of course, by the intrusions of the fairies and our awareness that when Lysander, once so desirous of Hermia, falls under the influence of Puck's magic potion, he proclaims love instead for Helena. Nevertheless, the lovers' triumph over Egeus is satisfying.

The theme of one generation's relationship to the next buttresses all of Shakespeare's history plays. In both the first Henriad (*Henry VI, 1, 2, & 3*, and *Richard III*) and the second (*Richard II, Henry IV, Parts 1 & 2*, and *Henry V*), we remain aware of how every king, as well as every prospective holder of the throne, acts in response to the principles and actions of previous occupants.

In *Richard III*, for example, no character better exemplifies the passage of values and animosities than Queen Margaret. She is the only character who appears in all four plays of the tetralogy, and as the wife of the murdered Henry VI, she carries with her the memory of when she wielded power, and the desire to see punishment wreaked on those who have wrested that power from her. She and the Duke of Gloucester, soon to be Richard III, exchange memorable abuse, because she blames him most for her suffering. She has been banished, but she remains near the Court, hovering over the action like an avenging fury:

> . . . but I do find more pain in banishment
> Than death can yield me hereby my abode.
> A husband and a son thou ow'st to me—
> And thou a kingdom—all of you allegiance.

The sorrow that I have, by right is yours,
And all the pleasures you usurp are mine.
                    (I, iii, 167–173)

Here is one member of an older generation who has lived long enough to experience the suffering of her children passed back to her.

In *Richard II*, the dying John of Gaunt, uncle to the King and otherwise the most eminent man in England, warns Richard of the dangers he faces:

O had thy grandsire with a prophet's eye
Seen how his son's son should destroy his sons,
From forth thy reach he would have laid thy shame,
Deposing thee before thou wert possess'd,
Which are possess'd now to depose thyself.
                    (II, i, 104–108)

Gaunt recognizes the extent of Richard's criminal actions, including the robbing of the kingdom's treasury and the murder of the Duke of Gloucester, who was not only Gaunt's brother, but Richard's uncle. Gaunt therefore reflects back to the heritage of Edward III, their grandfather who conquered so much of Europe, and his son, Edward, the Black Prince, who predeceased his father, forcing the placement of the boy, Richard, on the throne. Now that Richard threatens to lay waste to that glorious heritage, Gaunt sees the result of a grandson who failed to live up to standards of the previous generation.

Later, when Gaunt's son Bullingbrook has returned from the exile commanded by Richard, and has managed to depose the King, the Bishop of Carlisle warns how such an action will have repercussions extending far beyond this time:

The blood of English shall manure the ground,
And future ages groan for this foul act.
Peace shall go sleep with Turks and infidels,
And in this seat of peace tumultuous wars
Shall kin with kin and kind with kind confound.
                    (IV, i, 136–141)

When Bullingbrook at last takes the throne as Henry IV, we see how his actions will shape not only the policies of his nation, but also his personal life, which will be tested by his eldest son, Hal, at the moment reveling with "unrestrained, loose companions" (V, iii, 7), and whose behavior threatens to undo all that the new King has accomplished.

These tensions carry over into the opening scene of *Henry IV, Part 1*, when the King admires the bravery of Northumberland's son, Hotspur, and broods over the ongoing dereliction of Hal (I, i, 78–90). The entire pageant of the next ten acts, however, incorporating both parts of *Henry IV*, is in fact the growth of Hal into the greatest King in English history. At the same time that he prepares militarily to take over for his royal father, the Prince also studies, so to speak, with his spiritual father, Falstaff, the irresolute lord of the tavern. Fittingly, the setting of both plays alternates between the world of the Court and the taverns of Eastcheap. Henry IV is King of the former, Falstaff of the latter, and Hal learns from both. All the while, he readies himself to leave both paternal figures and set out on his own, armed with different lessons that both have imbued in him.

The inevitable separation of Hal and Falstaff becomes most apparent in *Part 1*, when Hal is ordered to return to the Court and join the upcoming military enterprise. As if conscious of the changing course of his life, Hal orders Falstaff: "Do thou stand for my father and examine me upon the particulars of my life" (II, iv, 376–377). After Falstaff merrily defends himself in the King's voice, Hal commands that they switch parts, to which Falstaff answers: "Depose me?" (II, iv, 435). In fact, Hal will soon do just that, succeeding his father and exiling Falstaff, and his stern lecture to Falstaff, in King Henry's voice, assures us that young Hal has the inner strength to assume the responsibilities of the crown. Meanwhile, Hal's manner darkens, and as his insults grow more pointed, Falstaff takes on Hal's persona and tries to defend himself and maintain his place in Hal's life:

> . . . but for sweet Jack Falstaff, kind
> Jack Falstaff, true Jack Falstaff, valiant Jack Falstaff,
> and therefore more valiant, being as he is old Jack
> Falstaff, banish not him thy Harry's company, banish
> not him thy Harry's company—banish plump Jack,
> and banish all the world.
>
> (II, iv, 475–480)

Hal's answer, though, is inevitable and painful: "I do, I will" (II, iv, 481). For Hal to assume his rightful place in the kingdom, he must reject the anarchic ways of his spiritual father and conform to the moral rigor that the position of King demands.

A few scenes later, Hal and Henry IV meet in an encounter that sets forever the course of Hal's life. After bemoaning the burdens he carries because of his own actions against Richard, the King berates his son: "For thou has lost thy princely privilege/ With vile participation" (III, ii, 86–87). Hal replies coolly: "I shall hereafter, my thrice-gracious lord/ Be more myself" (III, ii, 92–93). The line recalls an identical phrase from Henry IV (I, iii, 5), and more than ever we are conscious that this son is succeeding his father on several levels.

When Hal at last is crowned King, he becomes even more successful than his father. Just as Henry IV, when he was still Bullingbrook, managed to overcome Richard through superior political instincts and the affection of the masses, so Henry V demonstrates skills that permit him to exceed his father's achievements. We see this acumen, for instance, at the end of *Henry IV, Part 2*, when the rowdy Falstaff interrupts the coronation procession. In a moment that chills listeners both offstage and on, the new King cuts him off permanently: "I know thee not, old man, fall to thy prayers" (V, v, 47). Then with a bow to God and to new allies in the Court, Henry banishes Falstaff, the parent from whom he learned so much about the real lives of common people, but who must be dismissed if law is to flourish.

Nevertheless, in the final play of the tetralogy, the one that bears his name, Henry V is always cognizant of his father's place in history as a usurper who removed a divinely ordained King. Henry V is equally aware of his own place as the son of that usurper, and therefore as a king whose hold on the throne will remain perpetually under challenge:

> Not to-day, O Lord,
> O, not to-day, think not upon the fault
> My father made in compassing the crown!
> I Richard's body have interred new,
> And on it have bestowed more contrite tears,
> Than from it issued forced drops of blood.
> (IV, i, 292–297)

The weight of one generation passes inevitably to the next. For all of his success, Henry V never escapes his father's moral and political inheritance.

All of Shakespeare's romances reflect the theme of one generation living in response to the actions of the preceding generation—*Cymbeline* as much as any other. At the outset, we learn that Imogen has disobeyed her father, Cymbeline, King of Britain, by marrying his foster son, Posthumus, rather than her stepbrother, Cloten. The King's blindness about the comparative worth of these two men recalls King Lear's errors of such judgment, but in this play, Imogen also must deal with Cymbeline's wife, the Queen, whose malice is so strong that she orders her doctor, Cornelius, to concoct a slow-acting poison that she hopes will dispatch Imogen (I, v, 8–10). Moreover, we learn that Cymbeline's sons have been lost some twenty years ago, and thus we await the reuniting of all these disparate generational elements.

They are eventually brought together, in a series of events that in the play parallels the unity of Rome and Britain, at least for the several centuries before England split from the Catholic Church. The most stirring character of the story is Imogen, who, like Desdemona, suffers from unjust accusations by her husband, Othello; like Rosalind, retreats to the forest in the disguise of a man and thereafter unites the members of her family; and like Cordelia, ultimately forgives her father, King Lear. Nevertheless, Cymbeline is the fitting title figure, for his words and actions separate the two generations, and his growth restores them:

> It had been vicious
> To have mistrusted her; yet, O my daughter,
> That it was folly in me, thou mayst say,
> And prove it in thy feeling. Heaven mend all!
> (V, v, 65–68)

In all the plays previously discussed in this chapter, the younger generation must live with and ultimately overcome offenses by their ancestors. In only one of Shakespeare's plays does the younger generation commit blunders, while the older generation proceeds more thoughtfully—*All's Well That Ends Well.*

The entire story is problematic because of Bertram, Shakespeare's least likable hero. At the beginning, he mourns the death of his father and prepares to leave for France, when his mother, the Countess, offers advice:

> Thy blood and virtue
> Contend for empire in thee, and thy goodness
> Share with thy birthright! Love all, trust a few,
> Do wrong to none. Be able for thine enemy
> Rather in power than use, and keep thy friend
> Under thy own life's key.
> (I, i, 62–67)

Her tone resembles that of Polonius in *Hamlet*, when that courtier dispenses a series of moralistic sayings to his son, Laertes. The Countess, however, offers genuinely useful counsel, which Bertram unfortunately ignores. Thus we have a young man unwilling to learn from the experience of someone older and wiser.

Not long after, the King of France adds to the general state of mistrust of the young generation when he muses on remarks made by Bertram's late father:

> "Let me not live," quoth he,
> "After my flame lacks oil, to be the snuff
> Of younger spirits, whose apprehensive senses
> All but new things disdain; whose judgments are

Mere fathers of their garments, whose constants
expire before their fashions."

(I, ii, 58–63)

The faults described match precisely those of Bertram, who continually proves shallow and unfeeling. Moreover, his devotion to the scoundrel Parolles, whom Shakespeare describes as a "parasitical follower" and who constantly leads Bertram astray, reflects the callowness of youth, at least as depicted in this work. Even after Helena, the young woman who has grown up with the Countess, and who cures the King of his apparently fatal illness, asks to become Bertram's wife, he dismisses her:

She had her breeding at my father's charge—
A poor physician's daughter my wife! Disdain
Rather corrupt me ever!

(II, iii, 114–116)

Thus one crucial theme of the play is Bertram's rehabilitation. When Helena later reads Bertram's letter of rejection to her, the Countess's disappointment is moving:

He was my son,
But I do wash his name out of my blood,
And thou art all my child.

(III, ii, 66–68)

When in *King Lear* the title character expels his daughter Cordelia for her supposed insults, our sympathies are completely with Cordelia. Indeed, in most of Shakespeare's plays, when parents lay down decrees to which children must conform, we stand with the younger generation. Only in *All's Well That Ends Well* do we ally ourselves with the parents.

True, at the end of this play, Bertram apparently experiences a transformation, for after Helena claims him for her own, he admits to the King:

If she, my liege, can make me know this clearly,
I'll love her dearly, ever, ever dearly.

(V, iii, 315–316)

How sincerely he means these words is not easy to determine, but we recognize that at last he accepts the values of the older generation.

Of all Shakespeare's characters who must deal with generational conflict, none confronts the issue more sharply than Hamlet. First he must deal with the death of his father, which was followed closely by the remarriage of his mother, Gertrude, to his uncle, Claudius. These actions, in turn, are complicated by the loss of his own succession to the crown, as well as by his mother's wandering affections. We are conscious, therefore, of Hamlet's political disenfranchisement and emotional turmoil. These issues are compounded when the Ghost, old Hamlet, confronts his son with the reality of the murder Claudius committed: taking his brother's life. Hamlet is now faced with the prospect of extreme action: "Revenge his most foul and most unnatural murther" (I, v, 25). That order creates a predicament of overwhelming complication. Revenge is clearly the code of his father's generation, and Hamlet is being asked to shoulder it. At the same time, Hamlet is furious with his mother for her betrayal of her husband. Moreover, Hamlet himself is haunted by thoughts of her sexual behavior with Claudius, and in his disgust he joins the Ghost, who proclaims:

> So [lust], though to a radiant angel link'd,
> Will [sate] itself in a celestial bed
> And prey on garbage.
>
> (I, v, 55–57)

We cannot be certain as to the precise nature of Hamlet's sexual jealousy, but he is surely tormented by knowledge of his mother's new relationship. We remember, too, that Hamlet is the Prince of his nation, and thus whatever steps he takes have consequences that pervade the long-standing social and political structure of Denmark. In yet another cruel twist, Hamlet is beset by fear of the true nature of this Ghost:

> Be thou a spirit of health, or goblin damn'd,
> Bring with thee airs from heaven, or blasts from hell,
> Be thy intents wicked or charitable,
> Thou com'st in such a questionable shape
> That I will speak to thee.
>
> (I, iv, 40–44)

In his desire to do right, Hamlet wonders whether obeying the Ghost would be a violation of his own moral standards. Yet so eager is Hamlet for a solution to the problem of his own place and purpose in life, and so desperate is he for a path to follow, that he obeys whatever voice seems to give him a clear route to follow.

Finally, and this point is most controversial, we may wonder whether, despite all his claims to the contrary, Hamlet truly loved his father. After all, old Hamlet was a general, a warrior, and, to all immediate impressions, not unlike Claudius. On the other hand, Hamlet is a philosopher and poet, more content in the company of actors than among soldiers. Toward that end, we notice how the Ghost intimidates Hamlet into taking on responsibility for revenge:

I find thee apt,
And duller shouldst thou be than the fat weed
That roots itself in ease on Lethe wharf,
Wouldst thou not stir in this.

(I, v, 31–34)

Thus Hamlet is directed to a course of action, but he never carries it out. His own character, whether we judge the reason to be a strength or weakness, holds him back. Nonetheless, in his desire to act justly and loyally, he is burdened by social, ethical, political, theological, and sexual crises, all of which contribute to his fundamental conflict with the world of his forefathers. In that respect Hamlet becomes the epitome of many of Shakespeare's heroes, who must try to balance their own desires against the values of the surrounding society, as well as the values inherited from preceding generations. The nature of tragedy guarantees that such a battle will prove fatal.

Honor

The word "honor" generally is used with one of two implications: as adherence to a private moral code, or as public acclaim. Many of Shakespeare's characters are preoccupied with the latter denotation of this word, but rarely does their concern benefit anyone, most of all themselves. Instead, when they feel the overpowering need to achieve such esteem, they end up committing foolish or destructive acts. Indeed, so often does mention of "honor" lead to ruinous behavior that whenever we hear someone in Shakespeare's plays use the word, we anticipate the worst.

Consider Brutus, the hero of *Julius Caesar*. In the play's opening scene, Brutus reveals with virtually every line his overwhelming concern for how he is viewed by the Roman populace. Moreover, he ruminates over his status with a solemnity that suggests he has a huge ego waiting to be stroked. As he says to his best friend, Cassius:

> If I have veil'd my look,
> I turn the trouble of my countenance
> Merely upon myself. Vexed I am
> Of late with passions of some difference,
> Conceptions only proper to myself.
> (I, ii, 37–41)

Thus we are not surprised when Brutus adds:

> For let the gods so speed me as I love
> The name of honor more than I fear death.
> (I, ii, 88–89)

Cassius recognizes how such a preoccupation with honor makes Brutus vulnerable:

I know that virtue to be in you, Brutus,
As well as I do know your outward favor.
Well, honor is the subject of my story . . .
                    (I, ii, 90–92)

At the end of the scene, after Cassius has attempted to persuade Brutus to lead action against Caesar, Cassius concludes:

Well, Brutus, thou art noble; yet I see
Thy honorable mettle may be wrought
From that it is disposed . . .
                    (I, ii, 308–310)

With his insight into human nature, Cassius recognizes how a man obsessed with his image may be manipulated, even to act against what he knows to be proper.

Throughout the play, Brutus struggles to carry out an "honorable" strategy. Even on those occasions when he does not invoke the word "honor," we nonetheless feel its values directing him. For instance, when Cassius proposes that the conspirators against Caesar should take an oath, Brutus reacts with dismay. He wants to believe that all these men proceed with the same noble intentions as he does, so he insists that an oath would be a violation of the spirit of their enterprise (II, i, 114–140). When Cassius suggests that Antony should be killed along with Caesar, Brutus again demurs:

Let's be sacrificers, but not butchers, Caius.
We all stand up against the spirit of Caesar,
And in the spirit of men there is no blood . . .
                    (II, i, 166–168)

As Brutus seeks to carry out a gentlemanly assassination, his desperation to appear honorable at every step undoes him. Later, despite Cassius's pleas to the contrary, Brutus insists that Antony not only be allowed to speak at Caesar's funeral, but that he also be allowed to speak last. The result is calamitous.

We see this same vulnerability to the allure of honor in Caesar himself. When one member of the conspiracy, Decius, comes to Caesar's home to persuade him to go to the forum, Caesar refuses, for he has heard Calphurnia relate her dream of Romans bathing in blood from Caesar's statue. When, however, Decius suggests that the citizenry of Rome will laugh at Caesar when they hear the reason for his absence (II, ii, 92–107), Caesar's sense of honor is tapped, and he immediately changes his mind.

The most dramatic use of the word "honor" occurs in the scene after

Caesar's death, when Brutus stands up before the Roman mob to justify his actions:

> Believe me for mine
> honor, and have respect to mine honor, that you
> may believe.
>
> (III, ii, 14–16)

With no legitimate explanation at hand, Brutus is forced to rely on his own public reputation. The words themselves thus sound hollow, but even more telling is that they are offered in flat prose, not elegant blank verse.

Antony surely recognizes this emptiness, for in his own oration over the corpse of Caesar, he mentions "honorable" so often in his characterizations of Brutus and the other conspirators that the word loses all dignity. Indeed, after hearing Antony invoke "honorable" some dozen times over approximately 150 lines, we can never take the word seriously again. It retains forever the connotation of hypocritical self-promotion.

The concept of "honor" appears throughout Shakespeare's tragedies. In the opening scene of *Titus Andronicus*, character after character speaks of honor as if it were a magic word that automatically elevated every action to nobility. Saturninus, son of the late Emperor, speaks of honor to Rome (I, i, 7, 13); Marcus speaks of his brother Titus's military and political achievements (I, i, 35–45); Titus himself, the aging general, insists on couching all his decrees under the banner of "honor" (I, i, 150, 156, 198).

In *Hamlet*, the Prince, who is unable to rouse himself to action against his uncle, Claudius, offers this testament in his last soliloquy:

> Rightly to be great
> Is not to stir without great argument,
> But greatly to find quarrel in a straw
> When honor's at the stake.
>
> (IV, iv, 53–56)

When all other reasons for action fail, this contemplative man seeks to find motivation in his wounded pride. The claim makes him sound as if he acts only to avoid personal humiliation, not to support a righteous cause.

In *Othello*, the Moor is perpetually conscious of how he presents himself to Venetian society. As a stranger, probably the only free black man in the city, and husband to Desdemona, he is sensitive about his status. Perhaps here is one reason he accepts his ensign Iago's insinuations about Desdemona's supposed infidelity. The concept of "honor," therefore, pervades the text, although the word itself occurs most notably in the final moments. After Othello has strangled his wife, and the two of them are discovered in their bedroom, he looks down at her lifeless body, then turns to the others for exoneration:

> An honorable murder, if you will;
> For nought I did in hate, but all in honor.
>
> (V, ii, 294)

This tragic excuse reminds us how empty the claim of honor can be.

We are reminded again in *Coriolanus*, in which Martius, the title character, fights not for his own renown, but for that of his mother, Volumnia. As she says in her opening lines:

> If my son were my
> husband, I should freelier rejoice in that absence
> wherein he won honor than in the embracements of his
> bed where he would show most love.
>
> (I, iii, 2–5)

The image of a mother substituting her son for her husband is already discomfiting. That she compounds the unpleasantness by imagining the military honors that he might win further taints the idea of such triumph. We realize that Volumnia lives vicariously through her son's exploits, that she seeks glory not for him, but so she can bask in his reflected light.

Throughout the play, such references to honor recur, but the reminder is perhaps most painful in Act V, after Martius, now bearing the title "Coriolanus," has been accused of treachery, fled the Roman side, and allied himself with his old enemy, the Volsces, who are readying themselves for war against Rome. Volumnia pleads with her son to restrain himself:

> Thou hast never in thy life
> Show'd thy dear mother any courtesy,
> When she, poor hen, fond of no second brood,
> Has cluck'd thee to the wars, and safely home
> Loaden with honor.
>
> (V, iii, 160–164)

Her desire for his honor, she explains, justifies everything. No matter how unhappy he may be, because she has inspired him to achieve public acclaim, she expects him to obey her. Her pleas, however, fall short, and Coriolanus's subsequent flouting of her wishes soon leads to his demise.

Honor is equally valuable to Hector in *Troilus and Cressida*. In this play, Shakespeare's topsy-turvy version of the Trojan War, scarcely a decent character is to be seen, and the pervasive spirit of the work may be found in the oft-repeated line of Thersites, the cynical Greek, whose very presence belittles the most famous episode in military history: "Lechery, lechery, still wars and lechery, nothing else holds fashion" (V, ii, 194–195). This senseless carnage is taking place, we are reminded regularly, because the Greek commander Menelaus's wife, Helen, ran off with the Trojan prince Paris. In the midst of the war, Hector, Paris's brother and the greatest of the Trojan heroes, can no longer tolerate the loss of life:

> Thus to persist
> In doing wrong extenuates not wrong,
> But makes it more heavy.
> (II, ii, 186–188)

Suddenly, though, Hector switches his point of view:

> My spritely brethren, I propend to you
> In resolution to keep Helen still,
> For 'tis a cause that hath no mean dependance
> Upon our joint and several dignities.
> (II, ii, 190–193)

Troilus then clarifies his brother's perspective:

> Why, there you touch'd the life of our design!
> Were it not glory that we more affected
> Than the performance of our heaving spleens,
> I would not wish a drop of Troyan blood
> Spent more in her defense. But, worthy Hector,
> She is a theme of honor and renown,
> A spur to valiant and magnanimous deeds,
> Whose present courage may beat down our foes,
> And fame in time to come canonize us . . .
> (II, ii, 194–203)

How ironic that Troilus himself has stood outside most of the fighting thus far. We may interpret this exchange to mean that Helen herself is worthless, but that since the Trojans are already fighting and dying for her, they have no choice but to continue. Besides, if they win, how much honor that victory will furnish. We can only speculate how many bloody conflicts throughout the history of the world have continued because of such misguided motivations.

In the midst of the turmoil, Hector is challenged by Achilles, his Trojan counterpart, but Andromache, Hector's wife, urges him not to fight:

> . . . for I have dreamt
> of bloody turbulence, and this whole night
> Hath nothing been but shapes and forms of slaughter.
> (V, iii, 10–12)

His wife's warning is but one piece of evidence which suggests to Hector that by going into battle, he will probably die. Nonetheless, he is devoted to his city and its cause, and therefore his acceptance of inevitable defeat might exude tragic dignity. When he articulates his reasons, however, they seem far more mundane:

> Mine honor keeps the weather of my fate.
> Life every man holds dear, but the dear man
> Holds honor far more precious-dear than life.
> (V, ii, 26–28)

In the center of a war that is raging because of the humiliation of one cuckolded fool, and while dozens of selfish, egoistic men pout, whine, and bully, all the while seeking their own sexual gratification, Hector's attempts to obey a superior moral code seem sadly out of place.

To note how the word "honor" may be used in countless inappropriate contexts, we need only consider any of Shakespeare's history plays, where conspiracies, treacheries, assassinations, and other despicable acts are couched in the most elevated terms. Here we shall focus on *Henry IV, Part 1*, in which the concept of honor swirls around two characters, Hotspur and Falstaff.

In the opening scene, Henry IV first speaks of Hotspur, more formally known as Henry Percy. He is the son of Northumberland, the leader of the nobles who supported Henry in his usurpation of the English throne:

> Yea, there thou mak'st me sad, and mak'st me sin
> In envy that my Lord Northumberland
> Should be the father to so blest a son—
> A son who is the theme of honor's tongue,
> Amongst a grove the very straightest plant . . .
> (I, i, 78–82)

The King further contrasts this aggressive soldier with his own son, who is currently wasting time and energy among the scoundrels of the taverns in Eastcheap. Yet the more we see of Hotspur, the more we grow suspicious of the man and the honor he claims to seek.

For instance, in Act II, Hotspur joins with his father and his uncle, Worcester, to rail against Henry IV's policies. In the midst of his anger, Hotspur bursts out:

> By heaven, methinks it were an easy leap,
> To pluck bright honor from the pale-fac'd moon,
> Or dive into the bottom of the deep,
> Where fadom-line could never touch the ground,
> And pluck up drowned honor by the locks . . .
>   (I, iii, 201–205)

The more Hotspur talks, the more we realize that his goal is not the good of his country, nor even the achievement of power for his colleagues, but simply glory for himself. Because of his own ego, he has refused to turn over prisoners to King Henry. Ultimately, Hotspur is revealed to be the symbol of a chivalric tradition that is as outdated as the feudal world it complements. Just as Richard II, Henry IV's predecessor on the throne, was out of touch with political reality, so is Hotspur, in his own way, equally obsolete. In this scene, his closing rallying cry rings particularly hollow:

> O, let the hours be short,
> Till fields, and blows, and groans applaud our sport!
>   (I, iii, 301–302)

He anticipates a gallant death. But to what end? The only one he articulates is his own honor.

In dramatic opposition to Hotspur is Falstaff, the Prince of Wales' joyously hedonistic companion, whose reflections on honor sound different indeed:

> What
> is honor? A word. What is in that word honor?
> What is that honor? Air. A trim reckoning!
> Who hath it? He that died a' Wednesday. Doth he
> feel it? No. Doth he hear it? No. 'Tis insensible
> then? Yea, to the dead. But will['t] not live with the
> living? No. Why? detraction will not suffer it.
> Therefore I'll none of it, honor is a mere scutcheon.
> And so ends my catchism.
>   (V, i, 133–141)

The speech is crucial for several reasons, not the least of which is that it reveals so much of Falstaff's character: his wit, insight, and cowardice. It is equally important, however, as part of Shakespeare's vision of war, to be examined more closely in the chapter on that subject. The futility of the spectacle may be wrapped up in the meaninglessness of glory for "he that died a' Wednesday." Above all, Falstaff loves life. The pursuit of honor, at least as Shakespeare dramatizes it, often leads to ignoble death.

We see as much in the fate of Sir Walter Blunt, one of the King's staunchest allies. He dies at the battle of Shrewsbury, slain by the valiant Scot Douglas, and at that moment, Blunt may appear to have died an "honorable" death. Yet as Falstaff waddles onstage, his presence lampoons both the savagery of the battle and any cause for which it is exerted: "There's honor for you!" (V, iii, 32–33) he says over the dead Blunt.

The death of Hotspur is also grimly ironic. When the one-on-one combat between Hal and Hotspur finally takes place, Hotspur is defeated after a brutal struggle. Gazing down on the corpse, the Prince generously calls Percy "great heart" (V, iv, 87), but also notes that the dead soldier is food "For worms" (V, iv, 87). Thus after all the talk of honor, after all the bunkum and braggadocio, Hotspur is left to rot.

The word "honor" appears hundreds of times in Shakespeare's plays, almost always with unpleasant consequences. Many of the characters who invoke it, like Brutus, Othello, and Hector, are respected figures whose moral code turns into a drive to secure public renown, the other kind of "honor." In their efforts to do so, however, these decent people who seek to gain so much only lose themselves.

Innocence

In the world of tragic drama, we accept that every play will conclude with the death of at least one major character. What we find much harder to accept is that other characters, some quite peripheral to the main action, may also forfeit their lives: not because of some transgression they commit, or any fault of their own, but simply because they come too close to the maelstrom and are unable to escape. That such innocent figures pay the ultimate penalty for their unfortunate station leaves us both pained and puzzled.

Consider Shakespeare's earliest tragedy, *Titus Andronicus*, his most brutal work and one gorged with slaughter and savagery. In the midst of the horror, a son is born to the villainous Moor, Aaron, and Tamora, Queen of the Goths, who is also the wife of Saturninus, Emperor of Rome. At the news of this birth, Aaron, until now a heartless schemer, becomes impassioned with love for his offspring, as when he cautions Demetrius and Chiron, Tamora's sons, who have threatened to kill the dark-skinned child. They believe his existence shames their mother, but Aaron warns them to keep their distance:

> Stay, murtherous villains, will you kill your brother?
> Now, by the burning tapers of the sky,
> That shone so brightly when this boy was got,
> He dies upon my scimitar's sharp point,
> That touches this my first-born son and heir!
> (IV, ii, 88–92)

Aaron's devotion, though, does not blunt his violent edge. He is determined that his son shall survive, and therefore asks the nurse who has brought him the infant: "But say again, how many saw the child" (IV, ii, 140). When the nurse replies that, beside herself, only the Queen and the midwife know of the baby's existence, Aaron instantly kills her. The nurse does nothing wrong. Indeed, all her actions are benign; yet she dies. What does the senseless passing of so harmless a soul tell about the nature of the world?

The suffering of innocents strikes us harder when the victims are children. Such is the case in *The Winter's Tale*, when Leontes, King of Sicilia, becomes obsessed with the thought that his wife, Hermione, has had an affair with his best friend, Polixenes, King of Bohemia. One of the targets of Leontes' anger is his son, Mamillius, whom Leontes suddenly suspects is not his own. Mamillius tries to soothe his father's anxiety: "I am like you [they] say" (I, ii, 207). The boy always charms us, as when he jokes with his mother's ladies about women's faces (II, i, 12–13). Perhaps this humor is meant as an ironic echo of Leontes' accusations, but nonetheless Mamillius is a winning presence. Nothing, however, can assuage Leontes' fury, and he bans Mamillius from Hermione's company (II, i, 59–60). When a servant reports that Mamillius has become ill, Leontes cannot acknowledge that his own behavior has caused the boy's condition, but instead blames Hermione herself: "To see his nobleness, / Conceiving the dishonor of his mother!" (II, iii, 12–13). As Leontes' obsession grows, we hear no word of Mamillius. Even when the oracle whom Leontes had sought for counsel exonerates Hermione, the King still refuses to accept her innocence:

> There is no truth at all i' th' oracle.
> The sessions shall proceed; this is mere falsehood.
>   (III, ii, 140–141)

No one has time to respond to this outrageous breach of order, for a servant rushes in to reveal the death of Mamillius. Finally Leontes relents, accepting his son's passing as punishment for his own sins: "I have too much believ'd mine own suspicion" (III, ii, 151).

At this point, we understand that in the great scheme of things, Mamillius's death has shaken Leontes out of his madness and forced him to take responsibility, but we still ask why the boy had to be sacrificed. At the end of this romance, the entire royal family of Sicilia is joyfully reunited: Leontes, Hermione, their long-lost daughter, Perdita, even the loyal attendant, Paulina. Yet we remember Mamillius, who does not return. Even in the fantasy world of the romance, where Shakespeare allows himself the most outrageous plot twists, he insists on the sacrifice of Mamillius. Is he suggesting that the death of such an innocent is necessary for the ultimate redemption?

One more innocent child who suffers a seemingly pointless death is Macduff's son in *Macbeth*. After Macbeth demands that the witches disclose his future, three images pass before him. None suggests that Macduff's offspring is a threat. Yet so possessed is Macbeth by the necessity to murder all who might oppose his reign that he resolves to take action:

> The castle of Macduff I will surprise,
> Seize upon Fife, give to th' edge o' th' sword
> His wife, his babes, and all unfortunate souls
> That trace him in his line.
>
> (IV, i, 150–153)

In the next scene, we meet Macduff's son, who has inherited his father's boldness. Speaking of the condition of the country, the young man states:

> Then the liars and swearers are fools; for
> there are liars and swearers enow to bear the honest
> men and hang up them.
>
> (IV, ii, 56–58)

This pessimism is affirmed by his mother, who is alerted to danger but questions why any of them should be victims:

> But I remember now
> I am in this earthly world—where to do harm
> Is often laudable, to do good sometime
> Accounted dangerous folly.
>
> (IV, ii, 74–77)

Her prediction is fulfilled moments later, when Macbeth's thugs slaughter the family. Once more we ask what kind of a world tolerates such brutality against the blameless.

Children are not the only innocents in Shakespeare's plays who suffer. In *Henry VIII*, his final history play, Katherine, the first wife of the King, is a victim of his chief advisor, Cardinal Wolsey. She is intelligent, incisive, and sympathetic to the needs of the King and his people, but her life is cut off because she is subject to the whims of one more powerful than she.

For instance, when the King, under Wolsey's prodding, grows suspicious about the Duke of Buckingham, Katherine points out that the surveyor who casts doubt on Buckingham's loyalty was once fired by the Duke (I, ii, 171–176). When Henry ignores this caution, Katherine finds herself stranded: a noble, if ineffective figure, forced to survive the cutthroat world of court politics. Nevertheless, she retains the admiration of those around her. As Norfolk says of her, when Wolsey urges a divorce:

> . . . That, like a jewel, has hung twenty years
> About his neck, yet never lost her lustre;
> Of her that loves him with that excellence
> That angels love good men with; even of her
> That when the greatest stroke of fortune falls
> Will bless the King.
>
> (II, ii, 31–36)

Henry, however, is desperate to separate from his wife, for he assumes that marriage to another woman will given him the male heir he desires. Still, he retains affection for Katherine: ". . . our queen, before the primest creature/ That's paragon'd o' th' world" (II, iv, 230–231). Moreover, after the decree of divorce, when Henry establishes his independence from the Church in Rome, Katherine maintains dignity:

> There's nothing I have done yet, o' my conscience,
> Deserves a corner. Would all other women
> Could speak this with as free a soul as I do!
>
> (III, i, 30–32)

Thereafter she continues to speak of her love for her husband (III, i, 179–181). As she nears death, she even expresses sympathy for Wolsey, the man who brought her to ruin, but who has been executed for the machinations he conducted in the name of the King: "So may he rest, his faults lie gently on him!" (IV, ii, 31). When Katherine dies, she speaks as ever generously, without bitterness, and proclaims her innocence (IV, ii, 160–173). In the end, we think of her as one who unintentionally crossed a dangerous man, Wolsey, leading to circumstances under which decent people may be destroyed.

Occasionally, however, innocence carries strength. In *Pericles*, for instance, Marina, daughter of Pericles, is sold by pirates to a brothel. Her steadfast morality disarms Lycimachus, the local Governor, who, after hearing her story, offers money and departs:

> Fare thee well, thou art a piece of virtue, and
> I doubt not but thy training hath been noble.
>
> (IV, vi, 111–112)

Marina's resistance enrages the keepers, and to avoid further incidents the Bawd orders Boult to rape the girl, but Marina's powers are such that she puts off this threat as well. First she appeals to Boult's self-worth:

Neither of these are so bad as thou art,
Since they do better thee in their command.
(IV, vi, 161–162)

Then she promises to teach him skills that she has acquired (IV, vi, 181–185). So strong is her faith that without force or legal compulsion, she disarms him. In the world of romance, purity has that power.

In the world of the tragedies, however, innocence does not end so happily, and here we think particularly of three young women. None is totally apart from the primary action of her play. In fact, all three are intimately involved. All are also essentially blameless, but because of their willingness to embrace men who accept responsibility, all three surrender their lives.

One is Ophelia in *Hamlet*, daughter of Polonius and sister to Laertes. From her first appearance, we recognize her predicament, for both her father and brother warn her against becoming close to Hamlet, the man she loves. As Laertes says:

His greatness weigh'd, his will is not his own,
[For he himself is subject to his birth . . .
(I, iii, 17–18)

Nonetheless, Ophelia's affection pulls her into the whirlwind of the Prince's madness, and eventually he turns his fury against her. "I did love you once" (III, i, 114) he says, but we cannot be sure if this statement is part of his "antic disposition," a calculated statement meant to be overheard by Polonius and King Claudius, an unintentional confession, or some combination thereof. In any case, for the rest of their encounter, Hamlet berates Ophelia, spitting antagonism at her as a woman and as the embodiment of the corruption in all women:

You jig and amble, and you [lisp], you nick-
name God's creatures and make your wantonness
[your] ignorance.
(III, i, 144–146)

Hamlet's rejection, in combination with his accidental murder of her father, proves too great a burden for Ophelia, and afterwards she appears in a state of distraction, talking nonsensically and singing the sort of obscene verses to which Hamlet earlier condemned her (IV, i). Her subsequent suicide, as described by the Queen (IV, vii, 166–182), is the inevitable result of her condition. She never acts maliciously; indeed, she tries to do right by everyone for whom she cares. None of them, however, has the capacity to do right by her.

Desdemona also suffers because of her faith in the man she loves—in this case, Othello. Perhaps she is not quite so innocent as other characters, for from the start she clarifies that she is an independent spirit prepared to shoulder responsibilities (I, iii, 180–188). Furthermore, she does interfere in her husband's business affairs, although with gentle firmness, when Cassio, Othello's lieutenant, seeks pardon for the ruckus in the street that caused Othello to fire him. Yet when she advocates Cassio's cause, Desdemona becomes determined:

> Tell me, Othello, I wonder in my soul
> What you would ask me that I should deny,
> Or stand so mamm'ring on.
>
> (III, iii, 68–70)

Still, Desdemona is in no way guilty of the infidelity that Othello, thanks to Iago's meddling, comes to believe of her, and while Othello grows more enraged, she maintains her purity of spirit. As she says to Iago:

> Unkindness may do much,
> And his unkindness may defeat my life,
> But never taint my love.
>
> (IV, ii, 159–161)

Desdemona's faith stands in contrast to the worldly wisdom of her confidante, Emilia, who sneers about men:

> What is it that they do
> When they change us for others? Is it sport?
> I think it is.
>
> (IV, iii, 96–98)

Even Othello, despite his jealousy, recognizes his wife's goodness. As he prepares to kill her, he asks her to pray against any sins she may have committed, then adds: "I would not kill thy soul" (V, ii, 32). Moreover, after he has strangled her, Desdemona manages to gasp a few final words: "A guiltless death I die" (V, ii, 122). Though earlier she may have been too bold for her own protection, Desdemona remains a victim of Iago's malevolence and Othello's blindness. Had she been more callous and less devoted, she might have survived by fighting against forces around her. Instead, by maintaining claims of her innocence, standing by her values, and trusting the man to whom she devoted her life, she is destroyed, an undeserving victim of the misdeeds of others.

We may say the same of Cordelia in *King Lear*. Although in the first scene of the play she risks everything by refusing to submit to the demands of King Lear, her father, and proclaim publically her love for him, Cordelia's integrity elevates her above virtually all onstage:

> It is no vicious blot, murther, or foulness,
> No unchaste action, or dishonored step,
> That hath depriv'd me of your grace and favor . . .
> (I, i, 227–229)

Expelled from Lear's sight, Cordelia leaves as a noble martyr to his pride and obstinancy.

When she returns from banishment, only to be captured along with her father by the forces of Edmund, the bastard son of the Duke of Gloucester, Cordelia speaks for all the innocents in Shakespeare's plays who suffer the consequences of a world where evil holds sway: "We are not the first/ Who with best meaning have incurr'd the worst" (V, iii, 3–4). Despite such words, which imply that her death is imminent, we hope that Cordelia will survive, for once her sisters, Goneril and Regan, have died, along with Regan's husband, Cornwall, and Edmund himself, no more punishments await. We trust that perhaps some small measure of solace may be achieved if Lear and Cordelia are allowed to live out their lives in tranquility. Nevertheless, Shakespeare insists that Cordelia's innocence must be destroyed, and therefore Edmund's directive that she be hanged is carried out before his retraction can be communicated.

The sight of Lear entering with the dead Cordelia in his arms may be the most heartbreaking image in all of Shakespeare's plays, and not only because we are losing a character for whom we have profound affection and respect. Rather, her death suggests that even though justice triumphs here, the frightful cost includes the loss of those who did nothing to deserve punishment and who tried to live as decently as they could. The destruction of such innocence in *King Lear* and all the other plays considered in this chapter therefore raises questions about the ultimate meaning of life and the nature of the universal order.

Intoxication

Amidst the titanic themes that dominate Shakespeare's works, the consumption of alcohol may seem of small import. The subject, however, raises a number of intriguing questions, most immediately concerning the playwright's own ambivalence. Throughout his plays, he presents figures who drink lustily, as well as others who demur from all liquor. In general, members of the former category resonate sympathetically, while those in the latter group are far less likeable. Yet this dichotomy is not always clear. Some drinkers are distinctly unpleasant folks, while those who abstain, even if not loveable, demonstrate redeeming qualities.

Consider, for instance, Cassio in *Othello*. He has been appointed by Othello to be his lieutenant, a rank above Iago, an ensign, who mocks the young man's inexperience:

> (A fellow almost damn'd in a fair wife),
> That never set a squadron in the field,
> Nor the division of a battle knows
> More than a spinster . . .
>
> (I, i, 21–24)

Cassio also exudes courtliness, as when he describes Othello's marriage to Desdemona:

> . . . he hath achiev'd a maid
> That paragons description and wild fame;
> One that excels the quirks of blazoning pens,
> And in th' essential vesture of creation
> Does tire the [ingener].
>
> (II, i, 61–65)

The words are gracious, and the construction smooth; yet these lines are so polished that Cassio takes on an air of excessive elegance. This quality, in combination with his lack of battle savvy, suggests foppishness.

That image is amplified when Cassio reveals his susceptibility to alcohol (II, iii, 41–42). Iago seizes on the point of vulnerability, and within minutes Cassio is reduced to singing lewd verses and otherwise degrading himself. The theatrical gambit is familiar. Whatever the work, whether tragic or comic, as soon as a character admits to an inability to hold liquor, we become confident that this figure will soon begin drinking and staggering across the stage. Here, however, the gimmick confirms our judgment of Cassio: although he presents a veneer of uprightness, something less winning lurks beneath.

That unattractiveness comes to the fore when we learn that Cassio frequents the home of Bianca, a prostitute in Cyprus. As Cassio jokes about her with Iago, who knows that Othello overhears them and assumes the conversation to be about Desdemona, Cassio reveals his coarseness:

> I marry [her]! What? A customer! Prithee
> bear some charity to my wit, do not think it so un-
> wholesome. Ha, ha, ha!
> (IV, i, 119–121)

In the context of earlier passages, his attempt at humor suggests that he is trying to foster some rugged, masculine geniality with Iago. Yet when Bianca storms back to return Othello's handkerchief (IV, i, 148–155), which Cassio gave to her at Iago's urging, Cassio withers comically under her assault: "How now, my sweet Bianca, how now? how now?" (IV, i, 156–157). Here is his true character: fearful and distinctly unmilitary. Thus his contempt for drinking masks hypocrisy and sanctimoniousness.

A different variation on this theme may be found in *Twelfth Night*, where Malvolio, steward to Olivia, is the priggish moralist, who chastizes her uncle, the rowdy Sir Toby, along with his comrades, Sir Andrew and Maria, for their late-night revelry:

> My masters, are you mad? Or what are you?
> Have you no wit, manners, nor honesty, but to gabble
> like tinkers at this time of night? Do ye make an
> alehouse of my lady's house, that ye squeak out your
> coziers' catches without any mitigation or remorse
> of voice? Is there no respect of place, persons, nor
> time in you?
> (II, iii, 86–92)

Sir Toby replies eloquently:

> Art thou more than a steward? Dost
> thou think because thou art virtuous there shall be no
> more cakes and ale?
>
> (II, iii, 114–116)

At first blush, this accusation against Malvolio seems fair, for he is an arrogant puritan with designs on Olivia's money. But Malvolio also captures the essence of Sir Toby, who has, in fact, no respect for "place, persons, and time." Nor does he have respect for his supposed friends, as we see when Sir Toby sets Sir Andrew up for humiliation and perhaps injury in a fight with Viola, still disguised as Cesario (III, iv). Indeed, the more we see of Sir Toby, the uglier he stands. The more he drinks, the crueler he becomes. He also refers to Malvolio as "an enemy to mankind" (III, iv, 98) a harsh verdict. Moreover, gulling Malvolio to convince him of Olivia's infatuation is amusing at the start, but when Malvolio is imprisoned in a dungeon and reduced to a helpless, raving victim who doubts his own sanity, the humor wears thin (IV, ii). Upon reflection, we realize that Malvolio, the teetotaler, never acts immorally; he is simply pompous and unpleasant. Sir Toby, the drinker, appears convivial and fun-loving, but demonstrates a viciousness that undercuts whatever offbeat charm his inebriation offers.

Such conflicting feelings reflect our attitude toward characters in *Antony and Cleopatra* as well. The play is split between two locales: Rome and Egypt. The former stands for reason, duty, and sobriety, while the latter offers passion, intuition, and intoxication. Antony is a distinguished Roman general, perhaps the greatest man in the world. That quality is surely part of the lure felt by Cleopatra, Queen of Egypt and the most eminent woman in the world. Yet from the start, Antony is viewed by his colleagues as something of a wastrel: ". . . the bellows and fan/ To cool a gipsy's lust" (I, i, 9–10). He also evinces an inordinate capacity for conviviality, as he regularly retreats from his responsibilities. Part of Antony's greatness is that he is capable of playing both roles, general and lover. His tragedy is that he is compelled to try to carry out both roles, which clash irreconcilably.

In opposition to Antony stands Octavius Caesar, another one of three rulers of the Roman Empire, and seemingly everything Antony is not. Indeed, he scorns Antony's tendency to self-indulgence, as Octavius reveals in conversation with Lepidus, the third and weakest member of the triumvirate:

> From Alexandria
> This is the news: he fishes, drinks, and wastes

> The lamps of night in revel; is not more manlike
> Than Cleopatra; nor the queen of Ptolomy
> More womanly than he . . . You shall find there
> A man who is th' [abstract] of all faults
> That all men follow.
>
> (I, iv, 3–10)

To an extent, Caesar's judgment is accurate: Antony's faults are severe. We enjoy Antony, however. We relish his wit and capacity to win a woman so mercurial and fascinating as Cleopatra. We also dislike Caesar, who is cold and intolerant of human weakness.

The disparity between the two personalities becomes clearer when they share a dinner on Pompey's yacht. As the celebration turns riotous, Lepidus falls into a stupor, while Antony also drinks with enthusiasm, along with his aide, Enobarbus. Only Caesar refuses to imbibe:

> But I had rather fast from all, four days,
> Than drink so much in one.
>
> (II, vii, 102–103)

The disgraceful behavior of the others hardly befits men competing to rule the world. Yet Caesar's abstinence is not ingratiating. Then Antony says:

> Come, let's all take hands,
> Till that the conquering wine hath steep'd our sense
> In soft and delicate Lethe.
>
> (II, vii, 106–108)

How can we regard this man as a serious leader?

His dissolution takes on a sadder edge when we place it in the context of the entire play. By the end, he has sacrificed his life and his cause for Cleopatra. Meanwhile, Octavius Caesar has triumphed, at least politically, for he will eventually take the throne of Rome as Augustus Caesar and, in essence, rule the world. True, Antony's love for Cleopatra becomes in its own way immortal. Still, although we admire Caesar's military skills, we never like him, nor does anyone onstage. What price victory? we ask. And what price love?

The theme of intoxication in Shakespeare's plays cannot be fully understood without examination of Sir John Falstaff. Although we shall consider him only as he appears in the history plays, he is also at the center of *The Merry Wives of Windsor*, which Shakespeare supposedly wrote at the behest of Queen Elizabeth, who wanted to see the fat knight in love. In that rural comedy, however, Sir John is a buffoon rather than a wit, the victim of nasty jokes perpetrated by figures of minimal stature.

To appreciate him fully, therefore, we shall focus on *Henry IV, 1 & 2*, where he looms physically and spiritually over everyone and everything.

From his opening lines, we are conscious that here is a figure devoted to drinking, as well as to womanizing, eating, pimping, and thieving. Yet he retains our affection and admiration. Why? Because he never denies what he is; indeed, he celebrates himself. As he says to his youthful companion, the Prince of England: "Why, Hal, 'tis my vocation. Hal, 'tis no sin for a man to labor in his vocation" (I, ii, 104–105). The line echoes a Biblical reference often reiterated by Protestant divines. In a world dominated by duplicity and trickery, Falstaff's directness is therefore a beacon. True, he continually fabricates stories, but he joyously acknowledges doing so. Thus we feel in him a humanity and generosity of spirit that are utterly endearing.

So is his affection for Hal. In *Henry IV, Part 1*, the two take on roles, Hal initially playing himself, then his father, Henry IV. Falstaff, on the other hand, enacts the King, then Hal, but always attempts to justify his life. Speaking of himself, but in the voice of the King, Falstaff says to Hal:

> If that man should be
> lewdly given, he deceiveth me; for, Harry, I see
> virtue in his looks. If then the tree may be known by
> the fruit, as the fruit by the tree, then peremptorily I
> speak it, there is virtue in that Falstaff; him keep
> with, the rest banish.
>
> (II, iv, 426–431)

The tone is light, but the underlying implication is genuine. Later, ostensibly as Hal, but actually in his own voice, Falstaff says of himself to Hal, now playing the King:

> That he is old,
> the more the pity, his white hairs do witness it, but
> that he is, saving your reverence, a whoremaster, that I
> utterly deny. If sack and sugar be a fault, God
> help the wicked! If to be old and merry be a sin, then
> many an old host I know is damn'd.
>
> (II, iv, 467–472)

Falstaff suggests that he is essentially harmless, that his actions do little damage to anyone. He also wishes Hal to remember that by associating with Falstaff, the Prince has gained understanding of the nation and its people: not just the nobles and the wealthier citizens, but the poor and vulnerable.

We might accept this vision Falstaff offers of himself, but other events alter our perspective. When Henry IV prepares to confront a rebellion led by Northumberland and his son, Hotspur, Falstaff is assigned to put together his own force in support of the King, and brings forth a bunch of ragtag civilians too poor to bribe their way out of service. Hal belittles their pathetic state, but Falstaff answers callously:

> Tut, tut, good enough to toss, food for
> powder, food for powder; they'll fill a pit as well as
> better. Tush, man, mortal men, mortal men.
> (IV, iii, 65–67)

Suddenly Falstaff's minor extortions do not seem harmless, for now he condemns helpless men to die in combat.

During the battle of Shrewsbury, Falstaff waddles in and out of the action, commenting derisively on the absurdity of it all (see the chapter on *Honor*). But Hal does need assistance, and when he calls on Falstaff to provide a sword, Sir John instead pulls from his sheath a bottle of sack. The gesture amuses us, but not Hal, who is fighting for his life and his father's throne (V, iii, 50–55).

Later, Falstaff's antics seem less objectionable, especially after Hal slays Hotspur in a ferocious one-on-one confrontation. When the dust has settled, Falstaff, all the while pretending to be dead, stands up, stabs the corpse of Hotspur in the leg, and slings the body over his shoulder. When he encounters Hal, the Prince protests this fraudulence, but Falstaff claims the kill as his own: "Lord, lord, how this world is given to lying!" (V, iv, 145–146). Hal's brother, Prince John, reacts with suspicion: "This is the strangest tale that ever I heard" (V, iv, 154). Hal's response, the equivalant of a forgiving shake of the head, becomes our own: "This is the strangest fellow, brother John" (V, iv, 155). Falstaff then follows in search of whatever prizes may come his way:

> I'll follow, as they say, for reward. He that
> rewards me, God reward him! If I do grow great, I'll
> grow less, for I'll purge and leave sack, and live
> cleanly as a nobleman should do.
> (V, iv, 162–165)

The promise is empty, but we hardly care. Falstaff has long exhausted the possibility of reform, but he is such delightful company that, like the Prince, we forgive him everything. One day, the Prince will not be able to do so, because when he assumes the throne, he will have to abandon this irreverent figure, as Hal clarified earlier: "I do, I will" (II, iv, 481). That separation, however, will not occur until the end of *Part 2*.

In that play, we must deal once again with the relative values of drinking, and two figures who represent the polarities. One is the Prince's brother John. Faced with yet another rebellion against his father, John gathers representatives from the opposing force, then promises pardons if they dismiss their troops: "Go, my lord,/ And let our army be discharged too" (IV, ii, 91–92). Moments later, John reverses himself and tells the rebels:

> Good tidings, my Lord Hastings! for the which
> I do arrest thee, traitor, of high treason,
> And you, Lord Archbishop, and you, Lord Mowbray,
> Of capital treason I attach you both.
> (IV, ii, 106–109)

Without a single shot, John has disarmed the enemy. Yet to accomplish this end, he violated the truth. Yet he did triumph. Yet he did break his word.

In the next scene, Falstaff comments upon the character of this young man:

> Good faith, this same young sober
> blooded boy doth not love me, nor a man cannot make
> him laugh, but that's no marvel, he drinks no wine.
> There's never none of these demure boys come
> to any proof, for thin drink doth so over-cool their
> blood, and making many fish-meals, that they fall into
> a kind of male green-sickness, and then when they
> marry, they get wenches. They are generally fools and
> cowards, which some of us should be too, but for
> inflammation.
> (IV, iii, 87–96)

He concludes his tirade with this advice:

> If I had a thousand
> sons, the first humane principle I would teach them
> should be, to forswear thin potations and to addict
> themselves to sack.
> (IV, iii, 122–125)

How are we to take this oration? Falstaff is correct: John is a gloomy soul. Still, he does conquer an entire army, admittedly by deceptive means, but without damage to his own forces. Thus we respect him as an operator, even if we do not care for him as a friend.

Perhaps that is how Shakespeare views this entire subject. Just as he has affection for drinkers, so he presents nondrinkers as unlikeable. At the same time, we are always conscious that sheer revelry is not enough to guide someone, especially someone with responsibility, through life. Drinkers may be entertaining, but they lack the political and military ruthlessness that more often than not, at least in Shakespeare's eyes, carries the day. Thus again we ask familiar questions: What price victory? What price happiness?

Justice

One of the major concerns that pervades the Shakespearean canon is the nature of justice. The issue is dramatized primarily from two perspectives. Under some circumstances, the letter of the law and the spirit of the law collide, so that a specific legal decision, though in accord with official statutes, may nonetheless seem unjust. Under these conditions, Shakespeare suggests, the law should be regarded as a living entity, which must be tempered by understanding. Second, we confront the relationship between earthly and divine justice, a conflict sometimes expressed metaphorically in the image of the "wheel." We must, therefore, place matters of the day-to-day world against those of eternal import.

Both aspects of this theme are paramount in *Measure for Measure*, in which Vincentio, Duke of Vienna, temporarily takes leave from his post as Chief Magistrate and gives all authority to Angelo, whom the Duke regards as a man of strict morality: in the Duke's words, "Lord Angelo is precise" (I, iii, 50). Angelo fulfills this expectation by sentencing young Claudio to death for impregnating his fiancée, Juliet, outside marriage. Escalus, an older lord, petitions for the sentence to be reduced, suggesting that all of us are vulnerable to temptation. Angelo, though, remains relentless:

> 'Tis one thing to be tempted, Escalus,
> Another thing to fall. I not deny
> The jury, passing on the prisoner's life,
> May in the sworn twelve have a thief or two
> Guiltier than him they try. What's open made to justice,
> That justice seizes.
>
> (II, i, 17–22)

He thus refuses to compromise a legal principle.

In desperation, Isabella, Claudio's sister, who is about to enter a strict

151

religious order, visits Angelo to beg for her brother's life. In her attempt at persuasion, she poses the matter differently:

> How would you be
> If He, which is the top of judgment, should
> But judge you as you are?
>   (II, ii, 75–77)

She tries to turn Angelo's eyes toward forgiveness rather than vengeance, invoking a Christian spirit of charity. Angelo, however, maintains his judgment:

> Be you content, fair maid,
> It is the law, not I, condemn your brother.
> Were he my kinsman, brother, or my son,
> It should be thus with him: he must die to-morrow.
>   (II, ii, 79–82)

Angelo tries to convince us, and perhaps himself, that the law is unshakeable, and that as a judicial officer he has no power to offer mercy of his own. The rest of the play, however, dramatizes precisely the opposite: that justice and mercy are forever intertwined.

First, however, Angelo is compelled to recognize aspects of himself that have hitherto remained dormant, for in his denial of Isabella's request, Angelo finds himself strangely aroused by her:

> What's this? what's this? Is this her fault, or mine?
> The tempter, or the tempted, who sins most, ha?
>   (II, ii, 162–163)

We are offended by Angelo's lust, but at the same time possibly sympathetic to a man possessed by feelings that he has never before known. Then again, what seems to attract Angelo most is Isabella's purity, and that desire is ugly. It becomes more so two scenes later, when Angelo clarifies to Isabella the only terms under which he will pardon Claudio:

> You must lay down the treasures of your body
> To this supposed, or else let him suffer—
> What would you do?
>   (II, iv, 96–98)

Facing such a dilemma, Isabella has faith in her brother:

> Though he hath fall'n by prompture of the blood,
> Yet hath he in him such a mind of honor

That had he twenty heads to tender down
On twenty bloody blocks, he'ld yield them up,
Before his sister should her body stoop
To such abhor'd pollution.

(II, iv, 177–183)

She has confidence that her brother's sense of justice will match her own. Claudio, however, views their predicament differently:

What sin you do to save a brother's life,
Nature dispenses with the deed so far,
That it becomes a virtue.

(III, i, 133–135)

He regards nothing as more important than his own safety. Isabella, though, views the desecration of her body as a crime that shall stain her for eternity, and she becomes horrified when her brother places greater value on his mortal life than on her immortal soul:

O you beast!
O faithless coward! O dishonest wretch!
Wilt thou be made a man of my vice?
Is't not a kind of incest, to take life
From thine own sister's shame?

(III, i, 135–139)

Given the insoluble crisis that Shakespeare has established, the only resolution is for the Duke himself to return and untangle everything, as he does before the public. Earlier, Isabella seemed to relent to Angelo's wishes, but in a plot device familiar from many plays of the time, Mariana, once betrothed to Angelo, was substituted for Isabella. Even then, Angelo did not lift Claudio's sentence, and thus hypocrisy must be added to his catalogue of crimes. In light of all these sins, the Duke prepares to execute Angelo:

The very mercy of the law cries out
Most audible, even from his proper tongue,
"An Angelo for Claudio, death for death!"
Haste still pays haste, and leisure answers leisure;
Like doth quit like, and *Measure* still for *Measure*.

(V, i, 407–411)

Here the Duke concretizes the twin aspects of justice that we see in the play, leaving the matter of Angelo's fate to Isabella. After Mariana begs

153

for Angelo's life, Isabella relents, although with a curious manifestation of ego:

> Most bounteous sir:
> Look, if it please you, on this man condemn'd
> As if my brother liv'd. I partly think
> A due sincerity governed his deeds,
> Till he did look on me. Since it is so,
> Let him not die. My brother had but justice,
> In that he did the thing for which he died . . .
> (V, i, 443–449)

Because she sees all sides to the situation, and understands the fallibility of human beings, even one who has acted as despicably as Angelo, Isabella offers forgiveness, a gesture intended perhaps to guide all of us in our dealings with one another. The surprise appearance of Claudio, in whose place another prisoner was executed, completes the cycle of forgiveness, and the play ends with a series of marriages. Still, we are not permitted to forget the relentlessness of the law. Lucio, the "fantastic" or comic outsider who earlier had insulted the disguised Duke and whose lewd remarks and behavior typify the pervasive immorality of Vienna, is condemned to marry the prostitute, Kate Keepdown, then to be whipped and hanged. When Lucio protests the punishment, the Duke clarifies his judgment: "Slandering a prince deserves it" (V, i, 524). Thus we are left to ponder the nature of justice and legality.

Shakespeare dramatizes the potential cruelties of the law in other plays as well. In *Timon of Athens*, the title character generously dispenses money to all suitors, but when he bankrupts himself, and his creditors demand payment, an outraged Timon deserts mankind:

> Burn house! sink Athens! henceforth hated be
> Of Timon man and all humanity!
> (III, vi, 104–105)

He has always sought to act beneficently, so we sympathize with a stranger who earlier urged that Timon's debts be forgiven:

> But I perceive
> Men must learn now with pity to dispense,
> For policy sits above conscience.
> (III, ii, 85–87)

We also recognize, however, that Timon does not owe this disinterested observer any money. In the same play, the Athenian Captain Alcibiades defends a client accused of murder by claiming that the man has acted bravely in warfare (III, v, 74–84). One Senator, though, speaking for the rest, remains firm: "We are for law, he dies, urge it no more/On height of our displeasure" (III, v, 85–86). In both cases, we see the legitimacy of exonerating the defendant, but we also acknowledge how the law must be upheld.

The legal situation is more complicated in *The Merchant of Venice*, in which Shakespeare portrays Shylock, the Jewish moneylender, as devoted to income with a fanaticism that borders on madness. He agrees to lend money to Antonio, his bitter Christian enemy, but only on the condition that if the loan is not paid back on time, Antonio must forfeit a pound of flesh. When Antonio is unable to repay, Shylock moves to court and demands the full force of the law:

> If you deny me, fie upon your law!
> There is no force in the decrees of Venice.
> I stand for judgment. Answer—shall I have it?
> (IV, i, 101–103)

Portia, disguised as Balthazar, attempts to persuade Shylock to mercy:

> Therefore, Jew,
> Though justice be thy plea, consider this,
> That in the course of justice, none of us
> Should see salvation. We do pray for mercy,
> And that same prayer doth teach us all to render
> The deeds of mercy.
> (IV, i, 197–202)

She acknowledges universal human failings, and thus speaks in terms of both earthly justice and the ultimate reward of salvation. Shylock, though, fanatically reasserts his demand. After stretching the tension out for several minutes, Portia finally springs the trap she has held in reserve:

> Take then thy bond, take thou thy pound of flesh,
> But in the cutting it, if thou dost shed
> One drop of Christian blood, thy lands and goods
> Are by the laws of Venice confiscate
> Unto the state of Venice.
> (IV, i, 308–312)

The audience's view of this maneuver depends on its view of Shylock. No doubt the onlookers of Shakespeare's time would have been pleased at the unexpected reversal. Yet Portia's earlier call for mercy now is laden with irony: one, she is merciless to Shylock; and two, by prolonging the episode, she has put her husband, Bassanio, as well as Antonio and the entire sympathetic assemblage, through agony. Shylock's punishment is then compounded by Antonio, who demands that Shylock become a Christian. This conversion may be viewed as mildly generous in that it allows Shylock to follow the one potential path to heaven, but such beneficence is outweighed by the innate cruelty of robbing Shylock of the foundation of his life. However we view Shylock, we must acknowledge that although the punishment is legally defensible, it also reflects how the law may be used to destroy an individual.

The relationship between earthly justice and eternal reward may be seen in *Hamlet*, especially after King Claudius has just hurried out of the performance of "The Murder of Gonzago," which was presented with Hamlet's revisions to suggest that Claudius murdered old Hamlet. Now the King kneels in prayer, seeking forgiveness but understanding the impossibility of his request:

> O, what form of prayer
> Can serve my turn? "Forgive me my foul murther"?
> That cannot be, since I am still possess'd
> Of those effects for which I did the murther:
> My crown, mine own ambition, and my queen.
>   (III, iii, 51–55)

He cannot surrender the rewards of his crime; therefore he cannot receive pardon. Claudius then grasps one more truth:

> . . . And often 'tis seen the wicked prize itself
> Buys out the law, but 'tis not so above:
> There is no shuffling, there the action lies
> In his true nature, and we ourselves compell'd,
> Even to the teeth and forehead of our faults,
> To give in evidence.
>   (III, iii, 59–64)

Even if he could find forgiveness on the earthly plane, he would still deserve punishment from divine authority. Legal victory in this life does not guarantee absolution in the afterlife, where truth cannot be hidden under legalistic "shuffling." Thus despite his heinous crimes, Claudius's unsatisfied desire for repentance inspires sympathy from the audience. He is not a heartless villain beyond the bounds of morality, but a man in torment, prisoner to his own lusts.

Claudius's predicament may be contrasted with that of Hamlet, who enters and sees the praying King. Hamlet himself still searches for justice, for despite being convinced of Claudius's guilt, Hamlet cannot be certain of how to carry out legitimate punishment. Observing Claudius, Hamlet prepares to execute him, but suddenly holds back:

And now I'll do't—and so 'a goes to heaven,
And so am I [reveng'd]. That would be scann'd:
A villain kills my father, and for that
I, his sole son, do this same villain send
To heaven.
(III, iii, 74–78)

Hamlet begins to view himself not as merely a vehicle to carry out earthly justice, but as a divine agent. If Claudius is killed under such circumstances, he will escape the agonies that Hamlet's father now undergoes in purgatory. Thus Hamlet seeks more than mere revenge:

Up, sword, and know thou a more horrid hent:
When he is drunk asleep, or in his rage,
Or in th' incestious pleasure of his bed,
At game a-swearing, or about some act
That has no relish of salvation in't—
(III, iii, 88–92)

We now begin to lose sympathy for Hamlet, for he has gone beyond his rightful position and taken on the role of divine revenger. Through much of the remainder of the play, he proceeds as though he has the right to kill in heaven's name. He says as much when he reveals the switching of letters to the King of England, the plot by which he leads his old schoolmates, Rosencrantz and Guildenstern, to execution: "Why, even in that was heaven ordinant" (V, ii, 48). He even coldly ascribes their death to their own willingness to obey the King's order to investigate Hamlet:

[Why, man, they did make love to this employment,]
They are not near my conscience. Their defeat
Does by their own insinuation grow.
'Tis dangerous when the baser nature comes
Between the pass and fell incensed points
Of mighty opposites.
(V, ii, 57–62)

Thus Hamlet tries to unite his earthly mission with divine approval. In his attempt, we realize the irreconcilable tension between the code of Hamlet's world, whereby revenge is considered not only just but necessary, and the Christian code by which murder is unacceptable. The very meaning and nature of justice, then, are beyond Hamlet's grasp, and Shakespeare's implication may be that they are often problematic beyond human resolution.

The nature of justice, both earthly and heavenly, dominates *King Lear*. In the opening lines of the play, the Earl of Gloucester, Lear's trusted friend, speaks of the "order of law" (I, i, 19), as though it is beyond challenge. The play shows us what happens when that order breaks down, and all traditional forms of judgement and punishment cannot be carried out.

We see such perversion in Act III, scene vii, when Cornwall anticipates the punishment that he, his wife, Regan, and her sister, Goneril, will inflict on Gloucester, whom they believe to be their enemy:

> Though well we may not pass upon his life
> Without the form of justice, yet our power
> Shall do a court'sy to our wrath, which men
> May blame, but not control.
>
> (III, vii, 23–26)

Cornwall implies that even without following proper legal procedure, those in power have the right to impose what they deem to be "justice." Yet at the end of the scene, one of Cornwall's servants, outraged by the blinding of Gloucester, stabs Cornwall fatally. We understand this action to be a manifestation of a greater sense of right, the imposition of divine justice on the course of events on earth. As Albany, Goneril's husband, exclaims:

> This shows you are above,
> You [justicers], that these our nether crimes
> So speedily can venge!
>
> (IV, ii, 78–80)

Does such knowledge make the unjust actions of life more bearable? Here is another issue that over the course of Shakespeare's plays lies unresolved.

Lear himself is haunted by perversions of justice. In the depths of madness on the heath, he fights to impose a sense of right and wrong on a world that he sees as breaking down:

> Thou rascal beadle, hold thy bloody hand!
> Why dost thou lash that whore? Strip thy own back,
> Thou hotly lusts to use her in that kind
> For which thou whip'st her.
>
> (IV, vi, 160–163)

To Lear at this moment, guilt is universal. We are all sinners, and none of us has the right to demand retribution. The only legitimate justice comes from heaven, where forces of right inevitably triumph. The dying Edmund acknowledges as much, having been defeated in combat by his brother, Edgar: "The wheel is come full circle, I am here" (V, iii, 175).

Yet the ending of *King Lear* leaves us more unsettled than ever. As Lear holds the dying Cordelia in his arms, he asks: "Why should a dog, a horse, a rat, have life,/ And thou no breath at all?" (V, iii, 307). Why does such suffering as we have witnessed exist in the world? How, then, can we speak of divine justice? The play provides no answer.

Throughout the plays of Shakespeare, the concept of justice remains complicated. The law exists for the protection of the citizens, as the Duke in *Measure for Measure* suggests. Yet it must be tempered by compassion, as the actions of Angelo confirm, and as verdicts in *Timon of Athens* hint. Even those who call for such compassion, including Portia in *The Merchant of Venice*, show how laws exercised legally may create abuses. Our perspective on the question of justice must also be put in the greater context of divine authority. As we see in *Hamlet*, human beings ought not to usurp such prerogatives. Finally, in *King Lear*, we see how any understanding of the nature of guilt and the power and legitimacy of retribution demand answers that may lie beyond our knowledge.

Language

No doubt Shakespeare's plays contain the richest, most eloquent language to be found in any literature outside the Bible. The virtuosity of the technique, in combination with the immense, imaginative vocabulary, is dazzling. Yet Shakespeare also evinces concern for the very nature of language, how the words his characters use, as well as the structure of their sentences and verse, reflect their personality.

In *Richard II*, for instance, the title character revels in his own extravagant usage, along with the expressions of others. In the opening scene, he orders that Bullingbrook, Richard's cousin, and Mowbray, the King's chief confidant, both of whom have accused each other of treason, be brought before him:

> High-stomach'd are they both and full of ire,
> In rage, deaf as the sea, hasty as fire.
>   (I, i, 18–19)

He is intrigued with their verbal eloquence rather than with their charges. This impression is reinforced after Bullingbrook offers a scathing condemnation of Mowbray's behavior, blaming him for "all the treasons for these eighteen years" (I, i, 95) and "the Duke of Gloucester's death" (I, i, 100). To these statements, Richard replies blithely, "How high a pitch his resolution soars" (I, i, 109). He cares more about the sound of the words than about the devastating indictments that stop just short of blaming Mowbray's superior, Richard himself, for treachery and murder.

When Richard sentences Mowbray to exile for life, Mowbray muses bitterly on that aspect of the punishment which will wound him the most:

The language I have learnt these forty years,
My native English, now I must forgo,
And now my tongue's use is to me no more
Than an unstring'd viol or harp . . .
(I, iii, 159–162)

For Mowbray, loss of language means loss of culture and heritage, a deprivation that will become more spiritual than physical:

What is thy sentence [then] but speechless death,
Which robs my tongue from breathing native breath?
(I, iii, 172–173)

In this play, then, language and self are inextricably tied.

No one embodies that theme more than Richard himself, for at many moments during his fall from the throne, he seems more involved with his mode of expression than with his place in the hierarchy of the kingdom. For example, in his lengthy explanation of why he interrupted the one-on-one trial by combat between Bullingbrook and Mowbray (I, iii, 123–143) the word "peace," first in line 132, then in line 137, is both subject and object of "fright" (137). Such tortuous syntax reveals the emptiness of Richard's conviction, as well as his verbal skills at masking such hollowness.

Subsequently, at the moment of abdication, Bullingbrook urges Richard to act quickly: "Part of your cares you give me with your crown" (IV, i, 194). Richard, however, focuses on Bullingbrook's word selection and, rather than face the usurpation, amuses himself with a series of puns:

Your cares set up do not pluck my cares down:
My care is loss of care, by old care done,
Your care is gain of care, by new care won;
The cares I give I have, though given away,
They tend the crown, yet still with me they stay.
(IV, i, 195–199)

Richard seems intent on showing that his linguistic skill, the mastery and understanding of language, manifests an innate royalty that the unimaginative Bullingbrook will forever lack.

Moments later, after Richard has shattered the looking glass in which he searched to find his image, Bullingbrook comments: "The shadow of your sorrow hath destroy'd/ The shadow of your face" (IV, i, 292–293). Bullingbrook struggles to match Richard's eloquence. The King, however, trumps Bullingbrook, so to speak, by reflecting on the double meaning:

Language

> Say that again.
> The shadow of my sorrow. Ha, let's see.
> 'Tis very true, my grief lies all within,
> And these external [manners] of laments
> Are merely shadows to the unseen grief
> That swells with silence in the tortur'd soul.
>
> (IV, i, 293–298)

Richard takes Bullingbrook's play on words and carries it further, demonstrating how Bullingbrook does not realize the subtleties and implications of his own witticism. Richard also uses the word "shadow" to imply that matters on the surface of life, such as possession of a throne, are of less consequence than inner feelings. The King's implication is that he, Richard, who is attuned to language and feeling, will always be superior to Bullingbrook, who is preoccupied with more obvious, less substantial issues.

Even when he is alone in prison, awaiting death, Richard gives attention to language:

> I have been studying how I may compare
> This prison where I live unto the world;
> And for because the world is populous,
> And here is not a creature but myself,
> I cannot do it; yet I'll hammer it out.
>
> (V, v, 1–5)

What stimulates him is the imagery of prison, not its reality. True, he is trying to come to grips with the course of his life, where he went astray, and how he might have acted differently and thereby succeeded. But above all, the metaphor spurs his mind.

Another play in which language dominates the proceedings is *Julius Caesar*. Especially striking in this text is how certain oratorical devices dominate the rhetoric of virtually every speaker in the play. For instance, in the first scene, the tribune Murellus tries to rouse the disordered mob into support for Pompey by accusing them of ignorance:

> You blocks, you stones, you worse than senseless things!
> O you hard hearts, you cruel men of Rome,
> Knew you not Pompey?
>
> (I, i, 35–37)

The anaphoric "you" creates an energy intended to envelope listeners in his passion, and the rhythm of the word patterns thereby becomes a weapon. Later, when orating over Caesar's corpse, Antony uses the identical verbal strategy, even invoking some of the same words:

> It is not meet you know how Caesar lov'd you:
> You are not wood, you are not stones, but men;
> And, being men, hearing the will of Caesar,
> It will inflame you, it will make you mad.
>
> (III, ii, 141–144)

Persuasion is the goal here, too, as, indeed, it is on the part of speakers throughout the play.

Consider another section of Murellus's tirade:

> Many a time and oft
> Have you climb'd up to walls and battlements,
> To tow'rs and windows, yea, to chimney-tops,
> Your infants in your arms, and there have sate
> The livelong day, with patient expression,
> To see great Pompey pass the streets of Rome . . .
>
> (I, i, 37–42)

He conjures up glorious memories, inviting his listeners to lose themselves in the maze of images. Here language creates a world of memory that allows Murellus to infuse the audience with feelings of greatness. Later Cassius, seeking to rouse action against Caesar, uses the same tactic with his friend Brutus, seeking to bring him to the side of the conspirators:

> Age, thou art sham'd!
> Rome, thou hast lost the breed of noble bloods!
> When went there by an age since the great flood
> But it was fam'd with more than one man?
>
> (I, i, 150–153)

The sense of the words is less significant than their sound, which is aimed at rousing Brutus to action with his own stature. That soaring ego, Cassius hopes, will salvage Rome's glory. Caught up in the speed and force of Cassius's language, Brutus does not stop to ponder what sentiments lie behind the glorious words.

We should also note Brutus's funeral oration over the murdered Caesar (III, ii, 13–34). Brutus has foolishly ordered that he be permitted to speak first, failing to grasp that the final address always has the most impact. In any case, his attempt to justify the actions of the conspirators falls far short of the mark, primarily because Brutus speaks in prose. His ideas lack the passion he seeks to communicate, so he is reduced to repeating the feeble word "honor" several times to legitimize what is, after all, a heinous act.

If any single character may be said to epitomize the power of language to define someone, that figure would be Parolles, Bertram's shifty confidant in *All's Well That Ends Well*. Like Falstaff in *Henry IV*, Parolles falls into the tradition of *miles gloriosus*, the "braggart soldier" from Roman comedy. More to the point, his name means "words" in French, and thus, not surprisingly, language is the key to his character, for he hides corruption and cowardice behind bombast. Yet whereas Falstaff helped humanize his young charge, Hal, Parolles tends to reinforce Bertram's bigotries. Lafew, the wise old lord who serves as Bertram's conscience for much of this play, even says of Parolles that "the soul of this man is his clothes" (II, v, 43–44). That image of dressing, of disguising one's nature, whether under words or raiment, is the essence of Parolles.

As we see when he counsels Bertram to run away rather than be trapped by the King's directives about war and women:

> Use a more spacious ceremony to the noble
> lords; you have restrain'd yourself within the list of
> too cold an adieu. Be more expressive to them, for
> they wear themselves in the cap of time, there do
> muster true gait; eat, speak, and move under the
> influence of the most receiv'd star, and though the
> devil lead the measure, such are to be follow'd.
> (II, i, 50–56)

Parolles is preoccupied with appearance rather than substance, with the veneer of bravery more than with its actuality; thus his use of words that are seemingly eloquent, but ultimately shallow, reflects his shamelessness.

The method for deceiving Parolles is most fitting. With Bertram's permission, two French lords send him off on a fraudulent mission to retrieve a drum, but before he exits, Parolles says with unintentional irony: "I love not many words" (III, vi, 84). The second lord sees him differently: "No more than a fish loves water" (III, vi, 85). In any case, just as Parolles is about to salvage any drum available, he is captured by French soldiers, whose nonsensical ravings fool Parolles completely. Instinctively turning coward, he promises to betray his comrades:

> Oh, let me live,
> And all the secrets of our camp I'll show,
> Their force, their purposes; nay, I'll speak that
> Which you will wonder at.
> (IV, i, 83–86)

Under questioning by these same troops, still threatening him in babble, Parolles reveals all he claims to know, and even confesses to have written a letter in which he insulted Bertram. The latter is outraged by this treachery, but so overwhelming is Parolles' parade of fraud that one lord is moved to admit: "I begin to love him for this" (IV, iii, 262). Yet when all have been unmasked, Parolles is still unrepentant: "Simply the thing I am/ Shall make me live" (IV, iii, 333–334). In his steadfastness to his own bluster, trickery, and general unscrupulousness, Parolles emerges with minor dignity, a quality that the perpetually slimy Bertram never achieves.

Of all Shakespeare's plays, the one that seems to revel most in the imaginative possibilities of language is *Love's Labor's Lost*. From the King's opening declaration (I, i, 1–23), phrased in overbearing, convoluted verse, the wordplay and sentence structure in this text is amazingly varied. Consider the "fantastical Spaniard" Armado, whose foppery and conceit are matched by his overblown speech, as the King suggests:

> One who the music of his own vain tongue
> Doth ravish like enchanting harmony . . .
>
> (I, i, 166–167)

We see as much in the letter read by his servant, Costard, who is accused of dallying with the maid, Jaquenetta, the object of Armado's affections:

> "So it is, besiged with sable-
> colored melancholy, I did commend the black op-
> pressing humor to the most wholesome physic of
> thy health-giving air; and as I am a gentleman, betook
> myself to walk . . ."
>
> (I, i, 231–235)

Here, too, sheer verbosity disguises intellectual and emotional hollowness.

When Armado accepts advice from the youthful Moth on affairs of the heart, their imagery of dance reflects the world of this play, in which most human activity, in particular courtship, is a stylized, insubstantial ritual. We can imagine Moth putting both himself and Armado through a series of physical contortions to communicate proper technique, but the comic highlight is Armado's own ludicrous sentiments:

> A most acute juvenal, volable and free of grace!
> By thy favor, sweet welkin, I must sigh in thy face:
> Most rude melancholy, valor gives thee place.
>
> (III, i, 66–68)

Contorted language is also characteristic of Holofernes the pedant, Shakespeare's satiric portrait of perhaps either the scholar John Florio or his own schoolmaster Thomas Jenkins. Here Holofernes comments on the seemingly simply activity of watching a hunt:

The deer was [as you know] *sanguis*, in
blood, ripe as the pomewater, who now hangeth like
a jewel in the ear of *caelo*, the sky, the welkin, the
heaven, and anon fallen like a crab on the face of
terra, the soil, the land, the earth.
                    (IV, ii, 3–7)

Moments later, he attempts to create romantic verse:

The preyful Princess pierc'd and prick'd a pretty pleasing pricket;
Some say a sore, but not a sore, till now made sore with shotting.
                    (IV, ii, 56–57)

This pretentiousness reflects the foolishness of Holofernes, and once
more we are conscious of how a melange of words can conceal a scarcity
of thought.

Holofernes' pomposity is contrasted by the tone of the letter from the
lord Berowne to his love, Rosaline:

If knowledge be the mark, to know thee shall sufffice;
Well learned is that tongue that well can thee commend,
All ignorant that soul that sees thee without wonder;
Which is to me some praise that I thy parts admire.
                    (IV, ii, 111–114)

From the beginning of the play, Berowne has tried to deny his romantic
feelings by scorning romance. How fitting, then, that as he falls more
deeply in love, his language becomes more direct, so much so that by
the end of the play, after the women have mocked their suitors who
have disguised themselves as Muscovites, Berowne dismisses poetic pre-
tension as an extension of male ego:

O, never will I trust to speeches penn'd.
Nor to the motion of a schoolboy's tongue,
Nor never come in vizard to my friend
Nor woo in rhyme, like a blind harper's song!
                    (V, ii, 402–405)

These lines are an accurate reflection of the presentation of language
throughout Shakespeare's plays. When we come across speakers who
cannot or will not articulate thoughts clearly, who hide behind clusters
of words and obscure constructions rather than speak forthrightly, their
deception manifests fundamental weakness.

We conclude here with the chief example of this phenomenon: Polonius in *Hamlet*. The advisor to King Claudius is at times a comic figure, as in his first lines, when he responds to the query about his son Laertes' plans:

> H'ath, my lord, wrung from me my slow leave
> By laborsome petition, and at last
> Upon his will I seal'd my hard consent.
> I do beseech you give him leave to go.
>
> (I, ii, 58–61)

Already we see the wordiness and convoluted manner that characterizes Polonius. More important, though, is the moral deviousness that his style masks. Like his sentences, Polonius perpetually meanders, skulking about the palace to spy on his daughter, Ophelia, and conjuring up theories to explain Hamlet's behavior. For instance, when he reads a letter from Hamlet to Ophelia, but obviously composed by the Prince in a purposefully graceless style, Polonius cannot resist remarking on the awkward use of language. Ironically, though, he remains blind to his own twisted expressions, as when he explains matters to the King and Queen:

> But what might you think,
> When I had seen this hot love on the wing—
> As I perceiv'd it (I must tell you that)
> Before my daughter told me—what might you,
> Or my dear Majesty your queen here, think,
> If I had play'd the deck or table-book,
> Or given my heart a [winking,] mute and dumb,
> Or look'd upon this love with idle sight,
> What might you think?
>
> (II, ii, 131–139)

He seems incapable of uttering a straightforward sentence. We are not surprised, therefore, at Polonius's manner of death: caught behind the curtain in Queen Gertrude's room, and stabbed by Hamlet who has taken him for Claudius:

> Thou wretched, rash, intruding fool, farewell!
> I took thee for thy better. Take thy fortune;
> Thou find'st to be too busy is some danger . . .
>
> (III, iv, 31–33)

Hamlet sees Polonius's fate as perfectly appropriate to the way the man conducted his life.

For Polonius and the other figures discussed here, as well as for virtually all characters in dramatic literature, language and personality reflect each other. In life, too, our words and syntactical constructions reveal more of ourselves than we can possibly know.

Love and Romance

In Shakespeare's plays, again as in life, romantic love takes many forms. In some cases, the bond is pure and seemingly inevitable, while in other instances, feelings are more bewildering. Yet the emotional attraction of one human being to another remains the most universal of themes, and Shakespeare allows us to see this force in all its wonder.

His most celebrated portrait of love, and the most famous in all literature, is *Romeo and Juliet*, in which the plot springboard is the ever-popular story line of love at first sight. Other elements, however, contribute to create a drama of astonishing impact. One reason for its power may be found at the very start, when the outcome is clearly laid out:

> The fearful passage of their death-mark'd love,
> And the continuance of their parents' rage,
> Which, but their children's end, nought could
>   remove . . .
>
> (Prologue, 9–11)

From this point on, references to death permeate the text, so that no matter how intense the love between these two young people becomes, we remain conscious of looming tragedy.

Such is the case even when we first hear of Romeo, who is described by his friend Benevolio, then by his mother Lady Montague, as wandering alone in the early morning and late at night (I, i, 116–129). He could be a figure from a comedy, for he is presented as a stereotypically infatuated Renaissance youth, an impression confirmed by Romeo's first statements about the immediate object of his affection, Rosaline:

> Why then, O brawling love! O loving hate!
> O any thing, of nothing first [create]!

171

O heavy lightness, serious vanity,
Misshapen chaos of well-[seeming] forms,
Feather of lead, bright smoke, cold fire, sick health,
Still-waking sleep, that is not what it is!
(I, i, 176–181)

His overdone oxymora (contrasting words in one image) reduce him to parody, a young man in love with the concept of love. Indeed, he recognizes this weakness in himself:

Tut, I have lost myself, I am not here;
This is not Romeo, he's some otherwhere.
(I, i, 197–198)

The suggestion that people who fall in love find themselves is familiar from other plays of Shakespeare. For instance, in *The Comedy of Errors*, Antipholus of Syracuse, a bemused newcomer to the city of Ephesus, comments on what he seeks:

So I, to find a mother and a brother,
In quest of them (unhappy), ah, lose myself.
(I, ii, 39–40)

He believes that he can find himself only through love, and at this moment he assumes that the source of that love will be a member of his family. Later, however, he "finds" himself through romantic love. In *Love's Labor's Lost*, the lord Berowne has agreed to abide by the King's directive to live a life of scholarship, without the interference of love, but eventually he realizes his folly:

[Let] us once lose our oaths to find ourselves,
Or else we lose ourselves to keep our oaths.
(IV, iii, 358–359)

Self-discovery through romance: the theme is intrinsic to Shakespeare's vision.

The transformation of Romeo from a comic figure to one of dignity begins during the ball at the Capulet home, where he anticipates an evening with Rosaline, but is struck instead by the masked Juliet: "O, she doth teach the torches to burn bright!" (I, v, 44). Moments later, he approaches her:

If I profane with my unworthiest hand
This holy shrine, the gentle sin is this,

My lips, two blushing pilgrims, ready stand
To smooth that rough touch with a tender kiss.
(I, v, 93–96)

What follows is a parry and thrust in the style of courtly love, as Juliet
tests Romeo's skill with words, while inviting him to pursue her. For
instance, he says:

O then, dear saint, let lips do what hands do,
They pray—grant thou, lest faith turn to despair.
(I, v, 103–104)

Juliet, in turn, challenges his request: "Saints do not move, though grant
for prayers' sake" (I, v, 105). As the two exchange conceits, Juliet gently
mocks Romeo, even as she encourages him. From the start, then, the two
seem a perfect match.

Shakespeare, however, never permits us to lose awareness of how their
love will resolve. Only a few lines later, for example, when Juliet discovers that Romeo is a Montague, and thus her family's enemy, she is
overcome with intimations of death: "My grave is like to be my
wedding-bed" (I, v, 135). After Romeo has spoken to her from below her
balcony, her fear recurs:

I have no joy of this contract to-night,
It is too rash, too unadvis'd, too sudden,
Too like the lightning, which doth cease to be
Ere one can say it lightens.
(II, ii, 117–120)

Still later, when Juliet anticipates Romeo's appearance, she continues to
worry:

Come, gentle night, come, loving, black-brow'd night,
Give me my Romeo, and, when I shall die,
Take him and cut him out in little stars,
And he will make the face of heaven so fine
That all the world will be in love with night
And pay no worship to the garish sun.
(III, ii, 20–25)

Yet part of the magic of this play is the determination of the two young
lovers. Despite fear of discovery, they share a night of physical passion,
and although the conventions of his theater prevented Shakespeare from
showing such private moments, we see Romeo and Juliet after their hon-
eymoon night, and understand how its consequences leave both so af-

fected that their personalities are temporarily altered. Juliet, normally the more thoughtful of the two, becomes giddy:

> Wilt thou be gone? it is not yet near day.
> It was the nightingale, and not the lark,
> That pierc'd the fearful hollow of thine ear . . .
>   (III, v, 1–3)

Seconds later, she tries to dissuade him from leaving:

> Yond light is not day-light, I know it, I;
> It is some meteor that the sun [exhal'd]
> To be to thee this night a torch-bearer
> And light thee on thy way to Mantua,
> Therefore stay yet, thou need'st not be gone.
>   (III, v, 12–16)

Only when Romeo relents ("Let's talk, it is not day" [III, v, 25]), does she revert to her rational self: "It is, it is! Hie hence, be gone, away!" (III, v, 26).

Still, the dominant sentiment in the play is the strength of love in the shadow of imminent death. Thus as Romeo stands over Juliet's apparently lifeless form in the crypt, he prepares to swallow poison:

> O, here
> Will I set up my everlasting rest,
> And shake the yoke of inauspicious stars
> From this world-wearied flesh.
>   (V, iii, 109–112)

The impact of all such lines is that the love between Romeo and Juliet is of such passion that it will carry on past their earthly lives.

Many of the elements of *Romeo and Juliet* may be found in a play that is contemporaneous with it, *A Midsummer Night's Dream*. Indeed, the words of the young man Lysander from the latter work apply to both: "The course of true love never did run smooth" (I, i, 134). From the start of *A Midsummer Night's Dream*, the familiar conflict between young love and older authority is apparent, for Hermia and her love Lysander seek to marry over the objections of her father, Egeus. The threat of death is also in the air, for when Hermia inquires as to the consequences if she does not marry Demetrius, Egeus's choice, her father states uncategorically: "Either to die the death, or to abjure/ For ever the society of men" (I, i, 65–66). In addition, when Hermia and Lysander are left alone, they indulge in overdone poetry similar to Romeo's (I, i, 136–141), and Hermia even broaches the theme of the fate:

> If then true lovers have ever been cross'd,
> It stands as an edict in destiny.
>
> (I, i, 150–151)

The most profound difference between the two plays, however, is that while the Prologue of *Romeo and Juliet* resounds with inevitable death, here all the action takes place under the eyes of Oberon, King of the Fairies, and his sprite, Puck. Thus when Hermia and Lysander run away, only to be joined by Demetrius and the woman who pursues him, Helena, we rest assured that no matter how emotions whirl and affections wander, all will resolve favorably. Nevertheless, hints of tragedy intrude. For instance, when Lysander and Hermia find themselves stranded in the woods, the two prepare to lie down for the night. Trying to wheedle his way closer, Lysander resolves: "And then end life when I end loyalty!" (II, ii, 63). Under the influence of Puck's magic juice, he will in fact prove disloyal, if only temporarily.

The affections between the lovers in *A Midsummer Night's Dream* are explored in other chapters (see "Appearance versus Reality," "Fidelity," "Marriage," and "Supernatural Phenomena"), but of particular interest here is that even when the multitude of confusions at last untangles, we remember the potential disaster the four have faced, especially during the performance of "Pyramus and Thisbe." Despite the absurdity of the mechanicals' (or laborers') presentation, the story is fundamentally like that of *Romeo and Juliet*, in which love between a young man and young woman is quashed by events beyond their control. Moreover, the circumstances of the deaths in "Pyramus and Thisbe" are startlingly close to the plot of the tragedy. When Pyramus mistakenly assumes that Thisbe is dead, the stricken youth stabs himself. Thereafter, Thisbe returns, only to find her lover's body, and so she, too, takes her life. In these two plays, therefore, Shakespeare presents youthful love, impassioned and impetuous, from both comic and tragic perspectives.

"Love at first sight" is one of the two most popular motifs that pervade the world's love stories. The other involves a man and a woman who begin their relationship as antagonists, then gradually draw together. The archetype of this plot is *The Taming of the Shrew*. Early on, the gentleman Petruchio unashamedly declares that his reason for visiting the city of Padua is to marry for money (I, ii, 75–76), but when he hears of the lady Katherine's notorious temper, he finds himself intrigued by her spirit as well (I, ii, 199–210). Meanwhile, Katherine has already denounced her father Baptista's treating her younger sister, Bianca, as his favorite:

She is your treasure, she must have a husband;
I must dance barefoot on her wedding-day,
And for your love to her lead apes into hell.
(II, i, 32–34)

Her resentment clarifies that she awaits a dynamic male to rescue her from the local mediocrities we have met.

Both characters, therefore, have pronounced themselves eager to fall in love, but so rough-edged are their personalities that their road to contentment cannot proceed smoothly. Not surprisingly, when they do meet, they swap insults, as Katherine dismisses him ("Asses are made to bare, and so are you" [II, i, 199]), and Petruchio resasserts himself ("Women are made to bear, and so are you" [II, i, 200]). They even exchange blows, until Petruchio sets down a rule: "I swear I'll cuff you, if you strike again" (II, i, 220). We accept that she is intrigued by his authoritative manner, but we also understand that her perverse nature, hardened by years of misery, prevents her from acquiescing too quickly. Therefore he must force her into marriage, but the surrender does not occur for some time.

Until that moment, their relationship is marked by an extreme form of courtship: starvation and denial of sleep at his house. Petruchio also treats the invited haberdasher so cruelly that Katherine and the audience both recognize what Peter, Petruchio's servant, articulates: "He kills her in her own humor" (IV, i, 180). Such treatment may be viewed as torture, but Petruchio interprets the procedure in his own fashion:

Ay, and amid this hurly I intend
That all is done in reverend care of her . . .
This is a way to kill a wife with kindness,
And thus I'll curb her mad and headstrong humor.
He that knows better how to tame a shrew,
Now let him speak; 'tis charity to shew.
(IV, i, 203–211)

Katherine and Petruchio eventually reach an equilibrium, demonstrated during their journey back to Padua, when he vacillates about whether the sun or moon shines down warmly, and she joins in what she realizes is a game:

Then God be blest, it [is] the blessed sun,
But sun it is not, when you say it is not;
And the moon changes even as your mind.
What you will have it nam'd, even that it is,
And so it shall be for Katherine.
(IV, v, 18–22)

Thereafter he relents, and the ground rules are established: He demands that she agree with him, but once she does, he defers to her. Katherine and Petruchio never define their relationship in those words, but their mutual affection is evident.

Mutual antagonism need not manifest itself physically, but however it appears, it suggests a hidden desire for romance. In *Much Ado About Nothing*, Beatrice (whose name means "blesser") and Benedick ("the blessed one") claim to despise each other. Yet that each talks of virtually nothing but the other reminds us that the opposite of love is not hate but indifference. As Benedick says:

> But it is
> certain I am lov'd of all ladies, only you excepted;
> and I would I could find in my heart that I had not a
> hard heart, for truly I love none.
>   (I, i, 124–127)

The more they gibe, the more we realize that each hopes the other will break down the barriers between them and allow their latent affection to bloom. Like Katherine, Beatrice invokes the phrase "lead his apes into hell" (II, i, 41), the proverbial punishment for old maids, and thus we suspect that despite her railing against men, Beatrice, too, is desperate to find one worthy of her. Moreover, one of her speeches contains several references to dancing, including "measure" (II, i, 69–80), and such imagery reflects the social conventions to which these two characters respond. Yet when they don masks and participate in a literal dance, Benedick recognizes Beatrice and talks about himself in the hope of hearing flattering remarks. Instead, she insults him:

> Why, he is the Prince's jester, a very dull
> fool; only his gift is in devising impossible slanders.
>   (II, i, 137–138)

We cannot be certain whether Beatrice also recognizes Benedick, but the scene works either way. In any case, she soon decides that they must dance and "follow the leaders" (II, i, 151), and Benedick responds in rhythm: "In every good thing" (II, i, 152). Their ultimate union is thus subtly inevitable.

What remains is for their friends to push them together, and how appropriate that the pair falls victim to verbal subterfuge. With Benedick listening, his friend Don Pedro describes Beatrice in the pangs of frustrated love:

> Then down upon her knees she falls,
> weeps, sobs, beats her heart, tears her hair, prays,
> curses: "O sweet Benedick! God give me patience!"
> (II, iii, 146–149)

Before long, Benedick is convinced that Beatrice is infatuated with him and resolves to pursue her. Subsequently, the women play a similar trick on Beatrice, letting her overhear warnings against her sharp tongue. Beatrice's reaction reveals that she, too, is eager to let down her guard:

> Stand I condemn'd for pride and scorn so much?
> Contempt, farewell, and maiden pride, adieu!
> No glory lives behind the back of such.
> And Benedick, love on, I will requite thee,
> Taming my wild heart to thy loving hand.
> (III, i, 108–112)

Her invitation to have her heart "tamed," another echo of Katherine, suggests that despite her protestations, she welcomes the chance to abide by certain conventions of her time. Thus the final dance that Beatrice and Benedick share (V, iv) fulfills our expectations.

Here, then, are two couples who overcome their passionate antagonism to enjoy equally passionate love affairs. Yet one more courtship should be mentioned, for it starts out with similiar intensity, then dissipates. In *Othello*, the title character is under pressure from Desdemona's father, Brabantio, to explain publically the courtship of Desdemona. In response, Othello tells how he related the essentials of his life: the travels and conquests that lifted him to his place of eminence. He then describes Desdemona's reaction to the narrative:

> My story being done,
> She gave me for my pains a world of [sighs];
> She swore, in faith 'twas strange, 'twas passing strange;
> 'Twas pitiful, 'twas wondrous pitiful.
> She wish'd she had not heard it, yet she wish'd
> That heaven had made her such a man. She thank'd me,
> And bade me, if had a friend that lov'd her,
> I should but teach him how to tell my story,
> And that would woo her.
> (I, iii, 158–166)

Here is the crux of their relationship. Desdemona has fallen in love not with a man, but with an image, an idealized version she drew from the stories he told her. Even Othello recognizes as much: "She lov'd me for the dangers I had pass'd" (I, iii, 167). He understands that she barely knows him, but that she finds him an object of fascination. He confesses, too, that he is taken with her primarily because she is taken with him: "And I lov'd her that she did pity them" (I, iii, 168). "Pity" in the Elizabethan context also has connotations of love; nonetheless, he does not really know her, either. The two have married as strangers, as if captivated by each other's portraits. Still, their attraction is understandable, for even the Duke is impressed by Othello's narrative: "I think this tale would win my daughter too" (I, iii, 171). We are aware, however, that when trouble surfaces in the form of lies and rumors spread by Iago, Othello's dissatisfied ensign, the two have no foundation of trust to support them through the crisis.

Thus Othello and Desdemona become victims of cosmopolitan Venice with its racial and social strictures. For contrast, as an example of courtship in an instinctive love that breaks down barriers, we should turn to *The Winter's Tale*, and Perdita and Florizel. Perdita, daughter of King Leontes of Sicilia and Hermione, but now living in Bohemia unaware of her history and royal parentage, speaks of herself as unworthy of Florizel's high station as Prince (IV, iv, 7–10), but he has partially removed the obstacles between them by changing into country attire. In addition, he tries to assuage her fears about how his father will regard her:

> Or I'll be thine, my fair,
> Or not my father's; for I cannot be
> Mine own, nor any thing to any, if
> I be not thine. To this I am most constant,
> Though destiny say so.
> (IV, iv, 42–46)

The contrast between these two characters and the title characters of *Romeo and Juliet* is striking. Juliet urges Romeo to "Deny thy father and refuse thy name" (II, ii, 34), but Romeo never manages to do so; rather, he surrenders to the pressures of family and "fate," unlike Florizel, who is willing to oppose both. Indeed, Romeo eventually bursts out: "Then I [defy] you, stars" (V, i, 24), but the gesture comes too late.

The relationship between Florizel and Perdita continues in this vein, as the two are joined by the disguised Polixenes, Florizel's father and the King of Bohemia, and Camillo, a lord of Sicilia. As Perdita distributes flowers, she takes on the qualities of a force of nature: sexual and passionate, yet pure, especially when she gives the flowers to Florizel and invokes images of fertility and growth (IV, iv, 112–129). Florizel responds with equal intensity:

> When you do dance, I wish you
> A wave o' th' sea, that you might ever do
> Nothing but that; move still, still so,
> And own no other function.
>
> (IV, iv, 140–143)

The image of dancing, familiar from the dialogue and actions of lovers from other plays, confirms that these two will continue with such unabated passion.

The ardor one person feels for another may not always be reciprocated, at least not at first. In *As You Like It*, the untutored peasant, Audrey, feels affection for Rosalind's grimly humorous servant, Touchstone, but he initially displays a decided lack of interest in her:

> Well, prais'd be the gods for thy foulness!
> sluttishness may come herafter.
>
> (III, iii, 40–41)

He does acknowledge, though, that he is attracted to her physically. Therefore she agrees to marry him, but Touchstone arranges for the wedding to be conducted by Sir Oliver Martext, a local vicar of dubious authority:

> I am not in the mind but I were
> better to be married of him than of another, for
> he is not like to marry me well; and not being well
> married, it will be a good excuse for me hereafter
> to leave my wife.
>
> (III, iii, 89–94)

Touchstone implies that he values Audrey only for temporary sexual gratification. Yet by the end of the play, when William, an innocuous country fellow, tries to claim Audrey for his own, Touchstone turns possessive, subduing the hapless William with a barrage of words (V, i, 46–57) and claiming Audrey for his own. Later, Touchstone not only insults a young page who has ambition to sing, but also leads Audrey away, this time to a legitimate marriage (V, iii, 1–6, 39–41). Apparently the power of romance has transformed even so crass a figure as Touchstone.

One instance in Shakespeare's plays where love is definitely not returned is *All's Well That Ends Well*, in which Helena, a gentlewoman raised by the Countess, is infatuated with the aristocratic count Bertram:

> 'Twere all one
> That I should love a bright particular star

And think to wed it, he is so above me.
In his bright radiance and collateral light
Must I be comforted, not in his sphere.

(I, i, 85–89)

He rebuffs her affection, but she remains undiscouraged, even after the gibes of Parolles, Bertram's manipulative confidant. In her words:

What power is it which mounts my love so high,
That makes me see, and cannot feed mine eye?
The mightiest space in fortune nature brings
To join like likes, and kiss like native beings.

(I, i, 220–223)

Throughout the play, heavenly influences are mentioned in relation to Helena. These references, in combination with her own awareness of the physical nature of things, make her a combination of the spiritual and the earthly. In that light, some of her actions are better understood.

Still, Helena's determination to marry Bertram remains surprising, especially after she has cured the King of France's seemingly fatal illness, and he has rewarded her by allowing her to select her husband. When she chooses Bertram, however, he scorns her:

She had her breeding at my father's charge—
A poor physician's daughter my wife! Disdain
Rather corrupt me ever!

(II, iii, 114–116)

Despite the King's claims that his own prestige is on the line, Bertram remains adamant: "I cannot love her, nor will strive to do't" (II, iii, 145). Bertram's reluctance is understandable, as he is being forced into marriage, but he is so rude that our sympathy goes to Helena, especially when Bertram prepares to send Helena to his mother with a letter detailing his hatred. At the same time, we wonder about Helena, who one scene later comments about Bertram's running away: "In every thing I wait upon his will" (II, iv, 54). Should we regard her patience as saintlike, or as evidence of ruthless persistence?

So desperate is Helena that she carries out a plan to switch places in bed with Diana, the woman Bertram desires. The matter of Helena's spirituality becomes more problematic here, but in her eyes, the ends justify the means:

Let us assay our plot, which if it speed,
Is wicked meaning in a lawful deed,

And lawful meaning in a lawful act,
Where both not sin, and yet a sinful fact.
                    (III, vii, 44–47)

At the conclusion of the play, though, these questions remain unresolved. Bertram, who believes Helena dead, is brought before the King. Initially, he expresses remorse, but when questioned about the ring given to him by Diana, which was given to her by Helena, he lies about its origin (V, iii, 93–95). Even after Diana is brought before him, Bertram remains contemptuous:

> My lord, this is a fond and desp'rate creature,
> When sometime I have laugh'd with. Let your Highness
> Lay a more noble thought upon mine honor
> Than for to think that I would sink it here.
>   (V, iii, 178–181)

When Helena finally appears, she marches directly to Bertram and claims him for her own: "Will you be mine now you are doubly won?" (V, iii, 314). Her challenge, which may be delivered with either icy calm or intense passion, reduces Bertram to two lines of helpless resignation:

> If she, my liege, can make me know this clearly,
> I'll love her dearly, ever, ever dearly.
>   (V, iii, 315–316)

Perhaps we are meant to believe that Helena's appearance, her rebirth, so to speak, causes Bertram's transformation. Nevertheless, he has been dislikable for so long that her love remains difficult to accept.

As we have considered, Shakespeare portrays love as having both physical and emotional dimensions, but rarely does he treat sexual relations between a man and a woman with dignity. Perhaps the play of Shakespeare's in which physical love is mocked most consistently is *Troilus and Cressida*. One compelling moment occurs when Troilus, son of Priam and therefore supposedly a leader of the Trojan side of the war, is waiting for his love, Cressida, Calchas's daughter. To Troilus, she is of far greater concern than military matters, and he can scarcely contain his anticipation:

> I am giddy; expectation whirls me round;
> Th'imaginary relish is so sweet
> That it enchants my sense; what will it be,
> When that wat'ry palates taste indeed
> Love's thrice-reputed nectar?
>   (III, ii, 18–22)

These poetic intentions, though, are unintentionally ironic, for we remember how the worldly Cressida spoke of sex:

> Women are angels, wooing:
> Things won are done, joy's soul lies in the doing.
> That she belov'd knows nought that she knows not this:
> Men prize the thing ungain'd more than it is.
>
> (I, ii, 286–289)

Thus when she enters feigning shyness and innocence, Troilus looks foolish, and even more so after the words of her uncle Pandarus, who has arranged the assignation: "So, so, rub on and kiss the mistress" (III, ii, 49–50). Troilus attempts to arouse her, but Cressida continues to act timid, all the while revealing her sophistication:

> They say all lovers swear more performance
> than they are able, and yet reserve an ability that
> they never perform . . .
>
> (III, ii, 84–86)

She pretends that she has heard rumors, but we suspect her comments are based on experience. After Pandarus interrupts, frustrated that the two are as yet talking, Cressida claims that she has always loved Troilus (III, ii, 114–115), then withdraws the claim, as if shocked at her own boldness: "Sweet, bid me hold my tongue . . ." (III, ii, 129). When at last he kisses her, she retreats in mock embarrassment (III, ii, 136–139), manipulating him unerringly. She even boasts indirectly of her skill at doing so:

> Perchance, my lord, I show more craft than love,
> And fell so roundly to a large confession,
> To angle for your thoughts, but you are wise,
> Or else you love not . . .
>
> (III, ii, 153–156)

Troilus remains impassioned, however, and the two express mutual fidelity, Cressida speaking with particular fervor (III, ii, 184–196). The emotion of this scene is comically blunted, however, by Cressida's entire performance, as well as by the joys of sexual fulfillment obliterated by Pandarus's final claim:

> If ever you prove false to one another . . .
>   Let all constant men be
> Troiluses, all false women, Cressids, and all brokers-
> between Pandars!
>
> (III, ii, 199–204)

That warning becomes actuality, while our view of physical love becomes jaundiced.

Even in the tragedy *Antony and Cleopatra*, the physical aspects of love are presented as more comic than romantic. Early on, Antony and his aide, Enobarbus, lounge about, commenting derisively about women's sexual capacity, in particular Cleopatra's:

> I have seen her die
> twenty times upon far poorer moment. I do think
> there is mettle in death, which commits some loving
> act upon her, she hath such a celerity in dying.
>
> (I, ii, 141–144)

The word "die," of course, has a dual meaning based upon an Elizabethan poetic metaphor implying sexual satisfaction.

In Shakespeare's comedies, romance always ends in marriage, and according to the conventions of that genre, we are expected to trust that thereafter all will be well. In tragedy, though, the death of a hero is essential, and therefore in *Antony and Cleopatra* physical love must be subordinate to the spiritual unity of two noble souls. That feeling dominates its final scenes.

Yet here is another romance tinged with foreshadowings of inevitable destruction, for from the beginning we are always aware that Antony cannot have both Cleopatra and leadership of the world. When he dies, Cleopatra's response suggests that their only salvation is a love beyond the realm of the earth:

> It were for me
> To throw my sceptre at the injurious gods,
> To tell them that this world did equal theirs
> Till they had stol'n our jewel.
>
> (IV, xv, 75–78)

Later she comments:

> His legs bestrid the ocean, his rear'd arm
> Crested the world, his voice was propertied
> As all the tuned spheres, and that to friends;
> But when he meant to quail and shake the orb,
> He was as rattling thunder . . . His delights
> Were dolphin-like, they show'd his back above
> The element they liv'd in. In his livery
> Walk'd crowns and crowners; realms and islands were
> As plates dropp'd from his pocket.
>
> (V, ii, 82–92)

All these images suggest a figure exceeding the boundaries of the planet. Cleopatra also envisions herself this way, as she prepares to die rather than be taken prisoner by Octavius Caesar:

> Husband, I come!
> Now to that name my courage prove my title!
> I am fire and air; my other elements
> I give to baser life.
>
> (V, ii, 287–290)

Even Caesar, who throughout the play has been insensitive to romance, speaks poetically over Cleopatra's body:

> Take up her bed,
> And bear her women from the monument.
> She shall be buried by her Antony;
> No grave upon the earth shall clip in it
> A pair so famous.
>
> (V, ii, 356–360)

Caesar recognizes that despite his military triumphs, Antony and Cleopatra have achieved a stature that grants them immortality. Such love as theirs, the play suggests, is worth all the transitory successes that the world affords.

In sum, Shakespeare's vision of romantic love is not easily categorized, for he dramatizes the experience as multifaceted and contradictory, frustrating and inspiring, exhilarating and tragic. Perhaps the only generalization that holds is that Shakespeare shows love to be eternally fascinating, the one aspect of life that spans the entire spectrum of humanity.

Machiavels

Villains are often the most intriguing characters in a dramatic or literary work, for it is their lust for money, power, love, or some more amorphous goal that propels the plot. Moreover, they almost always conceive the plan that they hope will fulfill their desire, and it is this plan to which the heroes or heroines react. Villains therefore furnish the intellectual and emotional energy that carries the narrative and commands our attention.

Shakespeare created a gallery of memorable villains, most of whom may be classified as "Machiavels." The name is taken from Niccolo Machiavelli (1469–1527), the Italian statesman whose book *Il Principe* (*The Prince*, 1513) contributed profoundly to the Renaissance view of political realism. Machiavelli's pragmatic advice on the administration of effective government became to the Elizabethans and many subsequent generations synonymous with diabolic conspiracy and unscrupulous manipulation. What gives Machiavels their unique flavor is that they carry out their schemes with glee; they relish their own ruthlessness. In addition, their wit, in combination with their intellect and freedom from moral restraint, creates an allure that may be at moments horrifying, but which is theatrically gripping.

One early example from Shakespeare's tragedies is Aaron the Moor from *Titus Andronicus*. As he explains:

> I will be bright, and shine in pearl and gold,
> To wait upon this new-made empress.
> (II, i, 19–20)

He plans to marry Tamora, the Queen of the Goths who has been recently engaged to Saturninus, the Emperor of Rome, the city that has conquered her people. The reasons for his cruelties otherwise remain cloudy. He comments to Tamora:

Vengeance is in my heart, death in my hand,
Blood and revenge are hammering in my head.
(II, iii, 38–39)

Never, however, does he give specific causes for his cynicism. Perhaps Shakespeare's audience would have assumed that his attitude is based on his blackness and resultant alienation.

Despite this vague motivation, Aaron contributes extraordinary moments. For instance, late in the play, a nurse enters with Tamora's newly born son. Because it is black and obviously Aaron's, Tamora has ordered it killed, but Aaron defends his offspring:

'Zounds, ye whore, is black so base a hue?
Sweet blowse, you are a beauteous blossom sure.
(IV, ii, 71–72)

This affection brings out another dimension of Aaron's character: a capacity for love. Nevertheless, Tamora's sons, Demetrius and Chiron, are outraged: "Thou has undone our mother" (IV, ii, 75), to which Aaron chortles: "Villain, I have done thy mother" (IV, ii, 76). His viciousness, pride, and glee, tempered by his affection for the infant, make him the most interesting figure onstage.

He remains so even when captured by Roman troops, and offers a litany of his crimes, including the murder of two sons of Titus Andronicus, the great Roman general:

I pried me through the crevice of a wall,
When, for his hand, he had his two sons' heads,
Beheld his tears, and laugh'd so heartily
That both mine eyes were rainy like to his ...
(V, i, 114–117)

After raving in thrilling detail about other evil schemes, Aaron concludes that he is sorry: "... that I had not done a thousand more" (V, i, 124). His exuberant malevolence remains commanding to the end.

One of Shakespeare's greatest Machiavels and, not incidentally, one of his greatest characters, is Richard III, who leads a play by his own name, but who appears in an earlier work that is part of Shakespeare's first tetralogy about English history, *Henry VI 1, 2, & 3* and *Richard III*. As young Richard of York, he enters at the end of *Henry VI, Part 2*, defending his father, the Duke of York, against accusations of treachery:

Oft have I seen a hot o'erweening cur
Run back and bite, because he was withheld,
Who, being suffer'd, with the bear's fell paw

Hath clapp'd his tail between his legs and cried;
And such a piece of service will you do,
If you oppose yourselves to match Lord Warwick.
(V, i, 151–156)

The vivid imagery, the veiled threat, the subtle wit, the boldness: the core of the enthralling character is already present. So are insults about Richard's hunchback and withered arm, offered by Clifford, his father's accuser:

Hence, heap of wrath, foul indigested lump,
As crooked in thy manners as thy shape.
(V, i, 157–158)

In *Henry VI, Part 3*, Richard moves closer to center stage, when his older brother Edward temporarily becomes King, and Richard is named Duke of Gloucester. One lengthy soliloquy communicates his rationalization that his deformity legitimizes any destruction he commits, as well as his skill in deceiving others:

Why, I can smile, and murther whiles I smile
And cry "Content" to that which grieves my heart,
And wet my cheeks with artificial tears
And frame my face to all occasions.
(III, ii, 182–185)

In a play where everyone else seeks power out of a sense of justice or moral imperative, Richard takes pride in his illegality and alienation. Later, after Clarence, Richard's other brother, deserts the King, one remark by Richard summarizes his attitude toward Edward's rule:

My thoughts aim at a further matter: I
Stay not for the love of Edward, but the crown.
(IV, i, 125–126)

Richard is true to one cause: himself. As he says after joyously murdering King Henry VI ("Down, down to hell, and say I sent thee thither—" [V, vi, 67]) and clearing another obstacle for himself in his plan to capture the throne:

Then since the heavens have shap'd my body so,
Let hell make crook'd my mind to answer it.
I have no brother, I am like no brother;
And this word "love," which greybeards call divine,

Be resident in men like one another,
And not in me; I am myself alone.

(V, vi, 78–83)

His pleasure in his own perversity is irresistible.

He truly comes into his own, however, in *Richard III*, in which Shakespeare follows Tudor propaganda by making Richard an archcriminal. Here Richard carries out one scheme after another with giddy relentlessness, simultaneously shocking and thrilling us. For instance, when he proposes marriage to Lady Anne, the widow of Edward, the son of Henry VI, Richard at first denies killing Edward, but then, in an astonishing gesture, reverses himself, opens his shirt, and invites her to stab him:

Nay, do not pause: for I did kill King Henry—
But 'twas thy beauty that provoked me.
Nay, now dispatch: 'twas I that stabb'd young Edward—
But 'twas thy heavenly face that set me on.

(I, ii, 179–182)

When she submits to his plea, then leaves, he reverts to his familiar tone and laughs at her susceptibility to his charms:

Was ever woman in this humor woo'd?
Was ever woman in this humor won?
I'll have her, but I will not keep her long.

(I, ii, 227–229)

As Richard moves from seduction to calculation without a moment's hesitation, he continually delights in his own skill. He says as much in the next scene, when plotting the downfall of everyone near him:

And thus I clothe my naked villainy
With odd old ends stol'n forth of holy writ,
And seem a saint, when most I play a devil.

(I, iii, 335–337)

The great historical controversy about Richard III concerns whether he killed his brother Edward's two sons. In this play, Richard is unquestionably responsible, as he connives to have the two boys sent to the Tower of London, ostensibly for their own safety. His self-appreciation is revealing:

Thus, like the formal Vice, Iniquity,
I moralize two meanings in one word.

(III, i, 82–83)

Such self-awareness places him squarely in the tradition of the Vice figure, one of the stock characters from medieval drama.

The greater the power Richard acquires, the more isolated he becomes. When his kingship is finally under attack, and his own downfall and death are imminent, he releases another aspect of his personality:

> I shall despair; there is no creature loves me,
> And if I die no soul will pity me.
> And wherefore should they, since that I myself
> Find in myself no pity to myself?
>
> (V, iii, 200–203)

The isolation and lack of feeling which were once the bulwark of his strength now partially humanize him. Such a realization on our part does not excuse his crimes, as the eleven ghosts who soon appear affirm. Still, Richard is a brilliant presence, and we are sorry to lose him.

One of the most intriguing Machiavels in Shakespeare's plays is Edmund in *King Lear*. The younger and illegitimate son of the Earl of Gloucester, Edmund stands to lose all inheritance to his older brother, Edgar, and this knowledge furnishes Edmund with motivation to wreak destruction:

> Wherefore should I
> Stand in the plague of custom, and permit
> The curiosity of nations to deprive me,
> For that I am some twelve or fourteen moonshines
> Lag of a brother?
>
> (I, ii, 2–6)

He refuses to accept the values of a society that refuses to accept him, and he also reveals contempt for any ethical order based on those values. When he later tricks Gloucester into believing that Edgar conspires against him, Gloucester looks to the heavens for explanation:

> These late eclipses in the sun and moon
> portend no good to us. Though the wisdom of nature
> can reason it thus and thus, yet nature finds itself
> scourg'd by the sequent effects.
>
> (I, ii, 102–106)

Like others on the roster of figures from the tragedies who at moments of crisis look to outside forces for explanation (see the chapter on "The Tragic Flaw"), Gloucester does not accept responsibility for his own actions. Edmund, however, looks at the situation more realistically:

> This is the excellent foppery of the world,
> that when we are sick in fortune—often the surfeits of
> our own behavior—we make guilty of our
> disasters the sun, the moon, and stars, as if we were
> villains on necessity, fools by heavenly compulsion,
> knaves, thieves, and treachers by spherical
> predominance; drunkards, liars, and adulterers by an
> enforc'd obedience of planetary influence, and all
> that we are evil in, by a divine throwing on.
> (I, ii, 118–126)

Edmund's self-reliance suggests his strength and insight into human nature. Yet such confidence in his own will also intimates a refusal to be bound by moral restraint, and to a Renaissance audience, such license was a fearsome threat.

One of the most fascinating aspects of Edmund's character is his relationship with Lear's two olders daughters, Goneril and Regan. As Goneril grows increasingly dissatisfied with her husband, Albany, whose compassion for Lear she despises, and after Regan's husband, Cornwall, is slain by a rebellious servant after the blinding of Gloucester, Edmund finds himself the object of both sisters' desire. He muses proudly on his luck:

> To both these sisters have I sworn my love;
> Each jealous of the other, as the stung
> Are of the adder. Which of them shall I take?
> Both? one? or neither? Neither can be enjoy'd
> If both remain alive . . .
> (V, i, 55–59)

He holds no emotional commitment to either. Rather, in the tradition of the Machiavel, he amuses himself as he basks in his own strength and sexual appeal.

When Edmund dies at the hands of the mysterious knight who turns out to be his brother, Edgar, Edmund's recognition of the end of his life, as well as the news of the deaths of Regan and Goneril, seems to touch something inside him:

> Some good I mean to do.
> Despite of mine own nature. Quickly send
> (Be brief in it) to th' castle, for my writ
> Is on the life of Lear and on Cordelia.
> (V, iii, 244–247)

Earlier he had condemned them both to death. Now, as if trying to make amends, he seeks freedom for them and absolution for himself. Neither is forthcoming, but at least Edmund achieves self-knowledge. He always understands his goals, and therefore we understand him.

Such is not the case with Don John in *Much Ado About Nothing*, who conspires to destroy the marriage of Hero, daughter to Leonato, and Claudio, a young lord of Florence. During his first appearance, he says of himself:

> I cannot hide what I am: I must be sad when I
> have cause, and smile at no man's jests; eat
> when I have no man's stomach, and wait for no
> man's leisure . . .
>
> (I, iii, 13–15)

Later, he adds: "Only to despite them, I will endeavour anything" (II, ii, 31–32). He does not want Hero for himself, and he seems to have forgotten his earlier jealousy of Claudio. He does not seek to understand or explain himself. Instead he remains curiously detached, as if he were watching himself act. We therefore remain at some distance from him, and in the final scene of the play, when word comes at the wedding of Hero and Claudio that Don John has been captured and will be returned for punishment, the dismissal of this final element of plot by the bachelor Benedick, "Think not on him till to-morrow" (V, iv, 127), seems appropriate.

The question of motivation is even sharper in the case of Shakespeare's supreme villain, Iago in *Othello*. From the start, the reason for his plan to destroy the marriage of Othello and Desdemona is a mystery, most importantly to Iago himself. The great romantic poet Coleridge described Iago as possessed by "motiveless malignity," but more explanation is needed. At the beginning of the play, Iago clearly resents the promotion of, and his own subservience to, Othello's young and inexperienced lieutenant, Cassio, whom Iago dismisses as unmanly and unworthy (I, i, 21–33). But Iago's hatred is more deep-seated than bitterness over the denial of professional advancement, for never during the rest of the play does he discuss military affairs. Instead he becomes preoccupied with obliterating the love between Desdemona and Othello, and the cause for his determination, his "peculiar end" (I, i, 60), as he calls it, must lie elsewhere.

Certainly he resents Othello for other reasons:

> I follow him to serve my turn upon him.
> We cannot all be masters, nor all masters
> Cannot be truly follow'd . . .

Were I the Moor, I would not be Iago.
In following him, I follow but myself.
                    (I, i, 42–58)

Iago sets himself up as an enemy to service and therefore to the social order. Still, we search for motivation. Perhaps the cause is racial, as Iago suggests when he shouts to Brabantio, Desdemona's father:

You heart is burst, you have lost half your soul;
Even now, now, very now, an old black ram
Is tupping your white ewe.
                    (I, i, 87–89)

This warning, however, also suggests Iago's preoccupation with matters sexual, and, indeed, his comments about sex become cruder and more frequent as he delights in mocking human affection, particularly love between a man and a woman. Speaking of Desdemona and Othello, he sneers to the would-be suitor Roderigo:

She must change
for youth; when she is sated with his body, she
will find the [error] of her choice.
                    (I, iii, 349–351)

Yet at one moment he claims to seek Desdemona for himself:

The Moor (howabeit that I endure him not)
Is of a constant, loving, noble nature,
And I dare think he'll prove to Desdemona
A most dear husband. Now I do love her too,
Not out of absolute lust (though peradventure
I stand accomptant for as great a sin),
But partly led to diet my revenge,
For that I do suspect the lusty Moor
Hath leap'd into my seat . . .
                    (II, i, 288–296)

Does he love her? He withdraws the remark as quickly as he makes it. Does Iago truly believe that Othello has slept with Emilia, Iago's wife, whom Iago himself seems to loathe? Or is he struggling to motivate himself to revenge? Certainly he recognizes Desdemona's quality and morality. Indeed, her goodness is part of the reason he wants to destroy her:

So will I turn her virtue into pitch,
And out of her own goodness make the net
That shall enmesh them all.

(II, iii, 360–362)

We must also weigh whether Iago, so vicious toward matters heterosexual, is a latent homosexual, jealous of Desdemona and desirous of Othello for himself. That impression is supported at least partially by his vivid description of sleeping with Cassio, whom, Iago claims, embraced him as if he were Desdemona (III, iii, 413–426). Is this narrative not only a lie, but a hidden fantasy? Iago ends that scene in a mock marriage pose, kneeling next to Othello while swearing "I am your own forever" (III, iii, 479). Does he, unbeknownst to himself, want such a vow to be carried out?

None of these aspects of Iago proves conclusively the sole reason why he acts as he does. Perhaps the most that we can conclude is that Iago, frustrated with his own social and sexual status, and unable to elevate himself, takes out his fury in destruction:

I have't. It is engendered. Hell and night
Must bring this monstrous birth to the world's light.

(I, iii, 403–404)

The mixture of joy and anger is both terrifying and thrilling.

Iago's plan takes off when he mentions to Othello a few casual coincidences involving Cassio and Desdemona, thereby cultivating the seeds of jealousy in Othello's mind. At first, Othello resists:

No, Iago,
I'll see before I doubt; when I doubt, prove;
And on the proof, there is no more but this—
Away at once with love or jealousy!

(III, iii, 189–192)

Iago, however, recalls Brabantio's warning (I, ii, 292): "She did deceive her father, marrying you . . . "(III, iii, 206). And before long, Othello reluctantly confesses: "And yet how nature erring from itself—" (III, iii, 227). With this admission, the climactic line of the play, Othello acknowledges the possibility of Desdemona's unfaithfulness; thereafter Iago, ever shrewd, drives him further and further into rage:

Would you, the [supervisor], grossly gape on?
Behold her topp'd?

(III, iii, 395–396)

Iago even mentions the missing handkerchief, the original token of love that Othello gave Desdemona, and the reference is diabolically cruel:

> I know not that; but such a handkerchief
> (I am sure it was your wive's) did I to-day
> See Cassio wipe his beard with.
> (III, iii, 437–439)

A few scenes later, when Othello, now over the edge, promises to poison Desdemona, Iago amends that suggestion, for poison, as the play's imagery reminds us, is Iago's weapon:

> Do it not with poison; strangle her in her bed,
> even the bed she hath contaminated.
> (IV, i, 207–208)

All these remarks confirm Iago's character as wittily monstrous. At one moment, however, he seems to evince a touch of humanity, when he comes across a tearful Desdemona and offers words of consolation: "Do not weep, do not weep. Alas the day!" (IV, ii, 124). Does he have remorse? Throughout this scene, his lines shorten, as if he is unable to articulate his thoughts. If we accept that Iago's wound is sexual and emotional, perhaps he does have a twinge of conscience, another sign of his complexity. In any case, the moment is transient, for with the appearance of Roderigo, Iago reverts to his boastful, talkative self.

Iago's final words are perfectly appropriate. When all has been revealed, and Desdemona lies strangled by Othello, with Emilia dead from Iago's stabbing, Othello orders Iago to explain himself. Iago bluntly replies:

> Demand me nothing; what you know, you know:
> From this time forth I never will speak word.
> (V, ii, 303–304)

What could he say, even if he wanted to justify his actions? The forces inside that drive him have always been beyond his comprehension.

The only one of Shakespeare's Machiavels who survives his play without death or formal punishment is Antonio in *The Tempest*. Years before the play begins, he joined in conspiracy to remove his brother, Prospero, from the throne of Milan. Now, stranded on Prospero's island, Antonio still seeks to overthrow those in authority. When Sebastian, brother to the King of Naples, asks: "But, for your conscience?" (II, i, 275), Antonio brushes him aside: "Ay, sir; where lies that?" (II, i, 276). As he explains cold-bloodedly (I, i, 276–290), he lives beyond ethical restraint. Thus even in exile, with seemingly no hope of rescue, Antonio plots revenge. At the end, when all families have been reunited, and Propsero has regained authority while invoking a general spirit of forgiveness (V, i, 132–134), Antonio leaves the stage silent, perhaps willing to live in accordance with Prospero's wishes, perhaps still plotting.

Such uncertainty adds to the power of the Machiavels' presence. Even when they explain their desires and reasons for acting as cruelly as they do, their willingness to inflict suffering is one of the most frightening aspects of Shakespeare's works. No matter how noble or joyous the ending of any play, the Machiavels reminds us of an ever-present evil that lurks in certain human hearts.

Madness

Lovers and madmen have such seething brains,
Such shaping fantasies, that apprehend
More than cool reason ever comprehends.
(V, i, 4–6)

So speaks Theseus, Duke of Athens, at the start of the final act of *A Midsummer Night's Dream*. Elsewhere we have considered elements of these lines (see "Appearance versus Reality"), but this chapter focuses specifically on Shakespeare's use of the theme of madness, or what we might call "delusion": how it can be an effective plot device, a reflection of passion run comically or dramatically out of control, or the result of misunderstanding that leads to tragic consequences.

The comic side of madness is apparent in *The Merry Wives of Windsor*, in which country ladies Mistresses Ford and Page realize that they are both the objects of Sir John Falstaff's attention. Thanks to Sir John's mischievous associates, Pistol and Nym, this information is revealed to the husbands as well. Page remains confident of his wife's loyalty, but Ford becomes obsessively suspicious (II, i, 185–188), and schemes to find out the truth. Disguised as Brook, he visits Falstaff and claims to seek his own fling with Mistress Ford. "Brook" carries off the deception, but in the process undergoes great anguish, as he confesses to Falstaff:

> Some say that, though she appear
> honest to me, yet in other places she enlargeth her
> mirth so far that there is shrewd construction made
> of her.

(II, ii, 221–224)

His delusion grows more intense when Falstaff acknowledges that he will meet with Mistress Ford, then comments on Ford's reputation:

Hang him, poor cuckholdly knave, I know
him not. Yet I wrong him to call him poor. They
say the jealous wittolly knave hath masses of money,
for the which his wife seems to me well-favor'd, I will
use her as the key of the cuckholdly rogue's coffer,
and there's my harvest-home.

(II, ii, 270–275)

Left onstage alone, Ford blusters furiously:

See the hell of
Having a false woman! My bed shall be abus'd, my
coffers ransack'd, my reputation gnawn at, and
I shall not only receive this villainous wrong,
but stand under the adoption of abominable terms,
and by him that does me this wrong.

(II, ii, 291–296)

In this context, these lines strike us as those of a buffoon. Mistresses Ford
and Page have charge of the situation, while the Falstaff of this sunny
play, unlike the brilliant, if corrupt, wit, of *Henry IV*, is a clown and later
the victim of cruelly childish pranks. But were the same words placed
in a darker context, they could reflect a mind preoccupied with infidelity
and betrayal. In subsequent plays, like *Othello* and *The Winter's Tale*, characters become so fixated on these emotions that they destroy themselves.
Here the actor playing Ford should hint at such depths of madness, but
we never regard the character's ravings seriously. Later, after "Brook"
listens to Falstaff relate the humiliation of being dumped in the laundry
basket, Ford accepts that not only has he been duped by his wife, but
that he has been a fool:

Hum! ha? Is this a vision? Is this a dream?
Do I sleep? Master Ford, awake! awake, Master
Ford! . . . Well, I will proclaim myself what I am.
I will now take the lecher; he is at my house.

(III, v, 139–145)

Not long after, he seeks forgiveness:

Pardon me, wife, henceforth do what thou wilt.
I rather will suspect the sun with [cold]
Than thee with wantonness.

(IV, iv, 6–8)

Such resolution fits the spirit of comedy.

A less sunny vision is offered in *The Comedy of Errors*, after the ill-tempered Antipholus of Epheseus beats his servant, Dromio, for failing to bring bail money. The suspicion that Antipholus may be mad brings on Dr. Pinch, immediately the victim of his own share of blows from Antipholus, who insists that he is in possession of his faculties. After corroboration, however, from Antipholus's wife, Adriana, and her sister, Luciana, as well as Dromio, Dr. Pinch orders that Antipholus be "bound and laid in some dark room" (IV, iv, 94). Such a threat does not bother us, for Antipholus is too self-possessed to suffer severe stress, but the potential for actual suffering is clear, and it is brought to fruition in *Twelfth Night*.

Madness pervades this play, as virtually every character either feels a touch of delusion or condemns someone else as deluded. For instance, the Countess Olivia is told by her gentlewoman, Maria, that Olivia's uncle, the hard-drinking Sir Toby, demands to see her. Olivia, however, has no patience: "Fetch him off, I pray you, he speaks nothing but madman; fie on him!" (I, v, 105–106). Later, when the stuffy steward Malvolio is awakened by the night reveling of Sir Toby Belch, his companion, Sir Andrew, Maria, and Feste the Clown, Malvolio bursts out:

> My masters, are you mad? Or what are you?
> Have you no wit, manners, nor honesty, but to gabble
> like tinkers at this time of night?
>
> (II, iii, 86–88)

Some time after, when Sebastian, Viola's brother, is accosted by Feste and Sir Andrew, who take him for Cesario, Viola's alter ego, Sebastian accuses them: "Are all the people mad?" (IV, i, 27). Only a few lines later, when Olivia virtually proposes to Sebastian after mistaking him for Cesario, Sebastian ruminates:

> What relish is in this? How runs the stream?
> Or I am mad, or else this is a dream.
>
> (IV, i, 60–61)

What all these uses of "mad" share is that its victims are isolated from humanity. Toby is set apart by his decadent behavior; Feste, Sir Andrew, and Maria, along with Sir Toby, are set apart by what Malvolio deems a disregard for proper decorum; and Sebastian is set apart by his inability to grasp the rules by which everyone else lives. Such isolation can be amusing, frustrating, or delicious, and thus we see how delusion in the form of self-absorption may be a burden or a joy.

In the matter of Malvolio, though, accusations of madness can be a weapon. Sir Toby, who despises the puritanical intruder, plays upon his ego and desire to marry Olivia by writing a letter that invites Malvolio to dress in yellow stockings with cross garters. Before he appears in such garb, Maria, who has conspired with Sir Toby, tells Olivia that Malvolio is "possess'd" (III, iv, 9), to which the Countess replies:

> I am as mad as he,
> If sad and merry madness equal be.
> (III, iv, 16)

In her own way, Olivia understands that love, too, is a form of "madness." But when she see her steward, Olivia is thrown by his attire and attitude toward her: "Why, this is very midsummer madness" (III, iv, 56), and she leaves Malvolio to the ministrations of Sir Toby and his cohorts, including Fabian, who knows the goal: "Why, we shall make him mad indeed" (III, iv, 133), while the manic Belch has the solution:

> Come, we'll have him in a dark room and
> bound. My niece is already in the belief that he's mad.
> We may carry it thus, for our pleasure and his
> penance, till our very pastime, tir'd out of breath,
> prompt us to have mercy on him; at which time we will
> bring the device to the bar and crown thee for a finder
> of madmen. But see, but see.
> (III, iv, 135–141)

Even before this prank is carried out, its cruelty is apparent. When it reaches fruition, Malvolio is trapped inside that dark room, pitifully denying the claims of madness to Feste, who has disguised himself as Sir Topas the curate. Malvolio's every word, though, seems to worsen his predicament. When he claims to be as sane as Feste, the latter replies:

> But as well! Then you are mad indeed, if you
> be no better in your wits than a fool.
> (IV, ii, 89–90)

Malvolio's tortured cries remind us that madness is perhaps the ultimate isolation, for whether it uplifts or imprisons us, it constricts our ability to communicate.

If accusations of madness can trap one character, so can its pose liberate another. Such is the case in *Titus Andronicus*, where the title character, torn by grief over the rape and mutilation of his daughter, Lavinia, is visited at his house by the perpetrators—Tamora, wife of Emperor Saturninus, and her two sons, Demetrius and Chiron. The Queen claims that she herself is Revenge, while her two offspring are Rape and Murder. When Titus apparently accepts this explanation, Tamora continues to plot the death of Titus and his son, Lucius. When, however, she steps away to confer with her two sons, Titus confides in us:

> I knew them all though they suppos'd me mad,
> And will o'erreach them in their own devices,
> A pair of cursed hell-hounds and their dame.
>   (V, ii, 142–144)

Such a position is strategy familiar from numerous revenge plays of Shakespeare's time, but here it works only to an extent because for much of the time, Titus borders on uncontrolled fury.

The act of appearing mad becomes most compelling and complicated when taken on by Hamlet, who does so after the Ghost of his father tells him, first, that Claudius committed his murder and, second, that Hamlet must take revenge. The Prince immediately confides to his closest friend, Horatio:

> As I perchance hereafter shall think meet
> To put an antic disposition on—
> That you, at such times seeing me, never shall,
> With arms encumb'red thus, or this headshake,
> Or by pronuncing of some doubtful phrase,
> As "Well, well, we know," or "We could, and if we would,"
> Or "If we list to speak," or "There be, and if they might,"
> Or such ambiguous giving out, to note
> That you know aught of me—this do swear,
> So grace and mercy at your most need help you.
>   (I, v, 171–180)

This moment is the crux of the play. Why does Hamlet need to adopt an "antic disposition"? What does he hope to achieve?

The possible answers to these questions are myriad, but perhaps they may all be embodied in the suggestion that Hamlet does not know how to proceed and hopes that his pose of madness will isolate him from events and people around him, including the Ghost. He may reason that if he is caught up in the throes of madness, he cannot be held responsible for his actions. No one can demand anything of him. In a sense, he frees himself from accountability.

But the strategy does not succeed, for the pose of madness is inconsistent, and we constantly wonder whether Hamlet is in control of himself, as when Ophelia reports to her father, Polonius, on the Prince's behavior and appearance:

He took me by the wrist, and held me hard,
Then goes he to the length of all his arm,
And with his other hand thus o'er his brow,
He falls to such perusal of my face
As 'a would draw it. Long stay'd he so.
At last a little shaking of mine arm,
And thrice his head thus waving up and down,
He rais'd a sigh so piteous and profound
As it did seem to shatter all his bulk
An end his being.
                                        (II, i, 84–93)

As we listen, we wonder about several points. Is Hamlet acting mad? Has he actually fallen into madness? Or does he believe he is not mad, but has become so infused with his role that he now *is* mad? The possibilities whirl round and round through the next three acts. In the meantime, Polonius muses on Hamlet's behavior and attitude: "Though this be madness, yet there is method in't" (II, ii, 205–206), while all those near Hamlet concoct their own explanation. Claudius insists that the death of Hamlet's father is the cause (II, ii, 7–10), but Gertrude, perhaps out of her own guilt, suggests:

I doubt it is no other but the main,
His father's death and our [o'erhasty] marriage.
                                        (II, ii, 56–57)

Polonius himself assumes that Hamlet is infatuated with Ophelia: "This is the very ecstasy of love" (II, i, 99).

We cannot be certain who is correct. Perhaps all are, to a degree. We can only watch Hamlet move in and out of madness, as he does with his old schoolmates, Rosencrantz and Guildenstern, who, at the King's command, seek to draw out the truth. For a few minutes, Hamlet banters with them, but then he breaks out in fury: "...be even and direct with me, whether you were sent for or no!" (II, ii, 287–288). When they continue to duck the issue, Hamlet releases what may have been building inside him:

I have of late—but
wherefore I know not—lost all my mirth,
forgone all custom of exercises . . .
                                        (II, ii, 295–297)

Is he pretending to be mad, or has the pose of madness left him bereft of energy and hope? Whatever our conclusion about this specific speech, we realize that Hamlet's madness, whether feigned or not, leaves him more deeply alone with his conscience and his memory.

Shakespeare dramatizes madness in yet another way in *Othello* and *The Winter's Tale*. In both, madness arises in the form of an obsessive jealousy, which Shakespeare makes intriguing by forcing us to wonder about the nature of that jealousy.

In *Othello*, the title character has married Desdemona, and all might proceed well were Iago not driven to wreak havoc. During the monumental Act III, scene iii, in which little physical action occurs, the tension exists in Othello's mind, as Iago, with casual innuendo, brings Othello to a fevered state. One early line captures the flavor of the process, as Othello says:

> [By heaven], thou echo'st me,
> As if there were some monster in thy thought
> Too hideous to be shown.
> > (III, iii, 106–108)

As Iago slips suggestions into their conversation, Othello seems to re-gather confidence:

> No, Iago,
> I'll see before I doubt; when I doubt, prove:
> And on the proof; there is no more but this—
> Away at once with love or jealousy!
> > (III, iii, 189–192)

Suddenly, however, Iago recalls the warning given by Brabantio, Desdemona's father (I, ii, 292): "She did deceive her father, marrying you . . ." (III, iii, 206). Now Othello feels even greater vulnerability: "And yet how nature erring from itself—" (III, iii, 227). This line may be regarded as the climax, for once Othello has acknowledged even the possibility of Desdoemna's being unfaithful, his collapse begins. As he says, speaking of Iago:

> Why did I marry? This honest creature, doubtless,
> Sees and knows more, much more, than he unfolds.
> > (III, iii, 242–243)

Before long, he even adopts some of Iago's vocabulary:

> O curse of marriage!
> That we can call these delicate creatures ours,
> And not their appetites.
> > (III, iii, 267–270)

His increasingly violent outbursts, his uneven sentence structure, and his cruder word choice become the manifestation of a madness that consumes Othello and leads to Desdemona's death.

The crucial question, however, and the most intriguing issue about the play, is whether Othello's madness is solely the result of Iago's insinuations and manipulations, or whether such fury lies within Othello from the start. Is Othello merely blind, or is he already inclined toward the direction in which Iago pushes him? Does Iago plant the seed of Othello's delusions of Desdemona's infidelity, or does Iago merely nurture, then harvest, the fruit of that seed?

Emilia, Iago's wife, offers one explanation for Othello's jealousy:

> But jealous souls will not be answer'd so.
> They are not ever jealous for the cause.
> But jealous for they're jealous. It is a monster
> Begot upon itself, born on itself.
>
> (III, iv, 159–162)

The cause is Othello's nature, she indirectly suggests. We probably agree when we consider how vulnerable he is: the only black man of his class in Venice, married to a white woman much younger than he. He is also a soldier, unaccustomed to the social world, and probably inexperienced with women. For instance, after requesting that Desdemona journey to Cyprus with him, he seems to excuse himself:

> Vouch with me, heaven, I therefore beg it not
> To please the palate of my appetite.
> Nor to comply with heat (the young affects
> In [me] defunct) and proper satisfaction;
> But to be free and bounteous to her mind.
>
> (I, iii, 261–265)

Why does he downplay the physical aspects of marriage? The likely answer is insecurity. All his military conquests have taken place outside this environment; now he is trying to survive in the drawing room society of Venice. Thus when we first meet him, Othello is lonely, friendless, and vulnerable to suggestion, possessed by insecurities which Iago can easily tap. When Othello begins to have the barest doubts about Desdemona's fidelity, he can only turn inward, where that doubt is intensified by his estrangement. Therefore the madness that gradually overcomes him is not sudden, not something of the moment, but the culmination of an ever-intensifying process.

In *Othello*, Shakespeare provides considerable evidence to explain a case of madness and obsessive jealousy. In *The Winter's Tale*, though, the character of Leontes, King of Sicilia, becomes similarly fixated without any substantial cause at all. He simply reacts to every playful remark uttered by his wife, Hermione, and his boyhood friend, Polixenes, the King of Bohemia. For instance, Polixenes speaks of his own wife and Hermione as "Temptations" (I, ii, 77), and Hermione picks up the cue:

> Yet go on,
> Th' offenses we have made you do we'll answer,
> If you first sinn'd with us, and that with us
> You did continue fault, and that you slipp'd not
> With any but with us.
> (I, ii, 82–86)

Moments later, Hermione flirts with Leontes, recalling their courtship, but she keeps her eye on Polixenes:

> Why, lo you now! I have spoke to th' purpose twice:
> The one for ever earn'd a royal husband;
> Th' other for some while a friend.
> (I, ii, 106–108)

At this moment, the atmosphere, sexually charged since the reference to nine months in the opening line of the scene, invades Leontes' personality, and he mutters:

> Too hot, too hot!
> To mingle friendship far is mingling bloods.
> (I, ii, 108–109)

Before long, he is compiling evidence, some of it doubtless imaginary:

> Is whispering nothing?
> Is leaning cheek to cheek? is meeting noses?
> Kissing with inside lip? stopping the career
> Of laughter with a sigh (a note fallible
> Of breaking honesty)? horsing foot on foot?
> Skulking in corners? wishing clocks more swift?
> (I, ii, 284–289)

Something in Leontes' makeup causes him to see every action in the worst light. Does he harbor frustrated sexual desire? All we know is that Leontes drives himself toward madness, although Camillo, one of Leontes' lords, explains matters to Polixenes as well as possible:

There is a sickness
Which puts some of us in distemper, but
I cannot name the disease, and it is caught
of you that yet are well.

(I, ii, 384–387)

By the next act, Leontes has banished his son and accused his wife in language and rhythms that sound much like Othello's:

. . . that she's
A bed-swerver, even as bad as those
That vulgars give bold'st titles; ay, and privy
To this their late escape.

(II, i, 92–95)

When Leontes insists on holding a trial for his wife, even the words of the oracle, which pardon Hermione and condemn Leontes, fail to soothe the obsessed King:

There is no truth at all i' th' oracle.
The sessions shall proceed; this is mere falsehood.

(III, ii, 140–141)

Only a report on the death of his son reaches him. He takes the event as punishment for his own transgressions and offers solace to Hermione, who has fainted at the shock of her son's passing:

I have too much believ'd mine own suspicion.
Beseech you tenderly apply to her
Some remedies for life.

(III, ii, 151–153)

Unlike Othello, Leontes returns to his senses, and the rest of *The Winter's Tale* reaffirms the redemptive powers of love. Nonetheless, the play makes us dwell on the uncertainties of the human mind, its susceptibility to madness, and the grip that delusion can have on an individual whose mental state leaves him vulnerable to attack.

Finally, we should consider one last aspect of this subject: the moment when madness turns into a kind of supersanity that allows a person or character to see more acutely than reason alone permits. The strongest example of such behavior is that of the title figure of *King Lear* who, under the humiliation imposed by his daughters and his loneliness when stranded in the open territory near Dover, acquires an understanding that previously was beyond him. Struggling to maintain sanity, Lear encounters the blind Gloucester, shepherded by his son Edgar, who is disguised as Mad Tom o' Bedlam. As Lear and Gloucester hold onto each other for support, Lear reflects bitterly:

> What, art mad? A man may see how this
> world goes with no eyes. Look with thine ears; see
> how yond justice rails upon yond simple thief. Hark
> in thine ear; change places, and handy-dandy, which
> is the justice, which is the thief?
>
> (IV, vi, 150–154)

He then offers a litany of corruptions in which the powerful are as guilty as those they punish (IV, vi, 157–172). Through this tirade, Lear indirectly catalogues the abuses he has committed as well as those that have been perpetrated against him, and his vision turns the world into a miasma of immorality, where no justice prevails. In this state, he challenges the way of life that he has supported and which has served his purpose during his life. The moment is one of profound revelation, as Edgar exclaims: "O, matter and impertinency mix'd,/ Reason in madness!" (IV, vi, 174–175). Here, then, is one step Lear takes toward regeneration, but how ironic that it comes when he seems blind to almost everything else.

Thus madness appears in many forms in the plays of Shakespeare. In rare instances, uncontrolled passion turns into a source of wonder, as the human mind releases hitherto undiscovered resources. In most other moments, though, particularly those of crisis, madness becomes destructive, and we grasp the capacity of the human spirit to consume itself with its own fury.

Male Friendship

One of the dominant motifs of Renaissance literature is the ideal of profound friendship between men. This theme pervades Shakespeare's plays, but always with intriguing variations on the nobility of two men whose spiritual and emotional bond supersedes worldly concerns. In some works, Shakespeare presents this relationship as having no sexual overtones, but in others we cannot be certain whether homoerotic elements are present. In either case, Shakespeare dramatizes how even a deep attachment is vulnerable to the changeability of life.

In *Julius Caesar*, Cassius and Brutus have been friends since boyhood. Their mutual affection has been strained, however, by Cassius's desire to wrest power from Caesar and Brutus's reluctance to participate in a coup. As the pair discuss the matter, Cassius turns Brutus's every comment into an opportunity to continue persuasion. For instance, when Brutus reacts to a roar from the unseen crowd: "I do fear the people/ Choose Caesar for their king" (I, ii, 79–80), Cassius pounces: "Ay, do you fear it?/ Then must I think you would not have it so" (I, ii, 80). When Brutus claims: ". . . I love/ The name of honor more than I fear death" (I, ii, 88–89), Cassius follows at once: "Well, honor is the subject of my story" (I, ii, 92).

Cassius then begins the temptation of Brutus, playing on the latter's ego by harkening back through Roman history to a legendary grandeur that Cassius knows Brutus reveres:

> O! you and I have heard our fathers say
> There was a Brutus once that would have brook'd
> Th' eternal devil to keep his state in Rome
> As easily as a king.
>
> (I, ii, 158–161)

Just as Cassius anticipates, Brutus accepts the compliments: "That you do love me, I am nothing jealous . . ." (I, ii, 162). But when Brutus leaves to contemplate further, Cassius reveals his intentions:

> Well, Brutus, thou art noble; yet I see
> Thy honorable mettle may be wrought
> From that it is dispos'd; therefore it is meet
> That noble minds keep ever with their likes;
> For who so firm that cannot be seduc'd?
>
> (I, ii, 308–312)

At these words, we ask whether Cassius and Brutus were ever as close as they claim, or have circumstances so contorted Cassius's values that he is willing to manipulate and betray his best friend?

Their alliance faces greater strain when the conspirators plan the assassination of Caesar. Brutus seeks to maintain what he sees as the high-minded goals of their mission, insisting, for instance, that Antony be spared. Cassius remains unconvinced: "Yet I fear him,/ For in the ingrafted love he bears to Caesar—" (II, i, 183–184). When Brutus does not let him even finish the thought, Cassius must relent. He finds doing so more difficult after the murder of Caesar, when Brutus, still seeking to act "honorably," allows Mark Antony to euologize Caesar's body after Brutus has spoken. Cassius anticipates disaster:

> You know not what you do. Do not consent
> That Antony speak in his funeral.
> Know you how much the people may be mov'd
> By that which he will utter.
>
> (III, i, 232–235)

Brutus, though, is immoveable, and again we wonder if the long-standing friendship of which these two speak was ever as profound as they have suggested. The more they talk, the more Brutus seems to be the prestigious one and Cassius the manipulator, trading on amity with Brutus to elevate himself.

By the end of the play, their relationship lies in tatters. With the forces of Cassius and Brutus fighting the armies of Antony for possession of Rome, the two friends are beset by squabbling over tactics. First Brutus accuses Cassius of bribery:

> Let me tell you, Cassius, you yourself
> Are much condemn'd to have an itching palm,
> To sell and mart your offices for gold
> To undeservers.
>
> (IV, iii, 9–12)

Cassius defends himself, but the two are reduced to quarrelling like small boys until Brutus dismisses Cassius: "Away, slight man" (IV, iii, 37). Cassius has no choice but to accept such humiliation. It grows greater when the two disagree over military tactics. Cassius, quite reasonably, wants to keep his army rested and to let the enemy come to them (IV, iii, 199–201). Brutus, however, advocates retreating, even though his soldiers will end up battling on two fronts (IV, iii, 203–212). Cassius tries to sway Brutus: "Hear me, good brother" (IV, iii, 212). Yet Brutus remains as resolute as ever, and such tactics reduce Cassius to helpless resignation:

> Now, most noble Brutus,
> The gods to-day stand friendly, that we may,
> Lovers in peace, lead on our days to age!
> (V, i, 92–94)

This line suggests that Cassius has, or once did have, genuine affection for Brutus. In any case, events have placed unsupportable burdens on that friendship, which thereafter collapses.

We see a different version of male friendship in *Twelfth Night*, when Sebastian is stranded in Illyria with his good friend, Antonio. Sebastian believes that his twin sister, Viola, has been drowned, and is determined to go to the court of Duke Orsino. Antonio, however, is equally resolved to serve his friend, to whom he proclaims total devotion:

> The gentleness of all the gods go with thee!
> I have many enemies in Orsino's court,
> Else would I very shortly see thee there.
> But come what may, I do adore thee so
> That danger shall seem sport, and I shall go.
> (II, i, 44–49)

The intensity of this attachment appears to be at least partly sexual, and in a play where Viola masks herself as a boy, and sexual attraction subsequently becomes a matter of considerable confusion, crossover between genders in terms of physical love would be appropriate. Indeed, when these two men next appear before us, Antonio's declaration of love is, if anything, more ardent:

> I could not stay behind you. My desire
> (More sharp than filed steel) did spur me forth . . .
> (III, iii, 4–5)

The depth of Antonio's passions becomes evident when he rushes to the defense of Viola (whom he mistakes for Sebastian) as she duels with the money-hungry Sir Andrew, who has been egged on by his crony, Sir Toby Belch. In response to Sir Toby's query as to who Antonio himself is, the intruder replies:

> One, sir, that for his love dares yet do more
> Than you have heard him brag to you he will.
> (III, iv, 316–317)

Although Antonio knows that he faces danger by exposing his identity in Illyria, he willingly does so to save the man he loves. Thus when Viola, not surprisingly, fails to recognize Antonio, his pain is profound:

> But O, how vild an idol proves this god!
> Thou hast, Sebastian, done good feature shame.
> In nature, there's no blemish but the mind;
> None can be call'd deformed but the unkind.
> (III, iv, 365–368)

His sense of betrayal is palpable. Later he articulates his affections more clearly, explaining why he rescued the person he thought was Sebastian:

> For his sake
> Did I expose myself (pure for his love)
> Into the danger of this adverse town,
> Drew to defend him when he was beset . . .
> (V, i, 82–85)

When Orsino inquires as to when Sebastian came to Illyria, Antonio explains their relationship:

> To-day, my lord, and for three months before,
> No, int'rim, not a minute's vacancy,
> Both day and night did we keep company.
> (V, i, 94–96)

Despite the intensity of this passion, Antonio is bound to be left alone, for in a comedy, we expect the men and women to match up, as most do here. Therefore, when all identities are revealed, Orsino leaves with Viola, and the countees Olivia with Sebastian. True, Antonio may exit with these couples, but we are aware that his love goes unrequited. Thus the affection of one man for another, however heartfelt it may be, defers to love between a man and a woman.

A less dignified portrayal of male love is dramatized is *Troilus and Cressida*. This play mocks just about every human institution, so we should not be surprised that the friendship between the greatest of Greek heroes, Achilles, and Patroclus, another Greek commander, should be equally disparaged. In *The Iliad*, from which much of the material in *Troilus and Cressida* was drawn, Patroclus and Achilles share a noble alliance. In this play, though, Patroclus is universally scorned as Achilles' lover, as Patroclus himself admits to Achilles:

> A woman impudent and mannish grown
> Is not more loath'd than an effeminate man
> In time of action. I stand condemn'd for this;
> They think my little stomach to the war
> And your great love to me, restrains you thus.
>> (III, iii, 217–221)

To this confession, Achilles assents:

> I see my reputation is at stake,
> My fame is shrowdly gor'd.
>> (III, iii, 227–228)

The relationship is later derogated by Thersites, the cynical Greek, whose contempt for everyone and everything sets the bitter tone for this play. To Patroclus's face, Thersites calls him Achilles' "masculine whore" (V, i, 17), but Achilles later demonstrates his affection for Patroclus when the young man's death finally rouses Achilles to action against the Trojan hero Hector, whom he derides as "thou boy-queller" (V, v, 45). The implication of his fury, like so much of the military conflict in this play, is that it emerges from frustrated sexuality. As Thersites contemptuously comments: "Lechery, lechery, still wars and lechery, nothing else holds fashion" (V, ii, 194–195). Thus here male love is reduced to the same base level as all other forms of affection.

The situation is more complicated in *The Merchant of Venice*, which begins with the merchant Antonio's unexplained melancholy. His comrades, Salerio and Solanio, first hypothesize that he worries about his ships at sea, but Antonio rejects that explanation. When they postulate that he is in love, however (I, i, 46), he quickly denies even the possibility of such a condition. But with the entrance of his friend Bassanio, Antonio becomes quietly impassioned. Bassanio admits: "To you, Antonio I owe the most in money and love" (I, i, 130–131). Still, he does not appreciate the depth of Antonio's answer to Bassanio's request for a favor:

> I pray you, good Bassanio, let me know it,
> And if it stand, as you yourself still do,
> Within the eye of honor, be assur'd

My purse, my person, my extremest means,
Lies all unlock'd to your occasions.
                                        (I, i, 135–139)

Bassanio then extols the virtues of Portia, the woman in Belmont whom
he desires to marry, and requests that Antonio lend him enough money
that Bassanio may pursue her. Antonio consents, but Bassanio remains
oblivious to Antonio's overtures, and we sense Antonio's frustration (I,
i, 177–185).

When the pair solicit funds from Shylock, the Jewish moneylender,
Antonio turns surprisingly vicious, and his hatred takes over his demeanor. One reason that the two share a mutual antagonism is that both
are, in their own way, outsiders, whose only recourse is devotion to
money. Shylock is alienated because of his religion. He hates and is hated
by the Christian world around him, and his distaste manifests itself in a
scorn for social interaction. He despises, for instance, all masques and
revels, as he says to his daughter, Jessica: "Let not the sound of shallow
fopp'ry enter/ My sober house" (II, v, 35–36). Antonio, too, is isolated,
for his devotion to Bassanio, whether sexual or not, does not fit into the
world of Venice, and thus no matter how much money he acquires, his
love remains unfulfilled, and he lives in bitterness. The extent to which
the two are similiar may be seen in Portia's remark in the later trial scene,
when she enters, sees the two men, and demands: "Which is the merchant here? and which the Jew"? (IV, i, 174).

The extent of Antonio's unhappiness is apparent after his ships have
failed to return, and he is unable to repay Shylock, who demands the
promised bond: a pound of Antonio's flesh. Prior to the trial, Antonio
sends Bassanio a plaintive letter, bewailing his plight, yet not seeking
any defense. Rather, he explains:

                    . . . all debts
        are clear'd between you and I, if I might but
        see you at my death. Notwithstanding, use your
        pleasure; if your love do not persuade you to come,
        let not my letter.
                                        (III, ii, 318–322)

Antonio's tone suggests that if Bassanio will come to watch him die, then
Antonio will be satisfied, as if knowledge that Bassanio will always be
haunted by Antonio's sacrifice would make death bearable. During the
trial itself, as accusations and pleas fly back and forth, Antonio is curiously passive:

        I am a tainted wether of the flock,
        Meetest for death; the weakest kind of fruit

Drops earliest to the ground, and so let me.
You cannot better be employ'd, Bassanio,
Than to live still and write mine epitaph.
                    (IV, i, 114–118)

Comparing himself to a castrated sheep, Antonio again seems detached from his plight, as if he would welcome death. The implication of both passages is that for Antonio, life without Bassanio, now married to Portia, is not worth living.

At the end of the trial, after Shylock's refusal to back down from his demand and Portia's subsequent intervention, Antonio escapes, having exacted all of Shylock's money and humiliated him further by forcing him to become a Christian. Still, the ending of the play is unsatisfying for Antonio, for Bassanio leaves with Portia, joined by the other couples (Nerissa and Gratiano, Jessica and Lorenzo), leaving Antonio alone again. His last lines (V, i, 286–288) suggest that his only solace will be money, hardly enough for one who clearly longs for love.

Perhaps the one male friendship in Shakespeare's plays that seems satisfactory to both partners may be found in a work where hardly anything else appears balanced: *Hamlet.* The relationship in question is between Hamlet and Horatio, who first appear together at the end of Hamlet's first brooding soliloquy: "But break my heart, for I must hold my tongue" (I, ii, 159). His isolation from everyone else in court adds to his suffering over the death of his father and his mother's marriage to her husband's brother, Claudius. When, however, he recognizes Horatio, Hamlet's manner changes (I, ii, 161), and the two openly discuss matters of the court. Horatio even becomes Hamlet's confidant about the existence of the Ghost and Hamlet's subsequent plan "To put an antic disposition on . . ." (I, v, 172). Hamlet must also confide his reasons for having a revised script of "The Murder of Gonzago" performed for the King, so after Claudius rushes out of the presentation, Hamlet eagerly seeks Horatio's confirmation: "O good Horatio, I'll take the ghost's word for a thousand pound. Didst perceive?" (III, ii, 286–287). Horatio also serves as Hamlet's sounding board in the graveyard, when the Prince, gradually reconciling himself to his inability to carry out the Ghost's orders for revenge, picks up the jester Yorick's skull and broods on the meaninglessness of all human endeavour (V, i, 182–212).

At the end of the play, when all the principals lie dead, Horatio is left to carry on. Hamlet urges him not to take the felicitous escape of an early death, but to remain to tell Hamlet's story (V, ii, 342–348). Horatio does so to the conquering Norwegian general Fortinbras, but omits Hamlet's instructions for the deaths of Hamlet's former friends Rosencrantz and Guildenstern. The oversight is understandable; Horatio's affection for Hamlet overpowers all other emotions.

So much else takes place in *Hamlet* that the friendship between Hamlet and Horatio may seem incidental, but that relationship provides the ballast in Hamlet's life, the one calming influence amid the chaos of Elsinore. Then, too, Horatio makes no demands on Hamlet, but is content to support his friend through a terrible ordeal. The other male friendships considered in this chapter, whether we view them as homoerotic or not, are burdened impossibly by forces that surround them. Thus in Shakespeare's plays, male friendship remains a goal worth striving for and a relationship that offers singular rewards, yet an ideal almost impossible to achieve.

Marriage

During Shakespeare's time, marriage was a male-dominated institution. A wife's legal rights were essentially nil, a husband had every social advantage, and thus a woman's status and happiness were based on her husband's behavior. The cruelty of this plight is articulated by Antipholus's wife, Adriana, in *The Comedy of Errors*:

> His company must do his minions grace,
> Whilst I at home starve for a merry look:
> Hath homely age th' alluring beauty took
> From my poor cheek? Then he hath wasted it.
> Are my discourses dull? Barren my wit?
> If voluble and sharp discourse be marr'd,
> Unkindness blunts it more than marble hard.
> (II, i, 87–93)

This excerpt reflects diverse emotions. Adriana communicates possessiveness, but she also needs to be loved. She fears that her husband has lost interest in her, but she knows that she still has much to offer him. She does not seek to rule her roving spouse, but she does desire his time, attention, and love. She feels bitter at his ill treatment, but is eager for his pleasure with her to be revived. Most important, Shakespeare makes us feel sympathy for Adriana's predicament—indeed, for the predicament of all wives.

Although Adriana's complicated expression of frustration appears in one of Shakespeare's earliest works, the issues it raises may be found in many of Shakespeare's plays, in which the portrait of marriage is more complex. Two general themes emerge: (1) women characters are often forced to accept men who are far less worthy they are; and (2) the most admirable couples are joined in a subtle balance of responsibility, affection, and authority.

To find situations in which a woman must settle for an undeserving husband, we might look at any of several plays. In some cases, we see the couple only during courtship; nonetheless, reasonable judgments can be drawn from the evidence.

In *A Midsummer Night's Dream*, for instance, neither of Hermia's suitors, Lysander and Demetrius, appears worthy of either her or her friend Helena. At the beginning of the play, Hermia's father, Egeus, derogates his daughter's love for Lysander (I, i, 22–45). Meanwhile, the young man stands silent, then pleads for Hermia's hand not by praising her, but by claiming that he, Lysander, is just as deserving as Demetrius, who insists on pursuing Hermia despite her intense dislike of him (I, i, 99–110). When Hermia and Lysander are left alone, he lays out his plan to escape into the woods with her, but soon reveals the scheme to Helena, with whom he seems to have had a dalliance in that same locale (I, i, 165–168). Moreover, the play is filled with references to male infidelity, such as Hermia's lines:

> By all the vows that ever men have broke
> (In number more than ever women spoke) . . .
> (I, i, 175–176)

Although many of the men's rudest words and actions occur when the two fall under the spell of the fairy king, Oberon, and his sprite Puck's magic juices, Lysander and Demetrius also alter their depth of emotion, as when a bewitched Lysander denounces Hermia, whom he formerly loved, with more passion than he ever musters to exalt her:

> Get you gone, you dwarf,
> You minimus, of hind'ring knot-grass made;
> You bead, you acorn.
> (III, ii, 328–330)

Finally, when Bottom and the other mechanicals (or laborers) perform their hilarious version of "Pyramus and Thisbe," it is Demetrius, still under the influence of Oberon's potion, who sneers at the drama. His attitude is contrasted by that of Duke Theseus and Queen Hippolyta, who understand the implications of this story of tragic love, however badly it is performed. At the sight of Bottom as Pyramus, mourning over what he assumes is the body of his dead lover, Theseus comments: "This passion, and the death of a dear friend, would go near to make a man look sad" (V, i, 288–289), while Hippolyta adds "Beshrew my heart, but I pity the man" (V, i, 290). We see comparatively little of this noble marriage, but even in a few lines like these, Theseus and Hippolyta reveal that they share fundamental values which suggest that their marriage has a strong foundation. We also see in them an equilibrium, a mutual respect that dignifies both husband and wife. We doubt that Lysander and Hermia, or Demetrius and Helena, will achieve such parity.

The contrast between the attitudes of men and women in courtship buttresses much of *Love's Labor's Lost*. For instance, the Princess of France, who knows of the King of Navarre's vow against the presence of women in his court, shows herself to be worldly about human nature and love:

> Beauty is bought by the judgment of the eye,
> Not uttr'd by the base sale of chapmen's tongues.
> (II, i, 15–16)

To no one's surprise, therefore, the King and his lords who seek to deny themselves love become infatuated with the Princess and her ladies. Eventually the men discover one another's foibles, and the jollity is infectious, as even the King of Navarre recognizes the truth: "But what of this, are we not all in love?" (IV, iii, 278). The women, however, remain frustrated, as Rosaline, one of the Princess's attendants, explains that she wishes she could make Lord Berowne, who for so long has scorned commitment, suffer for the games he plays and the foolish gifts and poetry he offers her:

> How I would make him fawn, and beg, and seek,
> And wait the season, and observe the times,
> And spend his prodigal wits in bootless rhymes,
> And shape his service wholly to my device,
> And make him proud to make me proud that jests!
> (V, ii, 62–66)

She feels frustrated by a woman's socially determined role in the rituals of courtship and marriage. She is also impatient with the casual relationships the men have maintained, for she seeks genuine affection. Later, as the Pageant of the Nine Worthies unfolds, the males in the onstage audience prove their shallowness by heckling the participants mercilessly. For example, when the clown Costard introduces himself ("I Pompey am—" [V, ii, 547]), Berowne nastily, and not particularly wittily, interrupts: "You lie, you are not he" (V, ii, 548). Earlier, the men endured humiliation by dressing as Muscovites and dancing with the women, who all along recognized them and mockingly flirted with them. Now Berowne derives perverse satisfaction by transferring that humiliation to the helpless actors. Yet Boyet, who has been Berowne's antagonist, finds such childishness attractive (V, ii, 549). The implication is that the men, as ever hollow, bond only by attacking others, while the women are moved by the efforts of the players.

The merriment of the performance is interrupted by a rare tragic moment in Shakespearean comedy: the announcement of the death of the Princess's father. The shock forces all to contemplate the uselessness of so much of what has occurred. Berowne offers words of conciliation (V, ii, 755–758), but the Princess and the other ladies demand more than apologies. Therefore the men are assigned to complete various trials for a year, after which time the women will consider capitulating in marriage. One consequence of this punishment is that the men will not simply be awarded the women, but must prove themselves worthy. We are left to decide whether such men will ever be capable of doing so.

Other couples that seem less than ideal pairings include the lost Viola and Duke Orsino in *Twelfth Night*. At the beginning of the play, he wallows in decadence:

> If music be the food of love, play on.
> Give me excess of it; that surfeiting,
> The appetite may sicken, and so die.
>
> (I, i, 1–3)

He thereafter disparages all women's love as inconstant:

> Alas, their love may be call'd appetite,
> No motion of the liver, but the palate,
> That suffer surfeit, cloyment, and revolt,
> But mine is all as hungry as the sea,
> And can digest as much.
>
> (II, iv, 97–101)

Ironically, Orsino is the one whose affections alternate between Countess Olivia and the disguised Viola. Thus at the end of the play, when he proposes marriage to Viola, the gesture is less than convincing, and we fully expect his eye to continue wandering.

In *Henry VI, Part 1*, Shakespeare presents a marriage that is hopeless from the start: the union between Henry VI, King of England, and Margaret, daughter to the King of Naples, which is arranged by Lord Suffolk, whose attraction to Margaret dooms the weak Henry. As Suffolk says:

> I'll undertake to make thee Henry's queen,
> To put a golden sceptre in thy hand,
> And set a precious crown upon thy head,
> If thou wilt condescend to be my—
>
> (V, iii, 117–120)

At this stipulation, Margaret retorts sharply "What?" (V, iii, 120), but Suffolk gracefully sidesteps: "His love" (V, iii, 121). We have no doubt, however, that both parties understand and accept his implication. The travesty becomes more apparent when Suffolk persuades Henry to ignore the marriage arranged by the trustworthy Protector, Lord Gloucester:

> For what is wedlock forced, but a hell,
> An age of discord and continial strife?
> Whereas the contrary bringeth bliss,
> And is a pattern of celestial peace.
>
> (V, v, 62–65)

Suffolk's motives are malevolent, but he also reminds us that for Shakespeare and his contemporaries, a royal marriage had social, political, and religious implications. In other plays, Shakespeare suggests that the same can be said of marriages between less exalted personages. Throughout *Henry VI, Part 2* and *Part 3*, however, the focus is on the universal destruction that can be caused by a king and queen who are ill-suited, and in this series of plays Margaret runs roughshod over her husband. One example occurs in *Part 2*, when she explodes at Gloucester and the other rivals who hope to use her domination of Henry for their own advancement:

> Beside the haughty Protector, have we Beauford
> The imperious churchman, Somerset, Buckingham,
> And grumbling York; and not the least of these
> But can do more in England than the King.
>
> (I, iii, 68–71)

Not long after, while everyone is aware of the ongoing struggle for the crown between the rival families, Henry VI offers his perspective:

> For my part, noble lords, I care not which,
> Or Somerset or York, all's one to me.
>
> (I, iii, 101–102)

The King's political vulnerability reflects his weakness as a husband and as a man.

Even when a nobleman is strong enough to try to stand up to a powerful wife, results can be calamitous. Macbeth is certainly not timid, as his success in battle suggests, and the witches' prediction that he will one day hold the throne inspires him to contemplate murder (I, iii, 130–142). Nonetheless, it is Lady Macbeth's urging that drives a reluctant Macbeth to act. In a curious way, Macbeth admires her will:

> Bring forth men-children only!
> For thy undaunted mettle should compose
> Nothing but males.
>
> (I, vii, 72–74)

Moreover, and perhaps strange to say, he loves her deeply. When later she asks to know his plans, Macbeth tries to shield her from the worst of his schemes: "Be innocent of the knowledge, dearest chuck,/ Till thou applaud the deed" (III, ii, 45–46). When he learns that she is in such torment over her crimes that she has been sleepwalking, he offers helpless sympathy:

> If thou couldst, doctor, cast
> The water of my land, find her disease,
> And purge it to a sound and pristine health,
> I would applaud thee to the very echo,
> That should applaud again.
>
> (V, iii, 50–54)

Yet his affection for his wife does not enable him to stand up to her misdirected efforts for his advancement.

Not all wives in Shakespeare's plays who challenge their husbands are presented as dangerous. To the contrary, they are often figures of conscience. In *Julius Caesar*, Brutus's wife, Portia, visits him after the company of conspirators departs. She recognizes that he is beset by conflicts, and asks the cause:

> You have some sick offense within your mind,
> Which, by the right and virtue of my place,
> I ought to know of . . .
>
> (II, iii, 268–270)

After he refuses to confide in her, she states her case more authoritatively:

> I grant I am a woman; but withal
> A woman that Lord Brutus took to wife.
> I grant that I am a woman; but withal
> A woman well reputed, Cato's daughter.
> Think you I am no stronger than my sex,
> Being so father'd and husbanded?
>
> (II, i, 292–297)

Her passion touches Brutus: "O ye gods!/ Render me worthy of this noble wife!" (II, i, 297–298). He knows that the scheme he has planned with the other conspirators is morally indefensible. Thus his avoidance of his wife's questions and his unwillingness to respect her as a partner reflect his shame, as well as his dishonesty in refusing to acknowledge his wrongdoing.

The same sort of male denial is apparent in the relationship between the Trojan hero Hector and his wife, Andromache, in *Troilus and Cressida*. Here is a play filled with distorted affections and values, but amid the chaos, the marriage of the son of the Trojan King Priam occasionally seems like an oasis of sanity. When, however, the challenge from the Greek hero Achilles finally is brought forth, Hector cannot resist, despite Andromache's warning:

> When was my lord so much ungently temper'd
> To stop his ears against admonishment?
> Unarm, unarm, and do not fight to-day.
> (V, iii, 1–3)

Hector responds with the timeless tactic of bullying. Rather than answer directly, he questions his wife's right to ask him anything at all:

> You train me to offend you, get you in.
> By the everlasting gods, I'll go!
> (V, iii, 4–5)

Once again, we encounter a husband whose unwillingness to treat his wife as an equal reflects his own weakness.

One more example of such behavior may be found in *Henry IV, Part 1*, in which Hotspur, who has been tossing sleeplessly in bed, belittles his wife's questions about the cause of such restlessness. He has been conspiring with his father, Northumberland, and his uncle, Worcester, to remove Henry IV from the throne, and Hotspur has never publically expressed doubts about the legitimacy of their cause. But the more firmly he refuses to answer his wife's queries, the more we sense his unspoken guilt:

> I must not have you henceforth question me
> Whither I go, nor reason whereabout.
> Whither I must, I must, and to conclude,
> This evening must I leave you, gentle Kate.
> (II, iii, 103–106)

A few lines later he adds: "Thou wilt not utter what thou does not know . . ." (II, iii, 111), but his attempt at pretending to protect her does not mask his awareness that the enterprise he intends to carry out is, at its core, illegal.

Perhaps the most puzzling marriage in all of Shakespeare's plays is between King Claudius and Queen Gertrude in *Hamlet*. Hamlet continually implies that Claudius is far inferior to Hamlet's late father, whom Claudius murdered, but we never see Claudius treat Gertrude with anything but kindness. Indeed, Claudius claims to his advisor Laertes, Polonius's son, that he tolerates Hamlet's violent behavior solely because of Gertrude's affections for her son (IV, vii, 11–12). Then Claudius adds:

> . . . and for myself—
> My virtue or my plague, be it either which—
> She is so [conjunctive] to my life and soul,
> That, as the star moves not but in his sphere,
> I could not but by her.
> (IV, vii, 12–16)

Claudius is ever the politician, but these words seem genuine, and nothing in the play contradicts them.

As for Gertrude, questions abound. Were she and Claudius lovers before Claudius killed her husband? Does she suspect that Claudius committed the crime? Does she know for certain that he did so? Was she an accomplice? At one point during her confrontation with Hamlet, the only scene where the two are alone, Gertrude verges on confession:

> O Hamlet, speak no more!
> Thou turn'st my [eyes into my very] soul,
> And there I see such black and [grained] spots
> As will [not] leave their tinct.
> (III, iv, 88–91)

But seconds later the Ghost orders Hamlet to desist from questioning Gertrude further, and the mystery remains unsolved. Does the Ghost fear learning the truth about her affections? Again, we do not know. On the surface, therefore, this marriage appears to be based on love, but like so much else in *Hamlet*, it remains an enigma.

What we see among the noble marriages, therefore, is a series of relationships that are out of balance, in which one partner or both fail to live up to their responsibilities. Sometimes the husband conforms to his wife's suggestions, sometimes not. On the other hand, among the marriages portrayed between non-nobles, the husband generally proves unfaithful or shallow. Can we, then, point to any other partnerships in Shakespeare's plays that we might deem healthy, where mutual respect does exist?

One would be in *Much Ado About Nothing*, in which the perpetually squabbling protagonists Beatrice and Benedick, having been tricked by their friends into believing that each is in love with the other, allow their true feelings to surface. We enjoy watching the deception, but even more intriguing is the reaction of the love-stricken pair when they realize that they have been duped. After Benedick muses: "They swore that you were almost sick for me" (V, iv, 80), Beatrice answers in a similar pattern: "They swore that you were well-nigh dead for me" (V, iv, 81). As they banter back and forth, each unwilling to confess passion, their playfulness is utterly winning, and as they dance together, literally holding each other in shared melody and rhythm, we feel that here are a man and woman allying themselves forever.

We feel the same way about one other couple, equally unlikely to be matched, but even more notorious for the volatility of their passions. Therefore to judge them happy may seem outlandish. After all, in *The Taming of the Shrew*, Petruchio forces his new wife Katherine to surrender to him by denying her food and sleep. But when she does give in, their sport has considerable charm, as when they encounter an old man on the road back to Padua. Katherine has previously conformed to Petruchio's claims about whether the sun or the moon shines on them. Now she glances at the ancient traveler, whom Petruchio has deemed a "gentlewoman" (IV, v, 29), and comments cheerfully:

> Young budding virgin, fair, and fresh, and sweet,
> Whither away, or [where] is thy abode?
> Happy the parents of so fair a child!
> (IV, v, 37–39)

So infused is she with their repartee that she goes Petruchio one step further, until he relents and admits his own error. Hereafter they never declare their love in so many words, but their mutual affection is always evident.

The quintessential statement about marriage, at least in this play, may be found as Katherine speaks before the assemblage at the final wedding banquet:

> Thy husband is thy lord, thy life, thy keeper,
> Thy head, thy sovereign; one that cares for thee,
> And for thy maintenance; commits his body
> To painful labor, both by sea and land:
> To watch the night in storms, the day in cold,
> Whilst thou li'st warm at home, secure and safe;
> And craves no other tribute at thy hands
> But love, fair looks, and true obedience—
> Too little payment for so great a debt.
> (V, ii, 146–154)

She advocates what for Shakespeare's time would be an equilibrium between husband and wife. True, the social mores of our day are far different from those of the Renaissance, and our perceptions of propriety have changed. Furthermore, we can have no doubt that Shakespeare believed a woman's place subordinate to that of her husband. But if that husband is entitled to authority, he is equally charged with the responsibility of dedicating his life to her happiness and welfare. When Katherine compares marriage to the political relationship between prince and subject (V, ii, 155), she clarifies that just as a society's health is based on a proper hierarchical structure, so the happiness of a marriage is inextricably tied to order. To have all in balance and proportion was an ideal of Shakespeare's age, and that is the ideal Katherine advocates.

Shakespeare therefore evinces a profound respect for how women, through the institution of marriage, contribute to the moral and emotional health of a culture. His tragic and historical plays end with a reestablishment of religious and political order, while his comedies and romances end with a celebration of marriage. Both forms of resolution, however, reflect the reestablishment of the social order. With that vision in mind, perhaps the words of the goddess Juno in *The Tempest*, blessing the ceremony uniting Miranda, the daughter of Prospero, and Ferdinand, son of Alonso, capture the spirit of an institution that is for Shakespeare a bulwark of harmony and civilization:

> Honor, riches, marriage-blessing,
> Long continuance, and increasing,
> Hourly joys be still upon you!
>
> (IV, i, 106–108)

Money

Like all of us, Shakespeare's characters are vulnerable to temptation, which, as in life, may lead to corruption. One of the most powerful enticements is money, which can become the object of such fixation that it overwhelms the rest of a person's character. True, as Shakespeare dramatizes this preoccupation, it is not always strong enough to take exclusive hold of someone, but several of Shakespeare's plays remind us that the desire for money, like the desire for power, has the capacity to contaminate an individual or a society.

The lighter side of greed is apparent in some of Shakespeare's comedies. In *The Taming of the Shrew*, Baptista clarifies to several young men of Padua how he will reward the successful suitor of his younger daughter, Bianca: "I will be very kind, and liberal" (I, i, 98). He regards her as a commodity, as he later clarifies:

> 'Tis deeds must win the prize, and he of both
> That can assure my daughter's greatest dower
> Shall have my Bianca's love.
>
> (II, i, 342–344)

The shallow suitor Gremio, along with the servant Tranio, who is disguised as his master, Lucentio, another suitor, follows this directive by boasting of his own wealth; not surprisingly, Baptista concedes to the more promising claims of Tranio. Even then, however, Baptista adds a stipulation:

> I must confess your offer is the best,
> And let your father make her the assurance,
> She is your own, else you must pardon me;
> If you should die before him, where's her dower?
>
> (II, i, 386–389)

To be sure, during Shakespeare's time, monetary matters were a vital part of most marriage arrangements, but Baptista's greed overwhelms any concern he might have as to whether his daughter will marry happily as well.

We contrast this attitude with that of the visiting Petruchio, who enters claiming but one goal: "I come to wive it wealthily in Padua" (I, ii, 76). He then unashamedly negotiates with Baptista for the hand of Katherine, his older daughter, until Baptista relents:

> After my death, the one half of my lands,
> And in possession twenty thousand crowns.
>> (II, i, 121–122)

Yet so obvious is Petruchio's mission that we suspect something deeper lies within him, and that suspicion turns out to be correct. Indeed, as soon as he hears that Katherine has broken a lute over the head of Hortensio, the false music teacher, Petruchio is intrigued:

> Now, by the world, it is a lusty wench!
> I love her ten times more than e'er I did.
> Oh, how I long to have some chat with her!
>> (II, i, 160–162)

So taken is he with her independence and fury that he forgets about financial recompense. In fact, at the end of the play, when the husbands share a bet as to whose wife will follow orders, Baptista offers to increase Petruchio's dowry, but Petruchio is more occupied with Katherine herself (V, ii, 113–115). The implication of their relationship is clear: when true love exists, money becomes irrelevant.

This sentiment is echoed by the gentleman Fenton in *The Merry Wives of Windsor*, when he exchanges affection with Anne Page, daughter of Mistress Page:

> Albeit I will confess thy father's wealth
> Was the first motive that I woo'd thee, Anne;
> Yet wooing thee, I found thee of more value
> Than stamps in gold, or sums in sealed bag;
> And 'tis the very riches of thyself
> That now I aim at.
>> (III, iv, 13–18)

Fenton is one of the few characters in this play who realize the relative worth of money and human beings. For example, in the opening scene, Sir Hugh Evens, a Welsh parson, suggests that one of Sir John Falstaff's cronies, Shallow, might profit were his cousin, Slender, to marry Anne

Page. Later Ford, who suspects his wife is having a dalliance with Falstaff, listens in the guise of "Brook" as the fat knight boasts:

> I will
> use her as the key of the cuckholdly rogue's coffer,
> and there's my harvest-house.
>
> (II, ii, 273–275)

Ford is compelled to acknowledge his own manic sense of possession for both his money and his wife. Finally, so pervasive is the power of money that Page himself, an essentially decent man, dismisses Fenton over the lad's lack of income (III, iv, 68–70), as does the even shrewder Mistress Page, although she does so with a kind word (III, iv, 88–93). Still, at the end of this scene, Mistress Quickly, acting as marriage broker, emphasizes Fenton's quality:

> A kind heart he hath. A woman
> would run through fire and water for such a kind
> heart.
>
> (III, iv, 102–104)

After such praise, we are sure that scarcity of funds will not prevent this deserving couple from ending up together.

The corrupting power of money assumes far greater proportions in *The Merchant of Venice*, where the thoughts and language of the entire community are saturated with matters of finance, and no character escapes its influence. In the first scene, for example, friends Salerio and Solanio assume that the merchant Antonio's melancholy must be the result of the uncertain fate of his ships at sea (I, i, 8–40). He denies the connection, but the thought that money outweighs all other priorities has been established. It is developed by Antonio's friend Bassanio, who seems almost incapable of thinking or speaking without reference to income, as when he explains his predicament to Antonio in this same scene:

> To you, Antonio,
> I owe the most in money and in love,
> And from your love I have a warranty
> To unburthen all my plots and purposes
> How to get clear of all the debts I owe.
>
> (I, i, 130–134)

Even when he extols Portia, the lady he claims to love, images of money dominate Bassanio's vocabulary. He reveals that she is "richly left" (I, i, 161) and that she is, like "a golden fleece" (I, i, 170), the object of many suitors. The opening thus leads us to conclude that in Venice, money and happiness, or perhaps money and pleasure, are inextricably intertwined.

The issue of money grows with the entrance of Shylock, from whom Antonio seeks a loan of 3,000 ducats to help Bassanio in his courtship of Portia. Shylock's profession, one of the few permitted to Jews by law, is that of moneylender, and we note how similiar Antonio the merchant and Shylock the moneylender appear: both are emotionally desolate men whose sole comfort in life is their bank account. Antonio's love for Bassanio remains unrequited, while Shylock lives isolated because of his religion. We are not surprised, therefore, that the two men turn on each other. As Shylock notes bitterly:

> He hates our sacred nation, and he rails
> Even there where merchants most do congregate
> On me, my bargains, and my well-won thrift,
> Which he calls interest. Cursed be my tribe
> If I forgive him.
>
> (I, iii, 48–52)

Such a speech raises the question of whose hatred for whom emerged first, as well as the specific cause of this hatred. Is it solely religion, monetary practice, or some combination of both, complicated by the personal antagonism between two misfits? The answers to these questions are never clear.

The reality that money dominates the world of Venice, however, is never far from our thoughts, as when Lorenzo, the suitor of Jessica, Shylock's daughter, speaks of their love:

> She hath directed
> How I shall take her from her father's house,
> What gold and jewels she is furnish'd with,
> What page's suit she hath in readiness.
>
> (II, iv, 29–32)

Lorenzo seems an ordinary romantic hero, almost a cliche, in fact, eager to elope with the woman he loves and just as eager to leave her dictatorial father. His emphasis, however, on the financial reward of marrying Jessica also makes us view Lorenzo as another selfish Venetian. Portia, too, seems to think largely in financial terms. After Bassanio fulfills her father's legacy by selecting the leaden casket and thereby winning her hand, Portia expresses her joy with familiar terminology:

> Though for myself alone
> I would not be ambitious in my wish

To wish myself much better, yet for you,
I would be trebled twenty times myself,
A thousand times more fair, ten thousand times more rich,
That only to stand high in your account,
I might in virtues, beauties, livings, friends,
Exceed account. But the full sum of me
Is sum of something . . .

(III, ii, 150–158)

Furthermore, moments after they are engaged, Portia and Bassanio face their first crisis together: the repayment of Antonio's loan to Shylock.

In the climactic trial scene, money remains at the heart of the controversy, although Shylock's call for his bond, Antonio's pound of flesh, momentarily puts financial matters to the side. Even after Portia, pretending to be the lawyer Balthazar, offers Shylock three times the amount Antonio owes him, Shylock demands the literal bond. In Venice, then, the only force greater than money is out-and-out hatred. As Shylock himself says earlier about the Venetians:

You have among you many a purchas'd slave,
Which like your asses, and your dogs and mules,
You use in abject and in slavish parts,
Because you bought them . . .
The pound of flesh which I demand of him
Is dearly bought as mine, and I will have it.

(IV, i, 90–100)

He accuses them of dealing with human beings as barter, and justifies his ruthlessness as a product of the world they have created and in which he, to survive, must play by their rules. If he is corrupt, Shylock implies, he is so because the entire city is equally tainted. His defense is the most direct condemnation of the city and its way of life.

We move next to the world of Shakespeare's tragedies, where money plays a comparatively minor role. One brief, but signficant mention is in the opening scene of *King Lear*, when the Dukes of Burgundy and France vie for the hand of Lear's youngest daughter, Cordelia, who has just been expelled from the kingdom by her father. When confronted by the news that Cordelia has lost her dowry, Burgundy offers a shallow response:

Royal King,
Give but that portion which yourself propos'd,
And here I take Cordelia by the hand,
Duchess of Burgundy.

(I, i, 241–244)

He regards her as an object and evinces no sense of her intrinsic worth. France, however, states what is clear to the audience: "She is herself a dowry" (I, i, 241). His joy in marrying Cordelia embodies a theme so much at the heart of this play: the importance of the capacity to judge accurately the worth of people, to appreciate their true value, and not to be deceived by appearances.

That theme is also part of Shakespeare's last tragedy, *Timon of Athens*, which, coincidentally, concentrates more on the influence of money than does any of his other plays. Here King Timon rules with unbounded generosity, as the unnamed Poet, soliciting funds to support his art, explains:

> His large fortune,
> Upon his good and gracious nature hanging,
> Subdues and properties to his love and tendance
> All sorts of hearts . . .
>   (I, i, 55–58)

But the Poet also resents Timon's wealth, and anticipates his fall from power:

> When Fortune in her shift and change of mood
> Spurns down her late beloved, all his dependants
> Which labor'd after him to the mountain's top
> Even on their knees and [hands], let him [slip] down,
> Not one accompanying his declining foot.
>   (I, i, 84–88)

Another evaluation of Timon's generosity comes from the cynical philosopher Apemantus, who remains bewildered by Timon's generosity and his blindness to the obviously crass motives of those who petition him:

> O you gods! what a number
> of men eats Timon, and he sees 'em not! It grieves
> me to see so many dip their meat in one man's blood,
> and all the madness is, he cheers them up too.
> I wonder men dare trust themselves with men.
>   (I, ii, 39–43)

This bitter reflection leads us to ask why Timon should be so generous. He himself offers at least part of the answer, when he speaks at a banquet:

Money

> Why, I have often wish'd myself
> poorer, that I might come nearer to you. We are born
> to do benefits; and what better or properer can we call
> our own than the riches of our friends?
>
> (I, ii, 100–103)

These lines reveal Timon's ego, for he delights in giving. Why should he do so? Because his beneficence keeps the recipients subordinate to him, and the more generous he is, the more superior he feels. In addition, why should he be so casual about dismissing repayment from others? Because as long as people do not repay him, even if he tells them to forget the debt, they remain in his debt. Timon's generosity, therefore, is not only an expression of his link with humanity, but also an extension of his own authority. In this light, we understand the antagonism of those he supports, for no matter how free Timon may be with his wealth, such charity still makes the recipients conscious of their inferiority. For Timon, then, money becomes a vehicle for increasing his status and shrinking the dignity of others.

Yet he continues to think of himself as loving and beloved. Thus when the extent of Timon's debts are revealed, and creditors stand unyielding in their demands for restitution, Timon, astonished by the turnabout, demands of his servant, Flavius:

> How goes the world, that I am thus encount'red
> With clamorous demands of debt, broken bonds,
> And the detention of long since due debts,
> Against my honor?
>
> (II, ii, 36–39)

Even when all his resources are depleted, Timon refuses to acknowledge that action might be taken against him: "You shall perceive how you/ Mistake my fortunes; I am wealthy in my friends" (II, ii, 183–184). The irony of his vocabulary does not escape us. As much as Timon belittles money, he centers his life and thought around it. Moreover, Timon tries to turn his dismissal of money into a glorification of the human spirit; that attempt may be admirable, but it is also fatuous, especially after we have heard how eager his creditors are for retribution. As one of the servants of Timon's creditors remarks:

> No matter what, he's poor, and
> that's revenge enough. Who can speak broader than
> he that has no house to put his head in? Such
> may rail against great buildings.
>
> (III, iv, 62–65)

The result of such resentment is our understanding of the role of money in life. Even when it is dispensed generously, even when it is dismissed as trivial, it retains its power, for such is the corruptibility of human nature. Eventually Timon also recognizes this truth, and in raging misanthropy deserts civilization. In his madness, he digs for roots, but comes across gold instead:

> This yellow slave
> Will knit and break religions, bless th' accurs'd.
> Make the hoar leprosy ador'd, place thieves,
> And give them title, knee, and approbation
> With senators on the bench.
>
> (IV, iii, 34–38)

Infuriated by his loss of faith in humanity, he spends the rest of his life condemning all aspects of human existence. Earlier he threw money away with love: now he does so with hatred.

In conclusion, Shakespeare suggests that money is in itself harmless, but that given humanity's greed for power and our susceptibility to the attractions of hierarchical standing, money can become a dangerous weapon. Even when it is distributed with no strictures at all, as in *Timon of Athens*, the desire that human beings feel not only to secure their own place, but also to destroy those above them, inevitably brings destruction.

Mortality

To note that many of Shakespeare's characters live with awareness of the inevitability of death is to say little. After all, most individuals, whether in life or art, are conscious that one day they will die. What is of considerable interest, however, is which figures in Shakespeare's plays face this reality head-on, under what circumstances they do so, and with what attitude they proceed.

Shakespeare's comedies would seem to be an unlikely place to encounter such emotions. Yet a major reason why his lighter works have such depth is that the characters remain aware of all sorts of serious issues. Indeed, one way in which we may distinguish comedy from farce is that in farce characters generally feel nothing beyond physical sensation. They do not stop to reflect on the signficance of what they experience, nor on issues outside their immediate scope, and because the characters feel so little, the audience also remains detached. For instance, when watching a farce by a master of that form, such as the nineteenth-century Frenchman Feydeau, or a contemporary version, such as a television sitcom, we may laugh at characters scrambling in and out of bedclothes and bedrooms, but rarely do we think or care about the subtleties of their emotions. In comedy, on the other hand, even as we laugh, we reflect. When experiencing Molière's *The Misanthrope*, for example, we wonder about the nature of human vanity, loneliness, hypocrisy, and love. Thus in a discussion of any comic art, one crucial question to consider is whether the work belongs to the world of farce or comedy.

When dealing with Shakespeare's works, we encounter the highest form of comedy. To be sure, many of his comedies have farcical elements, including plot confusions, slapstick, and other physical fun, as well as bawdy humor. All these plays, however, have serious overtones that may bring our laughter up short.

In *The Comedy of Errors*, for example, Luciana complains to her sister, Adriana, about the apparent fickleness of Antipholus, the twin that both women assume to be Adriana's husband. In the midst of these shrill complaints, their servant, Dromio, who has been caught between conflicting demands by the brothers, returns to seek bail money to rescue his master. Separating himself from the confusion, he comments:

> Time is a very bankrout and owes more than he's worth to season.
> Nay, he's a thief, too: have you not heard men say,
> That Time comes stealing on by night and day?
> If ['a] be in debt and theft, and a sergeant in the way,
> Hath he not reason to turn back an hour in a day?
> (IV, ii, 58–62)

Such a glimpse of life's transience changes Adriana's attitude, and she gives Dromio the money at once. The speech also taps the audience's awareness that underneath the merry mix-ups on which this work is founded lie genuine emotion and pain.

A different strategy brings similar awareness at the end of *Love's Labor's Lost*. During the play's last scene, in the middle of the Pageant of the Nine Worthies, we reflect on the foolishness of the suitors and roles they took on to win over the women, who also played games designed to humiliate the men. Suddenly the lord Monsieur Marcade enters to announce the death of the Princess's father, the King of France. As the characters grasp the tragic situation, we, along with them, acknowledge the foolishness of so much of what has preceded. Lord Berowne, who all along has been the keenest of the men, puts matters in perspective:

> For your fair sakes have we neglected time,
> Play'd foul play with our oaths. Your beauty, ladies,
> Hath much deformed us, fashioning our humors
> Even to the oppos'd end of our intents . . .
> (V, ii, 755–758)

From this point on, the tone of the play grows grim, and the concluding song about the seasons and cycles of life makes us view the continuum of human existence under the shadow of mortality.

The same effect is achieved by one other song that concludes a comedy—Feste the clown's verses in *Twelfth Night*:

> When that I was and a little tine boy,
>   With hey ho, the wind and the rain,
> A foolish thing was but a toy,
>   For the rain it raineth every day.
> (V, i, 389–392)

These lines are an antidote to the egoism that has dominated the play. Irrespective of what we ourselves do, the world goes on, and the rain falls. Feste sees our lives as short and therefore laughable, for nothing we do matters. At the same time, because nothing we do matters, he sees our lives as short and sad.

No figure in Shakespeare makes awareness of mortality more poignant than that comic genius Sir John Falstaff, who dominates the action of *Henry IV, Parts 1 & 2*. In *Part 1*, he is sixty years old, grossly overweight, and prey to all sorts of illnesses, but during much of the action he fights off intimations of his own passing. Indeed, he speaks of himself instead as a young man, as when he is robbed by the Prince and Hal's cohort, Poins, on the highway near Gadshill: ". . . they hate us youth" (II, ii, 85), he bellows. Later in the tavern, though, he sighs:

> There lives not three good men
> unhang'd in England, and one of them is fat
> and grows old.
>
> (II, iv, 130–132)

Even as he offers such wistful comment, however, Falstaff is still entertaining himself and his companion Hal, who has yet to assume the responsibilities of the throne.

Part 2, however, offers a different spirit. Whereas *Part 1* focused on Hal's growth and his education at the hands of both his biological father, King Henry IV, and his spiritual father, Falstaff, *Part 2* dramatizes Hal's independence and the gradual fading of the two older men. At the start, Hal has essentially departed from Falstaff's world, the taverns of Eastcheap and elsewhere, so that Falstaff now finds himself desolate, without an audience or a partner in crime and revelry. In *Part 1*, he rumbled through the world with a boundless appetite for capons, sack, and wenches. In *Part 2*, his thoughts turn to himself, and from his first words we feel how aware he is about his health and the passing years: "Sirrah, you giant, what says the doctor to my water?" (I, ii, 1–2). In the presence of the stern Chief Justice, Falstaff maintains his swagger: "You that are old consider not the capacities of us that are young" (I, ii, 173–174). Nonetheless, the Chief Justice, a humorless purveyor of truth, refuses to let Falstaff avoid reality:

> Do you set down your name in the scroll
> of youth, that are written down old with all the
> characters of age? Have you not a moist eye, a
> dry hand, a yellow cheek, a white beard, a decreasing
> leg, and increasing belly? Is not your voice broken,
> your wind short, your chin double, your wit single,

and every part about you blasted with antiquity?
and will you call yourself young?
(I, ii, 178–185)

Still, Falstaff refuses to accept this vision of himself. Although he acknowledges that his body may be failing, his jokes become harsh. Nonetheless, he counts on his spirit to sustain him: "A good wit will make use of any thing. I will turn diseases to commodity" (I, ii, 247–248).

What turns Sir John truly wistful is the arrival of his two longtime comrades, Justices Shallow and Silence, whose musings drift inevitably to the passage of time. As Shallow says:

Jesu, Jesu, the mad days that I have spent!
And to see how many of my old acquaintances are dead!
(III, ii, 33–34)

After the exchange of memories, Falstaff sums up their predicament with unmatched simplicity and eloquence: "We have heard the chimes at midnight, Master Shallow" (III, ii, 214).

We never see Falstaff's death, but we see and hear the emotional blow that destroys him. After the death of Henry IV, Hal is to take the throne, and Falstaff assumes that the new King will grant him the same privileges that he enjoyed in the taverns:

I know the young king is sick for me. Let us
take any man's horses, the laws of England are at
my commandment. Blessed are they that have been
my friends, and woe to my Lord Chief Justice.
(V, iii, 135–138)

But at the coronation, after Falstaff calls out to his former charge, Henry V turns and utters these devastating words:

I know thee not, old man, fall to thy prayers.
How ill white hair becomes a fool and jester!
I have long dreamt of such a kind of man,
So surfeit-swell'd, so old, and so profane;
But being awak'd, I do despise my dream.
Make less thy body (hence) and more thy grace,
Leave gormandizing, know the grave doth gape
For thee thrice wider than for other men.
Reply to me not with a fool-born jest,
Presume not that I am the thing I was,
For God doth know, so shall the world perceive,

240

That I have turn'd away my former self;
So will I those that kept me company.
                    (V, v, 47–59)

The address compels Falstaff to confront his age, status, physical decay, and isolation from the young man he has always regarded as his son. Henry V concludes with banishment, as much a prelude to death as the King can inflict.

We should not be surprised that reflections on mortality are found in most of the tragedies. Yet those characters who do come to grips with the subject do so in ways that reflect their own personalities. In *Romeo and Juliet*, for example, moments before Juliet prepares to swallow the poison that will give her the appearance of death, she offers a nightmarish vision of the consequences of her action. First she weighs the possibility that the Friar, who concocted the scheme, might be willing to see her die to avoid his punishment (IV, iii, 24–27). Her mind then races in a phantasmagoria of death and ghosts, leaving herself trapped amid images of her past and family history (IV, iii, 36–59). The vision is appropriate to Juliet's life. She has struggled to break free of her family, but the pressure of their values has constricted her, and we should not be surprised that the nightmare she conjures up includes them.

A far different vision of mortality is offered by Cleopatra in *Antony and Cleopatra*. Indeed, she offers two contrasting pictures, both occurring after the death of Antony and moments before her own suicide. First she reflects on how she will be remembered by the populace:

> Saucy lictors
> Will catch at us like strumpets, and scald rhymers
> Ballad's out a' tune. The quick comedians
> Extemporally will stage us, and present
> Our Alexandrian revels: Antony
> Shall be brought drunken forth, and I shall see
> Some squeaking Cleopatra boy my greatness
> I' th' posture of a whore.
>   (V, ii, 214–221)

A woman who has lived her entire life on the stage of public view reflects how the mass of people in future centuries will regard her. She knows that she will be misunderstood; she also knows that she is helpless to change history's judgment of her. Here Shakespeare comments reflexively on his own art, for in his day, a boy did play the part of Cleopatra, and the last two lines force the audience to acknowledge the reality of that casting.

Cleopatra also looks forward to her afterlife with Antony:

> Methinks I hear
> Antony call; I see him rouse himself
> To praise my noble act. I hear him mock
> The luck of Caesar, which the gods give men
> To excuse their after wrath. Husband, I come!
> Now to that name my courage prove my title!
> I am fire and air; my other elements
> I give to baser life.
>
> (V, ii, 283–290)

She attempts to answer what may be the most profound question the play poses: is the love between Cleopatra and Antony worth the sacrifices each makes? At this moment, she insists that their love was superior to their world and the paltry concerns of those like Octavius Caesar, who survives to rule Rome and the world, but whom Cleopatra dismisses.

The title character of *Julius Caesar* offers his own view of mortality. When his wife, Calphurnia, cautions him about going to the forum on the fateful Ides of March (the fifteenth), Caesar tries to allay her fears:

> Cowards die many times before their deaths,
> The valiant never taste of death but once.
> Of all the wonders that I yet have heard,
> It seems to me most strange that men should fear,
> Seeing that death, a necessary end,
> Will come when it will come.
>
> (II, ii, 32–37)

Earlier we saw Caesar's superstition when he ordered Antony to touch Cleopatra during the race, so that she might prove fertile (I, ii, 6–8). We have also heard his shrewd estimates of political opponents, as when he judged Cassius: "He thinks too much; such men are dangerous" (I, ii, 195). Do we now see the dignity and nobility of the greatest man in the world? Or are his sentiments the arrogant musings of one who believes himself superior to the petty fears of other men?

Perhaps the darkest view of mortality is expressed by the title character of *Macbeth*. He speaks of the subject in two situations: in the first, he is feigning sorrow, while in the second, his emotions are genuine. Yet both statements reflect the same anguish.

The first occurs after the corpse of King Duncan has been discovered, stabbed by Macbeth, who tries to affect despair so as to avoid arousing suspicion:

> Had I but died an hour before this chance,
> I had liv'd a blessed time; for from this instant
> There's nothing serious in mortality;
> All is but toys: renown and grace is dead,

The wine of life is drawn, and the mere lees
Is left this vault to brag of.

(II, iii, 91–96)

Contrast these lines with the desolation inherent in his words upon hearing of the death of Lady Macbeth:

She should have died hereafter;
There would have been time for such a word.
To-morrow, and to-morrow, and to-morrow,
Creeps in this petty pace from day to day,
To the last syllable of recorded time;
And all our yesterdays have lighted fools
The way to dusty death. Out, out, brief candle!
Life's but a walking shadow, a poor player,
That struts and frets his hour upon the stage,
And then is heard no more. It is a tale
Told by an idiot, full of sound and fury,
Signifying nothing.

(V, v, 17–28)

The verse has the quality of a dirge, for the beats are heavier, suggesting more profound feeling. The first speech is too neat, as if it were the prepared recitation of one straining to appear melancholy. The second has a terrifying simplicity that reflects a mind beaten down by life and numbed by horrors he has seen and carried out. He no longer fears death; he may even welcome it.

Of all Shakespeare's characters, none is more preoccupied with thoughts of mortality than Hamlet, who throughout the play ponders implications of his death. The opening lines of his first soliloquy eloquently communicate his desire to escape life:

O that this too too sallied flesh would melt,
Thaw, and resolve itself into a dew!
Or that the Everlasting had not fix'd
His canon 'gainst [self-] slaughter!

(I, ii, 129–132)

So uncertain is his sense of self that death both attracts and repels him. Later, when the Ghost bids Hamlet follow him, the Prince dismisses his friend Horatio's fears:

I do not set my life at a pin's fee,
And for my soul, what can it do to that,
Being a thing immortal as itself?

(I, iii, 65–67)

Whatever terrors the Ghost holds for him are preferable to the uncertainty of Hamlet's life.

His fears, however, are apparent in the most famous soliloquy in dramatic literature: "To be, or not to be, that is the question" (III, i, 55). What follows is a meditation on the desire for death as relief from the burdens of life. Hamlet intuitively knows that he is not a killer or vehicle for revenge; thus he will never carry out the Ghost's commands. At the same time, he dreads an afterlife, for he cannot conceive carrying his responsibility through eternity.

Perhaps the most poignant reflections on mortality occur in the graveyard, where Hamlet broods upon the skull of Yorick, the King's jester:

> Where be your gibes now, your gambols,
> your songs, your flashes of merriment, that were
> wont to set the table on a roar?
>
> (V, i, 189–191)

Such recognition of the transience of things leads Hamlet directly to meditate on the life of another Prince, Alexander, who conquered the world, then had nowhere to turn:

> Alexander
> died, Alexander was buried, Alexander returneth
> to dust, the dust is earth, of earth we make loam,
> and why of that loam whereto he was converted might
> they not stop a beer-barrel?
>
> (V, i, 208–212)

That even the greatest military figure in the history of the world might be reduced to such standing suggests the unimportance of all human endeavour, a reduction Hamlet uses to comfort himself. Whatever he does, or fails to do, his life ultimately means nothing, and that awareness soothes his troubled conscience.

More than any other character in literature, Hamlet has been said to embody aspects of all of humanity. Little wonder, then, that his views of mortality should range so widely. In that sense, he encapsulates the reflections of the other characters that we have considered. Recognition of human mortality may bring perspective, comfort, relief, or sad recognition. Nonetheless, our knowledge of the brevity of human life, our understanding that our days are limited, both increases the urgency of human action and brings poignancy to our goals and dreams.

Nationalistic Pride and Prejudice

So ageless and overwhelming is Shakespeare's genius that we may forget that he was still very much a man of his place and time, and vulnerable to the same prejudices that were held by his countrymen. Thus Shakespeare often shows himself to be an Englishman of boundless pride, but also one with little tolerance for other cultures. The results are sometimes humorous and at other times disturbing, but always they make us aware that even so titanic an artist as Shakespeare may be susceptible to intense chauvinism.

Perhaps the nation for which Shakespeare has the least affection is France. The antagonism between the English and the French goes back at least as far as the Battle of Hastings in 1066, and Shakespeare seems to do all he can to perpetuate ill will between the two countries. In *Henry VI, Part 1*, for instance, the one heroic figure is the English general Talbot, whose courage in warfare distinguishes him from virtually everyone on the battlefield. As one messenger says:

> More than three hours the fight continued,
> Where valiant Talbot above human thought
> Enacted wonders with his sword and lance:
> Hundreds he sent to hell, and none durst stand him;
> Here, there and every where, enrag'd he slew.
> (I, i, 120–124)

Even his enemies are in awe of him:

> The French exclaim'd, the devil was in arms;
> All the whole army stood agaz'd on him.
> (I, i, 125–126)

245

The French, on the other hand, are portrayed as shallow cowards. Their Dauphin (or "Prince") Charles refers to "the forlorn French" (I, ii, 19), then mocks his own troops (I, ii, 22–24). The hollowness of the French, however, is most apparent in their treatment of the legendary Joan of Arc, here called "Joan of Pucelle." First Charles tries to disprove her claims of supernatural power by childishly hiding, but she recognizes him at once (I, ii, 66–67). Later, after she leads the French to triumph in battle, their victory is tainted, as Charles ruefully reflects:

> 'Tis Joan, not we, by whom the day is won;
> For which I will divide my crown with her.
> (I, vi, 17–18)

This attitude is contrasted with Talbot's continuing heroism. The implication is clear: the French are triumphant, yet small; the English defeated, yet heroic. We should also note Shakespeare's attitude toward Joan herself. She is traditionally characterized as a saint, but Shakespeare portrays her otherwise, as in Talbot's words:

> A witch by fear, not force, like Hannibal,
> Drives back our troops and conquers as she lists:
> So bees with smoke and doves with noisome stench
> Are from their hives and houses driven away.
> (I, v, 21–24)

Such dark qualities in the opposition partially excuse English failure; yet even Joan cannot contain contempt for her countrymen. When her one-time ally, the treacherous Burgundy, betrays her, she sneers: "Done like a Frenchman turn, and turn again" (III, iii, 85). The word "turn" implies sexual activity, but Pucelle is not praising Burgundy for his aggressive masculinity. Rather, she condemns him for being a political whore.

Shakespeare portrays the French even more coldly in *Henry V*, the play in which the greatest of all English Kings leads his outnumbered followers to the greatest of all English military triumphs, the battle of Agincourt. Still, Shakespeare underlies the conflict with a fascinating irony. From the opening scenes, Henry V clearly seeks to carry out war against France, but Shakespeare is careful not not to portray his country's hero as bloodthirsty. Instead, Henry solicits justification for the conflict from the Archbishop of Canterbury, whose obtuse explanation of Salic Law (which barred succession to a throne through a female line) earns this comic reiteration from the King: "May I with right and conscience make this claim?" (I, ii, 96). Eventually, Henry is assured that the war against France would have legitimate underpinnings, specifically the regaining of territories won by Henry's great-grandfather, Edward III (I, ii, 101–114).

Even after the commitment is made, Shakespeare makes the French especially deserving of attack by creating a fictional moment when the French insult Henry V, and the English in general, by presenting the King with a gift of tennis balls, equipment used in a sport then thought to be a frivolity in which English youth indulged excessively (I, ii, 250–257). Henry's cool response, framed around words that suggest images of tennis, implies that the rude gift has forced him to declare war (I, ii, 278–282). We, however, realize that he has planned the engagement all along. Thus while the conflict against France inspires the King's countrymen with patriotic fervor, we see the political craft behind his pose.

The contrast between the heroic English and the cowardly French is sharpened by the personal differences between Henry V and the Dauphin. The latter is characterized as a empty-headed braggart, distinguished primarily by his excessive devotion to his horse (III, vii, 11–18, 20–25). Even his own troops recognize his inadequacy, as the Constable comments about the Dauphin's reputed valor: "... never anybody saw it but his lackey" (III, vii, 110–112). Finally, the French foolishly mock the English King, assuming him to be the same wayward boy we knew as "Hal" in *Henry IV, Part 1*:

> What a wretched and peevish fellow is this
> King of England, to mope with his fat-brain'd follow-
> ers so far out of his knowledge!
> (III, vii, 132–134)

For Shakespeare's audience, such shortsighted remarks must have been exhilarating and contributive to the loyalty that surrounds Henry.

We should also note that before the climactic encounter, the French are portrayed as more conceited than usual. In the Constable's words: "Let us but blow on them,/ The vapor of our valor will o'erturn them" (IV, ii, 23–24). Thus when the victory at Agincourt takes place, it seems especially deserved. Shakespeare, though, is not content merely to present the facts. Historically, the badly outnumbered English troops suffered 400 deaths, while 10,000 French soldiers were killed, primarily because the English used lighter, more mobile armaments. Still, Shakespeare embellishes the truth by declaring that only twenty-five English died. Whenever the opportunity to belittle France presents itself, Shakespeare seems to seize it.

Elsewhere in his plays, Shakespeare mocks the French in another, less generous spirit, for he intimates regularly that venereal disease is a plague peculiar to that country. For instance, in *A Midsummer Night's Dream*, Peter Quince, the leader of the mechanicals (or laborers), comments derisively: "Some of your French crowns have no hair at all" (I, ii, 97), an allusion to the loss of hair suffered as a result of syphilis. The same pun may be found in *Measure for Measure* (I, ii, 52–54), a play that ostensibly dramatizes the squalid world of Vienna. Yet whenever sexual antics are at the fore, Shakespeare reminds us of his feelings against the French.

His feelings toward Italy and the natives of that country are scarcely warmer. The general portrait of them that emerges is one of hot-headed, immoral schemers who trust no one and who are themselves not to be trusted. In *Romeo and Juliet*, for instance, the city of Verona is subject to the feud that besets the two families. We never learn its cause, but throughout the work we are reminded that the hatred between the Capulets and the Montagues ravages the city. In the opening scene, after a fight has broken out, the Prince condemns all to punishment if further quarrelling disturbs the peace. He does not treat them respectfully, but rather scorns them as "beasts" (I, i, 83), and such distaste pervades Shakespeare's presentation of Italians in general.

Venice is dramatized with withering force in several plays. In *The Merchant of Venice*, the entire community overflows with hate and greed, a spirit reflected best by the merchant Antonio's ribald friend Gratiano, who offers a genial exterior, but who underneath demonstrates an undeniable ugliness. When we first meet him, he seems amusing:

> Let me play the fool,
> With mirth and laughter let old wrinkles come,
> And let my liver rather heat with wine
> Than my heart cool with mortifying groans.
> (I, i, 79–82)

In the courtroom, however, when Shylock, the Jewish moneylender, finds himself trapped by Portia, Bassanio's wife disguised as a lawyer, the onlooker Gratiano screams with sadistic glee:

> Beg that thou mayst leave to hang thyself,
> And yet thy wealth being forfeit to the state,
> Thou hast not left the value of a cord;
> Therefore thou must be hang'd at the state's charge.
> (IV, i, 364–367)

We observe similar behavior from other members of the community, such as Antonio's friends Salerio and Solanio, who jeer at Shylock (III, i) or from Shylock's servant, Launcelot Gobbo, who makes fun of his blind father (II, ii). Moreover, as mentioned in the chapter on "Money," the population of Venice is preoccupied with financial matters, and we find no one who values people in any other terms.

Shakespeare's Venice also has little tolerance for those who do not belong to its insulated society. The most obvious example is Shylock the Jew, who is ostrasized and subject to endless harassment. But others are equally scorned, even by a comparatively likeable figure such as Portia, who reveals her own dark side, first when she ruthlessly describes the parade of suitors who have come to win her hand (I, ii), then when she callously discusses the Prince of Morocco: "A gentle riddance. Draw the curtains, go. / Let all of his complexion choose me so" (II, vii, 78–79). She saves her cruelest gibes for Shylock in the courtroom (IV, i), after she tricks him into demanding the penalty of the pound of flesh.

The uglier aspects of Venice are also dramatized in *Othello*, in which the Moor is subtly, but clearly despised by certain elements. We should discount the bitterness of Othello's ensign, Iago, whose hatred of his general is matched by contempt for everyone else. But we cannot so easily dispatch the antagonism of Desdemona's father, Brabantio, who accuses Othello of bewitching his daughter: "Damn'd as thou art, thou has enchanted her" (I, ii, 63). Indeed, throughout the play we sense that although members of the Venetian aristocracy respect Othello's military exploits, they resent having to turn to a black man to lead their own forces against the Turks in Cyprus.

Perhaps Shakespeare's nastiest portrait of an Italian is Posthumus's acquaintance Jachimo in *Cymbeline*, in whom the playwright invests virtually every stereotypical defect that was in his day attributed to the Italian people. When Jachimo first sees Imogen, King Cymbeline's daughter, on whose infidelity he has wagered, he comments lewdly:

> All of her that is out of door most rich!
> If she be furnish'd with a mind so rare,
> She is alone th' Arabian bird, and I
> Have lost the wager.
> (I, vi, 15–18)

The bet itself, made with Imogen's husband, Posthumus, reflects Jachimo's capacity for ugly insinuation:

> I will lay you ten [thousand] ducats to your
> ring, that, commend me to the court where your lady
> is, with no more advantage than the opportunity of a
> second conference, and I will bring from thence that
> honor of hers which you imagine so reserv'd.
> (I, iv, 127–131)

Finally, the scheme he carries out reveals his capacity for machination. When he appears out of the trunk that earlier had been hauled into the sleeping Imogen's room, Jachimo contemplates the bracelet and the beauty of the sleeping woman from whom he steals it:

> I have enough;
> To th' trunk again, and shut the spring of it.
> Swift, swift, you dragons of the night, that dawning
> May bare the raven's eye! I lodge in fear;
> Though this a heavenly angel, hell is here.
>
> (II, ii, 46–50)

He seems to conduct a parody of a military invasion, a subtle parallel to the conflict between Rome and Britain surrounding this private action. His subterfuge and delight in evil make Jachimo the epitome of Shakespeare's anti-Italian feelings.

If Italians themselves are portrayed unattractively in Shakespeare's plays, the objects of their own prejudices are treated no more kindly. Throughout the works, Jews are mentioned in derogatory fashion, but the only complete Jewish creation is Shylock in *The Merchant of Venice*, in whom Shakespeare invests many characteristics that smack of anti-Semitism. Given that Jews were expelled from England centuries before Shakespeare's day and that only a small enclave survived in London, Shakespeare almost certainly had limited contact with followers of that religion. Nevertheless, his portrait of Shylock embodies a full range of prejudices. First, Shylock's overwhelming lust for money is apparent throughout the play. Shakespeare also makes Shylock unbearably didactic, as when he insists on instructing Antonio by recalling the labors of the Biblical Jacob (I, iii, 70–90). Shakespeare also emphasizes the character's antisocial bitterness, almost justifying Venice's dislike of him (II, v, 28–40). But most telling of all is Shylock's viciousness. He relishes his place as an outsider, as when he speaks of Antonio, who has long been his enemy, but who now seeks to borrow money:

> He hates our sacred nation, and he rails
> Even there where merchants most do congregate
> On me, my bargains, and my well-won thrift,
> Which he calls interest. Cursed be my tribe
> If I forgive him!
>
> (I, iii, 48–52)

To be sure, Shakespeare invests Shylock with pride, most notably in a speech which has become a famous statement against prejudice:

Hath not a Jew eyes? Hath not a Jew hands, organs,
dimensions, senses, affections, passions; fed with
the same food, hurt with the same weapons, subject
to the same diseases, heal'd by the same means,
warm'd and cool'd by the same winter and summer,
as a Christian is?

(III, i, 59–64)

The address, however, ends with this fearsome warning:

The villainy you teach
me, I will execute, and it shall go hard but I will
better the instruction.

(III, i, 71–73)

Thus Shylock, whatever sympathy he may garner as a victim of hatred, retains the capacity for ferocity. This characteristic manifests itself most notoriously in the stipulation that if Antonio cannot repay the loan, he must lose a pound of flesh. The threat confirms every bloodthirsty sterotype of Jews that permeated Shakespeare's day. Moreover, in court Shylock is terrifying in his insistence that this punishment be carried out, despite the offer to have the debt paid by others many times over (IV, i, 85–87). Perhaps Shakespeare sought to demonstrate how a victim of hatred becomes perverted under the weight of intolerance, but no doubt the playwright intended primarily to create a villain whom his audience would enjoy seeing destroyed.

Shakespeare is kinder to the Moors he creates, specifically Othello. For audiences of Shakespeare's day, the title "Moor" would have suggested a generic, dark-skinned African, and the playwright allows these figures a certain dignity. In *Titus Andronicus*, for instance, Aaron the Moor is the smartest character onstage, but beneath his wit exists a genuine lust for destruction. We see this quality when he leads Queen Tamora's sons, Demetrius and Charon, to take vengeance on Titus's daughter, Lavinia (II, i, 105–131), or when he chops off Titus's hand (III, i, 191). But *Titus Andronicus* is a play about human savagery, and amid this ruthless company Aaron seems at home. In the civilized world of Venice, however, Othello is isolated by his race, and we are perpetually conscious of his status as an alien. Othello speaks majestically, but the arc of the play follows the breakdown of his mind, as he blindly accepts Iago's misleading remarks about Othello's wife, Desdemona, and his lieutenant, Cassio, and becomes consumed with jealousy. The comparative ease with which Othello is manipulated by "honest Iago," particularly in Act III, scene iii, as well as the level of brutality to which Othello sinks in Acts

IV and V, suggests that Shakespeare envisioned the Moor with a formidable exterior, but prey to bestial forces latent within him.

For all the antagonism that Shakespeare has for cultures different from his own, he displays profound loyalty to Britain, and his plays are filled with such devotion. One example may be found in *Henry V*, when the King, rallying his troops before the Battle of Agincourt, recalls a roster of legendary heroes:

> Then shall our names,
> Familiar in his mouth as household words,
> Harry the King, Bedford, and Exeter,
> Warwick and Talbot, Salisbury and Gloucester
> Be in their flowing cups freshly rememb'red.
> (IV, iii, 51–55)

How could any audience members not feel the grandeur of such a litany? Furthermore, here again Henry V, ever the politician, seduces his listeners, both onstage and off, into trusting the sanctity of his cause. In the same play, we see how Fluellen (a Welshman), Gower (an Englishman), Macmorris (an Irishman), and Jamy (a Scotsman), all traditional enemies, join forces under Henry's inspired leadership. Thus Shakespeare glorifies loyalty to England as conquering all divisions between the various peoples of the British Isles.

In *King John*, the figure who embodies this spirit is, oddly enough, Philip, the illegitimate son of Richard the Lionhearted. When the weak-spirited King John falters in anticipation of the war against France, it is Philip, called "the Bastard" by Shakespeare, who unites the forces of England, rallying the troops around the grandeur of the English throne (V, ii, 127–158). Indeed, it is the Bastard who, after John's death, states in the final words of the play:

> This England never did, nor never shall,
> Lie at the proud foot of a conqueror,
> But when it first did help to wound itself,
> Now these her princes are come home again,
> Come the three corners of the world in arms,
> And we shall shock them. Nought shall make us rue,
> If England to itself do rest but true.
> (V, vii, 112–118)

The Bastard never takes the throne, but his patriotic tone rallies the spirit of a nation trying to resolve the uncertainty of a kingship in question. This play was written in approximately 1595, nearly forty years after Elizabeth I took the throne. As her reign neared its end, which would occur with her death in 1603, Shakespeare's audience feared that because the Queen was childless, the matter of succession might lead to chaos. We can therefore imagine how Shakespeare's audience took comfort from the Bastard's words that promise stability if the people of the country would only believe in themselves.

His plays also dramatize the consequences when discord threatens that English unity. In *Henry VI, Part 1*, while the country is at war with France, a messenger calls out to those competing for control of the English throne:

> Amongst the soldiers this is muttered,
> That here you maintain several factions;
> And whilst a field should be dispatch'd and fought,
> You are disputing of your generals . . .
> Awake, awake, English nobility!
> Let not sloth dim your honors new begot.
>
> (I, i, 70–79)

This counsel is ignored, however, and the cost is defeat, as Sir William Lucy, one of the lords, later laments:

> Thus while the vulture of sedition
> Feeds in the bosom of such great commanders,
> Sleeping neglection doth betray to loss
> The conquest of our scarce-cold conqueror,
> That ever-living man of memory,
> Henry the Fift. Whiles they each other cross,
> Lives, honor, lands, and all, hurry to loss.
>
> (IV, iii, 47–53)

The lesson is clear: factionalism at home has resulted in defeat abroad, undoing the triumphs of the late Henry V. Even his son, Henry VI, too weak to fight for himself, sees the crisis:

> O, what a scandal is it to our crown
> That two such noble peers as ye should jar!
> Believe me, lords, my tender years can tell,
> Civil dissension is a viperous worm
> That gnaws the bowels of the commonwealth.
>
> (III, i, 69–74)

Henry's pleas are ignored, though, and further defeat follows.

The most memorable expression of Shakespeare's patriotic fervor comes in *Richard II* from the dying John of Gaunt:

This royal throne of kings, this sceptred isle,
This earth of majesty, this seat of Mars,
This other Eden, demi-paradise,
This fortress built by Nature for herself
Against infection and the hand of war,
This happy breed of men, this little world,
This precious stone set in the silver sea,
Which serves it in the office of a wall,
Or as [a] moat defensive to a house,
Against the envy of less happier lands,
This blessed plot, this earth, this realm, this England . . .
(II, i, 40–50)

At this moment in history, as Shakespeare's audience knows, disorder will be unleashed by the rash behavior of Richard II and the usurpation of the throne by his cousin Bullingbrook, later Henry IV. Those events will lead to the internal quarrel among the country's noble families for possession of the throne, a sequence of bloody squirmishes in the middle decades of the fifteenth century that has come to be known as The War of the Roses. Gaunt's tribute, however, built around images from the Bible which imply that the nation is sovereign under God, affirms that whatever crises England faces, it will survive.

Thus Shakespeare's nationalistic fervor has two aspects. On the one hand, he is unashamedly antagonistic to other countries and cultures, and hardly ever do we read a kind word about them. On the other hand, he is boldly patriotic, and his praises to his country may be appreciated as meant to inspire not only the figures onstage, but also those in his audience, who vicariously experience the triumphs of their country's glorious past.

Nature

In Shakespeare's time, as well as in our own, "nature" has several implications. We may invoke the phrase "human nature" when we speak of the physical and psychological properties that belong to our species, as opposed to those of the lower orders of animals. We may speak of one man or one woman's "nature," and mean qualities that mark that individual's character. Or we may speak generally of "nature" itself to suggest the environment that surrounds humanity: the animals, plants, and inanimate objects that comprise the world in which we function.

This chapter will focus on the last of these meanings. For Shakespeare, "nature" is not a passive entity, lying in repose as human beings struggle through their daily lives; rather, it responds to our actions, and in some ways even influences them.

For instance, Shakespeare often dramatizes nature as a pastoral haven. In the final act of *The Merchant of Venice*, Lorenzo entices his wife, Jessica (daughter of Shylock, the Jewish moneylender), to escape into the magic of the night.

> How sweet the moonlight sleeps upon this bank!
> Here will we sit, and let the sounds of music
> Creep in our ears. Soft stillness and the night
> Become the touches of sweet harmony.
> (V, i, 54–57)

Here nature is a refuge from the realities of life. The same theme is reiterated in *As You Like It*, when the Duke, leader of a band that has sought refuge in the Forest of Arden, reflects on his home:

> Sweet are the uses of adversity,
> Which like the toad, ugly and venomous,
> Wears yet a precious jewel in his head;

And this our life, exempt from public haunt,
Finds tongues in trees, books in the running brooks,
Sermons in stones, and good in every thing.
                                        (II, i, 12–17)

One of the most alluring qualities of this pastoral life Shakespeare portrays is innocence, the subject when Touchstone, servant to Rosalind, daughter of the banished Duke, berates the befuddled farmer, Corin, about the differences between life in court and life in the country:

    Why, if thou never wast at court, thou
never saw'st good manners; if thou never saw'st
good manners, then thy manners must be wicked,
and wickedness is sin, and sin is damnation. Thou
art in a parlous sin, shepherd.
                                        (III, ii, 40–44)

Later, Touchstone demonstrates the same ill manners which he claims Corin possesses. That simple agrarian, however, matches his antagonist line for line:

              You told me you salute
not at the court, but you kiss your hands; that
courtesy would be uncleanly if courtiers were
shepherds.
                                        (III, ii, 48–50)

In his quiet way, Corin holds his own in the eternal conflict between the satisfactions of urban life versus those of a rural existence.

Yet simple dignity is not the only quality Shakespeare invests in the pastoral. In *The Winter's Tale*, the tranquility of the shepherd's world is marred by the presence of the thief Autolycus:

The lark, that tirra-lyra chants,
    With heigh, [with heigh,] the thrush and the jay!
Are summer songs for me and my aunts,
    While we lie tumbling in the hay.
                                        (IV, iii, 8–12)

That "aunts" is a euphemism for "whores" takes away some of the ditty's innocence. Yet whatever mischief he carries out, such as robbing the Clown who is about to enter with a lengthy grocery list, Autolycus remains a likeable rogue.

This setting takes on more serious implications, however, when the lost Princess Perdita offers flowers to a group of newcomers, including

Camillo, who is her father Leontes' exiled advisor, and the royal Polixenes, King of Bohemia, temporarily in disguise:

> Reverend sirs,
> For you there's rosemary and rue; these keep
> Seeming and savor all the winter long.
>   (IV, iv, 73–75)

The flowers she chooses, of which Polixenes approves because they are
appropriate to his age, invite a discussion on the quality of flowers from
nature versus those created by artifical crossbreeding. This subject, a version of the long-standing Renaissance debate on the value of the "natural" versus the "artificial," brings out Perdita's personality. A child of
nature, she argues for the purity of nature's flowers (IV, iv, 86–88), while
Polixenes suggests that the influence of humanity can improve nature's
art:

> This is an art
> Which does not need Nature—change it rather; but
> The art itself is Nature.
>   (IV, iv, 95–97)

The characters do not reach a conclusion. But Perdita's gifts to her love,
Florizel, who at the moment refers to himself as "Doricles," invoke a
series of images of fertility and growth (IV, iv, 112–129). Perdita, too,
may be understood as a product of nature: untamed, passionate, yet
pure.

In Shakespeare's comedies and romances, nature generally plays this
same role: as escape from the pressures of court and urban life. In the
tragedies, however, it takes on much greater stature. Shakespeare's audience believed in the reciprocal relationship between the microcosm,
our day-to-day world, and the macrocosm, the universe of stars and
planets surrounding us. According to this system of thought, the activities of the microcosm carried repercussions into the macrocosm, and
instances of this correlation abound in Shakespeare's tragic plays.

In *Julius Caesar*, for instance, after Brutus and Cassius have conducted
preliminary discussions about Caesar's apparent desire to gain control
of Rome, and after the plot has begun to form to assassinate Caesar,
Cinna and Casca, both potential conspirators, meet on a street in Rome,
amid thunder and lightning. Casca offers this explanation:

> Either there is a civil strife in heaven,
> Or else the world, too saucy with the gods,
> Incenses them to send destruction.
>   (I, iii, 11–13)

He later adds:

> Besides—I ha' not since put up my sword—
> Against the Capitol I met a lion,
> Who glaz'd upon me, and went surly by,
> Without annoying me . . .
> And yesterday the bird of night did sit
> Even at noon-day upon the market-place,
> Howling and shrieking. When these prodigies
> Do so conjointly meet, let not men say,
> "These are their reasons, they are natural":
> For I believe they are portentous things
> Unto the climate that they point upon.
>   (I, iii, 20–32)

For Shakespeare's audience, such events confirmed that the conspiracy against Caesar was intrinsically evil, for it had aroused the natural phenomena of the macrocosm to act unnaturally.

We see a different kind of unnatural event in *Hamlet*. The Ghost of Hamlet's father appears before the men on watch, including Horatio, Marcellus, and Barnardo. But when the Ghost hurries off, Marcellus comments:

> It faded on the crowing of the cock.
> Some say that ever 'gainst that season comes
> Wherein our Savior's birth is celebrated,
> This bird of dawning singeth all night long,
> And then they say no spirit dare stir abroad,
> The nights are wholesome, then no planets strike,
> No fairy takes, nor witch hath power to charm,
> So hallowed, and so gracious, is that time.
>   (I, i, 157–164)

The implication is clear: the actions of the natural world, here embodied in the crowing of the cock, inspire a direct response from the universe surrounding it. The sudden departure of the Ghost at a natural sound thus suggests the being's evil intention.

Some of the most graphic portraits of nature reacting to misdeeds in the microcosm take place in *Macbeth*. Indeed, from the witches' opening lines, the entire play seems consumed by rain, fog, and darkness, suggesting the moral horrors about to be perpetrated:

> Fair is foul, and foul is fair,
> Hover through the fog and filthy air.
>   (I, i, 11–12)

Immediately after Macbeth murders King Duncan, Macbeth whispers in horror to Lady Macbeth: "I have heard the owl scream and the crickets cry" (II, ii, 15). One scene later, the lord Lennox describes the unnatural consequences of the death of the King:

> The night has been unruly. Where we lay,
> Our chimneys were blown down, and (as they say)
> Lamentings heard i' th' air; strange screams of death,
> And prophesying, with accents terrible,
> Of dire combustion and confus'd events
> New hatch'd to th' woeful time. The obscure bird
> Clamor'd the livelong night. Some say the earth
> Was feverous and did shake.
> (II, iii, 54–61)

In the next scene, the catalogue of unnaturalness proceeds almost without control. As Lennox explains:

> Ha, good father,
> Thou seest the heavens, as troubled with man's act,
> Threatens his bloody stage. By th' clock 'tis day,
> And yet dark night strangles the travelling lamp.
> Is't night's predominance, or the day's shame,
> That darkness does the face of earth entomb,
> Where living light should kiss it?
> (II, iv, 4–10)

Here is as clear a statement as may be found in this play (indeed, in all of Shakespeare's plays) that the acts of humankind resound through the heavens. After the Doctor witnesses a stunned Lady Macbeth sleepwalking, he affirms this principle:

> Foul whisp'rings are abroad. Unnatural deeds
> Do breed unnatural troubles; infected minds
> To the deaf pillows will discharge their secrets.
> (V, ii, 71–73)

Even the ominous signs that indicate the final downfall of Macbeth, as predicted by the witches, smack of unnaturalness. First the messenger reports:

> As I did stand my watch upon the hill,
> I look'd toward Birnan, and anon methought
> The wood began to move.
> (V, v, 32–34)

Thus the unlawful and unnatural murder of King Duncan arouses the universe.

Perhaps no play of Shakespeare's is as involved with discussion and images of nature as *King Lear*. One of the earliest references occurs after the King has expelled his youngest daughter, Cordelia, for refusing to comply with his demand for a public expression of love for him. Even though his loyal servant, Kent, has urgently defended her, Lear refuses to bend:

> That thou has sought to make us break our [vow]—
> Which we durst never yet—and with strain'd pride
> To come betwixt our sentence and our power,
> Which nor our nature nor our place can bear . . .
>
> (I, i, 168–171)

Lear is speaking partially of his kingly "nature," but because he believes that the king is the link between the human and the divine, his words also carry the connotation of a more general "nature" of the world. Later, the Duke of France, one of two suitors for Cordelia, comments in wonder at her dismissal:

> Sure her offense
> Must be of such unnatural degree
> That monsters it, or your fore-vouch'd affection
> Fall into taint . . .
>
> (I, i, 218–221)

Here "unnatural" suggests "opposing nature," or opposing the natural scheme of things. France's implication is that "nature" is a benign entity, and that some "unnatural" act has created turmoil by violating this goodness. We recognize that Lear has committed the act.

The next significant mention of "Nature" is offered by Edmund, illegitimate son of Gloucester:

> Thou, Nature, are my goddess, to thy law
> My services are bound.
>
> (I, ii, 1–2)

Edmund here refers not to the benign order to which France referred, but to a brutish element in existence that can possess human beings and propel them into a drive for survival and power. In his terms, might makes right, and Edmund rationalizes that whatever he can achieve, at whatever cost, is justified by his triumph. Thus, in this play, two visions of nature clash: we watch goodness (embodied by Lear's youngest daughter, Cordelia; his servant Kent; Gloucester's older son, Edgar;

Lear's Fool; and Goneril's husband, Albany) battle ruthlessness (manifested in Lear's older daughters, Goneril and Regan; Gloucester's bastard son, Edmund; Regan's husband, Cornwall; and the sisters' servant, Oswald), with the world as the prize. Eventually good and light do triumph, or at least they emerge at the end. The price, however, leaves us to question whether we can judge the result to be a victory.

After Lear is expelled from Goneril's home, he journeys to the residence of his second daughter, Regan, but she treats him with similar heartlessness, for she demands that he surrender all his followers. In retaliation, Lear can only rage helplessly:

> No, you unnatural hags,
> I will have such revenges on you both
> That all the world shall—I will do such things—
> What they are yet I know not, but they shall be
> The terrors of the earth!
>
> (II, iv, 278–282)

Moments later, a colossal storm begins, reflecting in the macrocosm the unnaturalness of Lear's mind and the unnatural stage of the kingdom, with two daughters and their husbands in control, and war soon to begin. Later, with his world collapsing about him and the storm still blowing, Lear ponders:

> Then let them anatomize Regan; see what
> breeds about her heart. Is there any cause in nature
> that makes these hard hearts?
>
> (III, vi, 76–78)

He questions the core of his faith. How can nature, in whose benign qualities he has always believed, create monstrous children who commit such evil against their father?

That mystery is never solved, in this play or any other. Still, despite such insolubility, Shakespeare's contemporaries maintained belief in the relationship between human action and the nature around it. Perhaps we should now see such conviction as affirmation of faith in the meaning of both human existence and our struggles to act purposefully while living in the shadow of the vast space that surrounds us.

Order

The culture of Shakespeare's England reflected the long-standing medieval vision that the universe was created by God to be a perfect unity, within which every aspect of creation had its place. This "great chain of being," as it later came to be called, encompassed all of existence, from inanimate objects to the angels, and placed each in what were judged to be natural places of subordination. Within this order was a series of correspondences. As God was the highest among the angels, so the sun was the highest of the stars, fire the highest of the elements, the king the highest of human beings, the lion the highest of beasts, and the eagle the highest of birds. Furthermore, order within the political and social realm corresponded to that within the human body. Just as the surrounding world, the macrocosm, was said to be composed of four elements (fire, air, water, and earth), so human nature contained four parallel humors (choler, blood, phlegm, and melancholy). Any imbalance of these forces within an individual could lead to disorder that extended into the political and social realms, then into the universe itself.

During Shakespeare's lifetime, however, this medieval vision was challenged by the forces of the Renaissance and the Reformation, both of which inspired dispute about religious, political, social, and intellectual rights and freedoms. Each movement in its own way shifted responsibility away from institutions and more to the individual. In addition, the growing awareness of new lands and societies, especially throughout the Americas, caused European civilization to reflect upon the very nature of the human species, as well as on fundamental questions of morality and theology. All this turmoil was reflected in the central subject of Elizabethan literature: the struggle for order between individual lives and the social structure.

Shakespeare's plays dramatize this tension between old and new visions, between the world as a closed, structured system, and the capacity and responsibility of individuals to find their own way. Thus the plays

263

celebrate individuality, but they also reflect a contradictory belief that the exertion of individual will creates conflict.

The relationship of such conflict to drama is essential, for when theatrical characters exert their individual will, whether in the malevolent desire for power or wealth, or in the benign desire for love, the consequences include disorder, within both the characters themselves and the surrounding social structure. Such imbalance is the mainspring of Shakespeare's plots. Equally important, Shakespeare's audience wanted to see the resolution of that conflict manifested in the reestablishment of personal and social order.

In the comedies and certain romances, such imbalance tends to be localized. For example, in one of Shakspeare's earliest plays, *The Comedy of Errors*, the source of disorder is clarified from the opening lines, as the wandering Egeon requests that the Duke of Ephesus impose punishment on him:

> Proceeed, Solinus, to procure my fall,
> And by the doom of death end woes and all.
> (I, i, 1–2)

The Duke's response is equally somber, ending with the threat of death against Egeon for illegally visiting Ephesus without 1,000 marks for ransom. In return, Egeon narrates how his wife in Syracuse gave birth to twins, as did one of his serving women. On a sea voyage, a storm left the family alone on the ship, which itself split apart. Egeon was left with one son and a servant, and his wife with the other two boys. When the son whom Egeon raised turned eighteen, he set out in search of his brother, and Egeon has followed that quest.

All this information, dispensed in unwieldly fashion, sets up the fundamental disorder that besets Egeon's family. Thus we anticipate that by the end of the play, all will be resolved, and such is the case. Until then, confusion over the twin sons and servants abounds, but eventually the Abbess of Ephesus reunites everyone. We are also surprised to learn that she is Egeon's long-lost wife, Amelia (V, i, 345–346), one of only two instances in his plays when Shakespeare withholds information in this way (the other occurs in *The Winter's Tale*).

This fundamental movement from emotional disorder to order is characteristic of all of Shakespeare's comedies. In *Love's Labor's Lost*, the unbalancing exertion of will is the King's decree that his court will become a sanctuary for scholars to remain in isolation. By the end of the play, the men who have subscribed to this foolish scheme all end up in love. In *A Midsummer Night's Dream*, the initial source of disorder is the demand by Egeus that his daughter, Hermia, marry the young man whom Egeus has chosen for her, Demetrius, rather than the one she prefers,

Lysander. Eventually Lysander and Hermia are married, alongside Demetrius and the woman who loves him, Helena. In addition, such movement in the human world is paralleled by similar action in the world of the fairies, as Oberon and Titania, King and Queen of the fairies, initially quarrel over possession of the changeling boy, then reconcile. This coupling is also set against the royal marriage between Duke Theseus and Queen Hipployta. Thus at all levels of the story, we are conscious of marriage as a source of social harmony.

Sometimes Shakespeare's desperation to end a comedy with the restoration of order is almost palpable. In the final scene of *Measure for Measure*, the Duke unmasks himself from the monk's cowl under which he has moved undetected through Vienna, observing everyone's actions and words. In a burst of manipulation and decree, he wraps up all strands of the plot. Lucio, the sharp-witted "fantastic" who has unknowingly insulted the Duke, is condemned to marriage, then whipping and hanging. Claudio, earlier ordered to death for having impregnated Juliet outside marriage, is revealed to be alive and permitted to marry her. Mariana, once betrothed to Angelo, is allowed to marry him, even though the hypocritical Deputy stays so dislikeable that we wonder why Mariana remains devoted to him. Finally, after thanking his advisor, Escalus, and the prison Provost for their steadfast support, the Duke shocks everyone by proposing marriage to Claudio's sister, Isabella. True, he has rescued her, but she has already sought to enter a particularly strict religious order. Before she is permitted a reply, though, the play ends. We may not find all these unions dramatically persuasive, but we understand the underlying theme: social, political, and religious balance have been restored to the city.

One of Shakespeare's most famous statements about order occurs in *Troilus and Cressida*, when the Greek leader Ulysses, seeking to rally the Greek forces, speaks of the need for unity:

> The heavens themselves, the planets, and this centre
> Observe degree, priority, and place,
> Insisture, course, proportion, season, form,
> Office, and custom, in all line of order . . .
>   (I, iii, 85–88)

Because this play treats all matters ironically, from the great Trojan War to the sexual proclivities of the participants, Ulysses' speech must be regarded with suspicion. Indeed, he soon demonstrates an ulterior motive, when he speculates on what happens when order breaks down:

> Then every thing include itself in power,
> Power into will, will into appetite,

> And appetite, an universal wolf
> (So doubly seconded with will and power),
> Must make perforce an universal prey,
> And last eat up himself.
>
> (I, iii, 119–124)

According to Ulysses, the only way to avoid anarchy is mass fidelity to unquestioned authority, which must be accepted simply because it is authority. His oration exposes his lust for absolute power, and thus through Ulysses Shakespeare suggests how any call for conformity must be taken with skepticism.

Consider, then, the Archbishop of Canterbury's oration in *Henry V*, offered after the King has demanded theological justification for going to war against France:

> Therefore doth heaven divide
> The state of man in divers functions,
> Setting endeavor in continual motion;
> To which is fixed, as an aim or butt,
> Obedience; for so work the honey-bees,
> Creatures that by a rule in nature teach
> The act of order in a peopled kingdom.
>
> (I, ii, 183–189)

The logic here is dubious. Just because bees operate in strict order does not necessarily mean that human beings should do so. Moreover, our awareness that Canterbury has explained how a war with France would bring profit to his church makes us question his motives from the start. We also know that he seeks to curry the King's favor, and a public call for universal support of Henry's decision, with everyone obeying without question, fulfills that purpose. Altogether, then, Canterbury's statement should also be regarded skeptically.

Yet the need for order is always paramount throughout Shakespeare's works, including his final group of plays, the romances. In every example of this genre, a royal family is divided and children are lost, then reconciled after substantial time and travel. *Cymbeline* may be taken as representative. In the opening scene, two nameless gentlemen comment how Imogen, the daughter of King Cymbeline of Britain by a former wife, has disobeyed her father by marrying his foster son, Posthumus, rather than her stepbrother, Cloten, son of the manipulative new Queen. We also learn of Cymbeline's other two sons by that first wife (I, i, 56–65), who were lost twenty years ago. Thus from the start, we anticipate the reuniting of this royal family.

Such familial disorder is set against political turmoil, on both the personal and national levels. First, we have the schemer Jachimo's unseemly bet with Posthumus about his wife Imogen's fidelity, and Posthumus's even more unseemly willingness to accept the wager. When Jachimo apparently provides incontrovertible evidence of Imogen's unfaithfulness, i.e., the bracelet he stole while she was sleeping, Posthumus's fury (II, v, 19–35) should be understood not only as the expression of a proud, yet foolish man turned against the woman he loves, but also as the conquering of an Englishman by an Italian invader. In the midst of this story line, Posthumus joins with his friend, Philario, to consider the quarrel between Rome and Britain, and the issue of whether Cymbeline will pay tribute to the Roman Emperor. That crisis is temporarlly resolved, when the king's son, Cloten, in his one heroic moment, dismisses the Roman general Lucius's order for tribute:

> Britain's a world
> By itself, and we will nothing pay
> For wearing our own noses.
> (III, i, 12–14)

The allegorical implication is the importance of a united Britain against Rome, an image in contrast with the family split over the marriage of Imogen and the treachery and conflict that have ensued.

The plot of *Cymbeline* becomes bewilderingly complicated, but of concern here is how order is restored on a multitude of planes. Imogen suffers through exile in the forest but eventually returns to her husband, Posthumus, who berates himself over his susceptibility to Jachimo's scheme (V, v, 217–220). Thereafter Imogen and Cymbeline meet again (V, v, 260–273), and father and daughter exchange forgiveness. Finally, faced with his son's execution over the death of Cloten, the country lord Morgan reveals that he is the long-lost Belarius, and that the two young men he has raised as his own, Polydore and Cadwal, are indeed Guiderius and Aviragus, Cymbeline's sons and Imogen's brothers. Thus the instinctive solicitude they felt for her in the forest is understandable. Even Jachimo is so moved that he begs forgiveness, and Posthumus pardons him (V, v, 412–420). On the national level, Cymbeline agrees to pay tribute to Caesar, and the two empires of Rome and Britain are united. This alliance should not be viewed as Britain's capitulation, for in the play Britain triumphs militarily, but as a foundation of the English culture that started before Christianity, and which endured throughout Shakespeare's day. The order of the royal family and the state itself are thereby reaffirmed.

In the comedies and romances, the imbalance in character that breaks the order of things generally emerges from a desire for love. In the history plays, however, that force is a desire for power. Indeed, Shakespeare's two tetralogies based on English history from 1398 to 1485 may be said to be one long progression from disorder to order: from the removal of Richard II from the throne by Bullingbrook, one day to be Henry IV, to the destruction of Richard III and the unity of the two houses of Lancaster and York in the person of King Henry VII. Each individual play, however, also ends with a temporary restoration of order within the ensuing chaos.

For example, *Richard II* begins with mutual charges of treachery by Bullingbrook, the King's cousin, and Mowbray, the King's most trusted associate. Richard temporarily escapes the crisis by exiling both men, but after the death of John of Gaunt, the King's uncle and Bullingbrook's father, the King's greed and political miscalculation lead him to confiscate Bullingbrook's inherited lands and funds. This shattering of precedent provides Bullingbrook with the legal and political cover to break the command of exile and rally forces against the King. In the midst of the usurpation, one scene encapsulates many of the themes of the story, when the Gardener reflects on Richard's plight:

> He that hath suffered this disordered spring
> Hath now himself met with the fall of leaf.
>
> (III, iv, 48–49)

Not long after, the Bishop of Carlisle, the voice of orthodox religion in the play, berates those who would show loyalty to the newly crowned Bullingbrook:

> Disorder, horror, fear, and mutiny
> Shall here inhabit, and this land be call'd
> The field of Golgotha and dead men's skulls.
>
> (IV, i, 142–144)

Both the Gardener and Carlisle understand that chaos must be resolved.

Richard, though, seems to understand his situation best, and in a final soliloquy in prison, accepts the damage he has inflicted on himself and his kingdom:

> How sour sweet music is
> When time is broke, and no proportion kept!
> So is it in the music of men's lives.
> And here have I the daintiness of ear
> To check time broke in a disordered string;
> But for the concord of my state and time
> Had not an ear to hear my true time broke.
> I wasted time, and now doth time waste me . . .
>
> (V, v, 42–49)

In considering the unbalanced world he has created, Richard invokes two images that pervade Shakespeare's plays: time and music, both of which imply aspects of "order." Time reflects the progression of life, and the shattering of time is often said to manifest disruption of social procedure. In turn, the restoration of time implies the renewed balance of that procedure, as in one of the final lines of *Macbeth*, when Malcolm takes the throne: "We will perform in measure, time, and grace" (V, ix, 39). Music played in tune, on the other hand, has overtones of harmony, while music out of tune implies discord. For example, in *Othello*, the ensign Iago relishes his plots by commenting: "But I'll set down the pegs that make this music,/ As honest as I am" (II, i, 200–201).

Richard II ends with the new King Henry's vow to seek expiation for the tumult that grips his kingdom:

> Lords, I protest my soul is full of woe
> That blood should sprinkle me to make me grow.
> Come mourn with me for what I do lament,
> And put on sullen black incontinent.
> I'll make a voyage to the Holy Land,
> To wash this blood off from my guilty hand.
> March sadly after, grace my mournings here,
> In weeping after this untimely bier.
> (V, vi, 45–52)

The King recognizes what we do: the paradoxical consequences of his actions. On one hand, the removal of Richard II was necessary for the nation's political health; indeed, it began the modern political era in England. At the same time, removing a king, whose position, after all, was religiously ordained, was an act against God. Thus punishment, for both Henry personally and the country he governs, is inevitable.

We see such punishment in the form of disorder throughout the rest of the second Henriad, which details the reigns of Henry IV (1400–1413) and Henry V (1413–1422), and in the earlier Henriad, which dramatizes the later period (1422–1485), but which Shakespeare actually wrote first. In each play, rebels plot against the occupant of the throne, and the ruling powers temporarily subdue the insurrection at considerable loss of life. Yet as control of the throne moves back and forth from the Lancasters to the Yorks, many characters are conscious of how order must return. For instance, in *Henry VI, Part 3*, when the Yorkist Edward IV loses the crown to the Lancasters, the deposed King comments:

> Though Fortune's malice overthrow my state,
> My mind exceeds the compass of her wheel.
> (IV, iii, 46–47)

For the first time, Edward speaks of the larger scheme of life, that his fate is not the only issue. Moreover, the image of the wheel coming around suggests the inevitable reestablishment of order. The nightmarish decades climax with succession of murders carried out by Richard of York, first as the Duke of Gloucester, then as Richard III. After his death, the Earl of Richmond, soon to be King Henry VII, comments in the final speech of Richard III:

> All this divided York and Lancaster,
> Divided in their dire division,
> O now let Richmond and Elizabeth,
> The true succeeders of each royal house,
> By God's fair ordinance conjoin together.
>   (V, v, 27–31)

The long-awaited reordering of the kingship and the kingdom has been achieved.

The movement from disorder to order also underlies Shakespeare's tragedies; in each, we are conscious of how quickly chaos can spread through the political and social framework. In his first tragedy, *Titus Andronicus*, the opening lines reveal that the two sons of the late Emperor, Saturninus (the elder) and Bassianus, compete for the Roman throne. The misguided intervention of the eminent general Titus Andronicus on behalf of Saturninus is an attempt to restore order, but Titus unwittingly causes further disorder by sacrificing the son of Tamora, Queen of the defeated Goths. This brutality ensures more of the same, and the subsequent alliance between Tamora and Saturninus, who becomes infatuated with her, ensures that anarchy will grab hold of Rome. What follows is a grotesque pageant of murder, torture, and mutilation singular in Shakespeare, perhaps epitomized most graphically in the person of Lavinia, who is raped by Tamora's sons, then left with her hands cut off and her tongue removed (II, iv). At the end of the play, in a thematic purging, virtually all the principal characters are killed except Titus's son, Lucius, who assumes the throne of Rome, and restores order.

The theme of disorder appears more subtly in *Othello*, when Iago confides in his dupe, Roderigo, about Iago's seeming devotion to Othello:

> I follow him to serve my turn upon him.
> We cannot all be masters, nor all masters
> Cannot be truly followed.
>   (I, i, 42–44)

A few lines later, Iago adds:

> Were I the Moor, I would not be Iago.
> In following him, I follow but myself . . .
>
> (I, i, 57–58)

Iago sees himself as an enemy to the social contract, and Shakespeare's audience would have understood that the chaos Iago inspires is the inevitable outcome of his opposition to order in every form.

At the same time, devoted service is a hallmark of order. In *Timon of Athens*, the servant Flavius remains loyal to the King, and such devotion temporarily keeps the country unified:

> Happier is he that has no friend to feed
> Than such that do e'en enemies exceed.
> I bleed inwardly for my lord.
>
> (I, ii, 203–205)

Despite the affection and advice he offers, Flavius eventually fails to help Timon through the crisis the King himself creates by dispensing money away with excessive generosity. Still, Flavius's loyalty affirms the importance of noble service as essential to a healthy society.

The story of *King Lear*, too, is founded upon the unleashing of disorder. At the start of the play, Lear announces his plan to step down from the throne and divide his kingdom in three:

> We have this hour a constant will to publish
> Our daughters' several dowers, that future strife
> May be prevented now.
>
> (I, i, 43–45)

The terrible irony of this plan is that Lear means well. Yet his good intentions cannot legitimize a blunder of cataclysmic proportions. First, the kingship cannot be simply surrendered; the position is conferred by God for a lifetime. Furthermore, a divided kingdom inevitably yields to squabbling for authority, and such competition surfaces soon enough. Finally, Lear's fracturing of the royal family by the expulsion of his youngest daughter, Cordelia, leads to chaos throughout the extended family of his people, whose lives are irretrievably bound to his own. Thus Lear's actions in this opening scene propel his nation into tumult that takes the form of warfare between the surviving sisters, as well as with France, but even more memorably in the storm that mirrors the disorder of Lear's mind, his country, and the universe itself. Order is restored, but only with the purging of evil through the deaths of the elder sisters, Goneril and Regan, and their allies, as well as by the assumption of authority by Gloucester's benign son, Edgar, and Goneril's husband, Albany. That order is achieved at stunning cost, including the unexpected death of Cordelia. Nonetheless, the kingdom finds peace at last.

Finally, we come to *Hamlet*, in which the title figure sums up the theme of disorder as effectively as any character in Shakespeare's plays. Here is a young man mourning the death of his father, furious over the marriage of his mother to his hated uncle, then urged by his father's Ghost to take revenge on that uncle. Moreover, as Prince of Denmark, Hamlet not only bears responsibility for the political and military future of his country, but also must deal with the social, religious, and ethical consequences of his behavior. Finally, virtually every word he says and every movement he takes invite scrutiny from all sides. In short, disorder reigns supreme:

> The time is out of joint—O cursed spite,
> That ever I was born to set it right!
> (I, v, 188–189)

Like all of Shakespeare's tragedies, *Hamlet* ends with the restoration of order, as Fortinbras assumes the throne of Denmark. To be sure, he is the son of the dead King of Norway and therefore a descendant of the enemy of Hamlet's father. Yet Fortinbras's control puts the country back on plane, and his ascension is an affirmation of faith in the rightness of things.

Because all of Shakespeare's plays end with such order, when viewed together they suggest that whatever military, political, and intellectual conflicts may have shaken the society in which the plays were created, the overall vision of the world that emerges from them is one of unity and balance.

Politics

Shakespeare must have been fascinated with politics, the jockeying for authority that takes place within governmental institutions. The world of his plays is hardly democratic, but the strategies his characters employ to gain advantage over their opponents resonate with remarkable accuracy in all societies, our own as much as any other.

This theme is apparent especially in Shakespeare's earliest works. Consider the opening scene of *Henry VI, Part 2*, when at the urging of the Duke of Suffolk, the weak King is about to marry the poor but calculating Margaret of Anjou. After debate over the impending nuptials, of which no one approves, Humphrey, the Duke of Gloucester and the King's uncle and Protector, departs to avoid further squabbling with the King's great-uncle, the Bishop of Winchester, also known as Cardinal Beauford (I, i, 139–146). Immediately afterwards, though, Winchester speaks with the remaining nobles—Buckingham, Somerset, York, Warwick, and Salisbury—and all seem to unite. As Buckingham says:

> Cousin of Somerset, join you with me,
> And all together, with the Duke of Suffolk,
> We'll quickly hoise Duke Humphrey from his seat.
> (I, i, 167–169)

Yet as soon as the Cardinal leaves, Buckingham and Somerset join the remaining figures in a new conspiracy against both Gloucester and the Cardinal (I, i, 172–176). Then Buckingham and Somerset exit, leaving Salisbury, Warwick, and York to form their own team, ostensibly in support of Gloucester (I, i, 183–189).

This pattern of alliances, all in opposition, and all shifting back and forth, dominates the play. The supreme political principle in this court is self-promotion, and no one exemplifies that attitude better than the Duke of York, who takes personally the loss of territory demanded by the upcoming royal marriage, and who also has plans to grab the throne for himself and his family:

> A day will come when York shall claim his own,
> And therefore I will take the Nevils' parts,
> And make a show of love to proud Duke Humphrey,
> And when I spy advantage, claim the crown,
> For that's the golden mark I seek to hit.
>
> (I, i, 237–241)

Unlike the others, York believes that he has a historical right to the throne (as discussed in the chapter on "Divine Right"). Nonetheless, we see that no matter how much characters talk about moral and theological reasons, the heart of their personal doctrine is the drive for authority. Indeed, throughout the rest of the *Henry VI* plays, characters constantly switch sides, with their only principle being efficacy, i.e., where does the surest route to political advantage lie?

At the same time, the conspiracies against Gloucester suggest another troubling issue. As enemies plot about him, he tries to conduct himself morally in a society where immorality is rampant. We are therefore forced to ask if he can remain virtuous and survive, or is his only recourse to sink to the level of his opposition? The implications of this question are profound, extending far beyond the world of the history plays. Which course is preferable? Should Gloucester remain on what we might call "the high road," putting loyalty to the King and the throne ahead of his own aggrandizement? He believes that even should he lose this particular political battle, the justice of his cause will prevail. As he says when his wife is condemned for consorting with witches and thereafter exiled: "I cannot justify whom the law condemns" (II, iii, 16). Eventually, Gloucester, too, is put on trial and sentenced to death, but never does he resort to political treachery. His nobility is admirable, as is his fidelity to his country, but his refusal to rise against what he knows are evil forces frustrates us. Ultimately Gloucester's faith in the rightness of the universe is proven true, but not until decades after his own passing. Thus Shakespeare continues to ask which is preferable: maintaining moral standards or achieving political gain?

Even those who choose the latter, however, are not invulnerable to retribution. In the final play of this tetralogy, *Richard III*, Lord Buckingham casts his lot with Richard, who is first the Duke of Gloucester, then King. At one point, Buckingham predicts his own future, when he proclaims loyalty to the dying Edward IV, Richard's brother, but then whispers to Queen Elizabeth, Edward's wife:

> When I have most need to employ a friend,
> And most assured that he is a friend,
> Deep, hollow, treacherous, and full of guile
> Be he unto me!
> (II, i, 36–39)

This statement proves accurate, for Buckingham shortly allies himself with Richard, becoming what in contemporary parlance might be called a "front." Buckingham's strategy, however, comes at a severe price, and illustrates a phenomenon demonstrated throughout the history plays: a character who works for someone deceitful often becomes the victim of that deceit. Queen Margaret, the widow of Henry VI, warns Buckingham of that truth, when she speaks of Richard from the pain of experience:

> O Buckingham, take heed of yonder dog!
> Look when he fawns he bites, and when he bites,
> His venom tooth will rankle to the death.
> Have not to do with him, beware of him;
> Sin, death, and hell have set their marks on him,
> And all their ministers attend on him.
> (I, iii, 288–294)

To his regret, Buckingham disregards her.

His first mistake is extracting a promise from the future King, who claims:

> And look when I am king, claim thou of me
> The earldom of Herford, and all the moveables
> Whereof the King my brother was possess'd.
> (III, i, 194–196)

Richard's tone oozes resentment, for a man such as he cannot be pleased to be in political debt to anyone. Thus when Buckingham adds: "I'll claim that promise at your Grace's hand" (II, i, 197), he emphasizes his own priorities, insinuating that he and Richard are partners. Buckingham's second major misjudgment occurs after Richard orders the death of Edward's two young sons, whose existence endangers Richard's place on the throne. At first, Richard merely hints at his wishes, but when Buckingham fails to grasp the King's implication, Richard clarifies his intention: "I wish the bastards dead" (IV, ii, 18). For the first time, Buckingham hesitates:

> Give me some little breath, some pause, dear lord,
> Before I positively speak in this.
> I will resolve you herein presently.
> (IV, ii, 24–26)

Buckingham speaks as though Richard has offered a suggestion, not issued an order; thus the comment by Catesby, Richard's less talkative emissary, that the King "gnaws his lip" (IV, ii, 27) confirms that Buckingham has fallen from Richard's favor. Buckingham's last miscalculation is to press the King for that promised territory. With comic distaste, Richard dismisses the request: "I am not in the giving vein today" (IV, ii, 116). Buckingham barely controls his fury:

> And is it thus? repays me my deep service
> With such contempt? Made I him king for this?
> (IV, ii, 119–120)

So frustrated is Buckingham that he eventually leads troops against Richard, but is captured and condemned to death. He never expresses apology for the morality of his actions, but only regrets that his tactics proved unsuccessful (V, i, 12–28).

In the same play, we see another variety of political strategy, this followed by Lord Stanley. He never openly reveals alliance with or opposition to Richard, but speaks instead of his loyalty to the crown, the country, and the good of the populace. He is the professional politician, who never samples the intoxicating pleasures of absolute power, but who always enjoys the moderate pleasures of association with power. He never takes risks that might push him to the top, but he avoids risks that might leave him vulnerable from below. When we reflect that Stanley's son Richmond eventually brings down King Richard III, Stanley's neutrality becomes a lesson in political survival.

Perhaps the figure who best sums up the political environment in Shakespeare's early histories is Philip, the illegitimate son of Richard I, and the most heroic figure in *King John*. Shakespeare refers to him as "the Bastard"; nonetheless, he analyzes clearly the chief political drive of his time:

> Commodity, the bias of the world—
> The world, who of itself is peized well,
> Made to run even upon even ground,
> Till this advantage, this vile-drawing bias,
> This sway of motion, this commodity,
> Makes it take head from all indifferency,
> From all direction, purpose, course, intent . . .
> (II, i, 574–580)

Here "commodity" refers to those who act solely for personal convenience or advantage. Thus the Bastard denounces those leaders who put their own interests ahead of those of the country, as accurate an estimate of the major players in the first Henriad as Shakespeare offers.

In his Roman plays, particularly *Julius Caesar* and *Coriolanus*, politics is at the core of the drama, and several lessons may be drawn from the intrigue. For instance, while planning the conspiracy to overthrow Caesar, Cassius seeks his best friend Brutus's help for reasons that are unashamedly political. Casca agrees:

> O, he sits high in all the people's hearts;
> And that which would appear offense in us,
> His countenance, like richest alchymy,
> Will change to virtue and to worthiness.
> (I, iii, 157–160)

Cassius knows that given Brutus's reputation for integrity, his participation is an invaluable endorsement for their cause. Earlier, Cassius began to win Brutus over with that most blatant of political tools, flattery:

> I have heard
> Where many of the best respect in Rome
> (Except immortal Caesar), speaking of Brutus
> And groaning underneath this age's yoke,
> Have wish'd that noble Brutus had his eyes.
> (I, ii, 58–62)

Cassius knows that so huge an ego as Brutus's must be stroked. But such an ego may also insist on exerting itself, as Brutus does on several occasions. First he rejects the eminent Cicero's inclusion (II, i, 150–152). Then he refuses to kill Caesar's loyal follower Antony, claiming "Our cause will seem too bloody . . ." (II, i, 162). Brutus wants their group to be thought of as "sacrificers, but not butchers" (II, i, 166), but his idealism, Shakespeare suggests, has no place in the ruthless world of political struggle.

His miscalculations become even more blatant after the assassination of Caesar. Despite Cassius's objections, Brutus allows Antony first the opportunity to speak at Caesar's funeral, then the chance to talk last, always the choice position on any program. Are such errors the result of sheer political naivete? Or is Brutus so beset by his conscience that he goes out of his way to give Antony every opportunity for retribution? Whatever the reason, Brutus's lack of political adroitness is one of the dominant motifs of the play.

In contrast to Brutus is Antony, who proceeds through the political hazards without a misstep. After the assassination of Caesar, he approaches the conspirators gingerly, winning their trust. As discussed in the chapter on "Language," he manipulates the mob masterfully, so that when he finally gains a measure of control, he can ruthlessly exercise it, as when he dismisses his clumsy ally Lepidus:

> He must be taught, and train'd, and bid go forth;
> A barren-spirited fellow; one that feeds
> On objects, arts, and imitations,
> Which, out of use and stal'd by other men,
> Begin his fashion. Do not talk of him
> But as a property.
>
> (IV, i, 35–40)

Here is the cold determination that Shakespeare suggests must be endemic to any successful politician.

Political tactics are also at the heart of *Coriolanus*, in which the title character proves as ill-suited for that profession as Brutus does, but in a different way.

Martius, the triumphant general who earns the title "Coriolanus," despises the political arena. The question that pervades the play is whether he does so because of the innate qualities of that business or whether he himself is so warped, largely because of his upbringing by his mother, that he cannot bear to participate. Before Martius enters, we have an example of a politician supreme, Menenius, who calms the enraged plebeians and their cries for food by relating the infamous tale of the belly. This fable portrays the patricians as the stomach of the Roman political body, dispensing food to the rest, and the narrative unfolds with such enthusiasm that it appeases the mob's anger. Menenius's charm, however, is contrasted by Martius's coldness. The position of "consul," or leader of Rome, is virtually his for the asking, but he cannot subdue his contempt for the voters: "Who deserves greatness/ Deserves your hate . . ." (I, i, 176–177). Yet this unintentionally ironic line suggests that Martius berates the plebeians only to win their votes. After all, he is clearly hated; therefore he deserves greatness. Yet he cannot deal straightforwardly with the rules of the political arena.

For example, one of the rituals that each "candidate" must follow is revealing wounds before passersby, the equivalant of our contemporary rituals of kissing babies and "pressing the flesh." Martius follows tradition with great reluctance, and barely manages to hold his temper (II, iii, 60–150). For all his contempt, though, Coriolanus is hardly blind to political reality, as he proves when he berates Brutus and Sicinius, the representatives who have roused the masses against him:

Are these your herd?
Must these have voices, that can yield them now;
And straight declaim their tongues? What are your offices?
You being mouths, why rule you not their teeth?
Have you not set them on?
(III, i, 33–37)

Thus Coriolanus is hardly stupid. He simply has no taste for the sport, or at least for the other participants.

Both Brutus (in *Julius Caesar*) and Martius are unable to bring themselves to feel what others feel. Brutus is set apart by his compulsion to ponder, as well as an idealism that does not permit him to see human beings as they are. Martius suffers from such a loathing of the rest of humanity that he cannot bother himself to identify with their needs and feelings.

These flaws are not to be found in the most successful of Shakespeare's politicians: Henry IV and his son Henry V. We meet Henry IV first in *Richard II*, when he is still Bullingbrook and has cast his eye on the throne. Yet even this early, the King sees in Henry the political skills that Richard recognizes he himself lacks. As he says of Bullingbrook:

... How he did seem to dive into their hearts
With humble and familiar courtesy,
What reverence he did throw away on slaves,
Wooing poor craftsmen with the craft of smiles
And patient underbearing of his fortune,
As 'twere to banish their affects with him.
(I, iv, 25–30)

One of the fundamental changes in English life that this play reflects is that of the nature of the kingship, which moves from a completely autocratic position to one in which the holder of the throne must be willing to deal politically with all sorts of forces around him, including rebellious nobles and a restless, sometimes unruly, populace.

When Bullingbrook threatens to take the throne, he does so with political strategy: sending his father, Northumberland, to greet Richard with this warning:

Henry Bullingbrook
On both his knees doth kiss King Richard's hand,
And sends allegiance and true faith of heart
To his most royal person; hither come
Even at his feet to lay my arms and power,
Provided that my banishment repeal'd
And lands restor'd again be freely granted.

If not, I'll use the advantage of my power,
And lay the summer's dust with show'rs of blood
Rain'd from the wounds of slaughtered Englishmen . . .
                                        (III, iii, 35–43)

Bullingbrook seems to make his threats reluctantly. His tone implies that
if Richard refuses this generous offer, then the King himself will be responsible for the carnage that ensues.

Henry IV passes his political skills onto his son, Shakespeare's most
successful politician, Henry V. In his first appearance in *Henry IV, Part
1*, the Prince, here referred to as "Hal," carouses in carefree style with
the dissolute Sir John Falstaff and the other denizens of the tavern world,
but when alone, the young man proves coldly practical about his future:

So when this loose behavior I throw off
And pay the debt I promised,
By how much better than my word I am,
By so much shall I falsify men's hopes,
And like bright metal on a sullen ground,
My reformation, glitt'ring o'er my fault,
Shall show more goodly and attract more eyes
Than that which hath no foil to set it off.
I'll so offend, to make offense a skill.
Redeeming time when men least think I will.
                                        (I, ii, 208–217)

He plots every action, measuring how he will appear in the eyes of
others. From this moment on, Shakespeare portrays Hal as a calculator,
who seemingly never makes a move or utters a word without weighing
political implications. Moreover, the roles of Prince and later King soon
supersede the life of the man. Thus here is another question these plays
pose: can successful political figures ever separate themselves from the
offices they hold, or must they risk allowing their private lives to be
usurped by their public performances?

We have such a moment in *Henry IV, Part 2*, when Hal talks to his
crony Poins about the incipient death of Henry IV:

Marry, I tell thee it is not meet that I
should be sad, now my father is sick, albeit I could
tell to thee—as to one it pleases me, for fault of a
better, or call a friend—I could be sad, and sad
indeed too.
                                        (II, ii, 39–43)

He calibrates every emotion according to how it will affect his image. A
few lines later, he adds: "What wouldst thou think of me if I should

weep?" (II, ii, 52–53). The man himself has been lost under the public mask.

Even when Henry IV is near death, his relationship to his son, the future King, seems more like that of political guide than father, as in these words of counsel:

> Therefore, my Harry
> Be it thy course to busy giddy minds
> With foreign quarrels, that action, hence borne out,
> May waste the memory of the former days.
> (IV, v, 212–215)

The elder King is always conscious of his role as a usurper, and he reminds Hal that bringing the country together against a common enemy will eliminate domestic upset. How many leaders over the centuries have followed this advice?

After Hal gains the throne, more than ever he measures every word. When Falstaff rudely interrupts the solemn ceremony of coronation, Henry V expels the old man, but even during this painful moment, we are aware of the political machine that Hal has become, as when he adds:

> For God doth know, so shall the world perceive,
> That I have turn'd away my former self;
> So will I those that kept me company.
> (V, v, 57–59)

A couple of scenes earlier, Hal made peace with the Chief Justice, whose charges he had long avoided. That gesture, in combination with the sentiments of the speech to Falstaff, are the new King's way of confirming for his audience that he has left behind his wastrel youth and now embraces the responsibilities of office. Thus while he simultaneously discharges his best friend and assures his country of his commitment to the throne, his public and private personae have become indistinguishable.

In *Henry V*, the King remains a politician supreme. The skill with which he leads his country into war with France has already been considered in the chapter on "Language" (I, ii). Here other episodes are worthy of mention. First, the King becomes aware of a conspiracy against him led by Lord Scroop, the Earl of Cambridge, and Sir Thomas Grey. Rather than blatantly accuse them, he allows the three to pass judgment on another disorderly figure, whom the trio condemns to death (II, ii, 44–51). After the King quietly presents the accused with evidence, his passing of sentence seems not arbitrary, but perfectly in line with the precedent they themselves have set, and the King can afford to seem regretful:

> I will weep for thee;
> For this revolt of thine, methinks, is like
> Another fall of man.
> (II, ii, 140–142)

The judgment, of course, stands.

Later, when Henry's troops stand before the city of Harflew, the King seems to try to avert battle and the shedding of innocent blood:

> Therefore, you men of Harflew,
> Take pity of your town and your people,
> Whiles yet my soldiers are in my command,
> Whiles yet the cool and temperate wind of grace
> O'erblows the filthy and contagious clouds
> Of headly murther, spoil, and villainy.
> (III, iii, 27–32)

He shifts blame for any subsequent conflict onto the citizens of the town, as if to say that if he and his army were forced to fight and kill, they would do so reluctantly. He does not add, of course, that the only recourse for the town is surrender. Finally, after the defeat of the French at the historic battle of Agincourt, one way in which the triumphant English King seeks to seal the bond between the two countries is by marrying Katherine, the French King's daughter. Here Henry subtly hints to her of his stature:

> If thou would have such a one, take me! and take
> me, take a soldier; take a soldier, take a king.
> (V, ii, 165–166)

He modestly reminds her that not only is he royal, but he is also most likely the greatest man she will ever meet, and he reemphasizes the point (V, ii, 235–246) by reaffirming how much territory she may claim for her own, if only she will marry him. Not surprisingly, Katherine, like all of the king's audiences, is charmed into submission.

Throughout the plays in which he appears, Henry is an admirable King, but he grows a colder and less likeable person, and this schism confirms the great dilemma that Shakespeare dramatizes. To what extent, he seems to ask, does success in politics come at a terrible cost to character? Does politics demand such intense performance, such awareness of the arena, that one loses one's being? The plays do not offer an absolute answer, but that question, along with the others considered here, has timeless impact.

Power

One of the strongest motivations in the plays of Shakespeare is power, more specifically the desire to rule over others. Yet the implications of this drive resist simple explanation. Certain characters, for instance, become so consumed by the lust for power that they lose whatever ethical center they might have had. Other characters who seek power just as strongly are, in fact, the very ones who use it most effectively. Finally, those who reach positions of power inevitably undergo changes in personality and values, and not always in the manner prescribed by the nineteenth-century politician Lord Acton's famous dictum: "Power tends to corrupt, and absolute power corrupts absolutely." Rather, the pressures responsibility can prove insupportable for the most determined of souls.

Henry VI, Parts 1, 2, and *3* are dominated by figures who do not even bother to disguise their obsession to control their world. Consider the Earl of Suffolk, who in *Part 1* negotiates the marriage between Henry and Margaret of France, but who has far more sinister ambitions, based on his bond with Margaret. As he says at the close of *Part 1*, when the marriage is about to take place:

> Thus Suffolk hath prevail'd, and thus he goes,
> As did the youthful Paris once to Greece,
> With hope to find the like event in love,
> But prosper better than the Troyan did.
> Margaret shall now be Queen, and rule the King;
> But I will rule both her, the King, and realm.
> (V, v, 103–108)

Margaret also has ambition, as in *Part 2*, when she broods over her husband's reluctance to exert the force of the kingship over Gloucester, the king's Protector, and other nobles:

285

Beside the haughty Protector, have we Beauford
The imperious churchman, Somerset, Buckingham,
And grumbling York; and not the least of these
But can do more in England than the King.
(I, iii, 68–71)

That Margaret is a Frenchwoman, and thus an interloper in the English court, makes this whining more outrageous. She is opposed in this play by many members of the royal family, but principally by the Duke of York, who constantly reiterates his own ruthlessness in his quest for power. Here he explains his tactics to the wealthy and powerful Duke of Warwick:

Do you as I do in these dangerous days;
Wink at the Duke of Suffolk's insolence,
At Beauford's pride, at Somerset's ambition,
At Buckingham, and all the crew of them,
Till they have snar'd the shepherd of the flock,
That virtuous prince, the good Duke Humphrey.
'Tis that they seek and they in seeking that
Shall find their deaths, if York can prophesy.
(II, ii, 69–75)

This naked plotting is terrifying, but oddly exhilarating as well. True, the depiction of these characters, all of whom make their feelings utterly clear, is hardly subtle. Yet their personal energy, as expressed through the vividness of their language, is undeniable.

The Yorks eventually take temporary control of the throne, but just as the Lancasters, the descendants of John of Gaunt, suffer dissension in *Henry VI, Parts 1* and *2*, so the Yorks and their allies turn on one other in *Part 3*. The key moment occurs when Warwick, the strongest of the nobles (and known as the "Kingmaker"), who earlier had supported the York claim to the throne, learns from the French King Lewis that France will not support the Yorks because their hold on the crown is so feeble. Such practicality on Lewis's part reminds us that the struggle for power is not for idealists, but realists. In a remarkable turnaround, Warwick renounces King Edward and transfers loyalty to Warwick's own bitterest enemy, Queen Margaret:

And to repair my honor lost for him,
I here renounce him and return to Henry.
My noble Queen, let former grudges pass,
And henceforth I am thy true servitor.
(III, iii, 193–196)

Power

The two go so far as to allow their children to marry, but just so we are not deceived by this reversal, Warwick reminds us that the only genuine motivation for anyone in this court is power. Speaking of the King, he says:

> I was the chief that rais'd him to the crown,
> And I'll be chief to bring him down again;
> Not that I pity Henry's misery.
> But seek revenge on Edward's mockery.
> (III, iii, 262–265)

Eventually Henry returns to the throne briefly, but his final removal is orchestrated by the most charismatic and power-hungry figure to appear in *Part 3*: the Duke of York's crookbacked son, Richard, who eventually becomes Richard III. Here is an excerpt from his first soliloquy, which at this early moment is directed toward plotting the downfall of his philandering older brother, King Edward:

> Ay, Edward will use women honorably.
> Would he were wasted, marrow, bones, and all,
> That from his loins no hopeful branch may spring,
> To cross me from the golden time I look for!
> (III, ii, 124–127)

The uncontrollable lust for power overflows, as does Richard's ruthlessness, malicious wit, and delight in his capacity to scheme. By the end of the play, his intellectual exertions take the form of brutal violence, when he stabs the imprisoned Henry VI to death:

> I, that have neither pit, love, nor fear.
> Indeed 'tis true that Henry told me of;
> For I have often heard my mother say
> I came into the world with my legs forward.
> Had I not reason, think ye, to make haste,
> And seek their ruin that usurp'd our right?
> (V, vi, 68–73)

He has twisted his mind so that it matches the shape of his contorted body, all in the name of power. This motivation becomes the sole reason for his existence, as dramatized throughout the tetralogy's last play, the one that bears his name.

The bloody struggle for power between Suffolk, Margaret, the Duke of York and the other nobles of the Lancaster and the York families became known as the War of the Roses. Through these plays, Shakespeare clarifies that the reason such a conflict took place was the vacuum of leadership created by the weak rule of King Henry VI. When he assumed the kingship at the age of less than a year, after the death of his father, Henry V, the battle for the throne began immediately. This sentiment is expressed in *Part 1* by the Duke of Bedford, who cries to the Ghost of the dead King:

> Henry the Fift, thy ghost I invocate:
> Prosper this realm, keep it from civil broils,
> Combat with adverse planets in the heavens!
> (I, i, 52–54)

Through *Henry VI, 1, 2,* and *3,* the King remains so weak that he is abused by everyone, and on numerous occasions wishes himself freed from all responsibility. Here, from *Part 3*, when battle rages about him, is his most poignant call for release:

> O God! methinks it were a happy life
> To be no better than a homely swain,
> To sit upon a hill, as I do now,
> To carve out dials quaintly, point by point,
> Thereby to see the minutes how they run . . .
> (II, v, 21–25)

Occasionally Henry demonstrates vigor and insight, as in moments before his death at the hands of Richard, Duke of Gloucester:

> And thus I prophesy, that many a thousand
> Which now mistrust no parcel of my fear,
> And many an old man's sigh and many a widow's,
> And many an orphan's water-standing eye—
> Men for their sons, wives for their husbands,
> Orphans for their parents' timeless death—
> Shall rue the hour that ever thou wast born.
> (V, vi, 37–43)

More often, though, Henry is the woebegone idealist, too hapless to compete in so bloodthirsty an environment, and reduced to ineffectual, if noble, expressions of faith, as in this speech from *Part 2*:

> What stronger breastplate than a heart untainted!
> Thrice is he arm'd that hath his quarrel just;
> And he but naked, though lock'd up in steel,
> Whose conscience with injustice is corrupted.
> (III, ii, 232–235)

His foresight notwithstanding, the tragedy of Henry's reign and its aftermath is evidence of Shakespeare's conviction that only a strong central authority can lead England.

Yet the mere employment of power is not sufficient. It must be employed wisely. The historical Richard II, for instance, came to the throne at the age of nine. During his reign, he became infatuated with luxury, as well as susceptible to the influence of greedy sycophants, until finally he flaunted authority without regard for the consequences. Nonetheless, at the start of the play in which he is the title character, Shakespeare presents the King as uncomfortable with his position. Indeed, as Mowbray, the King's loyal officer, and Bullingbrook, the King's envious cousin, exchange charges of treason, Richard seems more concerned with the sheer drama of the moment than with the challenges to his rule. For instance, he ignores Bullingbrook's innuendos about eighteen years of treason, the approximate length of the King's reign (I, i, 95), and comments instead upon the speaker's theatrics: "How high a pitch his resolution soars!" (I, i, 109). Subsequently, rather than resolve the situation judiciously, Richard exiles both men, hoping to dissipate harsh feelings on all sides.

Richard takes other missteps, particularly after the death of John of Gaunt, Bullingbrook's father, when the King blithely confiscates the son's inheritance (II, i, 160–162), ostensibly to conduct the Irish wars. Even in these moments, however, we never feel Richard's eagerness to lead his nation. Rather he seems determined to indulge himself by doing what his office permits, and his carelessness is evident by his asking his weak uncle, the Duke of York, to rule in the King's absence (II, i, 221). Thus Shakespeare portrays Richard as a man born into power, but who never sought it and who never adjusts to its burdens.

That impression is confirmed when Bullingbrook returns from exile to reclaim his inheritance. Under attack from forces that Bullingbrook has rallied behind him, Richard quivers in panic:

> Have I not reason to look pale and dead?
> All souls that will be safe, fly from my side,
> For time hath set a blot upon my pride.
> (III, ii, 79–81)

The irony is that when Bullingbrook's challenge becomes too overwhelming, Richard truly comes into his own: not as a man competing to retain his place, but as one who romanticizes and theatricalizes his own downfall:

> With mine own tears I wash away my balm,
> With mine own hands I give away my crown,

With mine own tongue deny my sacred state,
With mine own breath release all duteous oaths . . .
God save King Henry, unking'd Richard says,
And send him many years of sunshine days!
What more remains?

(IV, i, 207–210; 220–222)

For Richard, therefore, power is a curse that he gratefully shakes off, but only after doing profound damage to himself and his country.

For Bullingbrook, the desire for power is complemented by an equally strong desire to use it. When he brings forth Bushy and Green, Richard's most disreputable advisors, Bullingbrook does not hesitate in having them executed (III, i). In his very next lines, however, he requests that York treat Richard's Queen with kindness. Thus from the start we see Henry IV's mixture of ruthlessness and compassion. It appears throughout *Henry IV, Parts 1* and *2*, as well. At the beginning of *Part 1*, for instance, Worcester, his brother Northumberland, and his nephew Hotspur, three members of the Percy family who supported Henry's ascension to the kingship, try to force the new King to yield to them the authority they anticipated. But Henry IV has more backbone than his erstwhile supporters expect, as when he interrupts Worcester:

Worcester, get thee gone, for I do see
Danger and disobedience in thine eye.
O, sir, your presence is too bold and peremptory,
And majesty might never yet endure
The moody frontier of a servant brow.

(I, iii, 15–19)

When the target of this scorn departs in furious silence, Henry turns back to Northumberland and calmly beckons: "You were about to speak" (I, iii, 20). No one onstage has any doubt who is in charge. Throughout *Henry IV, Parts 1* and *2*, Henry handles the conspiracies against him with equal dispatch. As he says to Worcester in *Part 1* before the climactic battle of Shrewsbury:

So tell your cousin, and bring me word
What he will do. But if he will not yield,
Rebuke and dread correction wait on us,
And they shall do their office. So be gone,
We will not now be troubled with reply,
We offer fair, take it advisedly.

(V, i, 109–114)

He will not be threatened into submission.

Yet responsibilities of power eventually prove unbearable for this King, too. In *Part 2*, he finds himself unable to sleep, and this disruption of the natural cycle of life leaves him, like Henry VI, envious of those who lead less pressured lives:

> How many thousand of my poorest subjects
> Are at this hour asleep! O sleep! O gentle sleep!
> Nature's soft nurse, how I have frighted thee,
> That thou no more wilt weigh my eyelids down,
> And steep my enemies in forgetfulness?
> (III, i, 4–8)

Henry concludes his soliloquy with a line that reflects the lives of countless leaders across the centuries: "Uneasy lies the head that wears a crown" (III, i, 31). Such obligation affects even Henry's son Henry V. In other chapters, we have considered the extent of his skills as a ruler (see "Divine Right," "Nationalistic Pride and Prejudice," and "Politics"). Here we note how he, too, nearly totters under the pressures of the decisions he must make. In *Henry V*, as his troops prepare to fight the French at the Battle of Agincourt, he dons a disguise to circulate among them so as to determine their mood, but the excursion turns into a moment of profound reflection. The encounter with the soldier Michael Williams forces Henry V to defend his policy of war, to the extent that he tries to dispense with responsibility altogether:

> Every subject's
> duty is the King's, but every subject's soul is his own.
> Therefore should every soldier in the wars do as every
> sick man in his bed, wash every mote out of his conscience; and
> dying so, death is to him advantage . . .
> (IV, i, 176–180)

Here the King confronts the most painful crisis any national leader can face: directing his countrymen into battle, where many of them will die. Henry tries to rationalize that he is not to blame for the result, but Williams is relentless in his judgment that the King must accept responsibility. When Henry points out that the King has said he will not be ransomed, that he will die fighting, Williams retorts:

> Ay, he said so, to make us fight cheerfully;
> but when our throats are cut, he may be ransom'd, and
> we ne'er the wiser.
> (IV, i, 192–194)

When the soldiers leave, and Henry reflects on the pageantry and trappings of kingship, he invokes the familiar image of sleep:

> No, not all these, thrice-gorgeous ceremony,
> Not all these, laid in bed majestical,
> Can sleep so soundly as the wretched slave . . .
>
> (IV, i, 266–268)

No ruler, even one as gifted as Henry V, can shoulder power with im-
punity.

Throughout his plays, Shakespeare dramatizes how a variety of characters handle this pressure. In *Measure for Measure*, the Duke temporarily
abdicates his position to Lord Angelo, seemingly for an experiment, as
he explains to the advisor lord Escalus:

> What figure of us think you he will bear?
> For you must know, we have with special soul
> Elected him our absence to supply,
> Lent him our terror, dress'd him with our love,
> And given his deputation all the organs
> Of our own pow'r.
>
> (I, i, 16–20)

Angelo's initial reaction to his new authority is rigidity. By enforcing a
long-forgotten law, he condemns young gentleman Claudio to death for
impregnating his fiancée, Juliet, out of marriage. But Angelo does not
prove steadfast in his morality; instead he finds himself smitten with
Isabella, Claudio's sister, who comes to plead for her brother's life, and
under this temptation, Angelo surrenders to corruption by offering to
spare Claudio if Isabella will sleep with him. Unbeknownst to Angelo,
his one-time betrothed, Mariana, is substituted for Isabella, but afterwards Angelo still refuses to grant clemency. Thus one implication of
this play is that even the strictest of moralists may be tainted by the
privileges of power.

King Lear dramatizes another form of corruption. Lear is innately a
good man, but in the first scene of Act I, he is challenged by his daughter
Cordelia, who refuses to comply with Lear's order to proclaim publically
her affection for him, so that she may gain a third of the kingdom he
plans to divide among his three daughters. The flouting of his authority
drives Lear into a rage:

> For by the sacred radiance of the sun,
> The [mysteries] of Hecat and the night;
> By all the operation of the orbs,

From whom we do exist and cease to be;
Here I disclaim all my paternal care . . .

(I, i, 109–113)

Rather than reflect calmly on his decision, Lear tries to justify himself by pointing to his stature. When his servant Kent objects, the King again resorts to his own grandeur as reason enough:

That thou has sought to make us break our [vow]—
Which we durst never yet—and with strain'd pride
To come betwixt our sentence and our power,
Which nor our nature nor our place can bear,
Our potency made good, take thy reward.

(I, i, 168–172)

Here is the arrogance of power, as a good man becomes so infused with authority that he assumes he must be correct simply because of who he is. Nor does he think about how his judgment will ravage his country and inflict suffering on his people. Moreover, even when he suspects he might be in error, he does not withdraw his decree for fear of demonstrating weakness. For Lear, therefore, the exercise of power becomes an end in itself.

Nonetheless, despite the dangers of power when it is badly used, Shakespeare is always conscious of the dangers of neglected authority. In his last play, *The Tempest*, Prospero, the former Duke of Milan, relates the circumstances under which his daughter, Miranda, and he were exiled:

I, thus neglecting wordly ends, all dedicated
To closeness and the bettering of my mind
With that which, but by being so retir'd,
O'er-prized all popular rate, in my false brother
Awak'd an evil nature, and my trust,
Like a good parent, did beget of him
A falsehood in its contrary, as great
As my trust was . . .

(I, ii, 89–96)

Thereafter Prospero's brother, Antonio, exiled him from Milan, and only through the beneficence of the loyal servant Gonzalo did Miranda and Prospero survive their journey to the island where they have lived all these years. Prospero suggests that he should not be blamed for becoming absorbed in study, that the emergence of Antonio's evil character was beyond Prospero's control. We, however, recognize that Prospero's failure led to his downfall and to a dark time for Milan. As the play continues, we also recognize that the strict obedience that Prospero demands from the other island's inhabitants—Miranda, the sprite Ariel, and the half-human Caliban—may be a reaction to his earlier imprudence. He is determined not to let his strength slip away again.

Thus the plays of Shakespeare offer conflicting views on the place of power in human life. Certainly authority lies at the heart of any society, there for the taking, and someone must seize it. The competition to do so may be literally deadly, but anyone who is not willing to compete probably does not deserve the prize. Even for the winners, though, the responsibility of wielding authority may prove debilitating. Yet it must be borne, and effectively, or else the society as a whole will suffer. Shakespeare offers no convenient solutions to this reality, no comforting illusions. Rather he invites us to see this aspect of our existence for what it is and how we must try to deal with it.

Reason versus Passion

Shakespeare's contemporaries regarded human beings as possessing many conflicting qualities. Two of these characteristics, however, were judged to be especially powerful influences on our behavior: first, we have the capacity to reason; second, we are vulnerable to instinctive drives and passions. The inner war between these two forces creates much of the unbalance in ourselves and our lives. Therefore we should not be surprised that much of Shakespearean drama reflects his characters' attempts to resolve that conflict.

One of the most delightful examples of a figure undergoing such difficulty is the bachelor Benedick in *Much Ado About Nothing*. At first, he announces his disdain for all love; in the long-standing tradition of comic drama, however, his antipathy masks a deep-seated desire that he does not acknowledge, but which we recognize whenever his counterpart, Beatrice, takes the stage. Benedick disparages her, but here is a case where hate and love reflect each other. The more Benedick rails, the more we want him to marry Beatrice, even when he denounces her with customary fury:

> She speaks poniards,
> and every words stabs. If her breath were as terrible
> as her terminations, there were no living near her,
> she would infect the north star. I would not
> marry her, though she were endow'd with all
> that Adam had left him before he transgress'd.
> She would have made Hercules have turn'd spit,
> yea, and have cleft his club to make the fire too.
>   (II, i, 247–254)

Later he rationalizes his attitude toward women while simultaneously downplaying his desires:

> One woman
> is fair, yet I am well; another is wise, yet I am
> well; another virtuous, yet I am well; but till all
> graces be in one woman, one woman shall not come
> in my grace. Rich she shall be, that's certain;
> wise, or I'll none; virtuous, or I'll never cheapen
> her; fair, or I'll never look on her; mild, or come
> not near me; noble, or not I for an angel; of good
> discourse, an excellent musician, and her hair shall
> be of what color it please God.
>
> (II, iii, 26–35)

Benedick desperately tries to control feelings that resist restraint, but when he overhears his friends' conversation in which they pretend to be convinced that Beatrice loves him, Benedick at last yields to passion:

> I may chance
> have some odd quirks and remnants of wit broken
> on me, because I have rail'd so long against marriage;
> but doth not the appetite alter? A man loves
> the meat in his youth that he cannot endure in his
> age. Shall quips and sentences and these paper
> bullets of the brain awe a man from the career of
> his humor? No, the world must be peopled. When
> I said I would die a bachelor, I did not think
> I should live till I married.
>
> (II, iii, 235–344)

At this moment, too, he tries to turn the attraction into a reasoned response. Yet we recognize the truth: that he was irrational when he turned away from love, irrational when he planned how to dispense his affections, and irrational now that he is prepared to surrender to those affections. In sum, watching him struggle to control his emotions is a delight.

Such a battle takes on a grimmer aspect in *The Two Gentlemen of Verona*, when one of the title figures, Proteus, tries to subdue his lust for Silvia, the beloved of his best friend, Valentine:

> Methinks my zeal to Valentine is cold,
> And that I love him not as I was wont:
> O, but I love his lady too too much,
> And that's the reason I love him so little . . .
> But when I look on her perfections,
> There is no reason but I shall be blind.
> If I can check my erring love, I will;
> If not, to compass her I'll use my skill.
>
> (II, iv, 203–214)

Two scenes later, Proteus has lost perspective:

> I cannot leave to love, and yet I do;
> But there I leave to love where I should love.
> Julia I lose, and Valentine I lose:
> If I keep them, I needs must lose myself;
> If I lose them, thus find I by their loss . . .
>
> (II, vi, 17–21)

He realizes that he is dominated by desires he can neither control nor understand. What we realize is that reason is always helpless against such overwhelming passion.

We see a soul in even greater torment in *Measure for Measure*, when the Deputy Angelo, who prides himself on his strict morality, is charged with enforcing the laws of Vienna. When Isabella comes before him, however, to plead for the life of her brother, Claudio, whom Angelo has condemned to death, Angelo finds himself attracted to her, as he confesses in an aside: "She speaks, and 'tis/ Such sense that my sense breeds with it" (II, ii, 141–142). Even though Angelo's lust is ugly, we may find ourselves empathic with a man in such a predicament:

> What's this? what's this? Is this her fault, or mine?
> The tempter, or the tempted, who sins most, ha?
> Not she; nor doth she tempt; but it is I
> That, lying by the violet in the sun,
> Do as the carrion does, not as the flow'r,
> Corrupt with virtuous season.
>
> (II, ii, 162–167)

Even more striking is Angelo's horror over the inspiration for what he judges to be his animalistic urges:

> What dost thou? or what art thou, Angelo?
> Dost thou desire her foully for those things
> That make her good?
>
> (II, ii, 172–174)

He is shocked to be aroused by her chastity, a quality that ought to make Isabella beyond desire, but which ironically arouses Angelo's lust. Therefore he orders her:

> Answer me to-morrow,
> Or by the affection that now guides me most,
> I'll prove a tyrant to him.
>
> (II, iv, 167–169)

Here is a stunning concession from a man who has heretofore insisted on the strictness of his own moral code.

The conflict between reason and passion appears most powerfully in Shakespeare's tragedies, where the inner war assumes titanic proportions. In *Othello*, for instance, the ensign Iago tries to talk himself and his dupe, Roderigo, into denying passion altogether. Speaking of lust, Iago says:

> If the [beam] of our
> lives had not one scale of reason to poise another of
> sensuality, the blood and baseness of our natures would
> conduct us to most prepost'rous conclusions.
> (I, iii, 325–328)

Yet even Iago is subject to these feelings, as he clarifies in a later soliloquy about Othello's wife, Desdemona:

> Now I do love her too,
> Not out of absolute lust (though peradventure
> I stand accomptant for as great a sin) . . .
> (II, i, 291–293)

He confesses his yearning, but immediately withdraws the sentiment, as if admitting the extent of his desire, even to himself, would violate his faith in his own mind.

The figure from this play in whom the battle between reason and passion rages most powerfully is the Moor, Othello. Initially he seems a man of unshakeable dignity, when in response to Iago's warning about threats to Othello's position, he answers calmly:

> Let him do his spite;
> My services which I have done the signiory
> Shall out-tongue his complaints.
> (I, ii, 17–19)

He has confidence in the universal authority of reason. Yet when Othello assumes command of the Venetian forces in Cyprus and is called from his bridal bed with Desdemona to quash a melee in the streets, he says of his rising anger:

> Now by heaven,
> My blood begins my safer guides to rule,
> And passion, having my best judgment collied,
> Assays to lead the way.
> (II, iii, 204–207)

His lines foreshadow the explosion of that passion, as occurs under Iago's prodding about Desdemona's possible jealousy (III, iii). During that episode, as Othello's suspicions burgeon, he tries to maintain rationality:

> Give me the ocular proof,
> Or by the worth of mine eternal soul,
> Thou hadst been better have been born a dog
> Than answer my wak'd wrath!
>
> (III, iii, 360–363)

Before much longer, though, he is consumed by emotion that overcomes his reason. Yet as Othello prepares to smother Desdemona, he attempts to turn even this act of madness into the product of clear thought:

> Yet I'll not shed her blood,
> Nor scar that whiter skin of hers than snow,
> And smooth as monumental alablaster.
> Yet she must die, else she'll betray more men.
>
> (V, ii, 3–6)

Still, no matter how measured he tries to appear in his own eyes, we see his uncontrollable fervor.

Of all Shakespeare's tragedies, the one in which reason and passion battle most profoundly is *Antony and Cleopatra*. The very structure of the piece reflects this conflict, as the action moves back and forth from Rome, which represents order and responsibility, to Egypt, which embodies emotion and pleasure. Throughout the play, Antony alternates between the two locales and the two aspects of his own character. Part of him feels a duty to uphold his position as military and political leader of the greatest empire on earth. The other side is drawn to the most fascinating woman he has ever met. The greatness of Antony is that he has the capacity to fulfill both roles. His tragedy is that in fulfilling one role, he cannot fulfill the other.

This tension becomes apparent in the opening lines of the play, as Philo, one of Antony's friends, suggests:

> . . . his captain's heart,
> Which in the scuffles of great fights hath burst
> The buckles on his breast, reneges all temper,
> And is become the bellows and the fan
> To cool a gipsy's lust.
>
> (I, i, 6–10)

Moments later, Antony articulates his dilemma:

> Let Rome in Tiber melt, and the wide arch
> Of the rang'd empire fall! Here is my space,
> Kingdoms are clay; our dungy earth alike
> Feeds beast as man; the nobleness of life
> Is to do thus [*embracing*] . . .
>
>   (I, i, 33–37)

He realizes that no matter what his sense of obligation, he is fatally attracted to Cleopatra. Even Octavius Caesar, Antony's Roman rival for power and a far less emotional man, intuits his competitor's crisis:

> From Alexandria
> This is the news: he fishes, drinks, and wastes
> The lamps of night in revel; is not more manlike
> Than Cleopatra; nor the queen of Ptolomy
> More womanly than he; hardly gave audience, or
> [Vouchsaf'd] to think he had partners. You shall find there
> A man who is th' [abstract] of all faults
> That all men follow.
>
>   (I, iv, 3–10)

Although Caesar understands Antony's situation, he cannot grasp how any man can allow himself to be so taken with a woman. For that reason, no matter how disciplined and iron-willed Caesar acts, we never sympathize with or care for him. Antony, on the other hand, despite his miscalculations, retains our good will, for in his vulnerability he seems profoundly human. Even when he agrees to marry Caesar's sister, Octavia, then reverts to his plan to return to Egypt (II, iii, 39–41), we appreciate that given his passionate nature, he has no choice.

Cleopatra, too, is beset by the conflict of reason versus passion:

> Though he be painted one way like a Gorgon,
> The other way 's a Mars.
>
>   (II, v, 116–117)

She is smitten with Antony at least partially because he is the most powerful man in the world, and she relishes having control over that man. At the same time, once he gives in to her wishes, once he relinquishes some of his power, he risks losing his allure.

Such confusion holds both Antony and Cleopatra. One powerful instance occurs after Cleopatra has urged Antony to oppose Caesar's forces at sea, primarily because she wishes her own troops to participate. At the high point of the battle, however, Cleopatra's forces desert, and Antony's follow. Afterwards, Antony berates himself:

> Egypt, thou knew'st too well
> My heart was to thy rudder tied by th' strings,
> And thou shouldst [tow] me after. O'er my spirit
> [Thy] full supremacy thou knew'st, and that
> Thy beck might from the bidding of the gods
> Command me.
>
> (III, xi, 56–61)

A few lines later, he adds:

> You did know
> How much you were my conqueror, and that
> My sword, made weak by my affection, would
> Obey it on all cause.
>
> (III, xi, 65–68)

He cannot control his love for Cleopatra, and although he recognizes that she is destroying him, no reasoning can free him. Thus once she says: "Pardon, pardon!" (III, xi, 68), Antony's fury evaporates:

> Fall not a tear, I say, one of them rates
> All that is won and lost. Give me a kiss.
> Even this repays me.
>
> (III, xi, 69–71)

When Antony later believes that Cleopatra has died after again betraying him in warfare, he once more forgives any transgression she might have committed:

> I will o'ertake thee, Cleopatra, and
> Weep for my pardon. So it must be, for now
> All length is torture; since the torch is out,
> Lie down and stray no farther.
>
> (IV, xiv, 44–47)

This duel between his reason, which beckons him to Rome, and his passion, which drives him irrevocably to Egypt, is the heart of Antony's life.

The conflict between reason and passion is also crucial to *The Tempest*, which is in many ways a meditation of the nature of the human character. The character in whom we see these forces compete most intently is Caliban, the native of the island whom Shakespeare characterizes as a "deformed slave" and who at times seems barely human. Yet he demonstrates enough perception that we wonder how to classify him.

For instance, the exiled Duke Prospero tries to justify his enslavement of Caliban by accusing his prisoner of attempting violence against Miranda, Prospero's daughter:

> I have us'd thee
> (Filth as thou art) with human care, and lodg'd thee
> In mine own cell, till thou didst seek to violate
> The honor of my child.
> (I, ii, 345–348)

The implication is that Caliban responded to humane treatment with bestial force. Caliban's answer, however, sounds clearly reasoned:

> O ho, O ho, would't had been done!
> Thou didst prevent me; I had peopled else
> This isle with Calibans.
> (I, ii, 349–351)

Miranda adds that she gave Caliban the gift of language (I, ii, 357–360), but he scorns such generosity as well:

> You taught me language, and my profit on't
> Is, I know how to curse. The red-plague rid you
> For learning me your language!
> (I, ii, 363–365)

Caliban thus emerges as a creature whose brute force subverts whatever intellect he can muster, whose passion overcomes his reason. Yet later it is Caliban who soothes the frightened jester Trinculo and butler Stephano:

> Be not afeard, the isle is full of noises,
> Sounds, and sweet airs, that give delight and hurt not.
> Sometimes a thousand twangling instruments
> Will hum about mine ears; and sometimes voices,
> That if I then had wak'd after long sleep,
> Will make me sleep again, and then in dreaming,
> The clouds methought would open, and show riches
> Ready to drop upon me, that when I wak'd
> I cried to dream again.
> (III, ii, 135–143)

Here he seems like a gentle figure who seeks only the tranquility of his own dreams.

How, then, are we to interpret Caliban? He is, like virtually all of Shakespeare's characters, a mixture. Indeed, the question of what proportion the forces of reason and passion share in human nature pervades Shakespeare's plays. The playwright shows human beings at their most noble and eloquent, but also at their most vicious and stupid. Whatever their social status, however, most seem to undergo some version of this conflict. Some understand the battle inside them, while others carry on obliviously. We in the audience, however, remain conscious of the complicated nature of our species: blessed with enough angelic reason to make us proud, but cursed by enough bestial passion to keep us humble.

Revenge

During Shakespeare's playwrighting career, revenge drama was one of the most popular theatrical forms. Its origins lay in Roman theater, notably in the plays of Seneca, but Shakespeare brought complexity to the genre. In general, revenge drama centers on a single figure who is inspired by one transgression to pursue a path of destruction that becomes more damaging than the act that provoked it. Because this revenge is fulfilled outside traditional moral order, the ethical code of the day proscribed that the story must conclude with the revenger's downfall. But Shakespeare also dramatizes revenge outside such formal structure, under circumstances when characters become so possessed by hatred that they lose all control.

In *Henry VI, Part 3*, for instance, Queen Margaret, wife of the ineffectual King Henry, leads her forces representing the crown and the Lancaster family against the insurgent army of the Duke of York, who seeks to put his own dynastic family on the throne. When Margaret captures York, she subjects him to humiliation, not because of a specific action, but because of his insolence in challenging her husband's authority. She dips York's handkerchief into the blood of his recently slain son, the Earl of Rutland, places a paper crown on York's head, and viciously belittles his ambition:

> But how is it that great Plantagenet
> Is crown'd so soon, and broke his solemn oath?
> And I bethink me, you should not be king
> Till our King Henry had shook hands with death.
> (I, iv, 99–102)

York responds with characteristic bitterness:

> She-wolf of France, but worse than wolves of France,
> Whose tongue more poisons than the adder's tooth!
> How ill-beseeming is it in thy sex
> To triumph like an Amazonian trull
> Upon their woes whom fortune captivates!
> But that thy face is vizard-like, unchanging,
> Made impudent with use of evil deeds,
> I would assay, proud queen, to make thee blush.
>
> (I, iv, 111–118)

York's accusations affirm a principal theme of revenge drama and one of the consequences of revenge as Shakespeare dramatizes it: the very act brings the revenger to an animalistic level.

Margaret, however, retains her vigor into the last play of the tetralogy, *Richard III*, when as the single surviving figure of all four works, she embodies both the history of her family's suffering and the spirit of vengeance. So enthralling is her voice and so vivid her hatred of Richard that her diatribe to Richard's mother, the Duchess of York and widow of the Duke whom Margaret humiliated, then murdered, deserves to be quoted in full:

> Bear with me; I am hungry for revenge,
> And now I cloy me beholding it.
> Thy Edward is dead, that kill'd my Edward;
> [Thy] other Edward dead, to quit my Edward;
> Young York he is but boot, because both they
> Match'd not the high perfection of my loss.
> Thy Clarence he is dead that stabb'd my Edward,
> And the beholders of this frantic play,
> Th' adulterate Hastings, Rivers, Vaughn, and Grey,
> Untimely smoth'red in their dusky graves.
> Richard yet lives, hell's black intelligencer,
> Only reserv'd their factor to buy souls
> And send them thither; but at hand, at hand,
> Ensues his piteous and unpitied end.
> Earth gapes, hell burns, fiends roar, saints pray,
> To have him suddenly convey'd from hence.
> Cancel his bond of life, dear God, I pray,
> That I may live and say, "The dog is dead."
>
> (IV, iii, 61–78)

Her final appeal for God to destroy Richard is a shocking climax to the most unbridled desire for murder declaimed by any character in all of Shakespeare's plays.

In some cases, revenge has no specific cause, but rather emerges from a general anger. In *Much Ado About Nothing*, when his crony Conrade asks Don John the Bastard, brother to the Prince of Aragon, to explain his sad demeanor, Don John can reply only:

> There is no measure in the occasion
> that breeds, therefore the sadness is without limit.
> (I, iii, 3–4)

Moments after, he adds:

> I cannot hide what I am: I must be sad when I
> have cause, and smile at no man's jests; eat
> when I have stomach, and wait for no man's leisure;
> sleep when I am drowsy, and tend on no man's
> business; laugh when I am merry, and claw no man
> in his humor.
> (I, iii, 13–18)

A bit later, Don John comes as close as ever to articulating a rationale for his plan to disrupt the marriage of Hero, Leonato's daughter, and the young lord Claudio:

> That young upstart
> hath all the glory of my overthrow. If I can cross
> him any way, I bless myself every way.
> (I, iii, 66–68)

He implies that the destruction for its own sake will gladden him. He cannot elevate his own status; therefore he chooses to destroy the lives of others.

This desire for blind revenge reaches its pinnacle in the character of Iago from *Othello*. In the opening scene, the title character's ensign claims that his reason for acting against his general is the appointment of Cassio as Othello's lieutenant (I, i, 8–30). But the discussion quickly turns away from military matters and never returns to that subject. Instead, Iago acknowledges his own self-interest: "I follow him to serve my turn upon him" (I, i, 42). Then he speaks of "my peculiar end" (I, i, 60), suggesting that Iago seeks not only to destroy the general, but also to buttress that revenge with reason, as he explains later on:

> I hate the Moor,
> And it is thought abroad that 'twixt my sheets
> [H'as] done my office. I know not if't be true,
> But I, for mere suspicion in that kind,
> Will do as if for surety.
> (I, iii, 386–390)

So bent is Iago on revenge that he willingly deceives himself. Thus at least one impact of the scene is how the capacity for revenge can push an individual into such a state that thought becomes subordinate to action.

When all his schemes approach fruition, Iago still cannot clarify his motives. All he says is: "This is the night/ That either makes me or foredoes me quite" (V, i, 128–129). He has never been able to articulate his goals, and here he cannot explain, even to himself, what satisfaction such success will bring. We may speculate that Iago's hatred of women, his anger at loss of promotion, his lust for Othello's wife, Desdemona, or, possibly, for Othello, or his general antagonism against a Moor is the foundation of his plot. But we also recognize that for Iago, none of these myriad sources is definitive.

Revenge also borders on the irrational in *The Merchant of Venice*, but here it has more definite sources. When the merchant Antonio requests of Shylock, the Jewish moneylender, the loan of 3,000 ducats for Antonio's friend, Bassanio, Shylock concocts a brutal punishment to be enforced if the loan is not repaid on time:

> . . . let the forfeit
> Be nominated for an equal pound
> Of your fair flesh, to be cut off and taken
> In what part of your body pleaseth me.
> (I, iii, 148–151)

Shakespeare's audience probably regarded this stipulation as a sign of Shylock's depravity. We, however, may interpret it more subtly. Shylock's hatred for Antonio is palpable, based on their mutual history as well as Shylock's general antagonism to Christian society. Furthermore, Shylock cannot risk attacking Antonio physically. With no other recourse, Shylock resorts to achieving vicarious revenge through the image of violating his enemy with a knife. Thus Shylock establishes his condition not with the hope of fulfilling it, but with the unconscious desire to communicate his detestation of Antonio and to make his target squirm.

Later Shylock tries to justify his desire for revenge, but the explanation comes, curiously, after he pleads for understanding (III, i, 59–64), and his monologue takes a sharp turn. Speaking of the similarity between Jews and Christians, he comments bitterly:

> And if you wrong us, shall
> we not revenge? If we are like you in the rest, we
> will resemble you in that. If a Jew wrong a Christian,
> what is his humility? Revenge. If a Christian wrong

a Jew, what should his sufferance be by Christian
example? Why, revenge. The villainy you teach
me, I will execute, and it shall go hard but I will
better the instruction.

(III, i, 66–73)

These lines have at least two implications: (1) Shylock clarifies that in
his view, revenge is a universal emotion, that no moral or religious principles can withstand its intensity; and (2) his last sentence suggests that
an individual possessed by that emotion loses all perspective, that the
desire for revenge, no matter what the cost to the revenger, can become
all-encompassing.

Such is indeed the result for Shylock. When Antonio's ships are apparently lost, Shylock sues to have the sentence carried out. In court, he
rejects all pleas for mercy:

So can I give no reason, nor I will not
More than a lodg'd hate, and a certain loathing
I bear Antonio, that I follow thus
A losing suit against him.

(IV, i, 59–62)

Here Shylock confesses that revenge has overtaken his better judgment.
Nor is he persuaded by Bassanio's offer to repay the debt several times
over:

If every ducat in six thousand ducats
Were in six parts, and every part a ducat,
I would not draw them, I would have my bond.

(IV, i, 84–87)

The reasonable alternative of huge financial settlement is lost, as the un-
stoppable craving for retribution batters sense.

Perhaps the play of Shakespeare's that most closely follows the tradition of revenge drama is his earliest tragedy, *Titus Andronicus*. Indeed,
so brutal is the action and so unrelenting the violence that critics have
speculated that Shakespeare may have been parodying the form. In any
case, in this play, one act of violence precipitates a whole series of actions, with the cycle ending only after the deaths of virtually every major
character.

The springboard to this savagery is the decision by Titus, the conquering Roman general, to sacrifice Alarbus, son of Tamora, Queen of
the conquered Goths. Titus intends for this gesture to mark the end of
the conflict between the two nations, and therefore he ignores Tamora's
pleas:

Andronicus, stain not thy tomb with blood!
Wilt thou draw near the nature of the gods?
Draw near them then in being merciful:
Sweet mercy is nobility's true badge.
Thrice-noble Titus, spare my first-born son!
(I, i, 116–120)

Were this play and the character of Titus more intricate psychologically, the general might hesitate to carry out his pronouncement, or at least weigh the moral issues. Instead he dismisses her petition, and Alarbus is carried off. Meanwhile, Titus's scheme to ensure that this sacrifice brings the war to a conclusion precipitates a more horrific response.

Ironically, though, the first murder is carried out by Titus against his own son, Mutius, who blocks his father's way when Bassianus, the rejected son of the late Emperor, and Marcus, Titus's brother, leave with Lavinia, Titus's daughter. Titus reacts on instinct, killing anyone, even his own son, who dares to challenge him. Nor does Titus's fury abate when he refuses to bury his sons with appropriate honors, and Marcus returns to offer advice: "Thou art a Roman, be not barbarous" (I, i, 378). This remark reverberates throughout the play, for once the ethos of revenge has taken over, all the characters, Romans and Goths alike, are reduced to the same barbaric level. The theme echoes later, when Titus and his youngest son, Lucius, plead for the lives of the boy's brothers. Although Titus has not yet seen the violence committed against his daughter, Lavinia, our knowledge that she has been raped and mutilated adds to the poignancy of Titus's reflection:

Why, foolish, Lucius, dost thou not perceive
That Rome is but a wilderness of tigers?
Tigers must prey, and Rome affords no prey
But me and mine.
(III, i, 53–56)

Revenge reduces all humanity, no matter how well-intentioned, to the level of beasts.

From this point on, we watch as Titus's mental state degenerates, until he sinks into madness, another familiar dramatic convention of revenge tragedy. Indeed, he becomes so obsessed that he maniacally defends a fly which Marcus kills, insisting that the innocent creature should have been spared (III, ii, 54–57). Titus's madness eventually takes the form of a craftiness that brings the orgy of revenge to a climax. Titus slaughters Tamora's two sons, Chiron and Demetrius, and serves their remains to their mother at dinner (V, iii). The deaths of Lavinia, Tamora, Titus himself, and finally Emperor Saturninus complete the spectacle. Still, no matter how shocking the action or clear the theme, the suddenness with which bodies drop, and the lack of introspection that pervades the play, ensures that this work is one of horror, not tragedy.

Such is not the case with Shakespeare's most profoundly reflective work based on the theme of revenge, *Hamlet*. The Prince's call to action occurs when the Ghost of his dead father appears and demands that Hamlet follow instructions: "Revenge his foul and most unnatural murther" (I, v, 25). The Ghost never specifies what form this revenge should take, but Hamlet assumes that his task is to prove himself to his father by killing Claudius, his father's brother, and now husband to Hamlet's mother, Gertrude. Hamlet initially seems eager to please the Ghost:

> Haste me to know't, that I with wings as swift
> As meditation, or the thoughts of love,
> May sweep to my revenge.
>
> (I, v, 29–31)

These words, though, sound surprisingly gentle from someone who has been ordered to carry out so daunting a task. Thus like Hamlet, we wonder if he is emotionally suited to discharge the duty. We also ask whether Hamlet, a poetic, sensitive young man, agrees to obey out of genuine love for so militaristic a father, or whether Hamlet feels instead that he ought to want to act to please old Hamlet and thereby become the courageous soldier the Prince has never shown himself to be. We also ask whether the Ghost that orders Hamlet to revenge is a benign figure, or whether the action he commands is essentially evil. Hamlet, too, ponders these questions, and thus he faces a dilemma of overwhelming complication. He loves his mother and hates his uncle. He respects and perhaps fears the Ghost of his dead father. He bears the weight of his own sensitive personality, as well as the legal, ethical, and religious sanctions against murder. Finally, he is a member of the royal family, and thus his actions resound through the kingdom. Hamlet articulates the crisis succinctly:

> The time is out of joint—O cursed spite,
> That ever I was born to set it right!
>
> (I, v, 188–189)

Hamlet's subsequent indecision initially manifests itself on the pose of madness, which becomes bewilderingly hard to decipher. We are never certain whether Hamlet is acting mad, whether the madness he thinks he is feigning has overtaken him, or whether he thinks he is still acting when he has lost control. One instance when his behavior loses us occurs during an assault on Polonius's daughter, Ophelia:

Get thee [to] a nunnery, why wouldst thou
be a breeder of sinners? I am myself indifferent honest,
but yet I could accuse me of such things that it were
better my mother hath not yet borne me.
(III, i, 120–123)

How literally are we to take any of this raving?

Whatever our answer, Hamlet's reluctance to commit revenge becomes most intense when he has the opportunity to kill Claudius, who seeks absolution for his crimes, but recognizes the impossibility of that reward:

. . . O, what form of prayer
Can serve my turn? 'Forgive me my foul murther?'
That cannot be, since I am still possess'd
Of those effects for which I did the murther:
My crown, mine own ambition, and my queen.
(III, iii, 51–56)

Hamlet, though, chooses not to kill the King when he is in prayer, but the reason startles us:

Why, this is [hire and salary], not revenge.
'A took my father grossly, full of bread,
With all his crimes broad blown, as flush as May,
And how his audit stands who knows save heaven?
But in our circumstance and course of thought
'Tis heavy with him. And am I then revenged,
To take him in the purging of his soul,
When he is fit and season'd for his passage?
(III, iii, 79–86)

Instead, Hamlet resolves to strike Claudius at a more opportune moment:

When he is drunk asleep, or in his rage,
Or in th' incestious pleasure of his bed,
At game a'swearing, or about some act
That has no relish of salvation in't . . .
(III, iii, 89–92)

We have long felt the tension between Hamlet's role as an earthly revenger and the Christian principle that justice belongs to heaven. At this moment, Hamlet exceeds his bounds by deciding that his crime should fulfill revenge not only in this world, but also in the next. By doing so, Hamlet assumes a new role in which he is free from the restraints of morality and justice, and he thereby commits a transgression of his own.

He also acquires a casualness about death that further lowers him in our estimation. He seems to feel no regret over the accidental slaying of Polonius, counselor to the King and the father of the woman Hamlet loves, Ophelia. Indeed, Hamlet dismisses the corpse: "Thou wretched, rash, intruding fool, farewell!/ I took thee for thy better" (III, iv, 31–32), then reaffirms his divine charge:

> I do repent, but heaven hath pleas'd it so
> To punish me with this, and this with me,
> That I must be their scourge and minister.
>   (III, iv, 173–175)

By declaring himself a heavenly avenger, he also denies any moral responsibility. Soon he coldly dispatches his old schoolmates Rosencrantz and Guildenstern to their deaths, rewriting the letter they are to give to the English King, and changing the directions from an order for Hamlet's death to one that commands the bearers' execution. Afterwards, he denies responsibility, as he explains to his friend Horatio:

> Why, even in that was heaven ordinant.
> I had my father's signet in my purse,
> Which was the model of that Danish seal . . .
>   (V, ii, 48–50)

So infused is Hamlet with power that he functions as if he is heaven's avenger and that all his actions are therefore justified. Nor does he feel guilt:

> Their defeat
> Does by their own insinuation grow,
> 'Tis dangerous when the baser nature comes
> Between the pass and fell incensed points
> Of mighty opposites.
>   (V, ii, 58–62)

By the final scene, Hamlet finds equilibrium when he exchanges forgiveness with Laertes, Polonius's son and brother to Ophelia, who, under the pressure of her father's death and Hamlet's seeming madness, has committed suicide. By then, however, Hamlet has lost the greater battle, as the responsibility to revenge has crushed him. As dramatized in other plays of Shakespeare, though, the spirit of revenge destroys many different figures. Indeed, Shakespeare suggests that the desire may turn into a disease, an all-controlling addiction that shatters a person's moral ballast and drives that individual beyond the bounds of rationality. Perhaps, then, we should look to two more lines. In *As You Like It*, the once villainous lord Oliver speaks of "Kindness, nobler ever than revenge" (IV, iii, 129), while in *The Tempest*, Shakespeare's final play, Prospero, the exiled Duke whose enemies have fallen into his power, comments "The rarer action is/ In virtue than in vengeance" (V, i, 27–28). These sentiments encapsulate the theme that Shakespeare dramatizes throughout his works, as well as reaffirm how revenge never alleviates suffering, but only intensifies it.

Supernatural Phenomena

Shakespeare and his contemporaries accepted belief in certain supernatural powers, but in presenting them onstage, the playwright did more than acknowledge the existence of these forces. Rather, he imbued them with personalities and motives, allowing other characters to react to them and thereby reveal their own values and morals. Thus the presence of supernatural forces not only offers opportunity for bold technical effects, or as much as the limitations of the theater permit, but also leads to intriguing thematic revelation.

Perhaps the most benign supernaturals are those in *A Midsummer Night's Dream*. The first one we meet is Puck, denounced by one fairy as a cruel prankster, but who describes himself as more playful than malicious:

> I am that merry wanderer of the night.
> I jest to Oberon and make him smile
> When I a fat and bean-fed horse beguile . . .
> (II, i, 43–45)

These figures are soon joined by Oberon, King of the Fairies, and Titania, his Queen, who accuse each other of affection for their mortal parallels: Theseus, the Duke of Athens, and Hippolyta, soon to be his wife. Titania also accuses Oberon of creating upsets in nature:

> But with thy brawls thou has disturb'd our sport.
> Therefore the winds, piping to us in vain,
> As in revenge, have suck'd up from the sea
> Contagious fogs, which, falling in the land,
> Hath every pelting river made so proud
> That they have overborne their continents.
> (II, i, 87–92)

She catalogues other climatic disturbances that have caused poor harvests and similar turmoil. These descriptions apparently paralleled real-life events of the time, and thus for Shakespeare's audience probably made the fantasy characters more believable.

Oberon and Puck then insinuate themselves into the lives of the four lovers: Hermia, Helena, Demetrius, and Lysander. Oberon becomes angry when he sees Demetrius spurn the affections of Helena, and therefore orders Puck to drop in the eyes of a "disdainful youth" (II, i, 261) a magic potion that causes the victim to fall in love with the next person he sees. To no one's surprise in a comedy, Puck mistakenly anoints Lysander, formerly enamored of Hermia, and confusion ensues, as affection by the males for the females shifts wildly. Here the influence of the supernatural brings out deeper feelings, especially from the men, who express their passions, whether for love or hate, far more deeply under the magical influence. When, for instance, drops are placed in Demetrius's eyes, he rhapsodizes to Helena with an ardor that he has never summoned before, even when he claimed to love Hermia:

> O, Helen, goddess, nymph, perfect, divine!
> To what, my love, shall I compare thine eyne?
> Crystal is muddy. O, how ripe in show
> Thy lips, those kissing cherries, tempting grow!
> (III, ii, 137–140)

Similarly, Lysander's antagonism to Hermia becomes more impassioned than any feelings of love he has articulated:

> Get you gone, you dwarf,
> You minimus, of hind'ring knot-grass made;
> You bead, you acorn.
> (III, ii, 328–330)

Eventually, with Puck's assistance, matters right themselves, when Lysander and Hermia, and Demetrius and Helena, pair off. We, note, however, that Demetrius remains under the influence of the magic juice.

A more interesting interference by Oberon and Puck concerns Titania, also the victim of this magic. In Oberon's words:

> I'll watch Titania when she is asleep,
> And drop the liquor of it in her eyes;
> The next thing then she waking looks upon
> (Be it lion, bear, or wolf, or bull,
> On meddling monkey, or on busy ape),
> She shall pursue it with the soul of love.
> (II, i, 177–182)

That object turns out to be Nick Bottom, the weaver, newly adorned with an ass's head, thanks to Puck. Titania, though, is smitten:

> I pray thee, gentle mortal, sing again.
> Mine ear is much enamored of thy note;
> So is mine eye enthralled to thy shape . . .
> (III, i, 137–139)

Titania's sudden infatuation affirms how one of the primary themes of this play applies to supernatural beings as well: that when we are in love, we see what we want to see. Even more enjoyable, though, is Bottom's reaction to this state of affairs, for he remains totally unflustered by the presence of the other fairies, and in response to their tender care merely expresses the desire to know them better (III, i, 182–202).

At first Oberon is amused by his wife's new romance, but eventually he tires of it. Or perhaps he envies her devotion:

> Her dotage now I begin to pity.
> For meeting her of late behind the wood,
> Seeking sweet favors for this hateful fool,
> I did upbraid her, and fall out with her.
> (IV, i, 47–50)

Whatever his reason, he removes the spell, so that she instantly regards Bottom with horror: "O, how mine eyes do loathe his visage now!" (IV, i, 79). She rejects that aspect of herself which was capable of seeing beauty in so preposterous a creature. Bottom, though, ever the unintentional poet, treasures his time in the world of fairies:

> I will get Peter Quince to write a
> ballet of this dream. It shall be call'd "Bottom's
> Dream," because it hath no bottom . . .
> (IV, i, 214–216)

His delight reminds us of the pleasures of the realm of imagination.

The presence of the supernatural in other plays of Shakespeare communicates darker themes. In *Richard III*, for instance, the besieged King is visited by ghosts of his many victims. For Elizabethans, such figures belonged to one of two categories: objective ghosts had the power to make themselves visible to several people, while subjective ghosts were figments of a single imagination. Here (V, iii) the ghosts, such as the young princes whom Richard ordered killed, are creations of his conscience, and as such they may be regarded as manifestations of guilt. So many apparitions take the stage in this scene, however, that the terror is blunted.

Such is not the case in *Julius Caesar*, when before the battle at Phillipi, the Ghost of Caesar forces the once noble Brutus to come to grips with his own conscience:

> Art thou some god, some angel, or some devil,
> That mak'st my blood cold, and my hair to stare?
> Speak to me what thou art.
>
> (IV, iii, 279–281)

The answer, "Thy evil spirit, Brutus" (IV, iii, 282), confirms what we have suspected: that Brutus's actions against Caesar have been indefensible. More important, the Ghost recalls something that Brutus uttered when he and the other conspirators plotted Caesar's assassination:

> Let's be sacrificers, but not butchers, Caius.
> We all stand up against the spirit of Caesar,
> And in the spirit of men there is no blood . . .
>
> (II, i, 166–168)

The appearance of Caesar's ghost affirms that the "spirit" of Caesar lives, that even though his body lies buried, his political heritage flourishes.

One of the most compelling supernatural presences in all of dramatic literature is the Ghost of Hamlet's father, a role apparently played by Shakespeare himself. From the first line of the play, its presence dominates the action, as the men on watch, Francisco and Bernardo, cannot be sure whether they see each other or a third figure. When they place their dilemma before Horatio, Hamlet's closest friend, and he beholds the apparition, he proposes three reasons why this Ghost might appear:

> If there be any good thing to be done
> That may to thee do ease, and grace to me,
> Speak to me.
> If thou art privy to thy country's fate,
> Which happily foreknowing may avoid,
> O speak!
> Or if thou hast uphoarded in thy life
> Extorted treasure in the womb of earth,
> For which, they say, your spirits oft walk in death,
> Speak of it, stay and speak!
>
> (I, i, 130–139)

The first of these possibilities turns out to be correct; yet the wording of Horatio's query poses intriguing questions. Will revenge against the Ghost's murderer, his brother Claudius, be "a good thing"? Will it bring "grace"? In essence, Horatio raises the difficult problem of whether this

Ghost is beneficent or malicious. When Horatio reveals his discovery to Hamlet, the Prince's reaction confirms this uncertainty. He repeatedly urges Horatio to describe the Ghost's appearance, noting the military apparel and the sorrowful manner. Yet Hamlet, too, is unclear how to respond to the Ghost's presence:

> My father's spirit—in arms! All is not well,
> I doubt some foul play. Would the night were come!
> Till then sit still, my soul. [Foul] deeds will rise,
> Though all the earth o'erwhelm them, to men's eyes.
>
> (I, ii, 254–257)

Hamlet has been searching for a purpose to his existence. Now he hopes that the Ghost will provide such meaning.

The Ghost does so, but the directive does not alleviate Hamlet's dilemma. At the start, the Ghost almost bullies Hamlet into action:

> And duller shouldst thou be than the fat weed
> That roots itself in ease on Lethe wharf,
> Wouldst thou not stir in this.
>
> (I, v, 32–34)

The menace inherent in these lines implies that the Ghost has never been satisfied with Hamlet's behavior, that now, at last, the son has opportunity to prove himself in his father's eyes. Then the Ghost confirms what Hamlet has suspected: "The serpent that did sting thy father's life/ Now wears his crown" (I, v, 38–39). The greatest anger, however, seems reserved for Claudius's marriage to Hamlet's mother, Gertrude, and her acceptance of him:

> But virtue, as it never will be moved,
> Though lewdness court it in a shape of heaven,
> So [lust], though to radiant angel link'd,
> Will [sate] itself in a celestial bed
> And prey on garbage.
>
> (I, v, 53–57)

Yet the Ghost orders Hamlet not to harm Gertrude:

> Let not the royal bed of Denmark be
> A couch for luxury and damned incest.
> But howsomever thou pursues this act,
> Taint not thy mind, nor let thy soul contrive
> Against thy mother aught.
>
> (I, v, 82–86)

The Ghost's attitude toward Gertrude is thus a peculiar mixture of fury and solicitude: fury that she has allowed herself to be seduced by Claudius, solicitude to ensure that judgment of her should be left to heaven. In this respect, the Ghost's attitude reflects our own uncertainty about her motivations. We are never certain whether Gertrude knows or even suspects that Claudius murdered her husband. We also wonder whether she and Claudius committed adultery before the murder and, if so, whether she was an accessory to the crime. In any case, what seems to enrage the Ghost more than the loss of his throne is his wife's marriage. Similarly, through the rest of the play, Hamlet seems preoccupied less with political and military matters and more with the sexual and emotional bonds between his mother and Claudius.

This attitude reaches a frenzy during Hamlet's confrontation with Gertrude, when he rails at length about her behavior. Showing her pictures of Claudius and old Hamlet, Hamlet cries out:

> Have you eyes?
> Could you on this fair mountain leave to feed,
> And batten on this moor? ha, have you eyes?
> You cannot call it love, for at your age
> The heyday in the blood is tame, it's humble,
> And waits upon the judgment, and what judgment
> Would step from this to this?
>
> (III, iv, 65–71)

Evidently Hamlet's barrage of accusation sparks something in Gertrude, for she appears ready to admit guilt:

> Thou turn'st my [eyes into my very] soul,
> And there I see such black and [grain'd spqts]
> As will [not] leave their tinct.
>
> (III, iv, 89–91)

Yet just as we, along with Hamlet, anticipate Gertrude's confession, the Ghost enters and interrupts Hamlet's rage, denying both him and us the chance to learn the answers to some of the most tantalizing questions the play provokes.

Thus the Ghost embodies much of the uncertainty in *Hamlet*. At first, it lifts Hamlet out of despair and apparently provides a definite course of action. Yet when this course proves untenable, the Ghost offers no escape or alternative. Simultaneously, the Ghost's attitude toward Gertrude becomes Hamlet's own attitude: fury tempered by love, yet still fueled by jealousy. This whirligig of emotion is at the core of the play.

The influence of the supernatural is equally powerful in *Macbeth*, where the witches are so strong a presence that at moments they seem to control the title character. After all, Shakespeare's audience believed that witches were in league with the devil and empowered to fly, vanish, conjure storms and images, and inflict disease. The play may also have been a tribute to King James I, formerly James VI of Scotland, who succeeded Elizabeth on the English throne, and whose interest in witches and other aspects of the supernatural was apparent in a book he wrote on the subject.

From the play's opening lines, the image of the witches is gripping, as they hint at their predilections:

> When the hurly-burly's done,
> When the battle's lost and won.
> (I, i, 3–4)

They regard human action with amused detachment, as if our lives were no more than "hurly-burly." The witches also express interest in "the battle": perhaps they mean the immediate conflict on the field before them, perhaps the conflict for the Scottish crown, or perhaps the conflict for mastery of Macbeth's soul. Whatever the target, their interest in what's "lost and won" seems sporting, as they clarify in comments about the sailor and his wife, and the vengeance wreaked upon that couple:

> I'll drain him dry as hay:
> Sleep shall neither night and day
> Hang upon his penthouse lid;
> He shall live a man forbid . . .
> (I, iii, 18–21)

Those punishments parallel the pains Macbeth suffers later. We also note the first witch's threat: "I'll do. I'll do, and I'll do" (I, iii, 10). The word "do" becomes crucial to this play, reflecting the central theme that no action can be carried out unto itself, that every one requires preparation and brings about consequences.

Do the witches control Macbeth, or does he have free will? The evidence suggests that the witches indeed tempt Macbeth, but that ultimately he acts according to the dictates of his character. When, for instance, the witches predict that he will be King and that another general, Banquo, will be father to kings, Banquo comments upon his colleague's reaction: "Good sir, why do you start, and seem to fear/ Things that sound so fair?" (I, iii, 51–52). At this point, we suspect that Macbeth has pondered such possibilities before. Perhaps the witches should be regarded as malicious meddlers, who desire only to play upon human vulnerabilities, to tap evil within. The subject they have chosen is Macbeth, whose frailties, particularly his ambition and capacity for violence, may be exploited.

Over the course of the play, however, Macbeth's attitude toward the witches changes. At the start, he is eager to believe them and fearfully asks them to speak (I, iii, 47). Indeed, after he congratulates Banquo on the prediction that his children will be kings, Macbeth greedily reasserts the witches' prophesy about himself: "And Thane of Cawdor too; went it not so?" (I, iii, 87). Later, though, after Macbeth has murdered King Duncan and seized the crown, the witches' guarantees no longer satisfy him:

> If't be so,
> For Banquo's issue have I fil'd my mind,
> For them the gracious Duncan have I murther'd,
> Put rancors in the vessel of my peace
> Only for them, and mine eternal jewel
> Given to the common enemy of man,
> To make them kings—the seeds of Banquo kings!
> (III, i, 63–69)

He has become so taken with himself that he assumes he can defy the witches by killing Banquo and his son, Fleance, who escapes the assassination attempt (III, iii). Finally, Macbeth rudely demands that the witches reveal his future: "How now, you secret, black, and midnight hags?/ What is't you do?" (IV, i, 47–48). Under his pressure, they present a series of apparitions and veiled truths, but Macbeth no longer cares. When the witches suggest that "none of woman born/ Shall harm Macbeth" (IV, i, 80–81), a reference to Macduff who was delivered by cesarean birth, Macbeth ignores the insinuation. Instead he sinks to his moral nadir by ordering the slaughter of Macduff's wife and children (IV, ii). He knows that they are no threat, but so deeply is Macbeth corrupted by violence that he crosses the boundaries of rationality. Thus the witches may be said to have triumphed.

The other principal supernatural force in this play is the Ghost of Banquo, who torments Macbeth when the newly crowned King hosts a royal banquet (III, iv). We may take this Ghost to be subjective, since Macbeth alone sees it and is so shaken that Lady Macbeth disperses the company.

One other possible intervention by the supernatural occurs in the scene previous to the banquet. In arranging the attack on Banquo and Fleance, Macbeth assigns the task to two murderers, but also advises them that they will be joined by "the perfect spy o' th' time" (III, i, 129). When this figure appears, he claims to have been sent by Macbeth (III, i, 1). He also hears the horses (III, iii, 8), knows Banquo's accustomed routes (III, iii, 12–14), recognizes Banquo (III, iii, 14), and realizes that Fleance has escaped (III, iii, 19). Could the third murderer be Macbeth himself? Not likely, since Macbeth remains at the castle preparing for the aforementioned gathering. Can we doubt, though, that this unidentified figure is some aspect of Macbeth? Spiritually, Macbeth is with his charges. He planned and ordered the murder, and in a play where the supernatural is such an integral part, the hypothesis that Macbeth's spirit functions in such a way seems reasonable.

Macbeth stands as perhaps Shakespeare's most intense foray into the spirit world, but in his final work the playwright also invoked imaginary beings to shape the world onstage. In *The Tempest*, the exiled Duke Prospero calls on his magic to summon various mythological goddesses to bless the union of his daughter, Miranda, and Ferdinand, son of King Alonso of Naples (IV, i). Those invoked include Iris, goddess of the rainbow and Juno's messenger; Ceres, goddess of agriculture; and Juno herself, queen of the gods. Joined by images of harvesters, they perform a ritual ceremony which ensures that the upcoming union will be fertile and otherwise blessed by nature. Yet even at this joyous moment, we note that Ceres requests that Venus and Cupid be excluded from the ceremony (IV, i, 87–91), along with the element of romantic love, or, in Iris's words, "Some wanton charm" (IV, i, 95). Prospero has always warned Miranda and Ferdinand to remain pure until after the wedding, and here is one more instance where unearthly characters reflect the more mundane matters of human existence.

Such is Shakespeare's strategy whenever he invokes supernatural figures. Theatrically, they provide irresistible energy. Thematically, they enlighten our sense of ourselves, as we see our lives and values reflected in a mysterious, ultimately unknowable, universe that surrounds our own.

The Tragic Flaw

In his *Poetics*, the Greek philosopher Aristotle used the term *hamartia* to explain that feature of the tragic hero which leads to his or her downfall. We have come to define the word as "tragic flaw," and we use it to mean a fatal weakness or error in judgment that propels a character to a tragic end. As an example, we might point to Euripides' *The Bacchae* and the unwillingness of King Pentheus to recognize the power of the god Dionysus. Shakespeare's tragic heroes, too, suffer from such flaws, as Hamlet explains:

> ... that these men,
> Carrying, I say, the stamp of one defect,
> Being nature's livery, or fortune's star,
> His virtues else, be they as pure as grace,
> As infinite as man may undergo,
> Shall in the general censure take corruption
> From that particular fault ...
>
> (I, iv, 30–36)

Shakespeare, however, develops this concept with an intriguing twist. Virtually all figures at the center of Shakespeare's tragic plays are called upon to resolve an extraordinary crisis. The exquisite dilemma of these characters is that their qualities of greatness, the ones that make them worthy of the positions they hold, also militate against the successful resolution of these crises. In other words, the strengths that raise the characters to the noblest heights become the points of vulnerability that lower them to the most profound depths.

This claim requires support, but even at first glance it should make sense. The essence of drama is the clash between an intriguing personality and a tantalizing situation that allows that personality to grapple with itself. In all of Shakespeare's plays, but particularly in the tragedies, we watch strongly motivated characters in predicaments that bring both attributes and liabilities to the fore.

Such interaction creates another quality that adds to the richness of Shakespeare's tragic plays. Often we are conscious of what the characters themselves do not know: how their individual instincts and drives shape their behavior. The result is constant dramatic irony, as characters proceed down a path that is not, strictly speaking, determined, but because of the characters' strengths and flaws, inescapable.

For example, from the opening moments of *Romeo and Juliet* when we see young Romeo, his outstanding characteristic is his passion, his willingness to release his emotions instantly and unconditionally. We hear a description of him wandering around Verona in a state of affection, then learn that he is in love with Rosaline, as he reminds everyone when he takes the stage:

> Why, such is love's transgression.
> Griefs of mine own lie heavy in my breast,
> Which thou wilt propagate to have it press'd
> With more of thine.
> (I, i, 185–189)

Romeo has turned himself into a parody of a Renaissance suitor. He maintains this attitude when he appears at the Capulet party and for the first time sees Juliet. Instantly, the direction of his passions changes:

> O, she doth teach the torches to burn bright!
> It seems she hangs upon the cheek of night
> As a rich jewel in an Ethiop's ear—
> Beauty too rich for use, for earth too dear!
> (I, v, 44–47)

The imagery is still familiar, but more direct and sincere, so we can believe that here is genuine love at first sight. After the two playfully exchange affections (I, v, 93–130), Romeo and Juliet each learns of the irony of their infatuation. Romeo realizes first: "Is she a Capulet/ O dear account! my life is my foe's debt" (I, v, 117–118). A few lines later, Juliet recognizes that Romeo is a Montague: "My only love sprung from my only hate!" (I, v, 138). The crisis is thus established.

Romeo deals with it as we might expect: with full passion. Evidence of this overflow occurs in the balcony scene, when he pursues Juliet in spite of the danger involved. She, on the other hand, tries to be practical: "How camest thou hither, tell me, and wherefore?" (II, ii, 62). Romeo remains in the throes of emotion: "With love's light wings did I o'erperch these walls . . ." (II, ii, 66), while Juliet reminds Romeo of the risk he takes: "If they do see thee, they will murther thee" (II, ii, 70). Still, Romeo cannot be rational: "Alack, there lies more peril in thine eye/ Than twenty of their swords!" (II, ii, 71–72). He chooses not to think but always to feel. Although we are moved by his devotion, we are equally amused by his refusal to face the seriousness of their situation.

Soon, however, Romeo's glory leads to his downfall, which occurs when Mercutio, Romeo's friend, and Tybalt, Juliet's cousin, fight (III, i). When Romeo attempts to intercede, he unwittingly allows Tybalt to strike a fatal blow, and Mercutio dies moments later. As always, Romeo reacts impetuously:

> O sweet Juliet,
> Thy beauty hath made me effeminate,
> And in my temper soft'ned valor's steel!
> (III, i, 113–115)

Without considering the consequences, he picks up a sword and challenges Tybalt, killing him. Only after Romeo's ally Benvolio shouts that the town is in an uproar does Romeo grasp the import of his action: "O, I am fortune's fool!" (III, i, 136). He blames the stars or blind fate, but we recognize how Romeo's own personality led him to this moment.

Near the end of the play, when his plan to rescue Juliet has seemingly gone awry, Romeo continues to rush headlong. After he finds Juliet's body in the Capulet family tomb and assumes that she is dead, he comments how lifelike she looks:

> Thou are not conquer'd, beauty's ensign yet
> Is crimson in thy lips and in thy cheeks,
> And death's pale flag is not advanced there.
> (V, iii, 94–96)

He adds: "Ah, dear Juliet, Why art thou yet so fair?" (V, iii, 101–102). Although the outcome of the play was revealed in the Prologue, Romeo's comments might temporarily raise hopes that he will do the obvious and pause to see if she awakens. Instead, with characteristic haste, he drinks poison and dies next to her, seconds before she revives. Once again, Romeo's most compelling trait proves his undoing.

We might say the same of Brutus, who becomes leader of the conspiracy in *Julius Caesar*. What distinguishes him from other characters in the play is his capacity for ethical examination and his pride in recognizing and carrying out the morally correct action. Yet this insistence upon cogitation and his determination to follow what he deems an honorable course destroys him and his enterprise.

We become aware of Brutus's point of vulnerability when he tries to deflect his best friend Cassius's inquiries:

> If I have veil'd my look,
> I turn the trouble of my countenance
> Merely upon myself. Vexed I am
> Of late with passions of some difference,
> Conceptions only proper to myself.
>
> (I, ii, 37–41)

Brutus is thoughtful and proud, almost to the point of excess. He is also private, and he believes himself to be the unquestioned judge of morality. In sum, he is a man ripe for a fall.

That fall comes closer when Brutus reflects upon Cassius's scheme to assassinate Caesar:

> It must be by his death; and for my part,
> I know no personal cause to spurn at him,
> But for the general. He would be crown'd:
> How that might change his nature, there's the question.
>
> (II, i, 10–13)

In fact, that is not the question. The real issue concerns the right of one citizen to murder another, but Brutus avoids this one, since he knows that the answer would doom the enterprise. Moreover, his refusal to discuss the matter with Portia, his wife, confirms his self-consciousness. Brutus knows that the murder of Caesar is indefensible. Yet his pride and relentless need to balance conflicting perspectives lead him to justify this tragic path.

Ironically, pride becomes Caesar's downfall as well. When the conspirators gather, and Cassius worries that Caesar might not go to the Senate that day (II, i, 193–201), the conspirator Decius reassures everyone:

> If he be so resolv'd,
> I can o'ersway him; for he loves to hear
> That unicorns may be betray'd with trees,
> And bears with glasses, elephants with holes,
> Lions with toils, and men with flatterers;
> But when I tell him he hates flatterers
> He says he does, being then most flattered.
>
> (II, i, 202–208)

That guarantee proves accurate. No wonder Caesar and Brutus have affection and respect for each other. They are prey to the same vulnerabilities of character.

Brutus's qualities also contribute to another dangerous aspect of his personality. He is removed from the realm of common men, a severe fault for a man who seeks a career in politics. He strives to elevate himself and his associates, but as a result lacks empathy for the plebeians. We see such behavior in the scene in which the conspirators gather, when Brutus scorns Cassius's request for a sworn oath and insists at preposterous length that everyone involved must by definition be loyal and high-minded (II, i, 114–140). No doubt he is trying to convince himself of what he says. We see the same sort of behavior in the central scene of the play, when Brutus tries to convince the Roman mob that the assassination of Caesar was legitimate. Taking the platform first (with poor tactics but typical generosity, Brutus has granted Mark Antony the privilege of speaking in the advantageous final spot), Brutus offers a literally prosaic defense:

> As Caesar lov'd
> me, I weep for him; as he was fortunate, I rejoice
> at it; as he was valiant, I honor him; but, as he was
> ambitious, I slew him.
> (III, ii, 24–27)

The words reflect the essence of Brutus. The rhetorical flourishes suggest scholarship and moral fiber, but the words are hollow, reflective of a man who thinks more shrewdly than others, but who fails to feel as others do. We also recognize that Brutus has enormous pride but little common sense.

In one of his final speeches before he falls on his sword, Brutus reflects:

> Countrymen,
> My heart doth joy that yet in all my life
> I found no man but he was true to me.
> I shall have more glory by this losing day
> More than Octavius and Mark Antony
> By this vile conquest shall attain unto.
> (V, v, 33–38)

How little he has learned. We sense that had he the opportunity to live again, he would make the same mistakes. As for his promise of future eminence, Brutus and Cassius have been judged among the most notorious traitors in history. One measure of their reputation is their place in the *Inferno* of the fourteenth century poet Dante: in the ninth and innermost circle of hell, along with Judas Iscariot, who betrayed Christ. All three are chewed and tortured in a mouth of Satan.

Shakespeare also seems aware of the predicament of men whose attributes warrant praise in one context, but condemnation in another. Macbeth, for instance, is a soldier of unsurpassed achievement. As King Duncan says of him, after hearing the sergeant's opening narrative about Macbeth's military successes: "O valiant cousin, worthy gentleman!" (I, ii, 24). Yet when Macbeth returns to a more civilized environment, this same instinct for violence becomes his undoing. When the witches tempt him with the thought of his achieving the throne, Macbeth is taken with the idea, although his conscience pains him:

> My thought, whose murther yet is but fantastical,
> Shakes so my single state of man that function
> Is smother'd in surmise, and nothing is
> But what is not.
>
> (I, iii, 139–142)

He is not eager to kill, fears the consequences of murder (I, vii, 1–28), and eventually talks himself out of the scheme, as he explains to Lady Macbeth:

> We will proceed no further in this business:
> He hath honor'd me of late, and I have bought
> Golden opinions from all sorts of people,
> Which would be worn now in their newest gloss,
> Not cast aside so soon.
>
> (I, vii, 31–35)

Under Lady Macbeth's mockery, however, his capacity for violence surfaces, and he imagines a knife drawing him onward to murder:

> I see thee yet, in form as palpable
> As this which now I draw.
> Thou marshall'st me the way that I was going,
> And such an instrument I was to use.
>
> (II, i, 40–43)

Macbeth recognizes that whether the knife is real or imaginary, it pulls him toward the crime he intends to commit. The impulse to kill in cold blood, essential on the battlefield, here turns into a cruel liability. What partially redeems Macbeth in our eyes, even as he commits the first of several murders, each more despicable than the last, is the inner pain that torments him, the conscience that battles his instinct for violence, but which cannot thwart that instinct.

The same predilection proves the undoing of Alcibiades' client in *Timon of Athens*. First we learn that the man is accused of murder, but Alcibiades, an Athenian Captain, claims the act was self-defense:

> But with a noble fury and fair spirit,
> Seeing his reputation touch'd to death,
> He did oppose his foe:
> And with such sober and unnoted passion
> He did behoove his anger, ere 'twas spent,
> As if he had but prov'd an argument.
> (III, v, 18–23)

An accusing Senator, however, reminds Alcibiades that his client has not led an exemplary life:

> He's a sworn rioter; he has a sin that often
> Drowns him and takes his valor prisoner.
> If there were no foes, that were enough
> To overcome him. In that beastly fury
> He has been known to commit outrages
> And cherish factions.
> (III, v, 67–72)

Alcibiades, however, notes that his client has killed in another context:

> Hard fate! he might have died in war . . .
> If by this crime he owes the law his life,
> Why, let the war receive't in valiant gore,
> For law is strict, and war is nothing more.
> (III, v, 74–84)

The same powers that won his client renown in battle, Alcibiades claims, are the ones for which he is condemned. Despite the sympathy Alcibiades arouses, the Senate refuses to pardon his client, and in a fit of pique Alcibiades stalks off, swearing revenge on Athens (V, iii, 110–116).

In his refusal to see his client's weakness, Alcibiades shows himself possessed by the same tragic flaw as the play's title character. Both men err in looking on human behavior with unqualified benevolence. Timon insists on dispensing money with endless generosity: "Methinks, I could deal kingdoms to my friends,/ And ne'er be weary" (I, ii, 220–221). Even when called upon by a strict legal system to repay the debts he has accrued, he never doubts that his beneficiaries will stand by him: "You shall perceive how you/ Mistake my fortunes. I am wealthy in my friends" (II, ii, 183–184). But he misjudges everyone, and in anger invites his creditors to a banquet, humiliates them by throwing water in their faces, then assaults them verbally for their demanding that he fulfill his obligations:

> Live loath'd, and long,
> Most smiling, smooth detested parasites,
> Courteous destroyers, affable wolves, meek bears,
> You fools of fortune, trencher-friends, time's flies,
> Cap-and-knee slaves, vapors, and minute-jacks!
> (III, vi, 93–97)

This explosion, coming right after Alcibiades' defeat, invites us to evaluate the two men together. Their insistence on judging humanity from only the kindest perspective might in another society prove ennobling, but in the Athens where they live, in which the law is ruthlessly enforced, their generosity is their undoing. As a result, both turn their back on society: Timon escapes to caves where he berates mankind, while Alcibiades resorts to the company of prostitutes and plans military vengeance against the city, a revenge curbed at the last moment.

The theme of a tragic flaw turning out to be a chief agent of a hero's downfall may be applied to Shakespeare's other great tragedies. Hamlet is a poet-philosopher, a man impassioned by words and ideas, a reflective, artistic soul. Yet he is called upon to carry out a revenge for which his own nature is unsuited. As a result, he turns his wit and anger against himself. His satiric gibes against the court become melancholy broodings on his own inadequacies, until he robs himself of all energy. By the end, he anticipates the death that will allow him to escape awareness that he has failed at being the son his father has always sought. As Hamlet says to to his friend Horatio before the fatal fencing encounter: "Thou wouldst not think how ill all's here about my heart—but it is no matter" (V, ii, 212–213).

Othello is a soldier whose pride and dignity have flourished in a life governed by military code. Even though he has traveled the world, however, he finds himself lost in cosmopolitan Venice, a city of unfamiliar manners and mores, where shadings of truth and morality hold sway. Yet he cannot believe that his values will not save him. As he says to Iago, his ensign, about Brabantio, the father of Othello's wife, Desdemona:

> Let him do his spite;
> My services that I have done the signiory
> Shall out-tongue his complaints.
> (I, ii, 17–19)

As a soldier, Othello is also unfamiliar with the world of women and the subtleties of male-female relationships. Thus he cannot deal with Iago's claims of suspicion about the fidelity of Desdemona, nor her petitions on behalf of Cassio, the lieutenant whom Othello has dismissed from office. In his final lines, Othello describes himself as "one that lov'd not wisely but too well" (V, ii, 344). We understand him to be perpetually at odds with the values of the society to which he tried to belong.

From King Lear's opening line, he shows himself to be accustomed to power. Indeed, we may be awestruck by the grandeur of a man so old, yet so determined to maintain control. Yet this fearsome will quickly becomes befuddled arrogance, when his youngest daughter, Cordelia, refuses to comply with his demand that she proclaim the depth of her love for him. Ironically, both Lear and Cordelia are too proud to bend. Thereafter, the King's brushing aside of counsel from his most loyal follower, Kent, compounds the error. By the time Lear realizes that his insistence on unchallenged authority has undone him, the throne has been lost.

Mark Antony in *Antony and Cleopatra* is one more hero undermined by his noblest qualities. All the characters around him agree that he has the political and military skills to lead the greatest empire on earth, but he also has the capacity to win the love of the most powerful, desirable woman on the planet, Cleopatra. Antony's stature emerges from these two aspects of his character. His tragedy emerges when circumstances demand that he sacrifice one of those aspects. He must surrender either Rome or Cleopatra, but he tries to hold both. His fall and death are therefore, inevitable.

The conflicts faced by all these tragic figures embody the clash between character and circumstance. In their attempts to draw from their strengths and thereby resolve the crises into which they are thrust, they bear the burden of their flaws. Yet while struggling toward an unavoidable end, they also affirm the essence of tragic drama and, indeed, of all tragic art.

War

No theme of Shakespeare's resounds more powerfully with modern audiences than his treatment of war. At first glance, he may seem to glorify the experience, for in several works, monumental battles provide a dramatic conclusion. Shakespeare, however, never romanticizes the reality of warfare. Indeed, he emphasizes the barbarism of this ever-present aspect of existence. To be sure, he presents individuals who perform bravely in combat, but these exploits never supersede the images of brutality and death that are intrinsic to this most horrible of human enterprises.

One way in which the playwright communicates the madness of war is through the structure of the plot. For Shakespeare, warfare represented the breakdown of the social order, and he portrays this chaos in brief, uneven scenes that reflect such madness. In the final acts of *Julius Caesar*, for instance, the forces of Brutus and Cassius, assassins of Caesar, are opposed by the armies of Antony and Octavius, two of the three generals who will shortly compete for leadership of Rome. During the battle, characters run off and onstage, seemingly out of control, as rumors of the deaths of various soldiers swirl about. First Cassius is discovered dead, then his ally Titinius (V, iii, 90–93), and gradually bodies drop with bewildering rapidity.

The same technique is used to sharper effect in *Antony and Cleopatra*, in which scenes are more jarring in their brevity. Before and during the battle of Actium, the action moves rapidly among Octavius Caesar's camp, Cleopatra's palace, and Antony's camp. This plot construction also mirrors Antony's own dilemma: he is caught between duty to Rome and love for Cleopatra. Meanwhile reports of triumph and defeat follow on top of one another (IV, iii–xiv), and like the characters themselves, we are never sure who is winning, nor where, nor why. Only when Antony bursts out in despair do we understand what we have witnessed:

All is lost!
This foul Egyptian hath betrayed me.
My fleet hath yielded to the foe, and yonder
They cast their caps up and carouse together
Like friends long lost.

(IV, xii, 9–13)

Antony's misinterpretation of Cleopatra's behavior, his conclusion that she has collaborated with his enemies, embodies the disorder of war.

Shakespeare presents such discord even more thrillingly in his history plays. In *Henry VI, Part 1*, the dominant figure is the Englishman Talbot, a paragon of a military hero. Even his enemies, the French, are in awe of him, as a messenger reports:

The French exclaim'd, the devil was in arms;
All the whole army stood agaz'd on him.
His soldiers, spying his undaunted spirit,
"A Talbot! a Talbot!" cried out amain,
And rush'd into the bowels of the battle.

(I, i, 125–129)

Courageous, yet noble, Talbot carries himself in a civilized manner through an uncivilized series of episodes. For instance, he speaks movingly about the slaying of a dear comrade, Bedford:

A braver soldier never couched lance,
A gentler heart did never sway in court;
But kings and mightiest potentates must die,
For that's the end of human misery.

(III, ii, 134–137)

Talbot's nobility is especially powerful before and during the battle of Bordeaux. After the French have rejected his offer to lay down their arms, Talbot anticipates the carnage to come:

Sell every man his life as dear as mine,
And they shall find dear deer of us, my friends.
God and Saint George, Talbot and England's right,
Prosper our colors in this dangerous fight!

(IV, ii, 53–56)

Moments later, Talbot orders his son to leave the battlefield, but the boy defies him, and stays to fight beside his father. After their reconciliation, Talbot's parting words become an elegy over every son who risks his life in battle:

In thee thy mother dies, our household's name,
My death's revenge, thy youth, and England's fame:
All these, and more, we hazard by thy stay;
All these are sav'd if thou wilt fly away.
                              (IV, vi, 38–41)

Equally moving are his words when he learns that his courageous son
has died:

And in that sea of blood my boy did drench
His overmounting spirit; and there died
My Icarus, my blossom, in his pride.
                              (IV, vii, 13–15)

No matter how heroic the pageant of war may seem to the historical
observer, the truth is the awful cost of human life.

In *Henry VI, Part 3*, which dramatizes the War of the Roses between
the York and Lancaster families for possession of the English crown, the
nightmarish quality of battle takes center stage, when a young man drags
in the body of a soldier he has killed, only to realize that the corpse is
that of his own father (II, v, 55–70). At this sight, the weak Henry VI
helplessly reflects on the irony:

O piteous spectacle! O bloody times!
Whiles lions war and battle for their dens
Poor harmless lambs abide their enmity.
                              (II, v, 73–75)

The imagery of lions fighting for their dens suggests that the King sees
all the destruction before him as pointless savagery, in which innocent
lambs, who have no stake in the outcome, nonetheless sacrifice their
lives. Seconds later, a nameless father pulls in one of his victims, whom
he discovers to be his own son:

O, pity, God, this miserable age!
What strategems! how fell! how butcherly!
Erroneous, mutinous, and unnatural,
This deadly quarrel daily doth beget!
                              (II, v, 88–91)

The word "quarrel" accentuates the private origins of this war that has
extended throughout the country, leading to the slaughter of countless
fathers and sons.

Shakespeare presents other aspects of war in *Henry IV, Part 1*, particularly through the contrasting figures of the rebel Henry Percy (Hot-

spur) and Sir John Falstaff, Prince Hal's tavern crony. Years earlier, Hotspur supported Henry IV in his usurpation of the throne from Richard II, but the new King has not proved as amenable to the Percy family as they expected. Hotspur resents such cavalier treatment and forsees deposing the newly enfranchised monarch in favor of Mortimer, once Richard's heir apparent, but now prisoner of the rogue Welshman Glendower:

> But I will lift the down-trod Mortimer
> As high in the air as this unthankful king,
> As this ingrate and cank'red Bullingbrook.
> (I, iii, 135–137)

Hotspur's motivation, however, extends beyond this cause:

> By heaven, methinks it were an easy leap,
> To pluck bright honor from the pale-fac'd moon,
> Or dive into the bottom of the deep,
> Where fadom-line could never touch the ground,
> And pluck up drowned honor by the locks,
> So he that doth redeem her thence might wear
> Without corrival all her dignities . . .
> (I, iii, 201–207)

Hotspur's private agenda includes a desire for individual glory, and his exploits are as much for self-gratification as for any political wrongs he seeks to redress. Indeed, he remains oblivious to the inevitable slaughter that his desire for retribution will bring:

> O, let the hours be short,
> Till fields, and blows, and groans applaud our sport!
> (I, iii, 301–302)

With all his dynamism, Hotspur is an attractive figure. But the more he speaks, the more we realize his foolishness. As Prince Hal himself says to the drawer Francis in the tavern:

> I am not yet of Percy's
> mind, the Hotspur of the north, he that kills
> me some six or seven dozen of Scots at a breakfast,
> washes his hands, and says to his wife, "Fie, upon this
> quiet life! I want work."
> (II, iv, 101–105)

Hotspur's pursuit of glory assumes a more manic quality after his father, Northumberland, communicates that he is ill and unable to fight. Hotspur's uncle, Worcester, hesitates (IV, i, 60–75), but Hotspur chooses to carry on relentlessly:

> Come let us take a muster speedily
> Doomsday is near, die all, die merrily.
>
> (IV, i, 133–134)

At last, before the great battle of Shrewsbury, toward which the play has been building, Hotspur's enthusiasm over meeting Prince Hal in battle verges on madness:

> O gentlemen, the time of life is short!
> To spend that shortness basely were too long
> If life did ride upon a dial's point,
> Still ending at the arrival of an hour.
> And if we live, we live to tread on kings,
> If die, brave death, when princes die with us!
>
> (V, ii, 81–86)

In a way, Hotspur is like war itself: from a distance, all medals, ribbons, and romance; up close, shocking brutality. When he dies in single combat with the Prince, Hotspur falls like the relic of a bygone age, a remnant of a chivalric spirit sadly out of place in the modern world.

His attitudes are also set off by values and words of the Prince's ribald companion, Falstaff, whose very presence mocks the military machine. We are first conscious of his influence when he brings forth his group of ragtag recruits before Hal (IV, ii), then describes how he tried to "press" better men into service:

> . . . and they have bought out their
> services; and now my whole charge consists of
> ancients, corporals, lieutenants, gentlemen of com-
> panies—slaves as ragged as Lazarus in the painted
> cloth, where the glutton's dogs lick'd his sores, and
> such as indeed were never soldiers, but discarded
> unjust servingmen, younger sons to younger brothers,
> revolted tapsters, and ostlers trade-fall'n, the cankers
> of a calm world and a long peace . . .
>
> (IV, ii, 22–30)

Hal scorns this bunch: "I did never see such pitiful rascals" (IV, ii, 64). But Falstaff answers blithely:

Tut, tut, good enough to toss, food for
powder, food for powder, they'll fill a pit as well
as better. Tush, man, mortal men, mortal men.
(IV, ii, 65–67)

He implies clearly that the quality of a soldier means little, for war requires only bodies to throw at the opposing army. Here is a side of
combat often unacknowledged, but in this play we see that wealthy and
noble men declare war, while poor and helpless men die in war—in this
case, to satisfy the frustrated egos of Hotspur, Worcester, and the rest.

When the battle begins, Falstaff's meanderings across the battlefield
shatter whatever dignity the proceedings might contain. First he comes
across the dead body of the King's loyal aid, Sir Walter Blunt, whom he
dismisses with a single remark: "There's honor for you" (V, iii, 31–32).
Earlier Falstaff had offered his "catechism" on honor, dismissing it as "a
mere scutcheon" (V, i, 140–141). That speech and this echo of it may both
be said to answer Hotspur, for whom honor in the form of military glory
becomes a cause unto itself (a subject explored further in the chapter on
"Honor").

When Hal rushes onstage, he demands that Falstaff give him a
weapon, but all Falstaff can bring forth is a bottle of sack, or wine. Hal
has no patience with such shenanigans: "What, is it a time to jest and
dally now?" (V, iii, 55). At this moment, our reaction is probably mixed.
On the one hand, Falstaff's carrying such supplies in combat is amusing.
At the same time, the Prince's life is in danger, and however misguided
the cause for which his opponents fight, we expect that Falstaff would
care enough to support the boy he so loves.

Finally, Falstaff parodies all military exploits when he stabs the corpse
of Hotspur, then picks up the body and carries it off with the expectation
of recompense (V, iv, 120–128). Even more outlandish is his demand for
reward, then his dramatizing the hard fight with Hotspur that he supposedly conducted (V, iii, 140–153). Afterwards, we have difficulty taking seriously any report of battlefield bravery.

Henry V climaxes with perhaps the most famous military triumph in
English history: the battle of Agincourt. Yet even though that victory is
presented as the product of extraordinary English skill and courage, and
even though Henry V is dramatized as a military leader of incomparable
inspiration, we are never allowed to forget that the universal result of
warfare is the death of hundreds or thousands of soldiers.

When King Henry stands with his forces at the Gate to Harflew, he
rouses his troops, beginning with: "Once more unto the breach, dear
friends, once more" (III, i, 1). The invitation sounds almost patrician.
Quickly, though, his tone changes:

> But when the blast of war blows in our ears,
> Then imitate the action of the tiger;
> Stiffen the sinews, [conjure] up the blood,
> Disguise fair nature with hard-favor'd rage . . .
>
> (III, i, 5–8)

He urges his troops to sink to the level of beasts. True, he ends with an uplifting sentiment:

> The game's afoot!
> Follow your spirit; and upon this charge
> Cry, "God for Harry, England, and Saint George!"
>
> (III, i, 32–34)

But such exalted words are undercut by the opening line of the next scene, as Bardolph, one of Falstaff's disreputable cronies, shouts: "On, on, on, on, on! To the breach, to the breach!" (III, ii, 1). King Henry may try to infuse his campaign with dignity, but Bardolph and the more repugnant mercenary Pistol clarify that their participation in the conflict serves only their own greed. For instance, Bardolph loots a conquered church and steals a holy relic, a crime for which the King must have him executed (III, vi, 107–113). Thus Henry temporarily reasserts order, but the underlying selfishness that motivates elements of his forces remains with us.

Even the supreme English victory is tainted by the intrinsic horror of warfare. At the conclusion of the action at Agincourt, Henry reflects on French losses:

> This note doth tell me of ten thousand French
> That in the field lie slain; of princes, in this number,
> And nobles bearing banners, there lie dead
> One hundred twenty-six; added to these,
> Of knights, esquires, and gallant gentlemen,
> Eight thousand and four hundred . . .
>
> (IV, viii, 80–85)

This passage continues with the names of many French nobles who died in the conflict, and therefore has at least two effects. One, it elevates Henry V by showing him to be not a crass boaster who finds joy in the suffering of his enemy, but a compassionate leader who mourns the terrible loss of life. On the other hand, earlier we saw Henry reluctantly issue a cruel directive:

> The French have reinforc'd their scatter'd men.
> Then every soldier kill his prisoners,
> Give the word through.
>
> (IV, vi, 36–38)

This decree invites the slaughter of countless of helpless, unarmed soldiers. Thus Henry's later sorrow over French losses reminds the audience that Shakespeare wanted Henry's image as an ideal general and King to remain untarnished.

The list of French dead, however, contributes in another way. It reminds us that no matter how gloriously the English triumph, the price of victory includes the death of thousands of men who did no more than fight for their country. That Shakespeare portrays the French as arrogant or buffoonish does not detract from the reality that so many of them die serving their nation's cause. This theme of loss is underscored most movingly by the French Duke of Burgundy, who appears before Henry V to appeal for peace. Speaking of France, he relates the tragic condition of the land:

> Her vine, the merry cheerer of the heart,
> Unpruned dies; her hedges even-pleach'd,
> Like prisoners wildly overgrown with hair,
> Put forth disorder'd twigs . . .
> And all our vineyards, fallows, meads, and hedges,
> Defective in their natures, grow to wildness.
> Even so our houses, and ourselves, and children,
> Have lost, or do not learn for want of time,
> The sciences that should become our country,
> But grow like savages—as soldiers will
> That nothing do but meditate on blood—
> To swearing and stern looks, defus'd attire,
> And every thing that seems unnatural.
>
> (V, ii, 41–62)

Here is the inevitable result of war: the "unnatural" destruction of a land and a people. Whatever individual heroism has occurred, Shakespeare suggests, the concomitant horror must never be forgotten.

Perhaps the starkest vision of war in all of Shakespeare's works may be found in *Troilus and Cressida*. Here is the playwright's version of the most famous military episode in history: the Trojan War. We are familiar with Homer's retelling of this event in *The Iliad*, but Shakespeare's portrait of the celebrated figures from legend and history is shockingly different. Here are no larger-than-life heroes fighting boldly in a struggle complicated by the interference of the gods. Here instead are petty, vicious plotters caught up in an endless conflict that never made much sense, and now, after seven years of slaughter, makes even less. As Shakespeare writes in the Prologue:

> Sixty and nine, that wore
> Their crownets regal, from th' Athenian bay
> Put forth toward Phrygia, and their vow is made
> To ransack Troy, within whose strong immures
> The ravish'd Helen, Menelaus' queen,
> With wanton Paris sleeps—and that's the quarrel.
>
> (Prologue, 5–10)

As it did in *Henry VI, Part 3*, the word "quarrel" diminishes the significance of the story.

Throughout the play, Thersites, a cynical member of the Greek army, comments on this folly, mocking even his own participation:

> Agamemnon is a fool to offer to command
> Achilles, Achilles is a fool to be commanded [of
> Agamemnon], Thersites is a fool to serve such a fool,
> and this Patroclus is a fool positive.
>
> (II, iii, 62–65)

Moments later, he adds:

> All the argument is a whore and a
> cuckold, a good quarrel to draw emulous factions and
> bleed to death upon.
>
> (II, iii, 72–74)

He captures the essence of this undertaking with a clear-sightedness that escapes all the other characters. Furthermore, such descriptions reduce this mammoth struggle to a pointless cartoon and leave us almost unable to take what follows seriously.

Yet we must do so, particularly when Hector, the noblest of the Trojans, is challenged to fight Achilles one-on-one. Despite warnings by his family, Hector cannot resist joining the horrific conflict, which Shakespeare dramatizes in familiar style by offering several short scenes. When Achilles and Hector at last engage each other, the Trojan's death seems inevitable, as does Achilles' brutalization of the body:

> Come tie his body to my horse's tail,
> Along the field I will the Trojan trail.
>
> (V, viii, 21–22)

Here is no glorious triumph, but the humiliation of a worthy foe, whose manner of death reflects the degeneracy of his world.

Perhaps the most memorable line of the play is offered by Thersites:

Lechery, lechery, still
wars and lechery, nothing else holds fashion. A
burning devil take them!

(V, ii, 194–196)

He not only captures the spirit of *Troilus and Cressida*, but also may be said to reflect the nature of warfare in Shakespeare's plays. Despite occasional moments of heroism, we often find that lechery, or what we might also term "greed," whether for power or territory, underlies much of the military conflict. Thus for Shakespeare, war represents the breakdown of order, the ultimate descent of humanity from civilization to brutishness.

Conclusion

Throughout this guide to the themes of Shakespeare's plays, attention has been focused on the characters and how they reveal themselves through language and action. That study has also led to conclusions about Shakespeare's presentation of so many aspects of life. Another issue, however, has pervaded every chapter: Does such discussion bring us closer to the playwright himself, to his beliefs and values? Can we really understand what Shakespeare thought and felt?

At first blush, the answer might seem to be "No." After all, we have comparatively few details of Shakespeare's own life, nor have we substantial material from diaries, letters, and other firsthand accounts, by either the playwright or his contemporaries, that might reveal more details of the man himself. Given such limitations, how can we actually "know" Shakespeare?

Upon reflection, however, we realize a remarkable truth: that through his writings, we have almost limitless access to Shakespeare's mind and heart.

True, most chapters in this book end with some confession of puzzlement as to Shakespeare's ultimate judgment on many subjects. In most other literary and dramatic works, we detect one voice that we assume belongs to the author. The plays of Shakespeare, however, offer multitudinous voices on virtually every subject. Yet that very complication is intrinsic to both our fascination with him and our understanding of him.

For instance, Shakespeare clearly valued the institution of marriage, but he offers both happy and unhappy examples. He presents numerous female characters who demonstrate admirable independence of spirit and intellect, but he frequently leaves them in relationships where they must subordinate their wishes to those of less than stellar partners.

Shakespeare dramatizes the skillful use of political power, but he also shows how figures who exert authority may easily fall into abuse of their jurisdiction. He presents not only the consequences of the failure to wield power effectively, but also how the great mass of people, though deserving of compassion and fair treatment, need to be strictly controlled.

He admires military heroism, but portrays warfare in all its horror and futility. He dramatizes the principles of Christianity, but offers many religious leaders who are prone to corruption. His characters carry prejudices against a variety of cultures, but the speakers, too, are often ugly, while the objects of intolerance may bring scorn on themselves, then moments later manifest another side that earns our sympathy.

He offers heroic men and women of every level, and monstrous men and women of every level. He dramatizes the most passionate love and the most terrifying hatred. He shows us pride, humility, vengeance, generosity, lust, loyalty, jealousy, foolishness, imagination, and cruelty. He also shows how many of these conflicting qualities, along with countless others, may clash inside the same characters.

In sum, Shakespeare presents a vision of life in all its wondrous confusions and contradictions. No aspect is beyond his interest, no individual or class outside his understanding. Yet he does not offer simple answers or perspectives. To read his plays is to encounter a depiction of ourselves so profound, so multifaceted, that we can never exhaust its bounty.

We therefore put aside the search for Shakespeare's personal qualities, for we may be confident that like any great artist, he revealed himself most fully through his work. Instead we enjoy his legacy: the most universal portrait of the human experience ever created. In the words of his contemporary, the poet and playwright Ben Jonson: "He was not of an age, but for all time!"

Further Reading

BIOGRAPHIES

Honan, Park. *Shakespeare: A Life*. New York: Oxford University Press, 1998.
O'Connor, Garry. *Shakespeare: A Popular Life*. New York: Applause Books, 1999.

THEATRICAL AND INTELLECTUAL BACKGROUND

Kastan, David, ed. *A Companion to Shakespeare*. Oxford: Blackwell Publishers, Ltd., 1999.
McDonald, Russ. *The Bedford Companion to Shakespeare: An Introduction with Documents*. New York: St. Martin's Press, 1996.
Tillyard, E. M. W. *The Elizabethan World Picture*. New York: Macmillan, 1943. Reprint: New York: Random House, 1961.
Wells, Stanley. *The Cambridge Companion to Shakespeare Studies*. Cambridge: Cambridge University Press, 1986.

GENERAL STUDIES

Cahn, Victor L. *Shakespeare the Playwright: A Companion to the Complete Tragedies, Histories, Comedies, and Romances*. Westport, CT: Greenwood, 1991. Reprint: Westport, CT: Praeger Publishers, 1996.
Charney, Maurice. *All of Shakespeare*. New York: Columbia University Press, 1993.
Goddard, Harold C. *The Meaning of Shakespeare*. Chicago: University of Chicago Press, 1951.
Kott, Jan. *Shakespeare Our Contemporary*. Garden City, NY: Doubleday, 1966.

THE TRAGEDIES

Bradley, A. C. *Shakespearean Tragedy*. New York: St. Martin's Press, 1992. (Originally published in 1904).
Garner, Shirley Nelson. *Shakespearean Tragedy and Gender*. Bloomington: Indiana University Press, 1996.

Margolies, David. *Monsters of the Deep: Social Dissolution in Shakespeare's Tragedies*. Manchester and New York: Manchester University Press, 1992.

Young, David. *The Action to the Word: Structure and Style in Shakespeare's Tragedies*. New Haven: Yale University Press, 1990.

THE HISTORIES

Holderness, Graham, ed. *Shakespeare's History Plays*: Richard II *to* Henry V. New York: St. Martin's Press, 1992.

Leggatt, Alexander. *Shakespeare's Political Drama: The History Plays and the Roman Plays*. London: Routledge, 1988.

Rackin, Phyllis. *Stages of History: Shakespeare's English Chronicles*. Ithaca, NY: Cornell University Press, 1990.

Saccio, Peter. *Shakespeare's English Kings*. New York: Oxford University Press, 1977.

THE COMEDIES

Barber, C. L. *Shakespeare's Festive Comedy*. Princeton: Princeton University Press, 1959.

Frye, Northrop. *A Natural Perspective: The Development of Shakespearean Comedy and Romance*. New York: Columbia University Press, 1995.

Ornstein, Robert. *Shakespeare's Comedies: From Romance Farce to Romantic Mystery*. Newark: University of Delaware Press, 1986.

Salingar, Leo. *Shakespeare and the Traditions of Comedy*. London: Cambridge University Press, 1974.

THE ROMANCES

Adams, Robert M. *Shakespeare: The Four Romances*. New York: W. W. Norton, 1989.

Foakes, R. A. *Shakespeare: The Dark Comedies to the Last Plays*. Charlottesville: University Press of Virginia, 1971.

Hunt, Maurice. *Shakespeare's Romance of the Word*. Lewisburg, PA: Bucknell University Press, 1990.

Traversi, Derek. *Shakespeare: The Last Phase*. London: Hollis & Carter, 1954.

Index

About the Author

VICTOR L. CAHN is Professor of English at Skidmore College, where he teaches courses in the history of drama, Shakespeare, and modern drama. Dr. Cahn's book *Shakespeare the Playwright: A Companion to the Complete Tragedies, Histories, Comedies, and Romances* (Greenwood 1991 & 1996) was selected as an Outstanding Academic Book by *Choice*. He has also written studies of contemporary British dramatists Tom Stoppard and Harold Pinter, and his numerous articles and reviews have appeared in such diverse publications as *Modern Drama, The Literary Review, The New York Times*, and *Variety*. An actor by avocation, Dr. Cahn is the author of several produced plays.